Computer Ethics and Professional Responsibility

To our wives
Aline Bynum and Anne Rogerson

Computer Ethics and Professional Responsibility

Edited
by

Terrell Ward Bynum

and

Simon Rogerson

Editorial material and organization © 2004 by Blackwell Publishing Ltd

BLACKWELL PUBLISHING
350 Main Street, Malden, MA 02148-5020, USA
9600 Garsington Road, Oxford OX4 2DQ, UK
550 Swanston Street, Carlton, Victoria 3053, Australia

The right of Terrell Ward Bynum and Simon Rogerson to be identified as the Authors of the Editorial Material in this Work has been asserted in accordance with the UK Copyright, Designs, and Patents Act 1988.

First published 2004 by Blackwell Publishing Ltd

3   2005

Library of Congress Cataloging-in-Publication Data

Computer ethics and professional responsibility / edited with extensive introductions and study questions by Terrell Ward Bynum and Simon Rogerson.
    p. cm.
    ISBN 1-85554-844-5 (hardcover : alk. paper) — ISBN 1-85554-845-3 (pbk.: alk. paper)
    1. Electronic data processing — Moral and ethical aspects. I. Bynum, Terrell Ward.
II. Rogerson, Simon.

QA76.9.M65 C657 2004
174'.90904 — dc21

                2002153908

ISBN-13: 978-1-85554-844-2 (hardcover : alk. paper) — ISBN-13: 978-1-85554-845-9 (pbk.: alk. paper)

A catalogue record for this title is available from the British Library.

Set in 10/12½ pt Photina
by Graphicraft Ltd, Hong Kong
Printed and bound in India
by Replika Press Pvt Ltd, Kundli

The publisher's policy is to use permanent paper from mills that operate a sustainable forestry policy, and which has been manufactured from pulp processed using acid-free and elementary chlorine-free practices. Furthermore, the publisher ensures that the text paper and cover board used have met acceptable environmental accreditation standards.

For further information on
Blackwell Publishing, visit our website:
www.blackwellpublishing.com

Contents

Notes on Contributors

Terrell Ward Bynum: Professor of Philosophy and Director, Research Center on Computing & Society, Southern Connecticut State University, New Haven, CT, USA; Co-Founder of the ETHICOMP Conference Series; Past Chair of the Committee on Professional Ethics of the Association for Computing Machinery

N. Ben Fairweather: Research Fellow and Resident Philosopher in the Centre for Computing and Social Responsibility, De Montfort University, Leicester, UK; Co-Editor of the *Journal of Information, Communication and Ethics in Society*

Elizabeth France: Telecommunications Ombudsman of the United Kingdom, Wilderspool Park, Warrington, UK; formerly the Information Commissioner of the United Kingdom, as well as the Data Protection Registrar of the United Kingdom

Krystyna Gorniak-Kocikowska: Professor of Philosophy and Senior Research Associate in the Research Center on Computing & Society, Southern Connecticut State University, New Haven, CT, USA; Co-Editor of the first Polish language textbook in Computer Ethics

Donald Gotterbarn: Professor of Computer Science and Director of the Software Engineering Ethics Research Institute, East Tennessee State University, TN, USA; Chair of the Committee on Professional Ethics of the Association for Computing Machinery; Fellow in the Center for Applied Philosophy and Public Ethics, Canberra, Australia

Chuck Huff: Professor of Psychology, St Olaf College, Northfield, MN, USA; Associate Editor of the journal *Computers and Society*; Associate Editor for Psychology of the journal *Social Science Computer Review*

Deborah G. Johnson: Anne Shirley Carter Olsson Professor of Applied Ethics, Department of Technology, Culture and Communication, University of Virginia, Charlottesville, VA, USA; President of INSEIT (the International Society for Ethics and Information Technology); author of the first major textbook on Computer Ethics

Walter Maner: Professor of Computer Science, Bowling Green State University, Bowling Green, OH, USA; Fellow of the Research Center on Computing & Society; pioneer in Computer Ethics (1970s and 1980s); author and conference organizer in Computer Ethics and Applied Ethics

James H. Moor: Professor of Philosophy, Dartmouth College, Hanover, NH, USA; Executive Committee Member, International Association for Computers and Philosophy; Past President, Society for Machines and Mentality; Associate Editor, *Minds and Machines*; pioneer in Computer Ethics (1970s and 1980s)

Peter G. Neumann: Principal Scientist, Computer Science Laboratory, SRI International, Menlo Park, California, USA; Co-Chair of the Committee on Computers and Public Policy of the Association for Computing Machinery; Moderator of ACM Risks Forum; Co-Founder of People for Internet Responsibility

Simon Rogerson: Professor of Computer Ethics and Director of the Centre for Computing and Social Responsibility, De Montfort University, Leicester, UK; Co-Founder of the ETHICOMP Conference Series; Co-Editor of the *Journal of Information, Communication and Ethics in Society*; Member of the Parliamentary Information Technology Committee of the United Kingdom

Eugene H. Spafford: Professor of Computer Science and Director of CERIAS (Center for Education and Research in Information Assurance and Security), Purdue University, West Lafayette, Indiana, USA; Co-Chair of the Committee on Computers and Public Policy of the Association for Computing Machinery; Recipient of the William Hugh Murray Medal for Computer Security

Richard Stallman: Founder of the GNU Project and the Free Software Foundation, Boston, MA, USA; Macarthur Foundation Fellow; Recipient of the Electronic Frontier Foundation Pioneer Award; Recipient of the Takeda Award for Social/Economic Betterment

John Weckert: Associate Professor of Information Studies at the Charles Sturt University, Wagga Wagga, Australia; Co-Founder of the Australian Institute for Computer Ethics; Academic Staff, Center for Applied Philosophy and Public Ethics, Canberra, Australia; Fellow in the Research Center on Computing & Society at Southern Connecticut State University, USA

Preface and Acknowledgments

This book has been several years in gestation. Our original plan in 1995 was to create two books; namely, a single-authored textbook written by Terrell Ward Bynum, and a collection of papers jointly edited by Simon Rogerson and Terrell Ward Bynum. As the project matured, the two planned books merged into one "hybrid" volume with components of both. Therefore, the reader will find editors' introductions that are longer and more extensive than those typical of edited readers. At the same time, however, there are also 16 articles by a variety of leading authors. To complement these materials, we added a number of relevant resources, including cases to analyze, basic study questions for each article, questions to stimulate further thought, and lists of suggested readings and websites.

Besides this textbook, our project generated a variety of related materials and resources. We have posted these on the web sites of the Research Center on Computing & Society (RCCS) at Southern Connecticut State University (www.computerethics.org or www.computerethics.info) and the Centre for Computing and Social Responsibility (CCSR) at De Montfort University in the UK (www.ccsr.cse.dmu.ac.uk). Readers of this volume are invited to visit these web sites to obtain additional study questions, example student papers, new cases to analyze, more lists of Internet resources, and a variety of other materials. We would like to express our gratitude to web masters Margaret Tehan (at RCCS) and Jennifer Freeman (at CCSR) for their expert assistance in creating the web-based materials for this project.

The contents of the present textbook, together with its related on-line resources, provide all the resources necessary to fulfill the "Social and Professional Issues" curriculum recommendations in "Computing Curricula 2001," a report by the Joint Task Force on Computing Curricula 2001 of the Computer Society of the Institute for Electrical and Electronic Engineers (IEEE-CS) and the Association for Computing Machinery (ACM). (For details, see Editors' Note on pp. xvi–xvii.)

To develop and improve instructional materials for this textbook, various readings and sample student questions were tested in Computer Ethics courses at Southern Connecticut State University from Autumn 1997 to Spring 2001. As a result, this book has benefited from the suggestions of many students, especially the following (in alphabetical order): Jane Berling, Ray Bodine, Tanisha Bolt, Richard Breisler, Diane Capaldo, Josh Cohen, Michael Conigliaro, Edward D'Onofrio, Lisa Doubleday, Chris Fusco, Justine Giannotti, Nancy Graham, Bryan Harms, Susan Heilweil, Mark Hussey, Russell C. Jennings, Emily Johns-Ahern, George Koltypin, Hom Q. Keung Jr., Mark Lindholm, Tara Malley, Ben Schenkman, Ismat Virani, Peter Winslow, and Andrew Zychek. In addition, Ray Bodine and Lisa Doubleday headed a special project to develop student study questions.

A number of colleagues at Southern Connecticut State University, at De Montfort University, and in the field of computer ethics generously offered their advice and assistance as this project developed. We would especially like to thank the authors whose papers are published in this book, including (in alphabetical order): N. Ben Fairweather, Elizabeth France, Krystyna Gorniak-Kocikowska, Donald Gotterbarn, Chuck Huff, Deborah Johnson, Walter Maner, James H. Moor, Peter G. Neumann, Eugene Spafford, Richard Stallman, and John Weckert. In addition, we are most grateful to all of the following for their assistance and encouragement: Jennifer Freeman, Ken W. Gatzke, Richard Gerber, Frances Grodzinsky, F. E. Lowe, Paul Luker, Armen Marsoobian, Keith Miller, J. Philip Smith, Margaret Tehan, and Richard Volkman.

Our respective universities have supported this project in a variety of ways, and we would like to express our appreciation. Southern Connecticut State University provided a sabbatical leave during the Fall 2001 semester, and the Connecticut State University System provided two research grants. Travel and research funds were provided by the Research Center on Computing & Society, as well as Dartmouth College and De Montfort University.

The editors and publisher gratefully acknowledge the permission granted to reproduce the copyright material in this book:

1 James H. Moor, "Reason, Relativity, and Responsibility in Computer Ethics." This chapter was originally presented as the keynote address at ETHICOMP96 in Madrid, Spain and later published in *Computers and Society*, 28:1 (March 1998), pp. 14–21. © 1998 by James H. Moor and reprinted by permission of the author.

2 Walter Maner, "Unique Ethical Problems in Information Technology." This chapter was originally presented as the keynote address at ETHICOMP95 in Leicester, UK. It was subsequently published in *Science and Engineering Ethics*, 2:2 (special issue, ed. Terrell Ward Bynum and

Simon Rogerson, April 1996), pp. 137–54. © 1995 by Walter Maner and reprinted by permission of the author.

4   Chuck Huff, "Unintentional Power in the Design of Computing Systems." This chapter was originally a paper presented at ETHICOMP95 in Leicester, UK and appeared in the proceedings of that conference, edited by Simon Rogerson and Terrell Ward Bynum and published by the Centre for Computing and Social Responsibility. Reprinted by permission of the author. © 1995 by Chuck Huff.

5   Donald Gotterbarn, "Informatics and Professional Responsibility." This chapter was first published in *Science and Engineering Ethics*, 7:2 (April 2001), pp. 221–30. © 2001 by Donald Gotterbarn and reprinted by permission of the author.

6   Simon Rogerson, "The Ethics of Software Development Project Management." This chapter is a revised version of "Software Project Management Ethics" which was published in C. Myers, T. Hall, and D. Pitt (eds.), *The Responsible Software Engineer* (Springer-Verlag, 1996), ch. 11, pp. 100–6. This version © 2002 by Simon Rogerson.

7   N. Ben Fairweather, "No, PAPA: Why Incomplete Codes of Ethics are Worse than None at All." This chapter was originally presented as a paper at the Conference on Computer Ethics, Linköping University, Sweden, 1997 and was later published in G. Collste (ed.), *Ethics in the Age of Information Technology* (Linköping University Press, 2000). © 2000 by N. Ben Fairweather and reprinted by permission of the author.

8   Donald Gotterbarn, "On Licensing Computer Professionals." Portions of this chapter were previously published in Joseph M. Kizza (ed.), *The Social and Ethical Effects of the Computer Revolution* (McFarland & Company Inc., 1996). © 2001 by Donald Gotterbarn and reprinted by permission of the author.

9   Peter G. Neumann, "Computer Security and Human Values." This article was originally the "track address" in the Security Track of the National Conference on Computing and Values held at Southern Connecticut State University, New Haven, CT in August 1991. © by Research Center on Computing and Society, Southern Connecticut State University and reprinted by permission of the author.

10   Eugene H. Spafford, "Are Computer Hacker Break-Ins Ethical?" This chapter was first published in the *Journal of Systems and Software*, 1992. An earlier version appeared in *Information Technology Quarterly*, IX (1990). © 1991, 1997 by Eugene H. Spafford, all rights reserved. Reprinted by permission of the author.

11   James H. Moor, "Towards a Theory of Privacy in the Information Age." This chapter was first published in *Computers and Society*, 27 (September 1997), pp. 27–32. © 1997 by James H. Moor. Reprinted by permission of the author.

12   Elizabeth France, "Data Protection in a Changing World." © 2002 by Elizabeth France. Printed here by permission of the author.
13   Deborah G. Johnson, "Proprietary Rights in Computer Software: Individual and Policy Issues." This chapter was originally presented as a paper at the National Conference on Computing and Values held at Southern Connecticut State University, New Haven, CT in August 1991. © by Research Center on Computing and Society, Southern Connecticut State University and reprinted by permission of the author.
14   Richard Stallman, "Why Software Should Be Free." © 1991 by The Free Software Foundation, Inc. Copying and redistribution are permitted without royalty; alteration is not permitted.
15   Krystyna Gorniak-Kocikowska, "The Computer Revolution and Global Ethics." This is a shortened version of "The Computer Revolution and the Problem of Global Ethics", presented at ETHICOMP95 and published in the conference proceedings, ed. Simon Rogerson and Terrell Ward Bynum. Reprinted in *Science and Engineering Ethics*, 2:2 (special issue, 1996), pp. 177–190. © 1995 by Krystyna Gorniak-Kocikowska and reprinted by permission of the author.
16   John Weckert, "Giving Offense on the Internet." This chapter was originally presented as a paper at The Computer Ethics Conference, Linköping University, Sweden. It was first published in G. Collste (ed.), *Ethics and Information Technology* (New Academic Publishers, 1998), pp. 104–18. © 1997 by John Weckert. Reprinted by permission of the author.

"The Software Engineering Code of Ethics and Professional Practice." © 1999 by the Institute of Electrical and Electronics Engineers, Inc. and the Association for Computing Machinery, Inc.

"The ACM Code of Ethics and Professional Conduct." © 1992 by ACM, Inc. Included here by permission.
"The ACS Code of Ethics." © Australian Computer Society. Included here by permission.
"The BCS Code of Conduct." © 2001 by British Computer Society. Included here by permission.
"The IEEE Code of Ethics." © 1997 by IEEE. Included here by permission.
"The IMIS Code of Ethics." © 2001 by IMIS. Included here by permission.

Michael Gros and Rabbi Dr Asher Meir of the Center for Business Ethics and Social Responsibility for allowing us to reprint materials related to the Napster case.

Every effort has been made to trace copyright holders and to obtain their permission for the use of copyright material. The publisher apologizes for any errors or omissions in the above list and would be grateful if notified of any corrections that should be incorporated in future reprints or editions of this book.

We are very grateful to Blackwell's editor Sarah Dancy and to our friend and colleague Donald Gotterbarn, who read the manuscript with care and offered a multitude of valuable suggestions for improvement.

In conclusion, we – "The Chester Boys" – would like to express special thanks to our wives, Aline W. Bynum and Anne Rogerson, to whom this book is dedicated. Without their unflagging encouragement and support this project could not have been completed.

List of Abbreviations

ABET	Accreditation Board for Engineering Technologies
ACM	Association for Computing Machinery
ACS	Australian Computer Society
AI	Artificial Intelligence
BCS	British Computer Society
CCPA	Court of Customs and Patent Appeals
CCSR	Center for Computing and Social Responsibility
CCTV	closed circuit television
CP	computing practitioner
CSAC/CSAB	Computer Sciences Accreditation Commission/Computer Sciences Accreditation Board
DIFF	tool to find differences between two computer files
EPR	electronic patient records
EU	European Union
FSF	Free Software Foundation
GNU	a Unix-like operating system ("GNU" means "GNU's not Unix")
ICT	information and communication technology
ID	(personal) identification
IDEA	international data encryption algorithm
IEEE-CS	Computer Society of the Institute for Electrical and Electronic Engineers
IMIS	Institute for the Management of Information Systems
I/O	input/output
IPR	intellectual property rights
IS	information systems
IT	information technology
LASCAD	London Ambulance Service Computer-Aided Dispatch Project
LCM	least common multiple

OECD   Organization for Economic Cooperation and Development
PAPA   privacy, accuracy, property, accessibility
RCCS   Research Center on Computing & Society
RMN   regional medical network
SIS   social impact statement
SoDIS   Software Development Impact Statement
SPM   structured project management
SWEBOK   Software Engineering Body of Knowledge
TCP/IP   transmission control protocol/internet protocol
TQM   total quality management
WIPO   World Intellectual Property Organization

Editors' Note: Computing Curricula 2001 Guidelines of IEEE-CS and the ACM

In 1991 the Association for Computing Machinery (ACM) and the Computer Society of the Institute for Electrical and Electronic Engineers (IEEE-CS) adopted a set of curriculum guidelines for undergraduate programs in computing. Those guidelines, entitled *Computing Curricula 1991* (CC1991), recommended the inclusion of significant "social and professional" content in any undergraduate computing curriculum:

> Undergraduates also need to understand the basic cultural, social, legal, and ethical issues inherent in the discipline of computing. They should understand where the discipline has been, where it is, and where it is heading. They should also understand their individual roles in this process, as well as appreciate the philosophical questions, technical problems, and aesthetic values that play an important part in the development of the discipline.
>
> Students also need to develop the ability to ask serious questions about the social impact of computing and to evaluate proposed answers to those questions. Future practitioners must be able to anticipate the impact of introducing a given product into a given environment. Will that product enhance or degrade the quality of life? What will the impact be upon individuals, groups, and institutions?
>
> Finally, students need to be aware of the basic legal rights of software and hardware vendors and users, and they also need to appreciate the ethical values that are the basis for those rights. Future practitioners must understand the responsibility they will bear, and the possible consequences of failure. They must understand their own limitations as well as the limitations of their tools. All practitioners must make a long-term commitment to remaining current in their chosen specialties and in the discipline of computing as a whole. (ACM and IEEE-CS 1991)

In 1998 a joint task force of the same two professional organizations undertook the job of updating and expanding CC1991 to take account of computer-related developments during the 1990s. The resulting new curriculum guidelines, entitled *Computing Curricula 2001* (CC2001), placed even more emphasis upon social and professional issues; and, for the first time in history, created a separate "Area" within the CS Body of Knowledge for the subfield of "Social and Professional Issues" (see www.acm.org/sigcse/cc2001). This Area of the CS Body of Knowledge includes ten social and professional "Knowledge Units" – seven "core" units and three "elective" ones (see IEEE-CS and ACM 2001):

SP1   History of computing (core)
SP2   Social context of computing (core)
SP3   Methods and tools of analysis (core)
SP4   Professional and ethical responsibilities (core)
SP5   Risks and liabilities of computer-based systems (core)
SP6   Intellectual property (core)
SP7   Privacy and civil liberties (core)
SP8   Computer crime (elective)
SP9   Economic issues in computing (elective)
SP10   Philosophical frameworks (elective)

The present textbook, together with its related web-based resources, provides pedagogical materials (readings, study questions, sample student papers, cases to analyze, bibliographies, and webliographies) to cover all ten of these Knowledge Units in the Social and Professional Issues Area of CC2001. (See the website of the Research Center on Computing & Society (www.computerethics.org or www.computerethics.info) and also the website of the Centre for Computing and Social Responsibility (www.ccsr.cse.dmu.ac.uk). Readers of this textbook are invited to send email (bynum@computerethics.org) with suggested additions and corrections to the web-based materials or to the book itself.)

Editors' Introduction:
Ethics in the Information Age

Thus the new industrial revolution is a two edged sword. It may be used for the benefit of humanity. . . . It may also be used to destroy humanity, and if it is not used intelligently it can go very far in that direction.

Norbert Wiener

The Information Revolution

Powerful technologies have profound social consequences. Consider, for example, the impact on the world of farming, printing, and industrialization. Each of these technologies, when first created, brought about social and ethical revolutions. Information and communication technology (ICT) is no exception. Indeed, as we noted elsewhere:

> Computing technology is the most powerful and most flexible technology ever devised. For this reason, computing is changing everything – where and how we work, where and how we learn, shop, eat, vote, receive medical care, spend free time, make war, make friends, make love. (Rogerson and Bynum 1995, p. iv)

The information revolution therefore is not "merely technological;" *it is fundamentally social and ethical.*

The reason why ICT is so powerful is well explained by James Moor in his classic paper "What Is Computer Ethics?" (see Moor 1985, as well as chapter 1 below). Computer technology, said Moor, is almost a "universal tool" because it is "logically malleable" and therefore can be shaped and molded to perform nearly any task. In industrialized nations this "universal tool" has altered many aspects of life, such as banking, commerce, employment, medicine, national defense, transportation, and entertainment. ICT has thereby had profound effects – both good and bad – upon community life, family life, education, freedom, and democracy (to name only a few examples).

It is clear that public policy-makers, leaders of business and industry, teachers, social thinkers – indeed every citizen – should have a keen interest in the social and ethical impacts of information and communication technology.

Computer Practitioners and Professional Responsibility

Computer practitioners and many of their professional organizations have recognized for decades that ICT has important social and ethical implications. Since the 1970s, for example, a number of professional organizations have established codes of ethics, curriculum guidelines, and accreditation requirements to help computer professionals understand and manage their special ethical responsibilities. For example, the Association for Computing Machinery (ACM), the Computer Society of the Institute of Electrical and Electronic Engineers (IEEE-CS), the British Computer Society (BCS), the Australian Computer Society (ACS), and the Institute for the Management of Information Systems (IMIS) have all developed and adopted codes of ethics (see the Appendix to Part III below). In the United States the Accreditation Board for Engineering Technologies (ABET) has long required an ethics component in the computer engineering curriculum; and in 1991, the Computer Sciences Accreditation Commission/Computer Sciences Accreditation Board (CSAC/CSAB) also adopted the requirement that a significant component of computer ethics be included in any computer sciences degree-granting program that is nationally accredited. Also in 1991, a joint task force of the ACM and IEEE-CS developed a set of curriculum guidelines, *Computing Curricula 1991*, for university programs in computing (ACM and IEEE-CS 1991). Those guidelines recommended the inclusion of significant "social and professional" content in any undergraduate computing curriculum. In 2001, a new joint task force of the same two organizations developed an updated set of guidelines (*Computing Curricula 2001*) with an even stronger emphasis on social and ethical issues (IEEE-CS and ACM 2001). For the first time in history, the social and professional issues of computer ethics were assigned an entire area of the "CS Body of Knowledge" (see Editors' Note above).

Given all of the above-described developments, it is clear that professional organizations in computer science recognize and insist upon standards of professional responsibility for their members.

ICT and Human Values

Today, in the early years of the information age, the *long-term* social and ethical implications of ICT are still unknown. Technology changes so rapidly that new possibilities emerge before the social consequences can be fathomed (Rogerson and Bynum 1995). New social/ethical policies for the information age, therefore, are urgently needed to fill rapidly multiplying "policy vacuums" (Moor 1985). But filling such vacuums is a complex social process requiring active participation of individuals, organizations, governments – and, ultimately, the world community.

Human relationships

Consider, for example, the impact of information and communication technology upon human relationships. How will families or friendships be affected by mobile phones, palm-top and lap-top computers, telecommuting to work and school, virtual-reality conferencing, cybersex? Will the efficiency and convenience of ICT lead to shorter work hours and more "quality time" with friends and family? – Or will it create instead a more hectic and breathless lifestyle which separates family and friends from each other? Will people be isolated, each in front of a computer screen hour after hour, or will they find new friendships and relationships in "virtual communities" in cyberspace – relationships based upon interactions that could never occur in regular space-time settings? How fulfilling and "genuine" can such relationships be, and will they crowd out better, more satisfying face-to-face relationships? What does all this mean for a person's self-realization and satisfaction with life? What policies, laws, rules, practices should be put in place? – and who should put them there?

Privacy and anonymity

One of the earliest computer ethics topics to arouse public interest in America was privacy. For example, in the mid-1960s the American government had already created large databases of information about private citizens (census data, tax records, military service records, welfare records, and so on). In the United States Congress, bills were introduced to assign a personal identification (ID) number to every citizen and then gather all the government's data about each citizen under the corresponding number. A public outcry about "big-brother government" caused Congress to scrap this plan and led the US President to appoint committees to recommend privacy legislation. In the early 1970s, major computer privacy laws were passed in the USA. Ever since then, computer-threatened privacy has remained as a topic of public concern.

The ease and efficiency with which computers and computer networks can be used to gather, store, search, compare, retrieve, and share personal information make computer technology especially threatening to anyone who wishes to keep various kinds of "sensitive" information (for example, medical records) out of the public domain or out of the hands of those who are perceived as potential threats. Developments such as commercialization and rapid growth of the Internet, the rise of the World Wide Web, increasing "user-friendliness" and processing power of computers, and decreasing costs of computer technology have led to new privacy issues, such as data-mining, data-matching, recording of "click trails" on the web, and so on (see Tavani 1999).

The variety of privacy-related issues generated by computer technology, combined with the belief of many thinkers that privacy is vital to human self-identity and autonomy, has led philosophers and other thinkers to re-examine the concept of privacy itself. For example, a number of scholars have elaborated a theory of privacy defined as "control over personal information" (see Westin 1967, Miller 1971, Fried 1984, and Elgesem 1996). On the other hand, philosophers Moor and Tavani have argued that control of personal information is insufficient to establish or protect privacy, and "the concept of privacy itself is best defined in terms of restricted access, not control" (Tavani and Moor 2001; see also chapter 11 below). In addition, Nissenbaum has argued that there is even a sense of privacy in *public spaces*, or circumstances "other than the intimate." An adequate definition of privacy, therefore, must take account of "privacy in public" (Nissenbaum 1998). As computer technology rapidly advances – creating ever new possibilities for compiling, storing, accessing and analyzing information – philosophical debates about the meaning of the word "privacy" will likely continue.

Questions of "anonymity and computing" are sometimes discussed in the same context with questions of privacy, because anonymity can provide many of the same desired results as privacy. For example, if someone is using the Internet to obtain medical or psychological counseling, or to discuss sensitive topics (such as AIDS, abortion, gay rights, venereal disease, political dissent), anonymity can afford protection similar to that of privacy. In addition, both anonymity and privacy on the Internet can be helpful in preserving human values such as security, mental health, self-fulfillment, and peace of mind. Unfortunately, both privacy and anonymity also can be exploited to facilitate unwanted and undesirable computer-aided activities such as money laundering, drug trading, terrorism, or preying upon the vulnerable. For example, lack of database matching may have hidden information that could have prevented the 9/11 terror attacks in the USA.

Intellectual property and ownership

In the information age, possession and control of information are keys to wealth, power and success. Those who own and control the information infrastructure are amongst the wealthiest and most powerful of all. And those who own digitized intellectual property – software, databases, music, video, films, literary and artistic works, educational resources – possess major economic assets. But digitized information is, as Moor has so aptly said, "greased data" – easily copied and altered, easily transferred across borders. As a result, "free" access, on the Internet, to copyrighted or patented intellectual property has become a major social issue. What new laws, regulations, rules, international agreements and practices would be fair and just, and who should formulate or enforce them? Should information like computer programs be owned at all?

A related issue concerns the creation and ownership of "multimedia" works that mix and combine several types of digitized resource. A single creation, for example, might make use of bits and snippets of photographs, video clips, sound bites, graphic art, newsprint, and excerpts from various literary and artistic works. How significant must a component of such a work be before the user must pay copyright royalties? Must the creator of a multimedia work identify thousands of copyright holders and pay thousands of copyright fees in order to be allowed to create and disseminate his or her work? What should the rules be and who should enforce them? How can they be enforced at all in the unbounded realm of cyberspace?

Work

Work and the workplace are being transformed by ICT. More flexibility and choice are now possible, such as "teleworking" at home, on the road, at any hour or location. In addition, new kinds of job and job opportunity are being created, such as webmasters, data-miners, cyber counselors, and so on. But such benefits and opportunities are accompanied by risks and problems, such as unemployment for computer-replaced humans, "deskilling" of workers who only need to push buttons, stress keeping up with high-speed machines, repetitive motion injuries, magnetism and radiation from computer hardware, surveillance of workers by monitoring software, and computerized "sweat shops" that pay "slave wages." A wide range of new laws, regulations, rules, and practices are needed if society is to manage these workplace developments efficiently and justly.

Social justice

As more of society's activities and opportunities enter cyberspace – business opportunities, educational opportunities, medical services, employment, leisure-time activities, and on and on – it will become harder and harder for people with little or no access to information technology to share in the benefits and opportunities of society. Someone with no "electronic identity" may have no social identity at all. Therefore social justice (not to mention economic prosperity) requires that society develops policies and practices to more fully include people who, in the past, have had limited access to computer resources: women, the poor, the old, persons of color, rural residents, persons with disabilities.

Consider the example of "assistive technology" for persons with disabilities. Various hardware and software devices have been developed in recent years to enable persons with disabilities to use information technology easily and effectively. As a result, people who would otherwise be utterly dependent upon others for almost everything suddenly find their lives transformed into happier, productive, "near-normal" ones. Visual impairments and blindness, hearing impairments and deafness, inability to control one's limbs, even near-total paralysis need no longer be major impediments to social participation and productivity. Given these dramatic benefits of assistive technology, as well as rapidly decreasing costs, does a just society have an ethical obligation to provide assistive technology to its citizens with disabilities?

Government and democracy

Information and communication technology has the potential to change significantly many relationships between individual citizens and governments – local, regional, and national. Electronic voting and referenda, as well as emailed messages to legislators and ministers, could give citizens more timely input into government decisions and law-making. Optimists point out that information technology, appropriately used, can enable better citizen participation in democratic processes, can make government more open and accountable, can provide easy citizen access to government information, reports, services, plans, and proposed legislation. Pessimists, on the other hand, worry that government officials who are regularly bombarded with emails from angry voters might be easily swayed by short-term swings in public mood, that hackers could disrupt or corrupt electronic election processes, that dictatorial governments might find ways to use computer technology to control and intimidate the population more effectively than ever before. What policies should be put in place to take account of these hopes and worries?

A primary goal of computer ethics

The above paragraphs identify only a small fraction of the social and ethical issues that computing technology has begun to generate in the information age. The vast majority of such issues are still unknown, and they will gradually come into view as powerful and flexible ICT makes new things possible. A primary goal of computer ethics is to identify and analyze resulting "policy vacuums" as well as to help formulate new social/ethical policies to deal with them in just and responsible ways.

Computer Ethics: Some Historical Milestones

Some important milestones in the history of computer ethics include the following.

1940s and 1950s

Computer ethics as a field of academic study was founded by MIT professor Norbert Wiener during World War Two (early 1940s) while helping to develop an anti-aircraft cannon capable of shooting down fast warplanes. The engineering challenge of this project caused Wiener and some colleagues to create a new field of research that Wiener called "cybernetics" – the science of information feedback systems. The concepts of cybernetics, when combined with digital computers under development at that time, led Wiener to draw some remarkably insightful ethical conclusions about the technology that we now call ICT. He perceptively foresaw revolutionary social and ethical consequences. In 1948, for example, in his book *Cybernetics: or Control and Communication in the Animal and the Machine*, Wiener said the following:

> It has long been clear to me that the modern ultra-rapid computing machine was in principle an ideal central nervous system to an apparatus for automatic control; and that its input and output need not be in the form of numbers or diagrams but might very well be, respectively, the readings of artificial sense organs, such as photoelectric cells or thermometers, and the performance of motors or solenoids. . . . we are already in a position to construct artificial machines of almost any degree of elaborateness of performance. Long before Nagasaki and the public awareness of the atomic bomb, it had occurred to me that we were here in the presence of another social potentiality of unheard-of importance for good and for evil. (pp. 27–8)

In 1950 Wiener published his monumental computer ethics book, *The Human Use of Human Beings*, which not only established him as the founder of computer ethics, but – far more importantly – laid down a comprehensive computer ethics foundation which remains today (more than half a century later) a powerful basis for computer ethics research and analysis. (However,

Wiener did not use the name "computer ethics," which came into common use more than two decades later.)

Wiener's monumental foundation of computer ethics was far ahead of its time, and it was virtually ignored for decades. In his view, the integration of computer technology into society will eventually constitute the remaking of society – the "second industrial revolution." It will require a multifaceted process taking decades of effort, and it will radically change everything. A project so vast will necessarily include a wide diversity of tasks and challenges. Workers must adjust to radical changes in the workplace; governments must establish new laws and regulations; industry and businesses must create new policies and practices; professional organizations must develop new codes of conduct for their members; sociologists and psychologists must study and understand new social and psychological phenomena; and philosophers must rethink and redefine old social and ethical concepts.

1960s

In the mid-1960s, computer scientist Donn Parker began to examine unethical and illegal uses of computers by computer professionals. "It seemed," Parker said, "that when people entered the computer center they left their ethics at the door." He collected examples of computer crime and other unethical computerized activities. He developed a code of professional ethics for the ACM. Over the next decade, Parker went on to produce books, articles, speeches, and workshops that relaunched the field of computer ethics, giving it momentum and importance among professional computer scientists and public policy-makers. Parker is, in this sense, the second founder of computer ethics after Norbert Wiener (see Parker 1968, 1979; Parker et al. 1990).

1970s

During the late 1960s, computer science professor Joseph Weizenbaum created a computer program that he called ELIZA. In his first experiment with ELIZA, he scripted it to provide a crude imitation of "a Rogerian psychotherapist engaged in an initial interview with a patient." Weizenbaum was shocked at the reactions people had to his simple computer program. Some practicing psychiatrists saw it as evidence that computers would soon be performing automated psychotherapy, and even computer scholars at his university became emotionally involved with the computer, sharing their intimate thoughts with it. Weizenbaum was concerned that an "information processing model" of human beings was reinforcing an already growing tendency among scientists, and even the general public, to see humans as mere machines. In the early 1970s, Weizenbaum undertook a book-writing project to defend the view that humans are much more than information processors. The project resulted in his book, *Computer Power and Human Reason* (1976), which is now considered a classic in computer ethics. Weizenbaum's book, plus his university courses and the many speeches he gave in the 1970s, inspired a number of thinkers and projects in computer ethics. He stands with Norbert Wiener and Donn Parker as a key person in the formative history of the subject.

In the mid-1970s, philosopher (and later computer science professor) Walter Maner began to use the term "computer ethics" to refer to *that field of applied ethics dealing with ethical problems aggravated, transformed, or created by computer technology.* Maner offered an experimental university course on the subject, and he generated much interest in university-level computer ethics courses by offering a variety of workshops and lectures at computer science conferences and philosophy conferences across America. In 1978 he also self-published and disseminated his *Starter Kit in Computer Ethics* (published two years later by Helvetia Press), which contained curriculum materials and pedagogical advice for university teachers to develop computer ethics courses. Maner's trailblazing course, plus his *Starter Kit* and the many conference workshops he conducted, had a significant impact upon the teaching of computer ethics across America. Many university courses were put in place because of him, and several important scholars were attracted into the field.

1980s and 1990s

By the early 1980s, a number of social and ethical consequences of information technology were becoming public issues in America and Europe: issues such as computer-enabled crime, disasters caused by computer failures,[1] invasions of privacy via computer databases, and major law suits regarding software ownership. Because of the work of Parker, Weizenbaum, Maner, and others, the foundation had been laid for computer ethics as an academic discipline. (Unhappily, Wiener's monumental achievements from the 1940s and 1950s were essentially ignored.) The time was right, therefore, for an explosion of activities in computer ethics.

In 1985, James Moor published his now-classic article "What Is Computer Ethics?"; and in that same year, Deborah Johnson published *Computer*

---

[1] In 1983, President Ronald Reagan of the USA gave his "star wars" speech, which sparked a negative reaction from computer professionals across the globe. One important consequence was the founding of the organization Computer Professionals for Social Responsibility (CPSR).

Ethics, the first textbook – and for more than a decade, the *defining* textbook – in the field. Also in the mid-1980s there were relevant books published in psychology and sociology. For example, Sherry Turkle wrote *The Second Self* (1984), a book on the impact of computing on the human psyche; and Judith Perrolle produced *Computers and Social Change: Information, Property and Power* (1987), a sociological approach to computing and human values.

During the late 1980s and throughout the 1990s, the field of computer ethics grew rapidly. Conferences, university courses, textbooks, research centers, journals, and research professorships were created. During this period, practical concern related to computer ethics continued to rise. Organizations regularly monitored the use and abuse of ICT. For example, since 1983 incidents of ICT abuse within the UK have been reported every three years by the Audit Commission. The reports provide evidence of the level of ICT abuse, the reasons for its occurrence, and the risks that organizations need to address. By the mid-1990s, the present editors were noting a "second generation" of computer ethics developments (Rogerson and Bynum 1996).

Overview of this Book

In this book, the term "computer ethics" is used very broadly to include areas of study sometimes referred to as "information ethics," "ICT ethics," "cyberethics," and "global information ethics."

The book is divided into four parts, each of which includes (1) an editors' introduction to provide background and context, (2) relevant essays by computer ethics thinkers, (3) a specific case to consider and analyze, (4) a set of helpful study questions, and (5) a short list of additional readings and web resources to deepen one's knowledge of the topic. (Supplementary materials can also be found on the web sites of the RCCS (www.computerethics.org or www.computerethics.info) and the CCSR (www.ccsr.cse.dmu.ac.uk).)

Part I, "What Is Computer Ethics?," discusses the nature of computer ethics as a field of study. In chapter 1, James H. Moor presents his influential account of the nature, goals, and methods of computer ethics. In chapter 2, Walter Maner defends his view that ICT creates unique ethical problems that would not have occurred without it. Part I concludes with a discussion and example analysis by Terrell Ward Bynum of case analysis in computer ethics.

Part II, "Professional Responsibility," examines computer ethics from the point of view of ICT professionals. In chapter 4, Chuck Huff discusses and illustrates the fact that designers of computer systems often have a larger social and ethical impact than they realize or intend. In chapter 5, Donald Gotterbarn argues that ICT professionals have specific duties and

responsibilities in light of their special knowledge and powerful impacts
upon the world. Should codes of ethics and standards of good practice guide
computer professionals in their judgments and actions? – and, if so, what are
the appropriate codes and standards? What can developers of information
systems do to ensure that ethical considerations are properly addressed? In
the concluding chapter of Part II, Simon Rogerson offers a specific method
to integrate ethical considerations into software project management.

Part III, "Codes of Ethics," discusses the various roles and functions of
ethical codes for ICT professionals. It also provides six example codes of
ethics from professional organizations in America, the United Kingdom,
and Australia. In chapter 7, N. Ben Fairweather examines the shortcomings of a popular list of four "ethical issues" with the acronym PAPA
(privacy, accuracy, property, and accessibility) (see Mason 1986), and
he warns about the dangers of the mistaken belief that a code of ethics
can provide a complete ethical algorithm or checklist. In chapter 8,
Donald Gotterbarn examines various objections to the licensing of computer professionals, explains the ethical advantages of such licensing,
and offers a model licensing plan that overcomes typical objections to
licensing.

Part IV, "Sample Topics in Computer Ethics," explores four computer
ethics issues that have frequently been in the news – computer security,
privacy, ownership of intellectual property, and globalization. These topics
illustrate the kinds of issue and method of analysis that thinkers in computer
ethics have addressed in recent years:

"Computer Security" examines, in chapters by Peter G. Neumann and
Eugene H. Spafford, a variety of issues associated with computer security
and crime, including, for example, viruses, worms, Trojan horses, hacking
and cracking, and important gaps between ideal and actual computer
system security.

"Privacy and Computing" examines, in chapters by James H. Moor and
Elizabeth France, the reasons why ICT has generated so many privacy-
related issues, various definitions of privacy, the role and importance of
privacy in society, the relation of privacy to human values, and important
differences between the American and European ways of approaching
computer privacy questions.

"Computing and Intellectual Property," in chapters by Deborah G.
Johnson and Richard Stallman, relates traditional theories of ownership
to major social controversies surrounding digitized intellectual properties,
copyrights, patents, and the relationship between ethics and the law.
Included is a discussion of "free software" and the roots of the "open source"
movement.

"Global Information Ethics," in chapters by Krystyna Gorniak-
Kocikowska and John Weckert, examines various ethical issues that arise

because of the global reach of the Internet. Because the Internet ignores national borders and crosses cultural boundaries, whose laws and values apply, and how can cultural clashes and misunderstandings be resolved? Should information available on the Internet be censored, and if so who should determine what is acceptable? Should people in one culture be concerned about offending someone in another culture? Should a new "global" ethics be created to resolve such issues?

References

ACM and IEEE-CS (1991). *Computing Curricula 1991.* Available at http://www. computer.org/education/cc1991/

Elgesem, D. (1996). "Privacy, Respect for Persons, and Risk." In C. Ess (ed.), *Philosophical Perspectives on Computer-Mediated Communication.* State University of New York Press.

Fried, C. (1984). "Privacy." In F. D. Schoeman (ed.), *Philosophical Dimensions of Privacy.* Cambridge University Press.

IEEE-CS and ACM (2001). *Computing Curricula 2001.* Available at http://www. acm.org/sigcse/cc2001/

Johnson, D. G. (1985). *Computer Ethics.* Prentice-Hall (2nd edn 1994; 3rd edn 2001).

Maner, W. (1980). *Starter Kit in Computer Ethics.* Helvetia Press (published in cooperation with the National Information and Resource Center for Teaching Philosophy). (Originally self-published by Maner in 1978.)

Mason, R. O. (1986). "Four Ethical Issues of the Information Age." *MIS Quarterly,* 10/1: 5–12.

Miller, A. R. (1971). *The Assault on Privacy: Computers, Data Banks, and Dossiers.* University of Michigan Press.

Moor, J. H. (1985). "What Is Computer Ethics?" In T. W. Bynum (ed.), *Computers and Ethics.* Oxford: Blackwell, pp. 266–75. (Published as the October 1985 issue of *Metaphilosophy.*)

Nissenbaum, H. (1998). "Protecting Privacy in an Information Age: The Problem of Privacy in Public". *Law and Philosophy,* 17: 559–96.

Parker, D. (1968). "Rules of Ethics in Information Processing." *Communications of the ACM,* 11: 198–201.

Parker, D. (1979). *Ethical Conflicts in Computer Science and Technology.* AFIPS Press.

Parker, D., Swope, S., and Baker, B. N. (1990). *Ethical Conflicts in Information and Computer Science, Technology and Business.* QED Information Sciences.

Perrolle, J. A. (1987). *Computers and Social Change: Information, Property, and Power.* Wadsworth.

Rogerson, S. and Bynum, T. W. (1995). "Cyberspace: The Ethical Frontier." *Times Higher Education Supplement, The Times,* June 9.

Rogerson, S. and Bynum, T. W. (1996). "Information Ethics: The Second Generation." The Future of Information Systems Conference, UK Academy for Information Systems, April. Available at http://www.ccsr.cse.dmu.ac.uk/resources/general/discipline/ie_sec_gen.html

Tavani, H. T. (1999). "Informational Privacy, Data Mining and the Internet." *Ethics and Information Technology*, 1: 137–45.

Tavani, H. T. and Moor, J. H. (2001). "Privacy Protection, Control of Information, and Privacy-Enhancing Technologies." In R. A. Spinello and H. T. Tavani (eds.), *Readings in CyberEthics.* Jones and Bartlett, pp. 378–91.

Turkle, S. (1984). *The Second Self: Computers and the Human Spirit.* Simon and Schuster.

Weizenbaum, J. (1976). *Computer Power and Human Reason: From Judgment to Calculation.* Freeman.

Westin, A. R. (1967). *Privacy and Freedom.* Atheneum.

Wiener, N. (1948). *Cybernetics: or Control and Communication in the Animal and the Machine.* Technology Press.

Wiener, N. (1950/1954). *The Human Use of Human Beings: Cybernetics and Society.* Houghton Mifflin, 1950 (2nd rev. edn, Doubleday Anchor, 1954).

PART I

What is Computer Ethics?

It is not enough that you should understand about applied science in order that your work may increase man's blessings. Concern for man himself and his fate must always form the chief interest of all technical endeavors.

Albert Einstein

Editors' Introduction

In the 1940s and early 1950s, the field of study that is now called "computer ethics" was given a solid foundation by Professor Norbert Wiener of MIT. Unhappily, Professor Wiener's works in computer ethics were essentially ignored for decades by other thinkers. In the 1970s and 1980s computer ethics was recreated and redefined by thinkers who did not realize that Wiener had already done so much work in the field. Today, more than 50 years after Wiener created computer ethics, some thinkers are still attempting to define the nature and boundaries of the subject. Let us briefly consider five different definitions that have been developed since the 1970s.

Maner's Definition

The name "computer ethics" was not commonly used until the mid-1970s when Walter Maner began to use it. He defined this field of study as one that examines "ethical problems aggravated, transformed or created by computer technology." Some old ethical problems, he said, were made worse by computers, while others came into existence because of computer technology. He suggested that we should use traditional ethical theories of philosophers, such as the *utilitarian* ethics of the English philosophers Jeremy Bentham and John Stuart Mill, or the *rationalist* ethics of the German philosopher Immanuel Kant.

Johnson's Definition

In her book, *Computer Ethics* (1985), Deborah Johnson said that computer ethics studies the way in which computers "pose new versions of standard moral problems and moral dilemmas, exacerbating the old problems, and forcing us to apply ordinary moral norms in uncharted realms." Like Maner before her, Johnson adopted the "applied philosophy" approach of using procedures and concepts from utilitarianism and Kantianism. But, unlike Maner, she did not believe that computers create wholly new moral problems. Rather, she thought that computers gave a "new twist" to ethical questions that were already well known.

Moor's Definition

In his influential article "What Is Computer Ethics?" (1985), James Moor provided a definition of computer ethics that is much broader and more wide-ranging than those of Maner or Johnson. It is independent of any specific philosopher's theory; and it is compatible with a wide variety of approaches to ethical problem-solving. Since 1985, Moor's definition has been the most influential one. He defined computer ethics as a field concerned with "policy vacuums" and "conceptual muddles" regarding the social and ethical use of information technology:

> A typical problem in Computer Ethics arises because there is a policy vacuum about how computer technology should be used. Computers provide us with new capabilities and these in turn give us new choices for action. Often, either no policies for conduct in these situations exist or existing policies seem inadequate. A central task of Computer Ethics is to determine what we should do in such cases, that is, formulate policies to guide our actions. . . . One difficulty is that along with a policy vacuum there is often a conceptual vacuum. Although a problem in Computer Ethics may seem clear initially, a little reflection reveals a conceptual muddle. What is needed in such cases is an analysis that provides a coherent conceptual framework within which to formulate a policy for action. (Moor 1985, p. 266)

Moor said that computer technology is genuinely revolutionary because it is "logically malleable":

> Computers are logically malleable in that they can be shaped and molded to do any activity that can be characterized in terms of inputs, outputs and connecting logical operations. . . . Because logic applies everywhere, the potential applications of computer technology appear limitless. The computer is the nearest thing we have to a universal tool. Indeed, the limits of computers are largely the limits of our own creativity. (Ibid.)

According to Moor, the computer revolution will occur in two stages. The first stage is that of "technological introduction" in which computer technology is developed and refined. This already occurred during the first 40 years after the Second World War. The second stage – one that the industrialized world has only recently entered – is that of "technological permeation" in which technology gets integrated into everyday human activities and into social institutions, changing the very meaning of fundamental concepts, such as "money," "education," "work," and "fair elections."

Moor's way of defining computer ethics is very powerful and suggestive. It is broad enough to be compatible with a wide range of philosophical theories and methodologies, and it is rooted in a perceptive understanding of how technological revolutions proceed.

Bynum's Definition

In 1989 Terrell Ward Bynum developed another broad definition of computer ethics following a suggestion in Moor's 1985 paper. According to this view, computer ethics *identifies and analyzes the impacts of information technology on such social and human values as health, wealth, work, opportunity, freedom, democracy, knowledge, privacy, security, self-fulfillment, etc.* This very broad view of computer ethics employs applied ethics, sociology of computing, technology assessment, computer law, and related fields. It employs concepts, theories, and methodologies from these and other relevant disciplines. This conception of computer ethics is motivated by the belief that – eventually – information technology will profoundly affect everything that human beings hold dear.

Gotterbarn's Definition

In the 1990s, Donald Gotterbarn became a strong advocate for a different approach to computer ethics. From his perspective, computer ethics should be viewed as a branch of *professional ethics*, concerned primarily with standards of good practice and codes of conduct for computing professionals:

> There is little attention paid to the domain of professional ethics – the values that guide the day-to-day activities of computing professionals in their role as professionals. By computing professional I mean anyone involved in the design and development of computer artifacts. . . . The ethical decisions made during the development of these artifacts have a direct relationship to many of the issues discussed under the broader concept of computer ethics. (Gotterbarn 1991, p. 26)

With this "professional ethics" approach to computer ethics, Gotterbarn co-authored the 1992 version of the ACM Code of Ethics and Professional Conduct and led a team of scholars in the development of the 1999 ACM/IEEE Software Engineering Code of Ethics and Professional Practice. (Both of these codes of ethics are included in this book in Part III.)

Each of these definitions of computer ethics has influenced this textbook to some extent. Part I makes special use of the ideas of Moor and Maner; later parts of the book bring in other ideas as well.

References

Gotterbarn, D. (1991). "Computer Ethics: Responsibility Regained." *National Forum: The Phi Beta Kappa Journal*, 71: 26–31.

Johnson, D. G. (1985). *Computer Ethics*. Prentice-Hall (2nd edn 1994; 3rd edn 2001).

Maner, W. (1980). *Starter Kit in Computer Ethics*. Helvetia Press (published in cooperation with the National Information and Resource Center for Teaching Philosophy). (Originally self-published by Maner in 1978.)

Moor, J. H. (1985). "What Is Computer Ethics?" In T. W. Bynum (ed.), *Computers and Ethics*. Blackwell, pp. 266–75. (Published as the October 1985 issue of *Metaphilosophy*.)

CHAPTER 1

Reason, Relativity, and Responsibility in Computer Ethics

James H. Moor

Searching for Ethics in the Global Village

As computing becomes more prevalent, computer ethics becomes more difficult and more important. As Terry Bynum and Simon Rogerson put it,

> We are entering a generation marked by globalization and ubiquitous computing. The second generation of computer ethics, therefore, must be an era of "global information ethics." The stakes are much higher, and consequently considerations and applications of Information Ethics must be broader, more profound and above all effective in helping to realize a democratic and empowering technology rather than an enslaving or debilitating one. (1996, p. 135)

I heartily concur with the concern that Bynum and Rogerson express about the global impact of computing. The number and kinds of applications of computing increase dramatically each year and the impact of computing is felt around the planet. The ubiquitous use of electronic mail, electronic funds transfer, reservations systems, the World Wide Web, etc. places millions of the inhabitants of the planet in a global electronic village. Communication and actions at a distance have never been easier. We are definitely in a computer revolution. We are beyond the introduction stage of the revolution in which computers are curiosities of limited power used only by a few. Now, entire populations of developed countries are in the permeation stage of the revolution in which computers are rapidly moving into every aspect of daily life.

James H. Moor, "Reason, Relativity, and Responsibility in Computer Ethics." This chapter was originally presented as the keynote address at ETHICOMP96 in Madrid, Spain and later published in *Computers and Society*, 28:1 (March 1998), pp. 14–21. © 1998 by James H. Moor and reprinted by permission of the author.

The computer revolution has a life of its own. Recently [i.e., in 1996], in northern California about one-sixth of the phone calls didn't connect because of excessive use of the Internet. People are surging to gain access to computer technology. They see it as not only a part of their daily lives but a necessary venue for routine communication and commercial transactions. In fact, the surge has become so great that America On Line, a prominent Internet service provider, offered its customers refunds because the demand for connection overwhelmed the company's own computer technology. The widespread desire to be wired should make us reflect on what awaits us as the computer revolution explodes around the world. The digital genie is out of the bottle on a worldwide scale.

The prospect of a global village in which everyone on the planet is connected to everyone else with regard to computing power and communication is breathtaking. What is difficult to comprehend is what impact this will have on human life. Surely, some of the effects will be quite positive and others quite negative. The question is to what extent we can bring ethics to bear on the computer revolution in order to guide us to a better world or at least prevent us from falling into a worse world. With the newly acquired advantages of computer technology, few would want to put the genie completely back into the bottle. And yet, given the nature of the revolutionary beast, I am not sure it is possible to completely control it, though we certainly can modify its evolution. Aspects of the computer revolution will continue to spring up in unpredictable ways – in some cases causing us considerable grief. Therefore, it is extremely important to be alert to what is happening. Because the computer revolution has the potential to have major effects on how we lead our lives, the paramount issue of how we should control computing and the flow of information needs to be addressed on an ongoing basis in order to shape the technology to serve us to our mutual benefit. We must remain vigilant and proactive so that we don't pillage the global village.

Although almost everyone would agree that computing is having a significant, if not a revolutionary, impact on the world, and that ethical issues about applications of this surging technology should be raised, there is disagreement about the nature of computer ethics. Let me describe two positions with which I disagree. These two positions are both popular, but represent opposite extremes. I believe they mislead us about the real nature of computer ethics and undercut potential for progress in the field. The first view I will call the "Routine Ethics" position. According to the Routine Ethics position, ethical problems in computing are regarded as no different from ethical problems in any field. There is nothing special about them. We apply established customs, laws, and norms, and assess the situations straightforwardly. Sometimes people steal cars and sometimes people steal computers. What's the difference? The second view is usually called "Cultural Relativism." On this view, local customs and laws determine what is right and wrong, but, because computing technology such as the World Wide Web crosses cultural boundaries, the problems of computer ethics are intractable. Free speech is permitted in the United States but not in China. How can we justify a standard for or against free speech on the World Wide Web? Routine Ethics makes computer ethics trivial and Cultural Relativism makes it impossible.

I believe that the views of both Routine Ethics and Cultural Relativism are incorrect, particularly when used to characterize computer ethics. The former underestimates the changes that occur in our conceptual framework and the latter underestimates the stability of our core human values. The problems of computer ethics, at least in some cases, are special and exert pressure on our understanding. And yet our fundamental values, based on our common human nature, give us an opportunity for rational discussion even among cultures with different customs. The purpose of this chapter is to explain how it is possible to have both reason and relativity in computer ethics. Only with such an understanding is responsibility in computer ethics possible.

Logical Malleability and Informational Enrichment

Computers are *logically malleable*. This is the feature that makes computers so revolutionary. They are logically malleable in that they can be manipulated to do any activity that can be characterized in terms of inputs, outputs, and connecting logical operations. Computers can be manipulated syntactically and semantically. Syntactically, one can alter what the computer does by changing its program. And semantically one can use the states of a computer to represent anything one chooses, from the sales of a stock market to the trajectory of a spacecraft. Computers are general purpose machines like no others. That is why they are now found in every aspect of our lives and that is why a computer revolution is taking place.

Computers are also *informationally enriching*. Because of their logical malleability, computers are put to many uses in diverse activities. Once in place, computers can be modified to enhance capabilities and improve overall performance even further. Often, computerized activities become informationalized; i.e., the processing of information becomes a crucial ingredient in performing and understanding the activities themselves. When this happens, both the activities and the conceptions of the activities become informationally enriched.

The process of informational enrichment is gradual and is more manifest in some activities than in others. What is striking is how often and the extent to which it does occur. In a typical scenario a computer is introduced merely as a tool to perform a job or to assist in an activity. Gradually, the computer becomes an essential part of the methodology of doing the job or performing the activity. To do it properly is to use a computer. Over time, the job or activity is viewed increasingly as an informational phenomenon, so that information processing is taken as a salient or even defining feature.

Consider some examples of informational enrichment. At one time in the United States money was backed by gold. There was an exchange of paper bills, but the bills were merely coupons that could, at least in principle, be redeemed for gold or perhaps silver. For some time the US remained on the gold standard so that paper bills were markers for money. Monetary transactions were grounded in gold. Then the gold standard was dropped and the paper bills became the money. To have money was to have the paper, presumably backed by the good faith and trust in the government. Now paper has been augmented with credit cards and debit cards that can be read by computers. Of course, these cards are not the real money because one can always exchange the credits for paper money. But, it is likely that the use of paper money will decrease and the electronic tokens on the cards or in a bank's computer will become the money. Some cards now have chips embedded in them so that they can be loaded with electronic money which is then transferred as information to a merchant at the point of sale. We are headed for a cashless society. Monetary transactions are increasingly grounded in information. Money may come to be conceived as an elaborate computable function among people. In the computer age the concept of money is becoming informationally enriched.

As another example of informational enrichment, consider the evolving nature of warfare. Traditionally, in warfare different sides send people into battle who fight with each other at close quarters until one side has killed or captured so many that the other side surrenders. People are still sent to the battlefield, but warfare is rapidly becoming computerized. The stealth bomber used by the United States during the Gulf War [in 1991] was the result of computerized engineering. Computers designed the shape of the aircraft so that it would be nearly invisible to radar. The aircraft's design deprived Iraq of information. The Gulf War was about information and the lack of it. Bombs were dropped and guided by lasers and computers. Missiles were launched from ships and sought their targets by reading the terrain using computer guidance systems. The first objective of the armed forces under General H. Norman Schwarzkopf's command was to eliminate the ability of Iraq to communicate among its own forces or to use its aircraft detection systems. Schwarzkopf remarked after the war that it was the first time an enemy was brought to his knees by denial of information. As war becomes increasingly computerized, it may be less necessary or desirable to send men and women into the battlefield. Wars ultimately will be about the destruction of information or the introduction of misleading information. One side surrenders when it is not able to obtain and control certain kinds of information. This may not be a bad result. Better that data die, than people. As warfare becomes increasingly computerized, our concept of war becomes informationally enriched. The information processing model is seizing the high ground.

Informational enrichment can also affect ethical and legal practices and concepts. Consider the concept of privacy as it has evolved in the United States as an example (Moor 1990). Privacy is not explicitly mentioned in the Declaration of Independence or in the Constitution of the United States, though there are portions of these documents which implicitly support a notion of privacy as protection from governmental intrusion, particularly the physical invasion of people's houses. The notion of privacy has been an evolving concept in the US. For instance, in the 1960s and '70s the legal concept of privacy was expanded to include protection against government interference in personal decisions about contraception and abortion. Today, the concept of privacy includes these earlier elements but increasingly focuses on informational privacy. This shift in emphasis has been brought about because of the development of the computer and its use in collecting large databases of personal information.

The computer, originally viewed by many as little more than an electronic filing cabinet, rapidly revealed its potential. Once data is entered into a computer it can be sorted, searched, and accessed in extraordinarily easy ways that paper files cannot be in practical amounts of time. The activity of storing and retrieving information has been enhanced to the extent that all of us now have a legitimate basis for concern about the improper use and release of personal information through computers. The computerization of credit histories and medical records for use in normal business provides an ongoing possibility for misuse and abuse. Because of the widespread application of computer technology, our concern about privacy today goes far beyond the original concern about the physical intrusion of governmental forces into our houses. Now concerns about privacy are usually about improper access and manipulation of personal information by the government and many others who have access to computerized records. The original concept of privacy in the United States has become informationally enriched in the computer age.

Even concepts that begin as informational concepts can be informationally enriched. As an example, consider the legal concept of copyright. Legislation protecting the products of authors and inventors is authorized by the Constitution of the United States. Early copyright laws were passed to protect literary works, and patent laws were passed to protect inventions. Copyright laws in the US have been amended over the years to extend the length of protection to authors and to protect a wider and wider range of materials including music and photographs. But until the computer age the underlying conception of copyright was that it was intended to protect those items which could be read and understood by humans. For example, in the early part of the twentieth century an attempt to protect piano rolls by copyright was denied on the grounds that piano rolls were not in human readable form.

In the 1960s programmers began to submit copies of printouts of their programs for copyright protection. The printouts were in human readable form. But what programmers wanted to protect was not the printouts of programs but the programs as they existed on computers. However, the programs, as they existed on computers, were not in human readable form. If the human readable printouts were to count as surrogates to protect the machine versions of programs, copyright law had to be stretched. Moreover, if machine-readable programs were protectable by copyright, then it would seem that programs as instantiated on computer chips might be protectable by copyright as well. Copyright protection was so extended. Through the development of computing, the concept of copyright has become informationally enriched. Copyright extends not only to computer languages, but to computer languages in forms readable only by machines. Indeed, what is copyrightable today sometimes looks more like an invention than a literary work.

I have used the concepts of money, war, privacy, and copyright as examples of informational enrichment. There are many more. It is difficult to think of an activity now being done extensively by computers that has not been informationally enriched. In some cases this enrichment is so salient that our concepts shift somewhat. They too become informationally enriched. In the computer age, we live in a different world.

The Special Nature of Computer Ethics

I maintain that computer ethics is a special field of ethical research and application. Let me begin by describing computer ethics and then making a case for its special nature.

Computer ethics has two parts: (i) the analysis of the nature and social impact of computer technology and (ii) the corresponding formulation and justification of policies for the ethical use of such technology. I use the phrase "computer technology" because I take the subject-matter of the field broadly to include computers and associated technology, including software, hardware, and networks (Moor 1985).

We need thoughtful analyses of situations in which computers have an impact, and we need to formulate and justify policies for using them ethically. Although we need to analyze before we can formulate and justify a policy, the process of discovery often comes in the reverse order. We know that computing technology is being employed in a given situation, but we are puzzled how it should be used. There is a *policy vacuum*. For example, should a supervisor be allowed to read a subordinate's email? Or should the government be allowed to censor information on the Internet? Initially, there may be no clear policies on such matters. They never arose before. There are policy vacuums in such situations. Sometimes it may be simply a matter of establishing some policy, but often one must analyze the situation further. Is email in the workplace more like correspondence on company stationary in company files or more like private and personal phone conversations? Is the Internet more like a passive magazine or more like an active television? One often finds oneself in a *conceptual muddle*. The issues are not trivial matters of semantics. If someone's health status is discovered through email or an impressionable child is exposed to distressing material on the Internet, the consequences may be very damaging. Obtaining a clear conception of the situation from which to formulate ethical policies is the logical first step in analysis, although chronologically one's uncertainty about the appropriate policy may precede and motivate the search for conceptual clarification. Given a tentative understanding of the situation, one can propose and evaluate possible policies for proper conduct. The evaluation of a policy will usually require a close examination and perhaps refinement of one's values. Such policy evaluation may lead one back for further conceptual clarification and then further policy formulation and evaluation. Eventually, some clear understanding and justifiable policy should emerge. Of course, with the discovery of new consequences and the application of new technology to the situation, the cycle of conceptual clarification and policy formulation and evaluation may have to be repeated on an ongoing basis.

Because computers are logically malleable, they will continue to be applied in unpredictable and novel ways, generating numerous policy vacuums for the foreseeable future. Moreover, because computerized situations often become informationally enriched, we will continue to find ourselves in conceptual muddles about how precisely to understand these situations. This is not to say that we can't achieve conceptual clarity and that we can't formulate and justify reasonable policies. Rather, it is to point out that the task of computer ethics is, if not Sisyphean, at least ongoing and formidable. No other field of ethics has these features to the degree that computer ethics does. Computer ethics is not simply ethics rotely applied to computing. Typically, problems in computer ethics require more than straightforward application of ethical principles to situations. Considerable interpretation is required before appropriate policies can be formulated and justified. Of course, to say that computer ethics is a special field of ethics does not mean that every ethical problem involving computers is unique or difficult to understand. Stealing a computer may be a simple case of theft. A straightforward application of an ethical principle is appropriate. In such a situation there are no policy vacuums and no conceptual muddles. And to say that computer ethics is a special field of ethics does not mean that other fields of applied ethics do not have some instances of policy vacuums and conceptual confusion. Medical technology raises questions about what policy to follow for brain-dead patients and conceptual questions about what counts as life. What is special about computer ethics is that it has a continually large number of evolving situations which are difficult to conceptualize clearly and for which it is hard to find justified ethical policies. Doing computer ethics is not impossible, but doing it typically involves much more than rote application of existing norms.

I have argued that computer ethics is special but is the subject-matter truly *unique*? The answer depends upon what one means by "the subject-matter." If by "the subject-matter" one means "computing technology," then computer ethics is unique, for computing technology possesses unique properties (Maner 1996). I believe its most important property is logical malleability, which explains the ongoing wave of revolution and generation of ethical problems. If by "the subject-matter" one has in mind the occurrence of some novel ethical issues, then computer ethics is not unique because other fields of ethics sometimes consider novel situations which require revisions of conceptual frameworks and new policy formulation. If by "the subject-matter" one means "the overall range, depth and novelty of ethical issues generated by a technology," then computer ethics is unique. No other technology, as revolutionary as it may be for a given area, has and will have the scope, depth, and novelty of impact that computing technology has and will have. There is no mystery why computer ethics has a prominence that toaster ethics, locomotive ethics, and sewing machine ethics do not have.

In summary, what is unique about computer ethics is computing technology itself, and what makes computer ethics different as a field of ethics is the scope, depth, and novelty of ethical situations for which conceptual revisions and policy adjustments are required. Deborah Johnson, in her excellent introduction to computer ethics, avoids taking sides on the issue of the uniqueness of computer ethics and suggests that ethical issues surrounding computers are "*new species of old moral issues.*" Johnson goes on to say:

> The metaphor of species and genus encompasses the element of truth on each side of the debate in that a new species has some unique characteristics making it different from any other species, but at the same time, the species has generic or fundamental characteristics that are common to all members of the genus. (1994, p. 10)

Perhaps, the ambiguity in the question about the uniqueness of computer ethics suggests this middle ground approach. But I believe that Johnson's characterization of a problem of computer ethics as just another species of a fixed ethical genus is somewhat misleading because the conceptual uncertainty generated by some problems in computer ethics affects not only our understanding of the particular situation but also the ethical and legal categories that apply to it. As I have suggested, ethical and legal categories, such as privacy and copyright, can shift in meaning as they become informationally enriched. The novelty of the species sometimes infects the genus! Whether or not one regards computer ethics as unique, computer ethics is definitely a demanding field of ethics which requires more than routine application of principles.

Reasons within Relative Frameworks

I have been arguing against understanding computer ethics in terms of Routine Ethics because the application of computing technology regularly produces policy vacuums and informational enrichment which promotes conceptual shifts, if not outright conceptual muddles. Computer ethics is not rote. But, the rejection of Routine Ethics leaves many people uncomfortable. If ethics is not routine, how can it be done at all? Retreating to a position of Cultural Relativism will not solve the problem. According to Cultural Relativism, ethical issues must be decided situationally on the basis of local customs and laws. Two problems immediately confront us with such a position with regard to computer ethics. First, because computing activity is globally interactive, appealing to local customs and laws will not in general provide us with an answer to what we should do when customs and laws conflict. On the World Wide Web information flows without regard to particular customs. Which customs should we apply in regulating it? To pick the customs of any one culture seems arbitrary. Do we pick the customs of the culture in which the information appears on the computer screen or the customs of the culture from which the information originates? Second, all of the difficulties with Routine Ethics continue to apply. A policy vacuum may occur for every culture. A computing situation may be so novel that there are no customs or laws established anywhere to cope with it. Initially, an appeal to Cultural Relativism may seem like a sophisticated and plausible attempt to escape the parochial limits of Routine Ethics, but on closer inspection it has the limitations of Routine Ethics and more.

The shortcomings and difficulties with Routine Ethics and Cultural Relativism may make one cautious about doing applied ethics at all. If people differ in their ethical judgments, how can disagreements be avoided or resolved? It is for this reason, I think, that computer scientists and others are sometimes reluctant to teach computer ethics. Ethical issues seem to be too elusive and vague. It is more comfortable to talk about algorithms, data structures, memory locations, and networks because there are facts of the matter on these topics. The realm of values seems hopelessly virtual, never to be as substantial as the real realm of facts. But a safe retreat to a realm of pure facts where everything is black or white, true or false, is not possible. Every science, including computer science, rests on value judgments. If, for example, truth is not taken as a critical value by scientists, the enterprise of science cannot begin.

My position is that all interesting human enterprises, including computing, are conducted within frameworks of values. Moreover, these frameworks can be rationally criticized and adjusted. Sometimes they are criticized externally from the vantage point of other frameworks and sometimes they are critiqued internally. Some value frameworks, such as those in an emerging science like computer science, undergo rapid evolution. Other value frameworks are more stable. Value frameworks provide us with the sorts of reason we consider relevant when justifying particular value judgments. Human values are relative, but not simply in the shallow sense of Cultural Relativism. Our most basic values are relative to our humanity, which provides us with a shared framework in which to conduct reasoned arguments about what we ought to do.

My intent is not to search for a way to eliminate value disputes altogether, which I do not think is possible, but to show how some reasoned discussion about value issues is possible even when customs may be absent or in conflict. To say that values are relative means that they are not absolute; it does not mean they are random or uncommon or uncriticizable. Perhaps, reflecting about reasoning with relative values is like thinking about swimming for the first time. It seems impossible. Why doesn't one sink to the bottom? How can one move if the water moves when pushed? Why doesn't one drown? But, swimming without drowning is possible and so is reasoning with relative values. In fact, not only is it possible; we do it all the time. Given the relativity of values, is there any hope for rational discussion in computer ethics. Absolutely!

My presentation will be in two steps. First, I will discuss the ubiquity of non-ethical values and emphasize their use in every aspect of human activity – we cannot escape value decision-making even if we want to do so. I will use computer science itself as an example, though any interesting human enterprise could serve as an illustration. And, second, I will discuss the use of values in making ethical decisions. My position is that an accommodation between reasoned argument and relativity of values is possible. We can acknowledge the difference in values among people and among cultures and still engage in rational discussions about the best policies for using computer technology.

Let me begin by emphasizing the ubiquity of values in our lives. In every reasonably complex human activity decisions are made which require value choices at least implicitly. Cooks make value decisions about what constitutes a good meal. Businesspeople make value decisions about good investments. Lawyers make decisions about good jurors. All of these endeavors utilize facts, but the facts are always in the escort of values. Each discipline has its own cluster of values which members of the discipline use in making decisions. Even scientists, who pride themselves in establishing facts, must utilize values at least implicitly. In order to gather the facts, scientists must know what counts as good evidence, what counts as good methodology, and what counts as good explanation. Values permeate our lives. I am not speaking here primarily of ethical values. Rather, these are the values of daily activities that make our activities purposeful. Values are so much a part of what we do that we often don't reflect on the fact that values are at work when we make ordinary decisions. Value judgments cannot be escaped by any of us in work or play. Values saturate our decision-making and are necessary for the flourishing of the activities of life.

Even if one agrees that non-ethical values cannot be escaped in doing ordinary activities, there is still the concern that the relativity of values makes it impossible to have reasoned disputes. After all, cooks, business-people, lawyers, and scientists disagree among themselves. To examine the problem of relativity of values, let us use the activity of computer science as an example. In doing computer science, like other sophisticated human activities, one must make decisions and these decisions utilize, often impli-citly, sets of non-ethical values. These are the values of the discipline. For instance, a computer scientist knows what makes a computer program a good program. Here I am using "good" primarily in a non-ethical sense. A good computer program is one that works, that has been thoroughly tested, that doesn't have bugs, that is well structured, that is well documented, that runs efficiently, that is easy to maintain, and that has a friendly interface. All of the properties of a good program reflect values. They are the features that make one computer program *better* than another. Moreover, this set of related values, that constitutes a set of standards within computer science, is widely shared among computer scientists. Given these standards, rational discussions can be conducted about how to improve a particular computer program. Moreover, policies regarding good programming techniques can be reasonably justified relative to the set of standards. For instance, one might argue for a policy of using object-oriented programming on the grounds that it leads to fewer bugs and computer code that is easier to maintain.

Computer scientists, like everyone else, can have disagreements, includ-ing disagreements about the standards. But disagreements which might appear to be about values are sometimes merely disagreements about facts. If there is a disagreement about the justification of the policy to use object-oriented programming, the real disagreement may be about whether or not object-oriented programming really leads to fewer bugs and code that is easier to maintain. Such a dispute might be put to an empirical test. In this situation it is not a dispute about the importance of bug-free, easily maintainable code, but about how well object-oriented programming achieves these valued goals. Thus, disputes that initially may strike us as irreconcilable disputes about values may really be disputes about the facts of the matter subject to empirical adjudication.

Naturally, computer scientists can also disagree about the values that make up a good computer program as well. Some may rank documentation as essential and others may take it to be a less important optional feature. Depending upon the ranking of the different values, different judgments can be made regarding which programs are better than others and which policies about constructing computer programs are the most important. What I want to emphasize, however, is the degree of consensus that exists among computer scientists about what constitutes a good computer program. The specific rankings may differ somewhat from person to person, but a pattern of agreement emerges about the types of program that are the best. No computer scientist regards an ineffective, untested, buggy, unstructured, undocumented, inefficient, unmaintainable code with an unfriendly interface as a good program. It just doesn't happen. In a sense, the shared standards define the field and determine who is qualified and, indeed, who is in the field at all. If one prefers to produce buggy, "spaghetti code" programs, one is not doing serious computer science at all.

Discussions of the relativity of values sometimes engage in the "Many/Any Fallacy". This fallacy occurs when one reasons from the fact that many alternatives are acceptable to the claim that any alternative is acceptable. There are many acceptable ways for a travel agent to route someone between Boston and Madrid. It doesn't follow that any way of sending someone between these cities is acceptable. Traveling through the center of the Earth and going via the North Star are not included. Many different computer programs may be good, but not just any computer program is good.

To summarize, non-ethical values play a role in our decision-making in all interesting human activities, including computer science. No escape to a safe realm of pure facts, even in science, is ever possible. The standards of value of a discipline may be widely shared, implicit, and go unnoticed, but they are always there. Moreover, every discipline has sufficient agreement upon what the standards are to conduct its business. Without some consensus on what is valuable, progress in a discipline is impossible.

Core Values

Given that some consensus about values within communities with shared preferences exists, is there any basis for consensus about values among communities? Ethical judgments are made beyond the narrow bounds of special interest communities. Given differences among communities, let alone differences among cultures, how is it possible to ground ethical judgments? Ethical judgments about computing technology may seem even more dubious. Because computing technology generates policy vacuums, i.e., creates situations in which there are no established policies based on custom, law, or religion, we are confronted with the difficult task of justifying ethical policies about novel applications of computing technology even within a community.

To address these challenges, we must begin by asking whether we share any values as human beings. What do we have in common? I believe that there is a set of core values which are shared by most, if not all, humans. They are familiar to all of us. Life and happiness are two of the most obvious such values. At the very least, people want to avoid death and pain for themselves. Of course, in some situations people give up their lives and suffer pain to accomplish certain objectives. But, generally speaking, people do not intentionally hurt and kill themselves for no reason. There is a prima facie value on life and happiness for humans. Other core values (or core goods) for humans include ability, freedom, knowledge, resources, and protection. These values are articulated in different ways in different cultures, but all cultures place importance on these values to some extent. Obviously, some cultures may distribute these goods unequally among their members, but no culture disregards these values completely. No culture or individual human could continue to exist and disregard the core values completely. Humans need nourishment and cultures need to raise their young to survive. These kinds of activity require at least some ability, freedom, knowledge, resources, and protection. The fact that humans share some basic values is not surprising. These values provide some evolutionary advantages. Individuals and cultures that completely neglect the core goods will not exist for very long.

The core values provide standards with which to evaluate the rationality of our actions and policies. They give us reasons to favor some courses of action over others. They provide a framework of values for judging the activities of others as well. As we become acquainted with other cultures, differences often strike us. The members of other cultures eat different meals, wear different clothing, and live in different shelters. But at a more abstract level people are remarkably alike. Initially, we may find the habits of others to be strange, silly, or bizarre, but after investigation we don't find them to be unintelligible. Activities that may appear at first to be random or purposeless are in fact ordered and purposeful. This doesn't make the practices of others uncriticizable, any more than our own are uncriticizable, but it does make them understandable.

Discussions of relativism in ethics often include examples of the Many/Any Fallacy. Many different customs exist, and, so it is argued, any custom may exist. Not so! Some possible practices are ruled out and other practices (in some form or other) are required if a culture is to exist. Core human values are articulated in a multitude of delightful ways, but they also constrain the realm of possibilities. "Relative" doesn't mean "random."

To say that we share the core values is only a first step in the argument toward grounding ethical judgments. The most evil villain and the most corrupt society will exhibit core human values on an individual basis. Possessing core human values is a sign of being rational, but is not a sufficient condition for being ethical. To adopt *the ethical point of view*, one must respect others and their core values. All things being equal, people do not want to suffer death, pain, disability, interference, deception, loss of resources, or intrusion.

If we take as an ethical guideline to avoid harming others without justification, then the core values give us a set of standards by which to evaluate actions and policies. The core values provide a framework for analysis in computer ethics. By using the core-value framework, some policies for applying computer technology can be judged to be better than others. Let us consider a set of possible policies for the activities of a web browser as an example.

Possible policies for a web site

1 Destroy information on the user's hard disk by leaving a time bomb on the user's hard disk.
2 Remove information from the user's hard disk without the user's knowledge.
3 Leave a cookie (information about the user's preferences) on the user's hard disk without informing the user.
4 Leave a cookie on the user's hard disk and inform the user.
5 Do not leave or take any permanent information from the user's hard disk.
6 Give the user the information and ability to accept or decline cookies.

If we respect others and their core values, i.e., take the ethical point of view, then these policies can be ranked at least roughly. Policies 1 and 2 are clearly unacceptable. Nobody contacts a web site wishing or expecting to have his or her hard disk erased or information stolen. The information found on a hard disk is a resource of the user that requires respect and protection. Policy 3 is better than 1 or 2. People may benefit from having their preferences recorded so that the web site can tailor its responses more effectively the next time it is visited. Yet, information is being left on the users' hard disks without their knowledge. Some deception is involved. Policy 4 is better than 3 in that the user is informed about the activity. Policy 6 is better still in that the user has both the knowledge and the ability to allow or refuse the cookies.

Given these advantages, policy 6 is better than 5, though 5 would be a perfectly acceptable policy in that no harm is being caused to the user.

This analysis of the comparative strengths and weaknesses of these policies could be elaborated, but enough has been said to make several points. People may not agree on exactly how to rank these policies. Some may believe that the theft of information is worse than its destruction and so policy 2 is worse than policy 1. Some may believe that policy 6 creates some risks because of possible misunderstandings about what is being placed on a hard disk and so policy 5 is better than policy 6. But nobody would argue from an ethical point of view that policy 1 or 2 is acceptable. Most would agree that some of the other policies are acceptable and that some are better than others. Moreover, even when there is disagreement about the rankings, the disagreements may have as much to do with factual matters as with value differences. As a matter of fact, does the loss of information cause more damage than its destruction, and, as a matter of fact, do misunderstandings occur about what is or is not left on a hard disk? Apparent value differences may be open to empirical resolution.

The situation is parallel to the evaluation of computer programs. Computer scientists have substantial agreement that some computer programs are terrible and some are very good. There are disagreements about the rankings of some in the middle. Often reasons can be given about why some are better than others. Similarly, some policies for using computers are ethically not acceptable whereas others clearly are. People may have different rankings, but these rankings, assuming an ethical point of view, will have significant positive correlation. Moreover, people can give reasons why some policies are better than others. The core values provide a set of standards by which we can evaluate different policies. They tell us what to look for when making our assessments about the benefits and harms of different policies. They give us the reasons for preferring one policy over another. They suggest ways to modify policies to make them better.

Responsibility, Resolution, and Residue

There are many levels of relativity in value judgments. Some of our values are relative to our being human. If we were angels or creatures from another dimension, our core values might be different. And then, of course, different cultures articulate the core human values differently. And different individuals within a culture may differ in their assessments of values. Indeed, some values of one individual may change over time. I have been arguing that such relativity is compatible with rational discussion of ethical issues and resolution of at least some ethical disputes. We are, after all, human beings, not angels or creatures from another dimension. We share core values. This provides us with a set of standards with which to assess policies even in situations in which no previous policies exist and with which to assess other value frameworks when disagreements occur.

Ethical responsibility begins by taking the ethical point of view. We must respect others and their core values. If we can avoid policies that result in significant harm to others, that would be a good beginning toward responsible ethical conduct. Some policies are so obviously harmful that they are readily rejected by our core-value standards. Selling computer software which is known to malfunction in a way which is likely to result in death is an obvious example. Other policies easily meet our standards. Building computer interfaces which facilitate use by the disabled is a clear example. And of course, some policies for managing computer technology will be disputed. However, as I have been emphasizing, some of the ethical policies under dispute may be subject to further rational discussion and resolution. The major resolution technique, which I have been emphasizing, is the empirical investigation of the actual consequences of proposed policies. For instance, some people might propose a limitation on free speech on the Internet on the grounds that such freedom would lead to an unstable society or to severe psychological damage of some citizens. Advocates of free speech might appeal to its usefulness in transmitting knowledge and its effectiveness in calling attention to the flaws of government. To some extent these are empirical claims that can be confirmed or disconfirmed, which in turn may suggest compromises and modifications of policies.

Another resolution technique is to assume an impartial position when evaluating policies. Imagine yourself as an outsider not being benefited or harmed by a policy. Is it a fair policy? Is it a policy which you would advocate if you were suddenly placed in a position in which you were affected by the policy? It may be tempting to be the seller of defective software, but nobody wants to be a buyer of defective software. And finally, analogies are sometimes useful in resolving disagreements. If a computing professional would not approve of her stockbroker's withholding information from her about the volatility of stock she is considering buying, it would seem by analogy she should share information with a client about the instability of a computer program which the client is considering purchasing.

All of these techniques for resolution can help form a consensus about acceptable policies. But when the resolution techniques have gone as far as they can, some residue of disagreement may remain. Even in these situations alternative policies may be available which all parties can accept. But, a residue of ethical difference is not to be feared. Disputes occur in every human endeavor and yet progress is made. Computer ethics is no different in this regard. The chief threat to computer ethics is not the possibility that a residue of disagreements about which policies are best will remain after debates on the issues are completed, but a failure to debate the ethical issues of computing technology at all. If we naively regard the issues of computer ethics as routine or, even worse, as unsolvable, then we are in the greatest danger of being harmed by computer technology. Responsibility requires us to adopt the ethical point of view and to engage in ongoing conceptual analysis and policy formulation and justification with regard to this ever evolving technology. Because the computer revolution now engulfs the entire world, it is crucial that the issues of computer ethics be addressed on a global level. The global village needs to conduct a global conversation about the social and ethical impact of computing and what should be done about it. Fortunately, computing may help us to conduct exactly that conversation.

References

Bynum T. W. and Rogerson, S. (1996). "Introduction and Overview: Global Information Ethics." *Science and Engineering Ethics*, 2/2: 131–6.
Johnson, D. G. (1994). *Computer Ethics*, 2nd edn. Prentice Hall, Inc.
Maner, W. (1996). "Unique Ethical Problems in Information Technology." *Science and Engineering Ethics*, 2/2: 137–54.
Moor, J. H. (1985). "What is Computer Ethics?" *Metaphilosophy*, 16/4: 266–75.
Moor, J. H. (1990). "Ethics of Privacy Protection." *Library Trends*, 39/1 & 2: 69–82.

Basic study questions

1. What is the "Routine Ethics" position regarding the nature of computer ethics? Why does Moor believe that this view "undercuts potential for progress" in computer ethics?
2. What is the "Cultural Relativism" position regarding the nature of computer ethics? Why does Moor believe that this view "undercuts potential for progress" in computer ethics? Why does the global nature of the World Wide Web make Cultural Relativism an ineffective approach to computer ethics?
3. What is the "Many/Any Fallacy"? How does the Cultural Relativism position commit this fallacy?
4. Explain the meaning of "logical malleability." Why does this feature of computer technology, according to Moor, make it revolutionary?
5. What does Moor mean by the term "informational enrichment"?
6. How has the concept of money become informationally enriched?
7. How has the concept of warfare become informationally enriched?
8. How has the concept of privacy in the USA become informationally enriched?
9. How has the concept of copyright become informationally enriched?
10. According to Moor, computer ethics has two parts. What are these two components of computer ethics?
11. What, according to Moor, is a policy vacuum? How does computer technology generate policy vacuums?

12. What is a conceptual muddle? How is informational enrichment related to conceptual muddles?
13. What, according to Moor, is a "core value"? List the core values that Moor mentions.
14. According to Moor, to make an ethical judgment one must do more than use core values; one must also "take the ethical point of view." What is "the ethical point of view"? (See also p. 66 below.)

Questions for further thought

1. What is the difference between a disagreement about facts and a disagreement about values? Give three examples that illustrate the difference.
2. Based upon Moor's description of the nature of computer ethics, describe a step-by-step procedure for making computer ethics decisions regarding the right thing to do in a given case of computer use. Be sure to take account of the role of core values.
3. Given Moor's account of the nature of computer ethics, why is computer ethics an especially important branch of applied ethics?

CHAPTER 2

Unique Ethical Problems in Information Technology

Walter Maner

Introduction

One factor behind the rise of computer ethics is the lingering suspicion that computer professionals may be unprepared to deal effectively with the ethical issues that arise in their workplace. Over the years, this suspicion has been reinforced by mostly anecdotal research that seems to show that computer professionals simply do not recognize when ethical issues are present. Perhaps the earliest work of this kind was done by Donn Parker in the late 1970s at SRI International (see Parker 1978).

In 1977, Parker invited highly trained professionals from various fields to evaluate the ethical content of 47 simple hypothetical cases that he had created based in part on his expert knowledge of computer abuse. Workshop participants focused on each action or non-action of each person who played a role in these one-page scenarios. For each act that was performed or not performed, their set task was to determine whether the behavior was unethical or not, or simply raised no ethics issue at all. Parker found a surprising amount of residual disagreement among these professionals even after an exhaustive analysis and discussion of all the issues each case presented.

More surprisingly, a significant minority of professionals held to their belief that no ethics issue was present even in cases of apparent computer abuse. For example, in Scenario 3.1, a company representative routinely receives copies of the computerized arrest records for new company employees. These records are provided as a favor by a police file clerk who happens to have access to various local and federal databases containing criminal justice information.

Walter Maner, "Unique Ethical Problems in Information Technology." This chapter was originally presented as the keynote address at ETHICOMP95 in Leicester, UK. It was subsequently published in *Science and Engineering Ethics*, 2:2 (special issue, ed. Terrell Ward Bynum and Simon Rogerson, April 1996), pp. 137–54. © 1995 by Walter Maner and reprinted by permission of the author.

Of the 33 individuals who analyzed this case, 9 thought disclosure of arrest histories raised no ethics issues at all. Parker's research does not identify the professions represented by those who failed to detect ethics issues, but most of the participants in this early study[1] were computer professionals. This left casual readers of Parker's *Ethical Conflicts in Computer Science and Technology* free to identify computer professionals as the ones who lacked ethical sensitivity. If some of them could not even recognize when ethical issues were present, it is hard to imagine how they could ever hope to deal responsibly with them. According to Parker (1976), the problem may have been fostered by computer education and training programs that encouraged, or at least failed to criminalize, certain types of unethical professional conduct. This perception of professional inadequacy is part of a largely hidden political agenda that has contributed to the development of various curricula in computer ethics. In recent years, the tacit perception that those preparing for careers in computing may need remedial moral education seems to have influenced some accreditation boards. As a result, they have been willing to mandate more and more ethical content in computer science and computer engineering programs. They may also be responding to the increased media attention given to instances of computer abuse, fraud, and crime. Others demand more ethical content because they believe that catastrophic failures of computer programs are directly attributable to immoral behavior (Gotterbarn 1991c, p. 74).

The growth of interest is gratifying, especially considering that, in 1976, I found it hard to convince anyone that "computer ethics" was anything other than an oxymoron.[2] No doubt Norbert Wiener would be pleased to see his work bearing late fruit (see Wiener 1960). At the same time, I am greatly disturbed when courses in social impact and computer ethics become a tool for indoctrination in appropriate standards of professional conduct. Donald Gotterbarn, for example, argues that one of the six goals of computer ethics is the "socialization" of students into "professional" norms (1991a, p. 42). The fact that these norms are often eminently reasonable, even recommended thoughtfully to us by our professional organizations, does not make

---

[1]   There was a follow-up study some years later that remedied some of the problems discovered in the original methodology (see Parker et al. 1990).

[2]   I coined the term "computer ethics" in 1976 to describe a specific set of moral problems either created, aggravated, or transformed by the introduction of computer technology. By the fall of 1977, I was ready to create a curriculum for computer ethics and, shortly thereafter, began to teach one of the first university courses entirely devoted to applied computer ethics. By 1978, I had become a willing promoter of computer ethics at various national conferences. Two years later, Terrell Bynum helped me publish a curriculum development kit we called the 'Starter Kit in Computer Ethics.' We found we could not interest the academic establishment in computer ethics, either philosophers or computer scientists, but we managed to survive as an underground movement within the American Association of Philosophy Teachers.

indoctrination any less repugnant. The goal cannot be simply to criminalize or stigmatize departures from professional norms. Consider an analogy. Suppose a course in human sexual relationships has for its goal the socialization of college students into 'high standards' of sexual conduct, and that this goal is enforced by contradicting or discrediting anyone who violates these standards. Most people would be quick to recognize that this curriculum is more political than academic, and that such an approach would tend to create a classroom environment where bias could overwhelm inquiry.

We stand today on the threshold of a time when well-intended political motives threaten to reshape computer ethics into some form of moral education. Unfortunately, it is an easy transition from the correct belief that we ought to teach future computer scientists and engineers the meaning of responsible conduct to the mistaken belief that we ought to train them to behave like responsible professionals. When Terrell Ward Bynum says, for example, that he hopes the study of computer ethics will develop "good judgment" in students, he is not advocating socialization (1991, p. 24). By "good judgment," he means to refer to the reasoned and principled process by which reflective moral judgments are rendered. From this correct position, it is a tempting and subtle transition to the mistaken position that computer ethics should cause students to develop good judgments, meaning that their positions on particular moral issues conform to the norms of the profession. This self-deceiving mistake occurs because there is an undetected shift in emphasis from the process to the products of moral deliberation.

My point is that a perceived need for moral education does not and cannot provide an adequate rationale for the study of computer ethics. Rather, it must exist as a field worthy of study in its own right and not because at the moment it can provide useful means to certain socially noble ends. To exist and to endure as a separate field, there must be a unique domain for computer ethics distinct from the domain for moral education, distinct even from the domains of other kinds of professional and applied ethics. Like James Moor, I believe computers are special technology and raise special ethical issues, hence that computer ethics deserves special status (see Moor 1985).

My remaining remarks will suggest a rationale for computer ethics based on arguments and examples showing that one of the following is true:

- that certain ethical issues are so transformed by the use of computers that they deserve to be studied on their own, in their radically altered form; or
- that the involvement of computers in human conduct can create entirely new ethical issues, unique to computing, that do not surface in other areas.

I shall refer to the first as the "weaker view" and the second as the "stronger view." Although the weaker view provides sufficient rationale, most of my attention will be focused on establishing the stronger view. This is similar to the position I took in 1980 and 1985, except that I no longer believe that problems merely aggravated by computer technology deserve special status (see Maner 1980; Pecorino and Maner 1985).

Levels of Justification for the Study of Computer Ethics

From weaker to stronger, there are at least six levels of justification for the study of computer ethics.

Level 1 We should study computer ethics because doing so will make us behave like responsible professionals. At worst, this type of rationale is a disguised call for moral indoctrination. At best, it is weakened by the need to rely on an elusive connection between right knowledge and right conduct. This is similar to the claim that we should study religion because that will cause us to become more spiritual. For some people, perhaps it may, but the mechanism is not reliable.

Level 2 We should study computer ethics because doing so will teach us how to avoid computer abuse and catastrophes. Reports by Parker (1989), Neumann (1995), and Forester and Morrison (1990) leave little doubt that computer use has led to significant abuse, hijinks, crime, near catastrophes, and actual catastrophes. The question is: Do we get a balanced view of social responsibility merely by examining the profession's dirty laundry? Granted, a litany of computer "horror stories" does provide a vehicle for infusing some ethical content into the study of computer science and computer engineering. Granted, we should all work to prevent computer catastrophes. Even so, there are major problems with the use of conceptual shock therapy:

- The cases commonly used raise issues of bad conduct rather than good conduct; they tell us what behaviors to avoid but do not tell us what behaviors are worth modeling.
- As Leon Tabak (1988) has argued, this approach may harm students by preventing them from developing a healthy, positive and constructive view of their profession.
- Most horror stories are admittedly rare and extreme cases, which makes them seem correspondingly remote and irrelevant to daily professional life.
- Persons who use computers for abusive purposes are likely to be morally bankrupt – there is little we can learn from them.
- Many computer catastrophes are the result of unintended actions and, as such, offer little guidance in organizing purposive behavior.

- A litany of horror stories does not itself provide a coherent concept of computer ethics.

Level 3   We should study computer ethics because the advance of computing technology will continue to create temporary policy vacuums. Long-term use of poorly designed computer keyboards, for example, exposes clerical workers to painful, chronic, and eventually debilitating repetitive stress injury. Clearly, employers should not require workers to use equipment that will likely cause them serious injury. The question is: What policies should we formulate to address problems of long-term keyboard use? New telephone technology for automatic caller identification creates a similar policy vacuum. It is not immediately obvious what the telephone company should be required to do, if anything, to protect the privacy of callers who wish to remain anonymous.

Unlike the first- and second-level justifications I have considered and rejected, this third-level justification does appear to be sufficient to establish computer ethics as an important and independent discipline. Still, there are problems:

- since policy vacuums are temporary and computer technologies evolve rapidly, anyone who studies computer ethics would have the perpetual task of tracking a fast-moving and ever-changing target;
- it is also possible that practical ethical issues arise mainly when policy frameworks clash; we could not resolve such issues merely by formulating more policy.

Level 4   We should study computer ethics because the use of computing permanently transforms certain ethical issues to the degree that their alterations require independent study. I would argue, for example, that many of the issues surrounding intellectual property have been radically and permanently altered by the intrusion of computer technology. The simple question, "What do I own?" has been transformed into the question, "What exactly is it that I own when I own something?" Likewise, the availability of cheap, fast, painless, transparent encryption technology has completely transformed the privacy debate. In the past, we worried about the erosion of privacy. Now we worry about the impenetrable wall of computer-generated privacy afforded to every criminal with a computer and half a brain.

Level 5   We should study computer ethics because the use of computing technology creates, and will continue to create, novel ethical issues that require special study. I will return to this topic in a moment.

Level 6   We should study computer ethics because the set of novel and transformed issues is large enough and coherent enough to define a new field. I mention this hopefully as a theoretical possibility. Frankly, after 15 years, we have not been able to assemble a critical mass of self-defining core issues. Joseph Behar, a sociologist, finds computer ethics diffuse and unfocused; Gary Chapman, when he spoke to the Computers and Quality of Life Conference in 1990, complained that no advances had been made in computer ethics (see Gotterbarn 1991b). There are various explanations for this apparent (or real) lack of progress (Behar 1993; Chapman 1990):

- Computer ethics is barely fifteen years old;[3] much of its intellectual geography remains uncharted.
- So far, no one has provided a complete and coherent concept of the proper subject matter for computer ethics.
- We have wrongly included in the domain of computer ethics any unethical act that happened to involve a computer. In the future, we must be more careful to restrict ourselves to those few acts where computers have an essential as opposed to incidental involvement.
- Because computer ethics is tied to an evolving technology, the field changes whenever the technology changes. For example, the use of networked computers presents moral problems different from those presented by the use of stand-alone computers. The use of mouse-driven interfaces raises issues different from those raised by keyboard-driven interfaces, particularly for people who are blind.
- We adopted, from clever philosophers, the dubious practice of using highly contrived, two-sided, dilemmatic cases to expose interesting but irresolvable ethical conflicts. This led to the false perception that there could be no progress and no commonality in computer ethics. New research may cause this perception to fade (see Leventhal et al. 1992).
- We have remained focused for too long on the dirty laundry of our profession.

On a hopeful note, the ImpactCS Steering Committee chaired by C. Dianne Martin is [in 1995] halfway through a three-year NSF-funded project that will likely generate a highly coherent picture of how the computer science curriculum can address social and ethical issues. ImpactCS intends to publish specific curriculum guidelines along with concrete models for implementing them.[4]

---

[3] I refer to the academic discipline of computer ethics as defined in Maner (1980).

[4] Integrating the ethical and social context of computing into the computer science curriculum: an interim report from the content subcommittee of the ImpactCS steering committee. See Rogerson and Bynum 1996. For further information on the ImpactCS project, contact Dr Chuck Huff in the Psychology Department at St Olaf College in Northfield, Minnesota 55057, USA (huff@stolaf.edu). The ImpactCS project was completed in 1998, and the results were published at http://www.student.seas.gwn.edu/~impactcs/pape3/pg1.html

The Special Status of Computer Ethics

I now turn to the task of justifying computer ethics at Level 5 by establishing, through several examples, that there are issues and problems unique to the field.

It is necessary to begin with a few disclaimers. First, I do not claim that this set of examples is in any sense complete or representative. I do not even claim that the kinds of example I will use are the best kinds of example to use in computer ethics. I do not claim that any of these issues is central to computer ethics. Nor am I suggesting that computer ethics should be limited to just those issues and problems that are unique to the field. I merely want to claim that each example is, in a specific sense, unique to computer ethics. By "unique" I mean to refer to those ethical issues and problems that are characterized by the primary and essential involvement of computer technology, exploit some unique property of that technology, and would not have arisen without the essential involvement of computing technology.

I mean to allow room to make either a strong or a weak claim as appropriate. For some examples, I make the strong claim that the issue or problem would not have arisen at all. For other examples, I claim only that the issue or problem would not have arisen in its present, highly altered form.

To establish the essential involvement of computing technology, I will argue that these issues and problems have no satisfactory non-computer moral analog. For my purposes, a "satisfactory" analogy is one that (a) is based on the use of a machine other than a computing machine and (b) allows the ready transfer of moral intuitions from the analog case to the case in question. In broad strokes, my line of argument will be that certain issues and problems are unique to computer ethics because they raise ethical questions that depend on some unique property of prevailing computer technology. My remarks are meant to apply to discrete-state stored-program inter-networking fixed instruction-set serial machines of von Neumann architecture. It is possible that other designs (such as the Connection Machine) would exhibit a different set of unique properties.

Next I offer a series of examples, starting with a simple case that allows me to illustrate my general approach.

Example 1: uniquely stored

One of the unique properties of computers is that they must store integers in "words" of a fixed size. Because of this restriction, the largest integer that can be stored in a 16-bit computer word is 32,767. If we insist on an exact representation of a number larger than this, an "overflow" will occur with the result that the value stored in the word becomes corrupted. This can produce interesting and harmful consequences. For example, a hospital computer system in Washington, DC, broke down on September 19, 1989, because its calendar calculations counted the days elapsed since January 1, 1900. On September 19, exactly 32,768 days had elapsed, overflowing the 16-bit word used to store the counter, resulting in a collapse of the entire system and forcing a lengthy period of manual operation (see Neumann 1995, p. 88). At the Bank of New York, a similar 16-bit counter overflowed, resulting in a $32 billion overdraft. The bank had to borrow $24 million for one day to cover the overdraft. The interest on this one-day loan cost the bank about $5 million. In addition, while technicians attempted to diagnose the source of the problem, customers experienced costly delays in their financial transactions (see ibid., p. 169).

Does this case have a satisfactory non-computer analog? Consider mechanical adding machines. Clearly they are susceptible to overflow, so it is likely that accountants who relied on them in years past sometimes produced totals too large for the machine to store. The storage mechanism overflowed, producing in steel the same result that the computer produced in silicon. The problem with this "analogy" is that, in a broad and relevant sense, adding machines are computers, albeit of a primitive kind. The low-level logical descriptions of adding machines and computers are fundamentally identical.

Perhaps your automobile's mechanical odometer gauge provides a better analogy. When the odometer reading exceeds a designed-in limit, say 99,999.9 miles, the gauge overflows and returns to all zeros. Those who sell used cars have taken unfair advantage of this property. They use a small motor to overflow the gauge manually, with the result that the buyer is unaware that he or she is purchasing a high-mileage vehicle.

This does provide a non-computer analogy, but is it a satisfactory analogy? Does it allow the ready transfer of moral intuitions to cases involving word overflow in computers? I believe it falls short. Perhaps it would be a satisfactory analogy if, when the odometer overflowed, the engine, the brakes, the wheels, and every other part of the automobile stopped working. This does not in fact happen because the odometer is not highly coupled to other systems critical to the operation of the vehicle. What is different about computer words is that they are deeply embedded in highly integrated subsystems such that the corruption of a single word threatens to bring down the operation of the entire computer. What we require, but do not have, is a non-computer analog that has a similar catastrophic failure mode.

So the incidents at the hospital in Washington, DC and the Bank of New York meet my three basic requirements for a unique issue or problem. They are characterized by the primary and essential involvement of computer technology, they depend on some unique property of that technology, and they would not have arisen without the essential involvement of computing technology. Even if the mechanical adding machine deserves to be considered as an analog case, it is still true that computing technology has radically altered the form and scope of the problem. On the other hand, if the adding machine does not provide a good analogy, then we may be entitled to a stronger conclusion: that these problems would not have arisen at all if there were no computers in the world.

Example 2: uniquely malleable

Another unique characteristic of computing machines is that they are very general purpose machines. As James Moor observed, they are "logically malleable" in the sense that "they can be shaped and molded to do any activity that can be characterized in terms of inputs, outputs, and connecting logical operations" (1985, p. 269). The unique adaptability and versatility of computers have important moral implications. To show how this comes about, I would like to repeat a story first told by Peter Green and Alan Brightman (1990).

> Alan (nickname "Stats") Groverman is a sports fanatic and a data-crunching genius.
>
> His teachers describe him as having a "head for numbers." To Stats, though, it's just what he does; keeping track, for example of yards gained by each running back on his beloved (San Francisco) 49ers team. And then averaging those numbers into the season's statistics. All done in his head-for-numbers. All without even a scrap of paper in front of him.
>
> Not that paper would make much of a difference. Stats has never been able to move a finger, let alone hold a pencil or pen. And he's never been able to press the keys of a calculator. Quadriplegia made these kinds of simplicities impossible from the day he was born. That's when he began to strengthen his head.
>
> Now, he figures, his head could use a little help. With his craving for sports ever-widening, his mental playing field is becoming increasingly harder to negotiate.
>
> Stats knows he needs a personal computer, what he calls "cleats for the mind." He also knows that he needs to be able to operate that computer without being able to move anything below his neck.

Since computers do not care how they get their inputs, Stats ought to be able to use a head-pointer or a mouth-stick to operate the keyboard. If mouse input is required, he could use a head-controlled mouse along with a sip-and-puff tube. To make this possible, we would need to load a new device driver to modify the behavior of the operating system. If Stats has trouble with repeating keys, we would need to make another small change to the operating system, one that disables the keyboard repeat feature. If keyboard or mouse input proves too tedious for him, we could add a speech processing chip, a microphone and voice-recognition software. We have a clear duty to provide computer access solutions in cases like this, but what makes this duty so reasonable and compelling is the fact that computers are so easily adapted to user requirements.

Does there exist any other machine that forces an analogous obligation on us to assist people with disabilities? I do not believe so. The situation would be different, for example, if Stats wanted to ride a bicycle. While it is true that bicycles have numerous adjustments to accommodate the varying geo-metry of different riders, they are infinitely less adaptable than computers. For one thing, bicycles cannot be programmed, and they do not have operat-ing systems. My point is that our obligation to provide universal accessibility to computer technology would not have arisen if computers were not uni-versally adaptable. The generality of the obligation is in proportion to the generality of the machine.

While it is clear that we should endeavor to adapt other machinery – elevators, for example – for use by people with disabilities, the moral intuitions we have about adapting elevators do not transfer readily to computers. Differences of scale block the transfer. Elevators can only do elevator-like things, but computers can do anything we can describe in terms of input, process, and output. Even if elevators did provide a com-parable case, it would still be true that the availability of a totally malle-able machine so transforms our obligations that this transformation itself deserves special study.

Example 3: uniquely complex

Another unique property of computer technology is its superhuman com-plexity. It is true that humans program computing machines, so in that sense we are masters of the machine. The problem is that our programming tools allow us to create discrete functions of arbitrary complexity. In many cases, the result is a program whose total behavior cannot be described by any compact function (see also Huff and Finholt 1994, p. 184). Buggy programs in particular are notorious for evading compact description! The fact is we routinely produce programs whose behavior defies inspection, defies understanding – programs that surprise, delight, entertain, frustrate, and ultimately confound us. Even when we understand program code in its static form, it does not follow that we understand how the program works when it executes. James Moor provides a case in point (1985, pp. 274–5). An interesting example of such a complex calculation occurred in 1976 when a computer worked on the four-color conjecture. The four-color problem, a puzzle mathematicians have worked on for over a century, is to show that a map can be colored with at most four colors so that no adjacent areas have the same color. Mathematicians at the University of Illinois broke the problem down into thousands of cases and programmed computers to consider them. After more than a thousand hours of computer time on various computers, the four-color conjecture was proved correct.

What is interesting about this mathematical proof, compared to traditional proofs, is that it is largely invisible. The general structure of the proof is known and found in the program, and any particular part of the computer's activity can be examined, but practically speaking the calculations are too enormous for humans to examine them all.

It is sobering to consider how much we rely on a technology we strain and stretch to understand. In the UK, for example, Nuclear Electric decided to rely heavily on computers as its primary protection system for its first nuclear power plant, Sizewell B. The company hoped to reduce the risk of nuclear catastrophe by eliminating as many sources of human error as possible. So Nuclear Electric installed a software system of amazing complexity, consisting of 300–400 microprocessors controlled by program modules that contained more than 100,000 lines of code (see Neumann 1995, pp. 80–1).

It is true that airplanes, as they existed before computers, were complex and that they presented behaviors that were difficult to understand. But aeronautical engineers do understand how airplanes work because airplanes are constructed according to known principles of physics. There are mathematical functions describing such forces as thrust and lift, and these forces behave according to physical laws. There are no corresponding laws governing the construction of computer software. This lack of governing law is unique among all the machines that we commonly use, and this deficiency creates unique obligations. Specifically, it places special responsibilities on software engineers for the thorough testing and validation of program behavior. There is, I would argue, a moral imperative to discover better testing methodologies and better mechanisms for proving programs correct. It is hard to overstate the enormity of this challenge. Testing a simple input routine that accepts a 20-character name, a 20-character address, and a 10-digit phone number would require approximately 1,066 test cases to exhaust all possibilities. If Noah had been a software engineer and had started testing this routine the moment he stepped off the ark, he would be less than 1 percent finished today even if he managed to run a trillion test cases every second (see McConnell 1993). In practice, software engineers test a few boundary values and, for all the others, they use values believed to be representative of various equivalence sets defined on the domain.

Example 4: uniquely fast

On Thursday, September 11, 1986, the Dow-Jones industrial average dropped 86.61 points, to 1792.89, on a record volume of 237.6 million shares. On the following day, the Dow fell 34.17 additional points on a volume of 240.5 million shares. Three months later, an article appearing in *Discover* magazine asked: Did computers make stock prices plummet? According to the article,

> [M]any analysts believe that the drop was accelerated (though not initiated) by computer-assisted arbitrage. Arbitrageurs capitalize on what's known as the spread: a short-term difference between the price of stock futures, which are contracts to buy stocks at a set time and price, and that of the underlying stocks. The arbitrageurs' computers constantly monitor the spread and let them know when it's large enough so that they can transfer their holdings from stocks to stock futures or vice-versa, and make a profit that more than covers the cost of the transaction. . . . With computers, arbitrageurs are constantly aware of where a profit can be made. However, throngs of arbitrageurs working with the latest information can set up perturbations in the market. Because arbitrageurs are all "massaging" the same basic information, a profitable spread is likely to show up on many of their computers at once. And since arbitrageurs take advantage of small spreads, they must deal in great volume to make it worth their while. All this adds up to a lot of trading in a little time, which can markedly alter the price of a stock. (*Discover* 1986)

After a while, regular investors begin to notice that the arbitrageurs are bringing down the value of all stocks, so they begin to sell too. Selling begets selling begets more selling. According to the chair of the NYSE, computerized trading seems to be a stabilizing influence only when markets are relatively quiet (*Science* 1987). When the market is unsettled, programmed trading amplifies and accelerates the changes already under way, perhaps as much as 20 percent. Today, the problem is arbitrage but, in the future, it is possible that ordinary investors will destabilize the market. This could conceivably happen because most investors will use the same type of computerized stock trading programs driven by very similar algorithms that predict nearly identical buy/sell points. The question is, could these destabilizing effects occur in a world without computers? Arbitrage, after all, relies only on elementary mathematics. All the necessary calculations could be done on a scratch pad by any one of us. The problem is that, by the time we finished doing the necessary arithmetic for the stocks in our investment portfolio, the price of futures and the price of stocks would have changed. The opportunity that had existed would be gone.

Example 5: uniquely cheap

Because computers can perform millions of computations each second, the cost of an individual calculation approaches zero. This unique property of computers leads to interesting consequences in ethics.

Let us imagine I am riding a subway train in New York City, returning home very late after a long day at the office. Since it is well past my dinner time, it does not take long for me to notice that everyone seated in my car, except me, has a fresh loaf of salami. To me, the train smells like the inside of a fine New York deli, never letting me forget how hungry I am. Finally I decide I must end this prolonged aromatic torture, so I ask everyone in the car to give me a slice of their own salami loaves. If everyone contributes, I can assemble a loaf of my own. No one can see any point in cooperating, so I offer to cut a very thin slice from each loaf. I can see that this is still not appealing to my skeptical fellow riders, so I offer to take an arbitrarily thin slice, thin enough to fall below anyone's threshold of concern. "You tell me how small it has to be not to matter," I say to them. "I will take that much and not a particle more." Of course, I may only get slices that are tissue-paper thin. No problem. Because I am collecting several dozen of these very thin slices, I will still have the makings of a delicious New York deli sandwich. By extension, if everyone in Manhattan had a loaf of salami, I would not have to ask for an entire slice. It would be sufficient for all the salami lovers to donate a tiny speck of their salami loaves. It would not matter to them that they have lost such a tiny speck of meat. I, on the other hand, would have collected many millions of specks, by which means I would have plenty of food on the table

This crazy scheme would never work for collecting salami. It would cost too much and it would take too long to transport millions of specks of salami to some central location. But a similar tactic might work if my job happens to involve the programming of computerized banking systems. I could slice some infinitesimal amount from every account, some amount so small that it falls beneath the account owner's threshold of concern. If I steal only half a cent each month from each of 100,000 bank accounts, I stand to pocket $6,000 in the course of a year. This kind of opportunity must have some appeal to an intelligent criminal mind, but very few cases have been reported. In one of these reported cases, a bank employee used a salami technique to steal $70,000 from customers of a branch bank in Ontario, Canada.[5] Procedurally speaking, it might be difficult to arraign someone

---

[5]   Kirk Makin, in an article written for the *Globe and Mail* appearing on November 3, 1987, reported that Sergeant Ted Green of the Ontario Provincial Police knew of such a case.

on several million counts of petit theft. According to Donn Parker: "Salami techniques are usually not fully discoverable within obtainable expenditures for investigation. Victims have usually lost so little individually that they are unwilling to expend much effort to solve the case" (1989, p. 19). Even so, salami-slicing was immortalized in John Foster's country song, "The Ballad of Silicon Slim":

In the dead of night he'd access each depositor's account
And from each of them he'd siphon off the teeniest amount.
And since no one ever noticed that there'd even been a crime
He stole forty million dollars – a penny at a time!

Legendary or not, there are at least three factors that make this type of scheme unusual. First, individual computer computations are now so cheap that the cost of moving a half-cent from one account to another is vastly less than half a cent. For all practical purposes, the calculation is free. So there can be tangible profit in moving amounts that are vanishingly small if the volume of such transactions is sufficiently high. Second, once the plan has been implemented, it requires no further attention. It is fully automatic. Money in the bank. Finally, from a practical standpoint, no one is ever deprived of anything in which they have a significant interest. In short, we seem to have invented a kind of stealing that requires no taking – or at least no taking of anything that would be of significant value or concern. It is theft by diminishing return.

Does this scheme have a non-computer analog? A distributor of heating oil could short all his customers one cup of oil on each delivery. By springtime, the distributor may have accumulated a few extra gallons of heating oil for his own use. But it may not be worth the trouble. He may not have enough customers. Or he may have to buy new metering devices sensitive enough to withhold exactly one cup from each customer. And he may have to bear the cost of cleaning, operating, calibrating, and maintaining this sensitive new equipment. All of these factors will make the entire operation less profitable. On the other hand, if the distributor withholds amounts large enough to offset his expenses, he runs the risk that he will exceed the customer's threshold of concern.

Example 6: uniquely cloned

Perhaps for the first time in history, computers give us the power to make an exact copy of some artifact. If I make a verified copy of a computer file, the copy can be proven to be bit for bit identical to the original. Common disk utilities such as DIFF can easily make the necessary bitwise comparisons. It is true that there may be some low-level physical differences due to track placement, sector size, cluster size, word size, blocking factors, and so on. But at a logical level, the copy will be perfect. Reading either the original or its copy will result in the exact same sequence of bytes. For all practical purposes, the copy is indistinguishable from the original. In any situation where we had used the original, we can now substitute our perfect copy, or vice versa. We can make any number of verified copies of our copy, and the final result will be logically identical to the first original.

This makes it possible for someone to "steal" software without depriving the original owner in any way. The thief gets a copy that is perfectly usable. He would be no better off even if he had the original file. Meanwhile the owner has not been dispossessed of any property. Both files are equally functional, equally useful. There was no transfer of possession. Sometimes we do not take adequate note of the special nature of this kind of crime. For example, the Assistant VP for Academic Computing at Brown University reportedly said that "software piracy is morally wrong – indeed, it is ethically indistinguishable from shoplifting or theft" (cited in Ladd 1989). This is mistaken. It is not like piracy. It is not like shoplifting or simple theft. It makes a moral difference whether or not people are deprived of property. Consider how different the situation would be if the process of copying a file automatically destroyed the original. Electrostatic copying may seem to provide a non-computer analog, but photocopied copies are not perfect. Regardless of the quality of the optics, regardless of the resolution of the process, regardless of the purity of the toner, electrostatic copies are not identical to the originals. Fifth- and sixth-generation copies are easily distinguished from first- and second-generation copies. If we "steal" an image by making a photocopy, it will be useful for some purposes, but we do not thereby acquire the full benefits afforded by the original.

Example 7: uniquely discrete

In a stimulating paper "On the Cruelty of Really Teaching Computer Science" (1989), Edger Dijkstra examines the implications of one central, controlling assumption: that computers are radically novel in the history of the world. Given this assumption, it follows that programming these unique machines will be radically different from other practical intellectual activities. This, Dijkstra believes, is because the assumption of continuity we make about the behavior of most materials and artifacts does not hold for computer systems. For most things, small changes lead to small effects, larger changes to proportionately larger effects. If I nudge the accelerator pedal a little closer to the floor, the vehicle moves a little faster. If I press the pedal hard to the floor, it moves a lot faster. As machines go, computers are very different.

A program is, as a mechanism, totally different from all the familiar analog devices we grew up with. Like all digitally encoded information, it has, unavoidably, the uncomfortable property that the smallest possible perturbations – i.e., changes of a single bit – can have the most drastic consequences (ibid., p. 1400).

This essential and unique property of digital computers leads to a specific set of problems that gives rise to a unique ethical difficulty, at least for those who espouse a consequentialist view of ethics. For an example of the kind of problem where small "perturbations" have drastic consequences, consider the Mariner 18 mission, where the absence of the single word NOT from one line of a large program caused an abort (see Neumann 1980, p. 5). In a similar case, it was a missing hyphen in the guidance program for an Atlas Agena rocket that made it necessary for controllers to destroy a Venus probe worth $18.5 million (see Neumann 1995, p. 26). It was a single character omitted from a reconfiguration command that caused the Soviet Phobos 1 Mars probe to tumble helplessly in space (ibid., p. 29). I am not suggesting that rockets rarely failed before they were computerized. I assume the opposite is true: that in the past they were far more susceptible to certain classes of failure than they are today. This does not mean that the German V-2 rocket, for example, can provide a satisfactory non-computer (or pre-computer) moral analogy. The behavior of the V-2, being an analog device, was a continuous function of all its parameters. It failed the way analog devices typically fail – localized failures for localized problems. Once rockets were controlled by computer software, however, they became vulnerable to additional failure modes that could be extremely generalized even for extremely localized problems.

"In the discrete world of computing," Dijkstra concludes, "there is no meaningful metric in which small change and small effects go hand in hand, and there never will be" (1989, p. 1400). This discontinuous and disproportionate connection between cause and effect is unique to digital computers and creates a special difficulty for consequentialist ethics theories. The decision procedure commonly followed by utilitarians (a type of consequentialist) requires them to predict alternative consequences for the alternative actions available to them in a particular situation. An act is good if it produces good consequences, or at least a net excess of good consequences over bad. The fundamental difficulty utilitarians face, if Dijkstra is right, is that the normally predictable linkage between acts and their effects is severely skewed by the infusion of computing technology. In short, we simply cannot tell what effects our actions will have on computers by analogy to the effects our actions have on other machines.

Example 8: uniquely coded

Computers operate by constructing codes upon codes upon codes – cylinders on top of tracks, tracks on top of sectors, sectors on top of records, records on top of fields, fields on top of characters, characters on top of bytes, and bytes on top of primitive binary digits. Computer "protocols" such as TCP/IP are comprised of layer upon layer of obscure code conventions that tell computers how to interpret and process each binary digit passed to it. For digital computers, this is business as usual. In a very real sense, all data is multiply "encrypted" in the normal course of computer operations.

According to Charlie Hart (1990), a reporter for the *Raleigh News and Observer*, the resulting convolution of codes threatens to make American history as unreadable as the Rosetta Stone. Historic, scientific and business data is in danger of dissolving into a meaningless jumble of letters, numbers, and computer symbols. For example, 200 reels of 17-year-old Public Health Service tapes had to be destroyed in 1989 because no one could determine what the names and numbers on them meant. Much information from the past 30 years is stranded on computer tape written by primitive or discarded systems. For example, the records of many World War II veterans are marooned on 1,600 reels of obsolete microfilm images picturing even more obsolete Hollerith punch cards.

This growing problem is due to the degradable nature of certain media, the rapid rate of obsolescence for I/O devices, the continual evolution of media formats, and the failure of programmers to keep a permanent record of how they chose to package data. It is ironic that state-of-the-art computer technology, during the brief period when it is current, greatly accelerates the transmission of information. But when it becomes obsolete, it has an even stronger reverse effect. Not every record deserves to be saved but, on balance, it seems likely that computers will impede the normal generational flow of significant information and culture. Computer users obviously do not conspire to put history out of reach of their children but, given the unique way computers layer and store codes, the result could be much the same. Data archeologists will manage to salvage bits and pieces of our encoded records, but much will be permanently lost.

This raises a moral issue as old as civilization itself. It is arguably wrong to harm future generations of humanity by depriving them of information they will need and value. It stunts commercial and scientific progress, prevents people from learning the truth about their origins, and it may force nations to repeat bitter lessons from the past. Granted, there is nothing unique about this issue. Over the long sweep of civilized history, entire cultures have been annihilated, great libraries have been plundered and destroyed, books have been banned and burned, languages have withered and died, ink has bleached in the sun, and rolls of papyrus have decayed into fragile, cryptic memoirs of faraway times.

But has there ever in the history of the world been a machine that could bury culture the way computers can? Just about any modern media recording device has the potential to swallow culture, but the process is not automatic and information is not hidden below convoluted layers of obscure code. Computers, on the other hand, because of the unique way they store and process information, are far more likely to bury culture. The increased risk associated with the reliance on computers for archival data storage transforms the moral issues surrounding the preservation and transmission of culture. The question is not, "Will some culturally important information be lost?" When digital media become the primary repositories for information, the question becomes, "Will any stored records be readable in the future?" Without computers, the issue would not arise in this highly altered form.

So, this kind of example ultimately contributes to a "weaker" but still sufficient rationale for computer ethics, as explained earlier. Is it possible to take a "stronger" position with this example? We shall see. As encryption technology continues to improve, there is a remote chance that computer scientists may develop an encryption algorithm so effective that the sun will burn out before any machine could succeed in breaking the code. Such a technology could bury historical records for the rest of history. While we wait for this ideal technology to be invented, we can use the 128-bit International Data Encryption Algorithm (IDEA) already available. To break an IDEA-encoded message, we will need a chip that can test a billion keys per second, throw these at the problem, and then repeat this cycle for the next 10,000,000,000,000 years (see Schneier 1993, p. 54). An array of 1,024 chips could do it in a single day, but does the universe contain enough silicon to build them?

Conclusion

I have tried to show that there are issues and problems that are unique to computer ethics. For all of these issues, there was an essential involvement of computing technology. Except for this technology, these issues would not have arisen, or would not have arisen in their highly altered form. The failure to find satisfactory non-computer analogies testifies to the uniqueness of these issues. The lack of an adequate analogy, in turn, has interesting moral consequences. Normally, when we confront unfamiliar ethical problems, we use analogies to build conceptual bridges to similar situations we have encountered in the past. Then we try to transfer moral intuitions across the bridge, from the analog case to our current situation. Lack of an effective analogy forces us to discover new moral values, formulate new moral principles, develop new policies, and find new ways to think about the issues presented to us. For all of these reasons, the kind of issues I have been illustrating deserves to be addressed separately from others that might at first appear similar. At the very least, they have been so transformed by computing technology that their altered form demands special attention.

I conclude with a lovely little puzzle suggested by Donald Gotterbarn (1991b, p. 27). There are clearly many devices that have had a significant impact on society over the centuries. The invention of the printing press was a pivotal event in the history of the transmission of culture, but there is no such thing as Printing Press Ethics. The locomotive revolutionized the transportation industry, but there is no such thing as Locomotive Ethics. The telephone forever changed the way we communicate with other human beings, but there is no such thing as Telephone Ethics. The tractor transformed the face of agriculture around the world, but there is no such thing as Tractor Ethics. The automobile has made it possible for us to work at great distances from our local neighborhoods, but there is no such thing as Commuter Ethics.

Why, therefore, should there be any such thing as Computer Ethics?

References

Behar, J. (1993). "Computer Ethics: Moral Philosophy or Professional Propaganda?" In M. Leiderman, C. Guzetta, L. Struminger, and M. Monnickendam (eds.), *Technology in People Services: Research, Theory and Applications*. The Haworth Press.

Bynum, T. W. (1991). "Computer Ethics in the Computer Science Curriculum." In T. W. Bynum, W. Maner, and J. Fodor (eds.), *Teaching Computer Ethics*. Research Center on Computing and Society.

Chapman, G. (1990). In response to a luncheon address by J. Perrolle, "Political and Social Dimensions of Computer Ethics." Conference on Computers and the Quality of Life, George Washington University, Washington, DC, September 14.

Dijkstra, E. (1989). "On the Cruelty of Really Teaching Computer Science." *Communications of the ACM*, 32/12 (December): 1398–1404.

Discover (1986). "Science Behind the News: Did Computers Make Stock Prices Plummet?" *Discover*, 7/12 (December): 13.

Forester, T. and Morrison, P. (1990). *Computer Ethics: Cautionary Tales and Ethical Dilemmas in Computing*. MIT Press.

Gotterbarn, D. (1991a). "A 'Capstone' Course in Computer Ethics." In T. W. Bynum, W. Maner, and J. Fodor (eds.), *Teaching Computer Ethics*. Research Center on Computing and Society.

Gotterbarn, D. (1991b). "Computer Ethics: Responsibility Regained." *National Forum: The Phi Kappa Phi Journal*, 71/3: 26–31.

Gotterbarn, D. (1991c). "The Use and Abuse of Computer Ethics." In T. W. Bynum, W. Maner, and J. Fodor (eds.), *Teaching Computer Ethics*. Research Center on Computing and Society.

Green, P. and Brightman, A. (1990). *Independence Day: Designing Computer Solutions for Individuals with Disability*. DLM Press.

Hart, C. (1990) "Computer Data Putting History out of Reach." *Raleigh News and Observer* (January 2).

Huff, C. and Finholt, T. (eds.) (1994). *Social Issues in Computing: Putting Computing in Its Place*. McGraw-Hill, Inc.

Ladd, J. (1989). "Ethical Issues in Information Technology." Presented at a conference of the Society for Social Studies of Science, November 15–18, in Irvine, California.

Leventhal, L., Instone, K., and Chilson, D. (1992). "Another View of Computer Science: Patterns of Responses Among Computer Scientists." *Journal of Systems Software* (January).

Maner, W. (1980). *Starter Kit in Computer Ethics*. Helvetica Press (published in cooperation with the National Information and Resource Center for the Teaching of Philosophy).

McConnell, S. (1993). *Code Complete: A Practical Handbook of Software Construction*. Microsoft Press.

Moor, J. (1985). "What Is Computer Ethics?" *Metaphilosophy*, 16/4: p. 266. (The article also appears in T. W. Bynum, W. Maner, and J. Fodor (eds.), *Teaching Computer Ethics*. Research Center on Computing and Society.)

Neumann, P. (1980). "Risks to the public in computers and related systems." *Software Engineering Notes* 5/2 (April): 5.

Neumann, P. (1995). *Computer Related Risks*. New York: Addison-Wesley Publishing Company.

Parker, D. (1976). *Crime by Computer*. Charles Scribner's Sons.

Parker, D. (1978). *Ethical Conflicts in Computer Science and Technology*. AFIPS Press.

Parker, D. (1989). *Computer Crime: Criminal Justice Resource Manual*, 2nd edn. National Institute of Justice.

Parker, D., Swope, S., and Baker, B. N. (1990). *Ethical Conflicts in Information and Computer Science, Technology, and Business*. QED Information Sciences.

Pecorino, P. and Maner, W. (1985). "The Philosopher as Teacher: A Proposal for a Course on Computer Ethics". *Metaphilosophy*, 16/4: 327–37.

Rogerson, S. and Bynum, T. (eds.) (1996). *Information Ethics: A Comprehensive Reader*. Blackwell Publishing.

Schneier, B. (1993). "The IDEA Encryption Algorithm." *Dr Dobb's Journal*, 208 (December): 54.

Science (1987). Computers Amplify Black Monday," *Science*, 238 (October): 4827.

Tabak, L. (1988). "Giving Engineers a Positive View of Social Responsibility," *SIGCSE Bulletin*, 20/4: 29–37.

Wiener, N. (1960). "Some Moral and Technical Consequences of Automation," *Science*, 131: 1355–8.

Basic study questions

1. Maner has two rationales for considering computer ethics to be an important field of research. One of these he calls "the weaker view" and the other "the stronger view." State these two rationales.

2. Maner presents six "levels of justification" for studying computer ethics. Briefly describe each level.
3. According to Maner, genuine computer ethics issues are "unique" to the field of computer ethics. What three characteristics, taken together, make them "unique" in Maner's sense?
4. Briefly describe Maner's "uniquely stored" case.
5. Briefly describe Maner's "uniquely malleable" case.
6. Briefly describe Maner's "uniquely complex" case.
7. Briefly describe Maner's "uniquely fast" case.
8. Briefly describe Maner's "uniquely cheap" case.
9. Briefly describe Maner's "uniquely cloned" case.
10. Briefly describe Maner's "uniquely discrete" case.
11. Briefly describe Maner's "uniquely coded" case.

Questions for further thought

1. What is the difference between "moral indoctrination" on the one hand and "instruction in ethics" on the other hand? What are the implications of this difference with regard to computer ethics education?
2. Discuss the nature and value of arguing by analogy. How does Maner use these ideas to argue for the "uniqueness" of certain issues in computer ethics?
3. At the end of his chapter, Maner asks why computer ethics should be a field of study when there is no comparable field for any other kind of technology. How does Moor answer this question in chapter 1 above? How would you answer this question?

CHAPTER 3

Ethical Decision-Making and Case Analysis in Computer Ethics

Terrell Ward Bynum

Pattern Recognition and Ethical Decision-Making

Most people have a remarkable capacity for certain kinds of pattern recognition. Consider for example the ability to pick out someone's face in a crowd or in a book of photographs. If you know someone well – say, your best friend or a close family member – you are very likely to be able to identify that person's face in a book of photos, even if it contains thousands of pictures of other people. Some people, of course, are better than others at this sort of task, but the overwhelming majority of people are very good at it. Similarly, most people are able to "read" the facial expressions and body language of others to determine how they are feeling. Again, some are "more sensitive" than others to these kinds of clues, but even the average person, in most circumstances, is good at "sensing" how others are feeling just by looking at their faces and seeing how they are behaving.

These pattern recognition skills constitute a kind of *knowledge*, but not the kind that is typically expressed in descriptive statements. For example, you obviously know what your best friend looks like because you can pick your friend out of a crowd; nevertheless you may be unable to describe your friend's face in words that would enable someone else to recognize that person in a crowd. Pattern recognition, therefore, is much like perception – you simply "see that" your friend is there in the crowd. You don't first create in words a long complicated description of your friend's face and then try to match that description to a face in the crowd.

I mention these pattern recognition capacities because I believe that they provide a clue to understanding how people normally make ethical judgments and why they make most of them quickly and correctly. The ability to detect ethical situations and make appropriate ethical judgments is apparently another example of pattern recognition. Often, a person can "see" that there is an ethical problem and can "see" that a proposed solution is adequate or inadequate. One is tempted to call this capacity "ethical intuition," though there is nothing mysterious about it, and it is certainly subject to explanation and improvement. Indeed, I argue below that many of the applied ethics tools and case analysis techniques offered by computer ethics thinkers can help to improve the ethical analysis skills of computer professionals, public policy-makers, and anyone else concerned with the many ethical issues of the "information age."

In this chapter, I use these ideas to develop and illustrate a case analysis method for computer ethics. My goal is to provide a method of analysis that is *natural* and *effective* – "natural" because it models the way people actually make ethical decisions in their everyday lives, and "effective" because it is informed and influenced by insights and helpful suggestions of a number of computer ethics and applied ethics scholars.

Four Important Questions

One of the most helpful descriptions of computer ethics can be found in James Moor's 1985 article "What Is Computer Ethics?" where he said the following:

> A typical problem in computer ethics arises because there is a policy vacuum about how computer technology should be used. Computers provide us with new capabilities and these in turn give us new choices for action. Often, either no policies for conduct in these situations exist or existing policies seem inadequate. A central task of computer ethics is to determine what we should do in such cases, that is, formulate policies to guide our actions. (p. 266)

Moor argued that computer technology is genuinely revolutionary because it is "logically malleable":

> Computers are logically malleable in that they can be shaped and molded to do any activity that can be characterized in terms of inputs, outputs and connecting logical operations. . . . Because logic applies everywhere, the potential applications of computer technology appear limitless. The computer is the nearest thing we have to a universal tool. Indeed, the limits of computers are largely the limits of our own creativity. (p. 269)

Moor's view, then, is that computer technology is powerful and revolutionary because it is logically malleable. It creates opportunities to do new things that people have never done before, and the question then arises whether we *should* do these things. Do already existing "policies for conduct" apply? If the answer is "yes," then presumably we should simply follow the existing policies. But if the answer is "no," we have to formulate new policies and ethically justify them. This is an important stage in the process of doing computer ethics, and I believe that we need a better understanding of four important aspects of the process if we are to arrive at a natural and effective method of case analysis:

1 What is a "policy for conduct" or a "policy to guide our actions" (to use Moor's words)?
2 How does one determine whether there are existing policies that adequately cover the situation in question?
3 How does one formulate new policies to deal with new situations that existing policies are unable to resolve?
4 How does one ethically justify newly formulated policies?

Policies to Guide One's Conduct

Usually, when a person makes an ethical decision or judgment, he or she does *not* seek the advice of a professional philosopher or attempt to use broad philosophical principles like Immanuel Kant's "categorical imperative," or Jeremy Bentham's "principle of utility," or the Buddha's "four noble truths." Indeed, the average person in most countries knows little or nothing about the sophisticated theories of "the great philosophers." Nevertheless, most people are quite successful at making ethical judgments and decisions when they wish to do so, because they understand the usual standards of right and wrong within their community, and they quickly adopt a traditional solution.

Ethical principles and practices are social phenomena created and sustained by complex social processes. Individuals do not need to reinvent ethics for themselves or memorize long lists of rules and laws. Instead, they are born into societies with complex networks of "policies for conduct" already in place. And as Aristotle noted in his *Nicomachean Ethics*, human beings are creatures of habit. When properly brought up and educated, they develop patterns of behavior consistent with and reinforced by the rules and values of their society. If they engage in behavior that goes against the rules, they are scolded and corrected at their mother's knee, or pressured and punished by peers, teachers, supervisors, government agents, and – in extreme cases – law enforcement officials. This is a very effective means of teaching values and shaping behavior, because the desire to avoid offending others and to avoid scorn and punishment are powerful motivating factors in human behavior. The capacity to avoid offending others is probably a trait "selected" by evolution and survival of the fittest. Making enemies, after all, is not an effective survival strategy! Human beings, therefore, are normally sensitive to criticism and wary of giving offense – "What would my friends and family say?" "What would the neighbors think?" "Would my colleagues and co-workers still respect me?" The above-mentioned capacity to read facial expressions and body language is related to this sensitivity about giving offense.

For these reasons, most people become remarkably adept at recognizing behavioral patterns that are approved and encouraged by their society; and they use their impressive pattern recognition skills to judge their own behavior as well as that of others. This explains how it is possible for people to make most of their ethical decisions quickly and correctly. It also explains why one's ability to make ethical judgments often seems to be a kind of "perception" or "intuition." Sometimes an action "just feels wrong" or "just seems right," though it may be difficult to say why. (Even antisocial "rebels," who explicitly choose to offend others, make use of these ethics-related pattern recognition skills.)

Rather than appealing to the abstract theories of famous philosophers, therefore, typical ethical decision-makers – including typical computer professionals – apply much less grandiose "policies for conduct." They often use personal values or standards derived from their family or local community. And if the decision-maker is a member of a profession, he or she may apply accepted "standards of good practice," or a professional code of ethics, or an employer's code of conduct. At the same time, of course, a large number of international, national, regional, and local laws may be relevant, and people usually try to stay within the law.

In a "reasonably just" society, where laws seem equitable and social institutions and traditions appear to be fair, this is a very efficient way to make good ethical judgments. In such a context, illegal activities and those that fly in the face of common practice are probably unethical. To guide one's actions and inform one's ethical judgments, therefore, one can use a variety of "policies for conduct" – a multileveled rich-textured fabric of overlapping laws, rules, principles, and practices. In 1997, in an article entitled "How to Do Computer Ethics," I attempted, with my colleague Petra Schubert, to provide a detailed list of such "policies for conduct" (see Bynum and Schubert 1997). That list included all of the following:

1 *International treaties and agreements* The broadest policies (in the geographic sense) to govern conduct are international rules and agreements such as international laws, government-to-government treaties, global business practices and agreements, and so on. Computing-related agreements include, for example, treaties governing ownership of intellectual property, security, and encryption of data.

2 *Laws* Nations, states, provinces, cities, and local governments all have thousands of laws, many of which apply to computer-related issues such as privacy of medical information, ownership of software, "hacking and cracking," creation and dissemination of malicious code such as computer viruses, and so on.

3 *Regulations* As well as laws themselves, there are thousands of government regulations laid down by various agencies and departments to

interpret and carry out the laws. Many of these regulations, of course, are concerned with computing.

4   *Standards of good practice*   Entire professional communities sometimes reach agreement on "standards of good practice" that every practitioner in that field is expected to uphold. In computing, to name only a couple of examples, there are standards of good practice for software engineering and standards for data encryption.

5   *Professional codes of ethics*   In addition to treaties, laws, government regulations, and standards of good practice, there are codes of ethics adopted by professional organizations. Such codes may apply, for example, to computer professionals who are members of such organizations as the Association for Computing Machinery (ACM), the British Computer Society (BCS), and the Institute for the Management of Information Systems (IMIS).

6   *Corporate policies*   Sometimes large corporations and organizations have their own rules of conduct for their employees; and these can include, for example, rules for the use of company computers, and standards for software testing and quality assurance.

7   *Community and personal values*   In addition to *formal* rules and regulations such as those listed above, an ethical decision-maker typically functions within a community that has a variety of *unwritten* "common practices" and mores. And of course family standards and personal values often influence ethical judgments as well.

In a reasonably just society, these "policies to guide one's conduct" are ethically empowering. When combined with pattern recognition skills, they enable people to make ethical judgments quickly and correctly in the vast majority of cases where ethical decisions are necessary or desired.

Of course, this way of proceeding has risks and limitations, because it is possible for laws to be unjust, for personal or family values to be biased and prejudiced, and for corporate policies to be ruthless or socially destructive. In addition, as Moor noted, the power and flexibility of ICT generate possibilities for which traditional policies are inadequate or missing (policy vacuums). For these reasons, "typical" or "customary" ways of making ethical decisions, although normally sufficient for most ethical judgments, are not completely reliable or effective. Fortunately, there are many resources and methods available to help one overcome these shortcomings and develop careful ethical analyses. As Walter Maner (2002) pointed out, an effective case analysis method can provide a variety of benefits: it can help guard against important omissions in our ethical considerations, assure careful consideration of relevant facts and issues, provide explanations and justifications when needed, raise awareness, increase sensitivity, deepen understanding, and help to teach and transmit professional culture.

Developing Ethical Judgment

In order to make a good ethical analysis, one must have "good ethical judgment." Centuries ago, Aristotle argued that the development of good ethical judgment depends upon experience (see his *Nicomachean Ethics*). Very young children, he noted, have no understanding of ethics, and they are motivated primarily by pleasure and pain, desire and passion. Parents, mentors, and the general community, according to Aristotle, are responsible for instilling appropriate habits into the children and instructing them about virtue and vice. By their teenage years, young people should have developed habits and behavioral patterns that are reasonably consistent with ethics and justice, and they should have acquired at least a rudimentary understanding of the nature of virtue and vice. Teenagers, however, are still very driven by passion and desire, and they surrender too easily to temptation. Even young adults, according to Aristotle, have not fully developed their ethical judgment skills. They need another two or three decades of experience before they can have an excellent ethical "eye." Aristotle's view is echoed in such well-known sayings as "wisdom comes with age" and the common practice in many cultures of relying upon elders of the community to make wise ethical decisions.

All of this is consistent with our assumption that good ethical judgment and decision-making involve pattern recognition skills and the ability to "see" what is right or wrong. To develop these skills, people need to have a breadth of experience; they need to have confronted and thought about a wide diversity of ethical problems and issues. Therefore, as Maner (2002) aptly noted, people who wish to develop their ethical analysis skills should welcome opportunities to learn from experience and engage in relevant conversations with trusted friends, colleagues, teachers, and mentors. They should seek experiences in which they cultivate moral awareness and sensitivity, clarify their value system and world view, observe human nature, engage in ethical behavior themselves, and learn some ethical theory. Of course, "there exists no general algorithmic method that will guarantee the validity of ethical deliberation." Nevertheless, "non-algorithmic 'heuristic' methods can guide and inform the process, making it significantly more robust and dependable" (Maner 2002; see also chapter 7 below, by N. Ben Fairweather).

A Suggested Method of Case Analysis

With the above points clearly in mind, we are now in position to consider a suggested "heuristic method" of ethical case analysis:

PRELIMINARY STEP − KEEP AN "ETHICAL-ANALYSIS LOG"   It is strongly suggested that you create an "ethical-analysis log" by writing down the details of your observations, conversations, findings, and suggestions as you proceed with your case analysis. Such a log can be very useful to students and to ICT practitioners alike. Students are likely to be asked to do this on exams and homework assignments; and ICT practitioners will find such an "ethics audit trail" extremely useful in their efforts to make decisions and justify them to themselves, their colleagues, clients and supervisors.

1. Take the ethical point of view

The first important "step" in any ethical analysis is to view the situation or problem from what is sometimes called "the ethical point of view." This involves adopting a perspective in which *equality, justice,* and *respect* all play important roles.

Equality   All human beings can suffer pain and sorrow and experience pleasure and joy. We all have needs, interests, and plans that can be served and advanced or thwarted and damaged. These are "ethically relevant considerations" that are part of our shared "human nature". (Supporters of the so-called "animal liberation movement" note that, to some extent at least, other members of the animal kingdom share these characteristics with humans, and so they also should be given some ethical consideration.)

Justice   Treating people equally is an important component of justice. That is why the image of "Justice" as a female character is usually depicted as blindfolded when using her "scales of justice." She cannot act in a biased manner if she cannot see which particular persons will benefit from her decisions. This requirement of treating people equally is reflected in common phrases such as "justice is blind," "equal in the eyes of the law," or "equal in the eyes of God." It explains why utilitarian philosopher Jeremy Bentham insisted that each person must count the same when one applies his utilitarian calculus; why John Locke argued that every person has the same inalienable rights of life, liberty, and property; why Immanuel Kant argued that one must "universalize" one's ethical "maxims;" why Aristotle used the same virtues and vices to ethically judge the lives and actions of all people regardless of their place in society; and why any person can learn the Buddha's "four noble truths" and follow "the eight-fold path."

Nearly all human beings have a very strong sense of justice. They are quick to take offense if others are seen as having unfair advantages and opportunities. Even young children cry "Unfair!" if their siblings or friends get special treatment that they are denied. Such sensitivity to injustice and bias can be very useful when one is attempting to identify ethical problems or envision possible solutions; and we will make effective use of this sensitivity in our case analysis method.

Respect   It is hard to overestimate the importance of respect in a human life. Lack of respect between individuals or cultures can lead to hate, rage, violence, and war. Loss of respect can severely damage a love relationship, a family, a friendship. In some cultures, loss of respect is even a reason to commit suicide. People need and cherish the respect of friends and loved ones; and they cannot function effectively on the job or in the community if they are not respected by their peers, their supervisors, and their neighbors. *Self-respect* and the resulting *integrity* that goes with it are aspects of ethical maturity and strength of character, while the loss of self-respect can be a catastrophe that destroys a happy life. It is not surprising that German philosopher Immanuel Kant made respect for persons the centerpiece of his ethical theory.

The ethical point of view   To determine whether an action or policy is ethically acceptable, or even ethically required, the first "step" is to "take the ethical point of view" which treats all human beings as "equal in the eyes of justice" and respects the ethical relevance of each person's needs and rights.

2. Develop a detailed description of the case to be analyzed

Before a just ethical judgment can be made, it is important to have a clear and detailed description of the relevant facts and considerations. If the case you are dealing with is described in a textbook or article, be sure that you understand the key words and phrases used to describe the situation. Ambiguous or vague terms should be clarified; and you should take note of the participants, their actions, roles, and relationships.

Limit your consideration to the facts that are actually presented or strongly implied in the case description. It is appropriate to presuppose common-sense knowledge as background information, but take care not to "invent" unusual or special "facts" not specified or strongly implied by the given case description. Such inappropriate additions to the case can dramatically alter the ethical circumstances and inappropriately influence your conclusions.

When dealing with a real case in everyday life – rather than a textbook exercise – the challenge is to gather and clarify the ethically relevant facts regarding the people involved and their actions, roles, and relationships. (Ethically relevant facts are ones that would lead to different ethical conclusions if left out of your considerations.) You need to estimate the time and resources you will have to gather the facts and to think about the circumstances. If time and resources are limited, you may have to make some reasonable assumptions to cover facts and information that cannot be gathered or verified.

3. Try to "see" the ethical issues and any "traditional" solutions that fit the case

After getting a clear and detailed description of the case, use your ethical "eye" to try to identify key issues and determine whether existing "policies to guide one's conduct" apply. If they do, you can simply select a traditional solution. There is little need for ethical analysis, because the proposed solution "just feels right" and "fits right in," and you can easily specify which policies apply.

The vast majority of ethical decisions that people make, including decisions that involve ICT, can be handled in this way without further ethical analysis. If the situation is unusual, however, and you appear to face a policy vacuum – or if there is need for a deeper or more thorough ethical understanding of the situation – you can take additional steps as follows.

4. Call upon your own ethical knowledge and skills

Any person who functions reasonably well in society makes use of a significant amount of ethical knowledge, perhaps much more than he or she may realize. For this reason, if you are faced with a "policy vacuum", or if you wish to achieve a more robust understanding of the ethical situation, there are several strategies that you can employ to tap into your own ethical knowledge and skills.

Think of precedents and analogies   As explained above, people are remarkably good at pattern recognition. Use this skill to your advantage by thinking about similar cases that you know about (or can imagine), possible precedents, analogies and disanalogies, examples and counter-examples that may cast light upon the case you are dealing with. How were similar cases handled in the past? What are the relevant similarities and differences between other cases and this one? Is this case so different that previous solutions do not apply?

Make use of your natural sensitivity about giving offense   Since most human beings are very concerned about offending others, you can turn your own sensitivity to advantage. Try to imagine who – if anyone – might object to the given situation and why. The objector is likely to be either someone who feels at risk or someone who has duties and responsibilities related to the kind of situation in question. The identity of the imagined objector, as well as the reason(s) for the imagined objection(s), may enable you to focus quickly upon the key issues that are likely to be central to the case. The more experience you have had with this kind of case, and the more you know about the parties and policies in question, the easier it will be to focus upon the heart of the problem and envision a workable solution. (This is a quick and informal version of the more systematic "stakeholder analysis" described below on p. 70.)

Engage in role-playing and apply your natural ability to sympathize   Imagine that you were a participant in the case. For each significant participant, put yourself "in the other person's shoes." How would you feel? How would you want the case to be resolved? What would be a just solution from your point of view? What if one of the participants were a friend of yours, or even your own child – what advice would you give? What resolution would seem fair to you? For each alternative action that might be taken, how could you justify that action to others who might object to it? Would you be proud to tell your family and friends about it, or announce it on television?

5. Get the advice of others

Take advantage of other people's ethical knowledge and perspectives. Ethical rules and practices are social phenomena, and no person is an island. Since every other person has had different experiences from yours, and sees the world from a different perspective, you can benefit from discussing the case with trusted friends, mentors, colleagues, and supervisors. Try to understand their views and compare them with yours.

6. Take advantage of one or more systematic analysis techniques

After taking all five of the above-described "steps" of ethical analysis, you are likely to have a very good understanding of the ethical situation – the various participants and their actions and relationships, the primary ethical issues involved, the various choices that were made (or should have been made), and the policies that were used (or should have been used) to make ethical judgments and decisions. In many cases, this will be a sufficient analysis for the intended purpose, and you can draw helpful ethical conclusions and, perhaps, make some useful recommendations to avoid or resolve similar cases in the future. (More will be said about these last two topics in "steps" 7 and 8 below.)

   If an even more robust ethical analysis is desired, there are many additional analysis techniques that you could use, including, for example, the following (these techniques are briefly explained here and are developed in more detail on the web sites associated with this textbook (see the Preface above)):

a. *Perform a "professional standards analysis"*   If the case in question involves actions and decisions of ICT professionals, it is likely that you will gain some ethical insights by systematically applying ethical principles from professional codes of ethics, such as the Software Engineering Code of Ethics and Professional Practice, or the ethical codes of organizations such as the ACM, the ACS, the BCS, and the IMIS (to name a few examples). (All five of these codes, as well as the IEEE code, are included below in the Appendix to Part III.) Such codes have been carefully developed to take account of professional standards of good practice and relevant laws and moral principles.

A good way to proceed is to select an appropriate code of ethics and then systematically examine the case in light of each ethical principle included in the selected code. You should ask such questions as: Did anyone violate any of the ethical principles in the code? If so, was the violation justified? Why do you say so? Does the case reveal a "policy vacuum" that could be filled by adding a new principle to the code? How could that new principle be stated and justified?

b. *Perform a "roles and responsibilities analysis"*   Every role that one fulfills in life comes with a set of duties and responsibilities, and many roles have associated rights as well. For example, a teacher is responsible for the instruction of students and the evaluation of their performance, and the teacher normally has the right to assign a grade to the student at the end of term. A doctor is responsible for diagnosing and treating patients and has the right to prescribe medication or therapy.

You can take advantage of the facts about roles and responsibilities by systematically considering the roles of various persons involved in the case. What are (or were) the roles of each person? What responsibilities and rights are (or were) appropriate to those roles, and are (or were) they properly carried out or respected? If ICT makes it possible for people to have new roles that did not exist before (policy vacuums), what should be the rights and responsibilities associated with those new roles and why?

c. *Perform a "stakeholder analysis"*   Actions and policies involved in a case typically affect the interests and well-being of a variety of people. Each person who is significantly affected, whether directly or indirectly, can be viewed as a "stakeholder" – that is, as someone who is significantly benefited or harmed, or someone whose rights are upheld or violated. (See chapter 6 below, by Simon Rogerson, for more discussion of stakeholder identification.)

You can gain a better understanding of the ethical issues in the case by systematically considering each stakeholder and the relevant benefits, harms, and rights involved. Were the benefits and harms distributed fairly? Were people's rights upheld and respected or trampled and violated? If ICT has generated new possibilities that were never encountered before, how should resulting benefits and harms be fairly distributed, and how could people's rights be properly respected? What new policies, if any, should be put in place and why?

d. *Perform a "systematic policy analysis"*   It is pointed out above that in every social context there exists a variety of "policies for conduct" that form a "multileveled rich-textured fabric of overlapping laws, rules, principles, and practices." These include international treaties and agreements, national and local laws, government regulations, professional standards of good practice, codes of conduct, corporate policies, and community and personal values.

You can take advantage of this rich array of "policies for conduct" by systematically considering each type of policy and its relevance to the case under consideration. What laws, regulations, and agreements are applicable? Were they properly followed? Are there standards of good practice or codes of ethics that apply in this case? What community and family values are relevant? How can the various policies be weighed and reconciled with each other? If ICT has created policy vacuums, what new "policies for conduct" should be put in place and why?

e. *Perform an "ethical-theory analysis"*   Under most circumstances, a person does not seek the advice of a professional philosopher or read "great philosophical works" when faced with an ethical decision to make or a case to analyze. Nevertheless, famous ethical theories have much to offer when one is seeking a better ethical understanding of the situation. For this reason, you can take advantage of some of the key ideas of these theories when developing a case analysis. Several example theories are sketched below. (More detailed explanations of these and others are available on the web sites associated with this textbook. See the Preface above.)

1   *Utilitarian ideas*   Jeremy Bentham was "the father of utilitarianism" and John Stuart Mill was his most famous disciple. These philosophers and their followers made *benefit* and *harm* the key ethical considerations. Two ethical principles capture the essence of their view:

THE PRINCIPLE OF UTILITY   Something is good ethically to the extent that it tends to promote benefit (including pleasure, happiness, advantage, etc.) and bad ethically to the extent that it tends to promote harm (including pain, unhappiness, disadvantage, etc.).

THE PRINCIPLE OF EQUALITY   Ethics does not permit someone to favor the rich over the poor, or the powerful over the weak, or men over women, or white persons over people of color, or the able-bodied over the disabled, etc. Regardless of a person's station in life, each person counts the same when the benefits and harms are added up.

The overall strategy of utilitarianism is to try to bring about the greatest benefit and least harm for the greatest number of people. It is important to note that risks and probabilities count also, because increased risk of harm is bad and increased probability of benefit is good.

You can make use of these ideas in your case analysis by examining for each person (regardless of his or her station in life) the likely benefits and harms for that person. The best course of action would be the one that is likely to bring about, for the greatest number of people, the most benefit and the least harm.

2   *Aristotelian ideas*   Key ideas in the ethical theories of Aristotle and his followers are virtues and vices. The virtues include positive character traits such as *courage, integrity, honesty, fidelity, reliability, generosity, responsibility, self-discipline, temperance, modesty*, and *persistence* (to name several examples). According to Aristotle, people who are appropriately raised by their families and their communities will usually develop patterns of behavior consistent with the virtues. And given appropriate experiences, they will come to recognize examples of virtue and vice.

Aristotle described the ethical virtues as rational character traits that occupy an appropriate middle ground between unreasonable extremes. *Courage*, for example, is a positive trait associated with rational control of fear. It lies between the excess of *cowardice*, associated with fear-driven behavior, and the deficiency of *foolhardiness*, associated with a lack of appropriate fear. *Good temper* is a virtue associated with rational control of anger; while the vice of *irascibility* is unreasonable proneness to anger, and the vice of *apathy to wrong doing* is unreasonable lack of anger about injustice.

To perform an Aristotelian analysis of a case, you should systematically identify the virtuous behavior of participants, as well as any examples of surrender to the vices.

3   *Kantian ideas*   Philosopher Immanuel Kant made respect for persons the central concept in his ethical theory. Because human beings are rational beings, said Kant, they have worth in themselves and do not need anything outside of themselves to give them worth. For this reason, the fundamental principle of Kant's ethics, which he called *the categorical imperative*, can be stated this way:

THE CATEGORICAL IMPERATIVE   Always treat every person, including yourself, as a being that has worth in itself, never merely as a being to be used to advance someone else's goals.

According to Kant, therefore, one must always respect the worth and dignity of a person, and never merely use him or her. Lying and cheating, for example, would be unethical because they involve merely using other people to achieve your own goals. Failure to uphold the rights of someone would be unethical because it would not show proper respect for the that person, and it would not allow the person to be a responsible agent taking responsibility for his or her own life.

In your case analysis, you can take advantage of Kant's ethical insight by asking whether each participant in the situation has been treated in a manner consistent with the categorical imperative.

7. Draw relevant ethical conclusions about the case

By engaging in all or most of the above-described "steps" of analysis, you are likely to have gained an impressive set of insights into the ethical issues and alternatives, putting you in a good position to draw relevant conclusions. What are the key ethical issues? Did anyone do anything unethical? Why do you think so? If the case involves possible future actions, what should those actions be, and what are the relevant ethical considerations that would justify them? If there are competing values or considerations, how would you rank them and why?

8. Draw relevant lessons about the future

If some of the participants in the case acted unethically, how can similar actions be prevented or decreased in the future? If you have identified any "policy vacuums" that need to be filled, what new policies would you recommend, and what are the ethical considerations that would justify them? It is worth noting that any new policies that you recommend will have the best chance of being adopted by the relevant community if they are similar in significant ways to already existing policies. A policy that "sticks out like a sore thumb" and seems to fly in the face of common standards of good practice would need a very persuasive ethical justification to be accepted.

A Sample Case to Analyze: The Extortionist Softbot

Given the above-presented "heuristic method of case analysis", we are now in position to consider a sample case (fictional, but realistic) and to develop an example case analysis. Our imagined case is this:

The case of the extortionist softbot

The term "softbot" is short for "software robot." A softbot resides within a computer or a network of computers and performs various "actions" there.

A "planner-based" softbot is a kind of "intelligent agent" that is assigned goals by a user and then employs artificial intelligence to create and carry out a plan to fulfill the user's goals. Planner-based softbots can travel through computer networks, such as the Internet, gathering information and using that information to perform various software-driven tasks.

CharityBot.com is a software company that creates planner-based softbots to help charitable organizations raise money. One of their most successful products is a "softbot template" called EMAILFUNDER, which can be used by charitable organizations to create their own customized softbots for soliciting donations over the Internet. EMAILFUNDER combines several software "agents" that perform various tasks:

E_RESEARCHER   This *research agent* crawls through the Internet gathering various kinds of information about individuals – information from web pages, databases, news services, credit agencies, chat rooms, and so on.

E_PROFILER   Using information from E_RESEARCHER, this *personal profile agent* creates profiles of individual people – their email addresses, employment records, economic status, credit ratings, leisure-time activities, social activities, friends and associates, and many other kinds of information.

E_MAEL_WRITER   The user provides a sample email message to this *email writing agent*, which then uses information from E_PROFILER to generate emailed solicitations asking people to donate money. E_MAEL_WRITER is artificially intelligent and is able to generate minor variations of the sample email message by using information from personal profiles and substituting relevant words. CharityBot.com considers this to be a major selling point of EMAILFUNDER because customized emails can play upon the interests of recipients, making them more likely to donate money to the charity.

MESSAGE_TESTR   This *statistical testing agent* keeps statistics about the success rate of each variation of the sample email message. After E_MAEL_WRITER has created a new version of the sample message and has emailed it to a thousand recipients, MESSAGE_TESTR determines the percentage of successful solicitations. If a particular message proves to be especially effective as a fundraiser, E_MAEL_WRITER is instructed to send out many thousands of copies. E_MAEL_WRITER and MESSAGE_TESTR, working together, can create and test dozens of message variations per week.

E_BANKR   This *electronic banking agent* receives credit-card based donations and deposits them electronically into the charity's bank account. It also automatically updates the charity's financial records to take account of the new funds.

Within weeks of hitting the market, EMAILFUNDER created a number of customized softbots that proved to be reasonably successful fundraisers for a number of charities. When Joe Biggheart, the chief fundraiser for a child cancer charity, learned about this, he decided to try EMAILFUNDER for a major fundraising project.

Joe leased a copy of EMAILFUNDER from CharityBot.com and attended a workshop to learn how to use it. During the workshop, Joe expressed some worries about the quality and appropriateness of email messages written by E_MAEL_WRITER. He also expressed some concern about possible privacy violations associated with personal profiles. The workshop leaders seemed annoyed by Joe's questions, and they quickly assured him that his worries were unfounded. Joe was surprised that they were annoyed, and he quickly changed the subject.

After the workshop, Joe dismissed his worries and initiated his fundraising project by providing a sample email message to his softbot and placing the softbot onto the Internet. Joe's sample message began as follows:

> Dear {recipient},
> We recently learned of your interest in children and health, and so we are writing to ask you to consider making a donation to the Children's Anti-Cancer Fund. We hope that you will be able to make a generous gift; and if you find it possible to give $1,000 or more, we will list your name on our "Web Site of Excellence" to honor you for your commitment to children and health.

After three days, Joe checked the electronic bank account of the Children's Anti-Cancer Fund and was pleased to find that nearly $1,000 had already been donated.

Because of a family crisis, Joe had to be away from the office for nearly a week. When he returned to the office, he was surprised to see how much money had been donated while he was away, and he anxiously read the computer-generated variation of his fund-raising letter to see why it had been so successful. Here is what he read:

> Dear {recipient},
> We recently learned of your interest in children and lust, and so we are writing to ask you to consider making a donation to the Children's Anti-Cancer Fund. We hope that you will be able to make a generous gift; and if you find it impossible to give $1,000 or more, we will list your name on our "Web Site of Excellence" to honor you for your commitment to children and lust.

Joe Biggheart was horrified to learn that his softbot, which was created by using EMAILFUNDER, had sent this computer-generated "extortion letter" to thousands of wealthy men who were regular visitors of pornographic web sites. As a result, several of those men donated large sums of money to the

Children's Anti-Cancer Fund. In addition, Joe discovered that his email box was filled with angry messages.

Joe immediately contacted CharityBot.com and told them about the disastrous email. A quick internal investigation revealed that the word "lust" had mistakenly been left off of the "words to avoid" list used by E_MAEL_WRITER. In addition, a preliminary investigation by one of CharityBot.com's software engineers revealed the strong possibility that a "bug" in the E_MAEL_WRITER software caused the word "impossible" to be substituted for "possible."

During the next few days, Joe and the Children's Anti-Cancer Fund were named in a dozen lawsuits, and three foreign countries sought to extradite Joe and others in order to try them for extortion and violations of privacy laws. A week later, the Children's Anti-Cancer Fund went out of business.

An Example Case Analysis

1. Take the ethical point of view

To begin an ethical analysis of this imagined case, we should start by "taking the ethical point of view," trying to avoid any bias or prejudice in our judgments and to view all those involved in a fair and even-handed way.

2. Develop a detailed case description

Our case description should "stick to the facts" that are actually mentioned or strongly implied; and we should avoid inserting additional "facts" that could significantly alter ethical judgments. Our description should identify the important participants and their roles in the case. The following description seems appropriate:

Participants and their roles

1   Humans

Joe Biggheart   Joe leased EMAILFUNDER from CharityBot.com, created a softbot using EMAILFUNDER, provided a sample email message to the softbot, and placed the softbot onto the Internet. Although he had some concerns about "the quality and appropriateness of email messages written by E_MAEL_WRITER" and about "possible privacy violations associated with personal profiles," he dismissed these worries when the CharityBot.com workshop leaders became annoyed and assured him that his worries were misplaced.

Recipients of the email message   A few sent large donations to the Children's Anti-Cancer Fund after receiving the "extortion" message; many recipients sent outraged email to Joe Biggheart; and a few brought a suit against Joe and his charity organization.

Software engineers from CharityBot.com   They originally created and tested EMAILFUNDER before it was marketed. Later they discovered that "lust" had mistakenly been left off of the "avoid these words" list used by E_MAEL_WRITER. One software engineer also determined that E_MAEL_WRITER probably had a program "bug" that caused the word "impossible" to be substituted for "possible".

Workshop leaders for CharityBot.com   They taught the workshop on using EMAILFUNDER, became annoyed with Joe's worries, and dismissed them as unfounded.

Prosecutors in some foreign countries   They attempted to extradite Joe Biggheart and other officers of his charity in order to try them for extortion and privacy violations.

2   Non-Human Agents

E_RESEARCHER   This software agent gathered information on the Internet about people who frequently visited pornography web sites.

E_PROFILER   This software agent created personal profiles of individuals from data provided by E_RESEARCHER.

E_MAEL_WRITER   This software agent created the "extortion" message by substituting the word "lust" for "health," as well as substituting "impossible" for "possible;" then it sent the resulting message to thousands of wealthy men who had frequented pornographic web sites.

3. Try to "see" the ethical issues

Now that we have a case description with which to work, we can use our "ethical eye" to try to spot problems and possible issues. What ethical questions instantly come to mind? What aspects of this case make you feel "uneasy" and or concerned, even if you cannot yet say why?

Ethical Questions
1   Joe's softbot created an email message that resulted in serious harm to lots of people. Who is responsible for this situation? Did anyone intentionally cause harm, or was it unintended?

2   If the harm was unintended, can anyone be blamed for being negligent or irresponsible? Or was this simply an unfortunate accident that could not have been foreseen or prevented?

Worries

1   Joe used a product created by CharityBot.com, and now he faces very serious problems. He was only trying to do good. It doesn't seem fair that Joe should bear all the blame by himself.
2   E_RESEARCHER and E_PROFILER, working together, can gather and list all sorts of information about people and their personal lives. This doesn't seem right.
3   It doesn't seem right that Joe should have to worry about laws in other countries besides his own.

4. Use your ethical reasoning skills

This is the "step" in which you try to think of precedents and similar situations; try to imagine who might be offended and why; and try to put yourself "in the other person's shoes."

Precedents and similarities   At first glance, this looks like a case of extortion and blackmail, because a message was sent that seemed to threaten the recipient if money is not paid. However, there is a very important difference, because we have no reason to believe that E_MAEL_WRITER knew what it was writing or was even capable of having intentions at all. And, given the fact that Joe Biggheart was "horrified" by the letter, we have good reason to believe that he did not intend to threaten anyone.

Objectors   All those people who were harmed are likely to raise objections, including people who received the "extortionist" email, all those who worked for the Children's Anti-Cancer Fund, children with cancer who were expecting help from the fund, Joe Biggheart, and many family members and friends of all these other objectors. Staff members and owners of CharityBot.com also might face damages. The objectors are likely to express their objections to law enforcement officials, officers of the Children's Anti-Cancer Fund, and managers and owners of CharityBot.com.

Key issues are likely to be (i) whether anyone intentionally caused harm, (ii) whether any laws were broken, (iii) whether anyone was culpably negligent, (iv) whether anyone should be punished and how, and (v) how people can be fairly compensated for their losses.

Standing "in the other person's shoes"   Recipients of the softbot's email who *never were* involved in child pornography or pedophilia, are bound to be furious, anxious to protect their reputations, and likely to want some compensation for their suffering. Recipients who *were* involved in child pornography or pedophilia are likely to feel relieved that the email was a mistake and hopeful that they will not be found out because of it. Joe Biggheart is likely to feel betrayed by CharityBot.com, whom he trusted to provide a reliable and safe software product. He may seek to blame everything on CharityBot.com and avoid any blame himself. Supporters of the Children's Anti-Cancer Fund, plus children with cancer and their families are likely to want the good work of the Fund to somehow be continued; and they are likely to ask the government to find a way to prevent such problems in the future.

5. Discuss the case with others

Other people may see the world from a different perspective, and they have had experiences that are different from yours. It is a good idea, therefore, to seek discussions with others about the case. For example, a lawyer or law student might see some legal issues that you overlooked, a computer security expert may offer some helpful suggestions about the risks of using softbots, and a friend who has been involved in a negligence lawsuit might have some helpful insights.

Interim Conclusions

Depending upon needs and circumstances, many case analyses can be concluded at this point by drawing relevant conclusions. For example, we can already draw the following inferences:

> Joe Biggheart was trying to do good for children who have cancer, and he did not intend to harm anyone; but Joe had some worries about risks and privacy that he dismissed too easily. He should have followed up on these.

> People at CharityBot.com did not take the risks of using softbots seriously enough. The software engineers may not have been concerned enough about such risks, the workshop leaders seem to have dismissed the risks too easily, and the company apparently did not inform its clients about the risks of using their products or similar ones from other companies. These problems may result in lawsuits against CharityBot.com filed by people who were harmed.

Of course, there is much more that could be said, and there are more ideas that can be developed from further analysis.

In addition to making these preliminary ethical judgments, we have hit upon some important *unresolved* computer ethics issues that society will have to face in the future. For example,

> Softbots are not ethically aware of what they do, yet they are given the capacity to perform all kinds of "actions". Society needs to figure out how to make softbots behave as if they were ethical agents, even though they aren't. Could there be "ethical rules" for softbots? (See Eichmann 1994) We apparently have identified some important "policy vacuums" here.

> When people (and softbots) from one country engage in actions on the Internet, they might be violating laws and rules in many other countries. Since no one can know all the laws and rules of all the countries of the world, how can anyone know whether he or she (or his or her softbot) is acting ethically on the Internet? A large set of "policy vacuums" seems to be lurking here.

For those who wish to pursue the implications of this case further, there are many additional analysis techniques available, and some of these are illustrated below. (Because of space limitations, only a few illustrations are given here. A more complete set of examples can be found on the web sites associated with this textbook (see the Preface above). The most definitive account of case analysis techniques that I know about is Maner's excellent article and associated web site "Heuristic Methods for Computer Ethics" (2002).)

6a. Perform a "professional standards analysis"

It is clear from our interim conclusions that several key ethical questions concern actions of ICT professionals working for CharityBot.com. Because of this, it will be helpful to select a relevant code of ethics and apply appropriate principles to the case. Let us use the Software Engineering Code of Ethics and Professional Practice (see Appendix A1 in Part III below) to analyze the actions of the software engineers who created EMAILFUNDER:

> According to principle 1.03 of the Software Engineering Code of Ethics and Professional Practice, software engineers should "*approve software only if they have a well-founded belief that it is safe, meets specifications, passes appropriate tests, and does not diminish quality of life, diminish privacy, or harm the environment. The ultimate effect of the work should be to the public good.*" It seems clear from our analysis above that the CharityBot.com software engineers violated this principle by failing to pay sufficient attention to, or ignoring, quality concerns and privacy risks.

> According to principle 1.04 of that same code of ethics, software engineers should "*disclose to appropriate persons or authorities any actual or potential danger*

to the user, the public, or the environment, that they reasonably believe to be associated with software or related documents." If the CharityBot.com software engineers did *not* know about the risks of using their products, they were negligent; and if they *did* know, they violated this principle by failing to notify their supervisors and clients.

6b. Perform a "roles and responsibilities analysis"

In addition to the software engineers who created EMAILFUNDER, several other people played important roles in this case. These include, for example, chief fundraiser Joe Biggheart and the workshop leaders from CharityBot.com. Let us consider their respective roles and responsibilities:

Joe Biggheart's roles and responsibilities   As chief fundraiser for the Children's Anti-Cancer Fund, Joe was responsible for selecting and carrying out fundraising projects that were legal and safe. Given his worries about the appropriateness of software-written email messages, and also about possible privacy violations, he should have been more persistent and investigated these concerns more fully. He dismissed these worries rather too quickly when the workshop leaders became annoyed with him.

Workshop leaders' roles and responsibilities   The CharityBot.com workshop leaders were responsible, not only for instruction of clients in the use of company products, they also should have taken more seriously the reliability and privacy questions that Joe raised in the workshop.

An important fact about this case is that *non-human agents* (e.g., E_MAEL_WRITER) were significant "actors" in this situation. They had roles and "responsibilities," but they were not ethical agents who could be held accountable in the usual sense of this term. As indicated above, this raises a number of questions about the "ethics" of software agents.

6c. Perform a "stakeholder analysis"

No one significantly benefited in this case, but a number of people were seriously harmed. These include Joe Biggheart, recipients of the emailed message, children with cancer and their families, staff members and stockholders of CharityBot.com, and staff members of the Children's Anti-Cancer Fund. Let us consider two of these stakeholders here. (A *complete* stakeholder analysis is normally recommended for an in-depth understanding of a case, but space limitations make that impossible here. See the web sites associated with this textbook for a more complete stakeholder analysis.)

Recipients of the message   Clearly, recipients of the "extortion" message suffered harm from it. Their privacy was invaded, most were shocked or at least annoyed, and surely some were embarrassed to have their interest in pornography revealed. A few of the recipients felt threatened enough to send large sums of money to the charity, and a number of the recipients were angry enough to initiate lawsuits.

Children with cancer   The children who were being helped, or would have been helped, by the Children's Anti-Cancer Fund were among the most seriously harmed. Some will likely find assistance elsewhere, but others may not; and some of the children might actually die from lack of proper medical care.

6d. Perform a "systematic policy analysis"

The above discussion has already identified a variety of "policies to guide one's conduct" which are relevant to this case. These include, for example, international extradition treaties, laws regarding extortion and negligence, and ethical principles included in professional codes of ethics. Let us consider two other types of policies.

International agreements   In addition to the extradition treaties mentioned above, there are other relevant international "policies." For example, international privacy agreements, such as the "Safe Harbors Agreement" between the United States and European countries, could help to resolve privacy violation questions about personal profiles created by E_RESEARCHER and E_PROFILER.

Corporate policies   Both CharityBot.com and the Children's Anti-Cancer Fund should have had policies in place to deal with privacy and security issues regarding the use of software. Both organizations would have benefited if such issues had been seriously addressed before the disastrous email was sent, and much harm could have been avoided.

6e. Perform an "ethical theory analysis"

Traditional ethical theories of the "great philosophers" can be seen as efforts to understand and systematize many important aspects of ethical practice. (This is similar to the role of "great scientific theories", which attempt to understand and systematize scientific practice.) For this reason, traditional ethical theories can often shed useful light upon a case that is being analyzed. Consider the following utilitarian, Aristotelian and Kantian points about the present case:

Utilitarian points   To behave in an ethical manner, according to the utilitarians, staff members of CharityBot.com, as well as those in the Children's Anti-Cancer Fund (especially Joe Biggheart) should have seriously considered the risks, as well as the possible benefits, of using softbots on the Internet – specifically the risks of using EMAILFUNDER. All of these participants appear to have focused primarily upon the possible profits and benefits, and insufficiently upon the risks. Failure to include a common sex-related word in the list of "words to avoid," as well as the likely existence of a serious software "bug," are indications that the CharityBot.com software engineers were careless. Also, given Joe Biggheart's worries about the appropriateness of software-written email, he should have established a means of checking messages before they were sent. For example, he could have arranged to have each new version of the message sent to his own email and approved by him before his softbot was permitted to send the message to thousands of targeted people.

Aristotelian points   Given what has been said above, it is likely that the CharityBot.com software engineers failed to achieve the kind of professional excellence that results from virtues like *reliability, responsibility,* and *persistence*. They seem, instead, to have indulged in the vices of *unreliability, irresponsibility,* and *lack of persistence*. Joe Biggheart, on the other hand, exhibited virtuous qualities like *generosity* and *compassion,* but he also apparently lacked sufficient *persistence* and *responsibility*. In addition, he should have had the *courage* to pursue his worries in spite of the annoyance they caused to the workshop leaders.

Kantian points   Staff members of CharityBot.com appear to have lacked proper respect for their clients and the people who are likely to be affected by their products. They did not take Joe Biggheart's concerns seriously when he expressed doubts about the reliability of software-generated messages or about possible privacy violations. They created and sold software that can be used systematically and effectively to invade people's privacy. They showed more concern for their own profits than for the dignity and worth of their clients and the people affected by their products. Joe Biggheart, on the other hand, did show respect and concern for the children and families served by his charity; although he (perhaps foolishly) trusted the people at CharityBot.com too much; and he allowed his focus upon fundraising and his fear of offending others to overshadow his respect and concern for recipients of his softbot's email.

7. Draw some key ethical conclusions

Given all that has been said above, we are now in a position to draw some conclusions:

A.   The primary cause of the disaster appears to be a number of ethical shortcomings at CharityBot.com. The software engineers, workshop leaders, and others in the company seem more concerned with profits than with the quality of their products and services. They don't have proper respect for their clients or the people affected by their products. They are willing to create and profit from products that seriously invade people's privacy. They appear to have no company policies that demand excellence, reliability, responsibility, and concern for the dignity and worth of persons. They place concern for company profits above the public welfare.

B.   A contributing cause of the disaster appears to be a lack of sufficient care and attention by the staff of the Children's Anti-Cancer Fund. The organization either lacked or failed to enforce policies that demand excellence and responsibility in carrying out one's duties. Joe Biggheart, in particular, even though he obviously cared about children with cancer and their families, appears to have had an attitude that was too casual when dealing with possible risks to the projects for which he was responsible. And he didn't have the courage or integrity to pursue his worries about quality and privacy.

8. Draw some lessons for the future

Items A and B above are the primary ethical conclusions of this case analysis. In addition, there are some lessons that can be learned:

*   Privacy will continue to be a major issue in computer ethics. The ease with which softbots on the Internet can gather personal information and assemble it into revealing profiles shows the continuing need for privacy in the information age. (See James Moor, "Towards a Theory of Privacy in the Information Age" in chapter 11 below.)
*   As softbots and other software agents become more sophisticated, they are empowered to make more and more "decisions" on their own, and also to perform many more "actions" without consulting their human creators. There seems to be an urgent need for the development of "agent ethics" to help regulate the behavior of computerized agents (See Eichmann 1994).

- Because the Internet is truly global and connects most countries of the world, it has become possible to act "locally" on one's home computer or office computer and nevertheless have a worldwide impact. When a person (or robot) is acting on the Internet, whose laws apply and whose values should be respected? Should everyone in cyberspace be subject to all the laws and rules of all the countries of the world? Could there be such a thing as a "global ethics"? (See Krystyna Gorniak-Kocikowska, "The Computer Revolution and the Problem of Global Ethics" in chapter 15 below.)

References

Bynum, T. W. and Schubert, P. (1997). "How to Do Computer Ethics: A Case Study – The Electronic Mall Bodensee." In M. J. van den Hoven (ed.), *Computer Ethics: Philosophical Enquiry – Proceedings of CEPE'97*. Erasmus University Press, pp. 85–95 (also available at http://www.computerethics.org).

Eichmann, D. (1994). "Ethical Web Agents." Proceedings of the Second International World Wide Web Conference: Mosaic and the Web, Chicago, IL, October 18–20, pp. 3–13. (Accessed on June 29, 2002 at the following web site: http://archive.ncsa.uiuc.edu/SDG/IT94/Proceedings/Agents/eichmann.ethical/eichmann.html.)

Maner, W. (2002). "Heuristic Methods for Computer Ethics". In J. H. Moor and T. W. Bynum (eds.), *Cyberphilosophy: The Intersection of Philosophy and Computing*. Blackwell Publishing (see also http://csweb.cs.bgsu.edu/maner/heuristics/toc.htm).

Moor, J. H. (1985). "What Is Computer Ethics?" In T. W. Bynum (ed.), *Computers and Ethics*. Blackwell Publishing, pp. 266–75. (Published as the October 1985 issue of *Metaphilosophy*.) (Also available at http://www.computerethics.org)

Basic study questions

1. What is "pattern recognition" and why does Bynum say that it is much like perception?
2. What does Bynum mean when he says that he wants his case analysis method to be "natural and effective"?
3. While discussing Moor's "What Is Computer Ethics?," Bynum raises four key questions. What are these questions?
4. Why, according to Bynum, are people so sensitive to offending others?
5. What are the different kinds of "policies for conduct" that, according to Bynum, people normally use to make decisions about what they ought to do?
6. What is Aristotle's account of how people develop good ethical judgment?
7. What, according to Bynum, is "the ethical point of view"?
8. According to Bynum, when developing a detailed description of a case, one should avoid inventing "facts not specified or strongly implied." Why?
9. What three strategies, according to Bynum, can help you "tap into your own ethical knowledge and skills"?

10. What is a "professional standards analysis"?
11. What is a "roles and responsibilities analysis"?
12. What is a "stakeholder analysis"?
13. What is a "systematic policy analysis"?
14. What is an "ethical theory analysis"?
15. What kinds of new policies have the best chance of being accepted by the community when new policies are developed to fill "policy vacuums"?

Questions for further thought

1. Does the idea of "ethics for robots" (including softbots) make any sense? If so, do robots have to be "conscious, thinking beings" before they could be ethical?
2. Given the fact that there are many different cultures of the world with very different value systems, does the concept of "global ethics" make any sense? How does this question relate to Moor's idea (see ch. 1 above) of "core values" – or to Gorniak-Kocikowska's work (see ch. 15 below)?
3. What is privacy, and why is this question ethically important?

ADDITIONAL READINGS AND WEB RESOURCES

Additional readings

Brey, P. (2000). "Disclosive Computer Ethics." *Computers and Society*, 30/4: 10–16.

Gotterbarn, D. (1991). "Computer Ethics: Responsibility Regained." *National Forum: The Phi Beta Kappa Journal*, 71: 26–31.

Johnson, D. G. (2000). "Introduction: Why Computer Ethics?" In D. G. Johnson, *Computer Ethics*, 3rd edn. Prentice Hall, pp. 1–25.

Moor, J. H. (1985). "What Is Computer Ethics?" *Metaphilosophy*, 16/4 (October): 266–75.

Rogerson, S. (1996). "The Ethics of Computing: The First and Second Generations." *The UK Business Ethics Network News* (Spring): 1–4.

Spinello, R. A. (2000). "Introduction." In R. A. Spinello, *CyberEthics: Morality and Law in Cyberspace*. Jones and Bartlett.

Web resources

Bynum, T. W. "Computer Ethics: Basic Concepts and Historical Overview," at http://plato.stanford.edu/entries/ethics-computer/

Centre for Computing and Social Responsibility, De Montfort University, UK, at http://www.ccsr.cse.dmu.ac.uk/index.html

Research Center on Computing and Society, Southern Connecticut State University, USA, at http://www.computerethics.org/

Tavani, H. T. "Computing, Ethics and Social Responsibility: A Bibliography," at http://cyberethics.cbi.msstate.edu/biblio/

PART II

Professional Responsibility

The work an unknown man has done is like a vein of water flowing hidden underground, secretly making the ground green.

Thomas Carlyle

Editors' Introduction

Computer practitioners – people who design, build, program, and service computerized devices, as well as those who plan and manage such activities – have enormous power to affect the world in good ways and in bad ways. Computer practitioners, therefore, also have an enormous responsibility to society at large, and especially to the people directly affected by the computer systems, networks, databases, and other information technology devices that computer practitioners create and control. For example, software engineers who develop computer programs to control airplanes, nuclear power plants, medical devices, and space stations are responsible for computer programs on which many lives depend. Given such important responsibilities, it is clear that computer practitioners should make judgments and decisions that are both ethical and professionally sound.

But what does it mean to be a *professional?* This term calls to mind well-educated practitioners, such as lawyers, doctors, teachers, accountants, and engineers, who have specific qualities and skills normally associated with being professional. For example, the term suggests:

1   Mastering an extensive body of knowledge and skills, usually acquired from formal education, as well as from a period of "apprenticeship." Doctors, lawyers, teachers, accountants, and engineers, for example, typically spend years as university students, as well as additional time acquiring practical experience working with more senior colleagues.
2   Providing an important service in order to advance or preserve a particular social value. For example, doctors preserve life and health, lawyers serve justice, teachers preserve and disseminate knowledge, accountants monitor financial legitimacy, engineers provide safe buildings, bridges, and other structures.
3   Exercising monopolistic control over relevant services to society. The monopoly is usually maintained by requiring a license or certificate to practice. For example, only licensed doctors may perform surgery or

prescribe medicine; only lawyers admitted to the bar may practice law; only certified teachers may teach in our schools, and so on.

4   Accepting a code of professional conduct that spells out professional responsibilities. In medicine, for example, there is the Hippocratic Oath adopted by most medical doctors around the globe. And in law, there are codes such as the American Bar Association's Model Rules of Professional Conduct.

Johnson (2001) and Spinello (1997) have rightly pointed out that these paradigm criteria for identifying professionals do not fully apply to computer practitioners. It is true, of course, that most people who earn their living as computer practitioners have acquired a relevant body of specialized knowledge from formal university study. In addition, many have also had extensive practical experience working under more senior colleagues. On the other hand, with regard to "advancing or preserving particular social values" there does not seem to be a specific value associated with computer practice – something comparable to health for medicine, or justice for law, or knowledge for education. Indeed, Moor has noted (see chapter 1 above) that computer technology is "logically malleable" in the sense that it can be shaped and molded to perform almost any task. So computer technology can be used to preserve and advance (or damage and destroy!) almost anything that society might value. Also, in general, computer practitioners do not currently need a license to practice (the state of Texas has recently introduced a license for software engineers), and so they do not have the kind of monopolistic control that doctors and lawyers exercise in most societies.

There are, of course, codes of conduct that various computer organizations have established for their members–organizations such as the Association for Computing Machinery (ACM), the British Computer Society (BCS), and the Institute of Electrical and Electronics Engineers (IEEE) (see Appendix to Part III below). Such codes are intended to guide the conduct of members, although none is backed by strong sanctions comparable to being disbarred from practicing the law or losing one's license to practice medicine. In this sense, computer practitioners are not strongly bound by their own codes of conduct, and they can continue to practice even if they regularly violate codes of conduct adopted by their official organizations.

According to Gotterbarn, stronger measures are needed:

Computing has matured to a point where it has standards, methods, and techniques which, if employed, would reduce the likelihood of many computing disasters. The world will no longer accept the view that bugs arise in programs by Spontaneous Generation. The bugs (errors) were put there by people who should know better. The failure to deliver quality products is unethical, even in computing. (Gotterbarn 1992)

Despite the fact that today's computer practitioners do not completely fulfill the paradigm characteristics of such professionals as doctors and lawyers, they do have many of the relevant characteristics and they are often thought of as professionals. In addition, they do have professional organizations, for example the ACM, the BCS, and the IEEE.

The Professional Context

Johnson has noted that computer professionals normally work in a complex context with a variety of laws, rules, policies and human relationships:

> [P]rofessionals function in a special context, a context that typically includes relationships with employers, clients, co-professionals, and the public. The context also involves legal, political, and economic constraints. Computer professionals, for example, are often employed by private corporations seeking a profit, constrained by law in a variety of ways, operating in a highly competitive environment, and so on. This context is usually very rich in complexity, and this cannot be ignored in analyzing ethical decision making. (Johnson 1994, p. 40)

The complexity of the professional context is important because ethical decision-making requires more than just following rules. For example, the *role* that one is fulfilling in a specific situation is often an important ethical consideration. *Roles carry related ethical responsibilities and obligations.* To mention some everyday examples: the role of a doctor, a parent, a bus driver, or a school- board member carry with them responsibilities and obligations that others do not have who are not in those roles. Parents, for example, have responsibilities toward their children that non-parents do not have; bus drivers are responsible for the safety of passengers on the bus and are obliged to do everything possible to maintain that safety; and school board members have specific responsibilities and obligations for student safety and education that the average citizen does not have.

The complex context in which a computer professional normally functions includes a variety of roles. Typically, such a person functions simultaneously as an employee, a consultant, a team member, and a citizen. Each of these roles carries with it certain duties, responsibilities, and obligations:

Employer-to-employee The relationship between an employer and an employee is a contractual one. On the one hand, the employee agrees to carry out assigned jobs, and on the other hand the employer agrees to pay compensation. It is the employer's responsibility to provide appropriate tools and a safe work environment, as well as to avoid asking the employee to do anything illegal. It is the employee's responsibility to be honest about his/her qualifications and experience, and to conscientiously perform the work assigned. The employee should be loyal to the employer in the sense that instructions are followed conscientiously, work is done diligently and co-operatively, and company trade secrets are not revealed to competitors. On the other hand, as Johnson rightly notes, "employers cannot demand (in the name of loyalty) every form of behavior that will serve the interests of the company" (Johnson 2001, p. 69).

Professional-to-professional   Most computer professionals today work as team members with others. Obviously, it is important for all members of a team to do their share of the work, to cooperate with the other members, to provide helpful advice and assistance, and so on. These professional-to-professional responsibilities come with team membership. In addition, of course, there will likely be other professionals who will have to maintain and upgrade later what the team is currently creating. Here again, there are additional professional-to-professional responsibilities.

Computer professionals normally belong to various organizations, such as the BCS, the ACS, the ACM, the IMIS, or the IEEE-CS. Insofar as the codes of ethics of such organizations embody the values, goals, and ethical commitments of the profession, members are responsible for upholding them. Often, fellow professionals help each other in securing jobs, contracts, promotions, and so on. Such loyalty to fellow professionals is good for the profession as a whole, but it can be carried too far if it leads to uncompetitive contract bids, unfair treatment of job applicants, and so forth.

Professional-to-client   Many computer professionals (or the teams in which they work) have clients – people or organizations with whom they have contracted to provide a computer-related product or service. The client comes to the professional for assistance because the professional has special knowledge that the client requires. What responsibilities arise from this professional-to-client relationship? The answer depends upon how one defines that relationship.

Bayles (1981) has pointed out that professional-client relationships can be understood using a variety of different models. Johnson (2001, ch. 3) uses three of Bayles's models to describe a range of possible relationships. At one extreme is the "agency" model in which the client makes all the significant decisions and the computer professional merely carries out those decisions. This model has the shortcoming that the special knowledge of the professional is not effectively used. As Johnson says, "Professional advice is needed not just to implement decisions but to help make the decisions" (2001, p. 71).

At the other extreme is the "paternalistic" relationship in which the professional makes all the decisions and the client is treated much like a child at the mercy of the professional's judgments. This model leaves out the special knowledge that the client has about how the computer product or service will be used. The computer professional needs to work closely with the client and share responsibility for making important decisions. This leads to the third – and intermediate – relationship between client and professional: the "fiduciary" relationship. As the name implies, trust is absolutely essential to this kind of working relationship:

> On this model both parties must trust one another. The client must trust the professional to use his or her expert knowledge and to think in terms of the interest of the client, but the professional must also trust that the client will give the professional relevant information, will listen to what the professional says, and so on. On this model, decision making is shared. (Johnson 2001, p. 71)

Professional-to-user   While working for an employer or a client, a computer professional often creates hardware or software intended for use by a range of people other than the individual or organization that has commissioned the work. An airplane manufacturer, for example, may hire a software firm to produce an avionics software package to help fly the airplane. Obviously, the users of the computer product – in this case the airplane crew – will be significantly affected by the product. If it works reliably and efficiently, the users will be well served; but if the product is defective, they may be harmed, perhaps even killed if the product fails to work as planned. For this reason, it is clear that computer professionals have responsibilities to users of their products, not just to employers and clients. These responsibilities include, for example, accepting jobs only if one is competent to perform them, exercising proper care and diligence, thoroughly testing the final product before delivering it to the customer, and so on.

Professional-to-society   The above example of avionics software illustrates a further point about responsibilities of computer professionals: their work can easily impact on thousands or even millions of people. The safety of passengers in an airplane, for example, and the safety of people who live and work under the flight path of the plane depend upon reliable functioning of software. If the software fails and the plane crashes, passengers could be killed or injured, as could people situated under the flight path of the plane.

The point of this example can be generalized: Computer technology is rapidly being adopted in all walks of life to perform jobs and provide services from medicine to education, from communications to manufacturing, from national defense to the entertainment industry. With such a huge impact upon the world and the future, computer professionals need to be socially responsible – to develop an understanding of the social impact of their profession, to develop responsible codes of conduct, and to educate future professionals with social responsibility in mind.

The professional-to-society relationship can be viewed as a contract. On the one hand, society grants the right to practice a profession, provides access to needed education, passes necessary laws, and provides police, fire, and other protective services. In return, the computer professional agrees to practice in a manner that benefits society. In this rapidly shrinking world, with global interaction on the Internet, the "society" that a computer professional serves is quickly becoming global. And environmentalists would even argue that computer professionals should take responsibility for the impact of their products and services not just upon human beings, but actually upon the whole earth, including plants and animals, forests, oceans, and other ecosystems. Computer ethics has become a globally important subject (see Gorniak-Kocikowska 1996, excerpts of which are included below as chapter 15.)

Conclusion

This part of the book explores the concept of "professional responsibility" as it applies to computer professionals. It also examines ways in which computer practitioners can more effectively identify and fulfill their social and ethical responsibilities.

In his article "Unintentional Power in the Design of Computing Systems," Chuck Huff examines ways in which computing systems generate negative effects and consequences that were not foreseen by their original designers. He also suggests ways to avoid such consequences.

In "Informatics and Professional Responsibility," Donald Gotterbarn extends and clarifies a distinction made by philosopher John Ladd (1989) between "negative" and "positive" responsibility. Gotterbarn illustrates the kinds of harm that can result from a negative, "reactive" understanding of professional responsibility among computer professionals. He then advocates a more positive, "proactive" sense of responsibility and illustrates the advantages and benefits of adopting such a perspective.

In his article "The Ethics of Software Development Management," Simon Rogerson examines typical software development practices. He argues that such practices normally do not effectively deal with relevant ethical issues, and he introduces eight ethical principles which can be applied to software development projects to ensure that appropriate ethical considerations guide software development.

This part of the book concludes with the famous case of the London Ambulance Service and the unhappy consequences of poor software development. The reader is invited to use the case analysis method from chapter 3 above to analyze this notorious software development disaster.

References

Bayles, M. (1981). *Professional Ethics*. Wadsworth.

Gorniak-Kocikowska, K. (1996). "The Computer Revolution and the Problem of Global Ethics." *Science and Engineering Ethics*, 2 (April): 177–90. (See also chapter 15 below.)

Gotterbarn, D. (1992). "You Don't Have the Right to Do It Wrong." Available at www-cs.etsu-tn.edu/gotterbarn/ArtPP4.htm (accessed December 7, 2002).

Johnson, D. G. (1994). *Computer Ethics*, 2nd edn. Prentice-Hall.

Johnson, D. G. (2001). *Computer Ethics*, 3rd edn. Prentice-Hall.

Ladd, J. (1989). "Computers and Moral Responsibility: A Framework for an Ethical Analysis." In C. C. Gould (ed.), *The Information Web: Ethical and Social Implications of Computer Networking*. Westview Press, pp. 207–27.

Spinello, R. A. (1997). *Case Studies in Information and Computer Ethics*. Prentice Hall.

CHAPTER 4

Unintentional Power in the Design of Computing Systems

Chuck Huff

For in much wisdom is much grief: and he that increaseth knowledge increaseth sorrow.

Ecclesiastes 1: 18

. . . computing professionals who design and develop systems must be alert to, and make others aware of, any potential damage.

ACM Code of Ethics 1992

Introduction

Why was the Hebrew scholar and author of Ecclesiastes so skeptical about the worth of knowledge? At least in our time, we find the rapid increase in knowledge to be both exhilarating and hopeful. As knowledge increases, we cure more diseases, connect more people, ease much poverty. Increases in knowledge certainly drive the technology industry and make "faster, better, more" almost a mantra of progress.

So it can be surprising to read words like those above. They smack of obscurantism, obstruction, willful ignorance. Surely attitudes like this can only come from unreconstructed technophobes. The implied advice is to avoid sorrow by avoiding knowledge – to retreat into ignorance. By the time you have done with this chapter, I hope to have convinced you that knowledge brings with it increased responsibility. If I succeed, you may have some sympathy for the weariness of the ancient scholar. You may still reject the implied advice.

Chuck Huff, "Unintentional Power in the Design of Computing Systems." This chapter was originally a paper presented at ETHICOMP95 in Leicester, UK and appeared in the proceedings of that conference, edited by Simon Rogerson and Terrell Ward Bynum and published by the Centre for Computing and Social Responsibility. Reprinted by permission of the author. © 1995 by Chuck Huff.

What sort of knowledge increases sorrow? At least for our purposes, it is the sort of knowledge that allows us to predict possible effects of the products we design. The sort of knowledge that makes us, at least in part, responsible for either producing or avoiding those effects. This knowledge makes our lives more complicated because it brings with it the sorts of "trouble" that involve more responsibility. Those who know about dangers or difficulties have a responsibility to take them into account. The ACM Code recognizes this in the second quotation at the beginning of this chapter. Computer professionals have a responsibility to design products that are safe and that perform well the functions for which they were designed.

For instance, the designers of the Therac-25 Radiation Therapy Machine (Jacky 1991; Leveson and Turner 1992) knew that the radiation their product generated could be delivered in dangerous dosages. Yet they produced a machine which, when used under the standard conditions in busy hospitals, could and did result in serious mistakes in dosage. Most analyses of the design process in this case agree that the designers were negligent in both the initial design and in following up on reports of malfunction. As a result, several people died and many were injured.

The great advance of the Therac-25 was that all of its controls had been moved into software. The operator now interacted with the machine solely through the computer terminal. Safety interlocks that might prevent lethal dosage levels were incorporated into the software, and eliminated from the hardware of the machine. This allowed easy reprogrammability of the dosage levels, and easy maintenance and upgrading of the machine. It also meant that the safety interlocks depended upon the reliability of the software. And not only the software, but also the software, as it was used by the technician. It turned out that, if the technician set the machine for one type of dosage (low-level electron beam) and then changed the setting to another type (high-level electron beam with a metal target interposed to alter the beam to low-level X-rays), the machine would switch to the high electron beam but not interpose the target quickly enough – thus directly irradiating the patient with lethal levels of the electron beam. When this happened, the computer screen would simply indicate "malfunction 54" for incorrect dosage. But since "malfunction 54" occurred up to 40 times a day for entirely innocuous reasons (e.g. the beam was slightly "out of tune"), technicians learned to ignore it. When a malfunction occurs this regularly in a busy medical facility, it is no wonder the technicians ignored it rather than stopping for the day to recalibrate (and thereby make patients wait).

Had the designers thought carefully about the conditions under which their product would be used, they could have made a better attempt to avoid the delivery of lethal or harmful dosages. Had they considered how widespread the use of their product could become, they might have designed a feedback process that would have sent "fixes" to these widespread sites.

They did not do these things. And in part they neglected to do them because they had construed their job narrowly as technically proficient design (Leveson and Turner 1992).

Levels of Constraint in Software Engineering

But isn't the job of the software engineer simply to be technically proficient and to make the best technical decisions he or she can, on time and within budget? Certainly, technical proficiency is crucial. And because technical proficiency is so difficult to achieve and to maintain, we often think it should be the only criterion by which work is measured. At least life would be simpler if this were so.

But there are very few technical decisions that are entirely constrained by math and physics. Those that are (like some issues in queuing theory) are still likely to be only portions of a larger project that has additional constraints. What are these additional constraints? Table 1 lists some of them. They range from thoroughly tested design standards to concerns about the "worth" of computing to society. Many are clearly in the domain of "engineering" popularly conceived. Some are clearly far from engineering. Level 1 constraints are commonly covered in training programs that serve as gateways into the field. But even at this level value judgments abound: which standards? how to resolve tradeoffs? Often, these decisions are not based on mathematical proofs or on physical constraints. They are based instead on criteria whose applicability is at least a matter for debate. And these debates are based on disagreements about what things we should value more. Thus, value judgments.

For example, the decision to implement all the safety interlocks on the Therac-25 in the software – and none in the hardware – was based (at least in part) on the value associated with having reprogrammable drivers for the machine. Easy reprogrammability is of value because it reduces costs on upgrades. It did not *have* to be done this way, but if you value flexibility and easy upgrading, you *should* design this way. In this instance, the designers mistakenly underestimated other, equally important values such as those associated with causing injury to patients.

Table 1   Constraints on the design of systems

Level 1	Systems design issues, standards, tradeoffs in design and performance
Level 2	Company policies, specifications, budgets, project timelines
Level 3	Anticipated uses and effects; interactions with other technologies and systems
Level 4	Larger "impact on society" issues (e.g., privacy, property, power, equity)

In this instance the designers underestimated the difficulty of controlling the dosage levels in a busy hospital radiation therapy room. Their neglect of this difficulty was based on their ignorance of the hurried and hectic conditions that occur in these settings. In a very important sense these designers had it "within their power" to design a safe product if they had inquired about the conditions under which their product would be used. Subsequent designs now take into account these difficulties (Jacky 1991).

Another, less catastrophic example may help. There is widespread concern about the gender imbalance in computer science in the United States (Martin and Murchie-Beyma 1992). The large majority of graduate students (and even larger majorities of professors) are men. Fewer undergraduate women are enrolling in computer science courses today, so it seems as though this imbalance is likely to continue. There is some consensus among researchers that a major reason women do not pursue careers in computer science or in related fields is that, from early adolescence onward, computing is defined as a male field and most uses of computing are portrayed as interesting only to males (Martin and Murchie-Beyma 1992).

A colleague and I were interested in this claim, and designed a study to determine the extent to which this portrayal of computing as a male domain infiltrated itself into the software that students might use in school. We had teachers design educational software for either boys, girls, or (gender unspecified) "children" (Huff and Cooper 1987). We then had the designers and independent raters rate those programs in terms of characteristics like time pressure, verbal interaction required, control given the user, etc. We found that programs designed for boys looked like games (with time pressure, eye–hand coordination, and competition most important), while programs for girls looked like "tools" for learning (with conversation and goal-based learning). So far, this is unremarkable. However, programs designed for "children" looked just like those designed for boys. Thus, programs designed for "students in general" were really programs designed for boys. Interestingly, 80 percent of the designers of our programs were female, many of whom expressed concern that educational software was male-biased. Thus, the portrayal of computing as a male domain is subtly and strongly woven into software itself, even by well-meaning, female educators.

This statement bears repeating on a more general level. The design of the software itself was affected by the social expectations of the designers. This is as true for this more subtle effect of gender bias in design as it is for the clearly mistaken (and clearly deadly) effects of the expectations of the designers of the Therac-25.

However, even if value judgments show up in the lower levels of system engineering, perhaps it is still possible to limit the work of the software designer to only those relatively simple value judgments that occur when choosing among algorithms or standards. Unfortunately, even a little knowledge about how computing systems are used will increase the sorrow of those who hope this. Look again at the two examples we have covered. In both cases issues from higher levels in the table of constraints worked their way down to the system design level. Choices about where to implement safety checks *should* have been made based upon better knowledge of the hectic work environment of radiation therapy. Choices about basic program characteristics *should* have been made based upon a broader assumption about who the users of the software would be. Thus, though it might be desirable to cleanly delineate the work of the software engineer, it is clearly impossible. Good engineering at the level of basic system design requires attention to many levels of constraint.

So, if you limit yourself only to considering constraints that are clearly at the "engineering" level, you can have an effect on the world that you would clearly prefer to have avoided. This is true, to a greater or lesser extent, for both of the examples we have seen here. And thus, to a greater or lesser extent, the designers of these products had power over the users of their products. They were unaware of the effect their design might have had. They certainly did not intend any negative effects from their design. But such effects occurred nonetheless.

Intentional Power

I call this power to harm others in ways that are difficult to predict *unintentional power*.[1] Obviously, the design decisions that software engineers make will affect the performance of a product, and such decisions thereby affect the users of that product. Many of these effects are intentional: the product works faster, is easier to maintain, has increased capability. Some are unintentional: the product is more difficult to maintain, it confuses or frustrates users, it kills users. In the same way that a large man may unintentionally thrust people aside as he carries an awkward package down a street, a software designer may unintentionally harm users of a product that she has designed for a good purpose. Both are exercising power. Both the software designer and the package carrier are affecting others intentionally and unintentionally.

To understand the issue of unintentional power, we must first get the most useful definition of this sort of power firmly in hand. To begin with, it is similar to both the physical science definition of power (the potential to do work) and our usual social definition of power (the ability to influence others). At this level, both definitions make it clear that intention is not important. In the one case it is simply irrelevant, and, in the other, we recognize that one

---

[1]   In this chapter, I am only looking at the negative effects of unintentional power. Obviously, positive effects are possible.

can have both intentional and unintentional influence on others (remember the package courier?).

Thus, we all have unintentional power associated with our actions whenever those actions have unintentional consequences. The issue then becomes, should we have been aware of the likelihood that those consequences would occur? Could we have foreseen them? Might we have been more careful? Here is an important principle about unintentional power; it carries with it a concomitant responsibility to be as aware as reasonably possible of the consequences of our actions.

The Problems of Unintentional Power

One difficulty with unintentional power in computing systems is that the designers are often far removed from the situations in which their power (now carried by the software they have designed) has its effect. Software designed in Chicago might be used in Calcutta. Software, or bits of software, might be reused for purposes other than ones its original designer envisioned. Software might be used in environments that are more complex or more dangerous than those for which it was initially designed. Thus, the person or persons with the power are removed from those who are affected. This makes it difficult for the designer to foresee possible consequences.

This distancing also makes it difficult for the users to recognize that it was, in fact, the designers who affected them. People are likely to blame themselves for the difficulties the software produces rather than to see it as an issue of bad design (Huff et al. 1991). After all, they are the ones closest to the harm, and it often doesn't occur to them that their software *was* designed by someone. Responsibility for harm, then, becomes difficult to assign and easy to avoid.

Another effect of distancing is that the response to the problem cannot be standardized for any particular domain of applications. The effects change too much from implementation to implementation. In response to a similar problem, computer professionals in human computer interaction have taken to field testing, iterative reviews, user-testing, and other methods to improve the odds that their products will fit into the particular domains for which they were designed (Borenstein 1991; Shneiderman 1992; Landauer 1995). There are simply far too many possible consequences to catch them all (on time and within budget).

Coping with Unintentional Power

Here, then, comes the rub: What is a "reasonable" attempt on the part of a designer to avoid the negative consequences of unintentional power?

Clearly, anyone who now designs software for radiation therapy should take into account the conditions under which their product will be used. We now know this because several people died from use of the Therac-25 Radiation Machine. I would submit, and I hope you agree, that this sort of "user-testing" is to be avoided. A general lesson we might draw from this is that designers of "safety critical" systems need to take more constraints into account than simply low-level design constraints. But surely we cannot expect a wide-ranging inquiry, looking at all the levels of constraint listed in table 1, before we decide to build any system?

But there are some things we can do, and that we should be expected to do. Research on the broader effects of computing has advanced enough to have some clear things to say about the dangers of ignoring the constraints listed earlier in this chapter. Software design is no longer in its infancy and should be expected to develop methods to deal with these constraints without bankrupting designers or their employers. Here are some beginning suggestions as to how we might go about addressing these issues.

Recognize the problem and attempt to limit its domain   Clearly we cannot address a problem we prefer to ignore. Some designers prefer to inflate the costs of looking at these issues (e.g., you mean we have to look at every possible implementation?), declare the problem too large and frightening to approach, and then to ignore it. Ignoring it will not make it go away. A better approach is to recognize the parameters of the problem, attempt to limit the domains where it can cause a problem, and to then address the problem within those limited domains. Developing standards (for safety critical computing, for computing interfaces, for data exchange, etc.) is one way to limit the domain.

Use developing methods to inform yourself of those effects worth predicting   Methods for quality-based (TQM) software design are now becoming available (Arthur 1992; Dunn 1994). In addition to these methods, the use of a social impact statement, or SIS (Shneiderman 1990; Huff 1996; Shneiderman and Rose 1996) can help you to determine what sorts of effect you should care about, as well as to investigate the constraints that will guide your solution. Neither TQM methods nor SIS approaches will make the decisions for you. Making these decisions depends upon the computing professionals' judgment about a particular project in a particular setting. This is what professionalism is about.

Make provision in the life-cycle of software to look for the effects   You simply cannot identify all the possible effects of a computing system ahead of release. For this reason, you should be ready to identify them after release, and as soon as possible after release. Software design methods currently incorporate a life-cycle design philosophy, and it is relatively easy to incorporate some of the methods from social impact statements into this life-cycle model.

Conclusion

The approaches I recommend are not a sea change in software engineering standards, but an evolutionary step. The standards are already designed to take account of late occurring effects, and to make designers aware of interactions between the software and some environmental issues. Quality design requires that we broaden our vision about the constraints we should consider in our designs.

You cannot make all designs safe under all conditions, but you can make them more safe, or more usable, or more equitable, under more conditions. Software engineers should take responsibility where these emerging methods allow them to, and should be humble about their ability to guarantee perfect functioning where they cannot measure or test performance in real conditions. By increasing knowledge about the social effects of software, and by adopting methods that allow us to anticipate these effects, we may be able to decrease sorrow, and thus confound the prophet's prediction. But we will do so at the expense of our own more simplistic approaches to software design.

References

Arthur, L. J. (1992). *Improving Software Quality: An Insider's Guide to TQM*. John Wiley.

Borenstein, N. S. (1991). *Programming as if People Mattered: Friendly Program, Software Engineering, and Other Noble Delusions*. Princeton University Press.

Dunn, R. H. (1994). *TQM for Computer Software*. McGraw-Hill.

Huff, C. W. (1996). "Practical Guidance for Teaching the Social Impact Statement (SIS)." In C. W. Huff (ed.), *Computers and the Quality of Life: The Proceedings of the Symposium on Computers and the Quality of Life*. ACM Press, pp. 86–9.

Huff, C. W. and Cooper, J. (1987). "Sex Bias in Educational Software: The Effects of Designers' Stereotypes on the Software They Design." *Journal of Applied Social Psychology*, 17: 519–32.

Huff, C. W., Fleming, J. F., and Cooper, J. (1991). "The Social Basis of Gender Differences in Human-Computer Interaction." In C. D. Martin, and E. Murchie-Beyma (eds.), *In Search of Gender-Free Paradigms for Computer Science Education*. ISTE Research Monographs, pp. 19–32.

Jacky, J. (1991). "Safety Critical Computing: Hazards, Practices, Standards, and Regulation." In C. Dunlop, and R. Kling (eds.), *Computerization and Controversy*. Academic Press, pp. 612–31.

Landauer, T. K. (1995). *The Trouble with Computers: Usefulness, Usability, and Productivity*. MIT Press.

Leveson, N. G. and Turner, C. S. (1992). *An Investigation of the Therac-25 Accidents.* Technical Report #92-108. Department of Information and Computer Science, University of California, Irvine.

Martin, C. D. and Murchie-Beyma, E. (eds.) (1992). *In Search of Gender-Free Paradigms for Computer Science Education.* International Society for Technology in Education.

Shneiderman, B. (1990). "Human Values and the Future of Technology: A Declaration of Empowerment." *Computers and Society,* 20/3: 1–6.

Shneiderman, B. (1992). *Designing the User Interface: Strategies for Effective Human–Computer Interaction.* Addison Wesley.

Shneiderman, B. and Rose, A. (1996). "Social Impact Statements: Engaging Public Participation in Information Technology Design." In C. Huff (ed.), *Computers and the Quality of Life: The Proceedings of the Symposium on Computers and the Quality of Life.* ACM Press, pp. 90–6.

Basic study questions

1. According to Huff, increased knowledge brings with it increased responsibility. How does this relate to designers of computer hardware and software?
2. Briefly describe the case of the Therac-25 Radiation Machine – what happened and why?
3. Briefly describe the four "levels" of constraint that Huff identifies with regard to the design of computerized devices.
4. When Huff and Cooper asked teachers to design educational computer programs for "children," what were the startling biased results?
5. The Therac-25 case and the educational software case both illustrate an important fact about computer design and unintended consequences. Explain.
6. What does Huff mean by "unintentional power"?
7. Explain why "unintentional power" brings with it "concomitant responsibility." How does the Therac-25 case illustrate this point?
8. Explain why "distancing" leads to "problems of unintentional power" and increases the chances of unintended harm.
9. To cope with the risks of "unintentional power," Huff offers three specific suggestions. What are they?

Questions for further thought

1. How much testing of a new computer product is "enough" to satisfy the requirements of ethics and responsibility?
2. Can professional codes of ethics help the designers of computer products create better computer products? Why do you think so?
3. Compare Huff's "addressing only the engineering level" (p. 102 above) with Gotterbarn's "crossword puzzle approach" to software engineering (p. 110 below).

CHAPTER 5

Informatics and Professional Responsibility

Donald Gotterbarn

Introduction

In the summer of 1991 a major telephone outage occurred in the United States because an error was introduced when three lines of code were changed in a multimillion-line signaling program. Because the three-line change was viewed as insignificant, it was not tested. This type of interruption to software systems is too common. Not merely are systems interrupted but sometimes lives are lost because of software problems. A New Jersey inmate under computer-monitored house arrest removed his electronic anklet. "A computer detected the tampering. However, when it called a second computer to report the incident, the first computer received a busy signal and never called back" (Joch 1995). While free, the escapee committed murder. In another case innocent victims were shot to death by the French police acting on an erroneous computer report (Vallee 1982). In 1986 two cancer patients were killed because of a software error in a computer-controlled X-ray machine. Given the plethora of these kinds of story, it is not surprising that informatics and computing have not enjoyed a positive image.

How can such problems result from the actions of moral software developers? The existence of such cases is a problem, but that is not my major concern in this chapter; rather, my concern is the narrow concept of responsibility which contributes to these disasters. I argue that, although informatics has been undergoing a rapid development, there has been no corresponding development in the concept of responsibility as it applies to computing practitioners (CPs). Computing is an emerging profession that will not succeed until it has expanded its sense of responsibility. I describe a

Donald Gotterbarn, "Informatics and Professional Responsibility." This chapter was first published in *Science and Engineering Ethics*, 7:2 (April 2001), pp. 221–30. © 2001 by Donald Gotterbarn and reprinted by permission of the author.

broader concept of responsibility that is consistent with professionalism in computing.

The focus of cases such as the ones cited above is computer failures. In the early days of computing, CPs sought immunity from blame for their failure to develop reliable systems. CPs developed their own special language. Flaws in computer programs were not errors introduced by the programmer, but were "bugs" found in the program. Notice how the emphasis is on finding the "bug" and not on determining how it got into the program or on taking preventative action so that similar "bugs" will not get into future programs. Another favorite exculpatory euphemism used by CPs is "computer error." "I am not to blame. It was a computer error." The developer's exemption from responsibility for undesirable events is sometimes based on relocating the responsibility in the client who failed to adequately specify what was "really" needed. If the specifications are precise and the client cannot be used to exempt the developer from responsibility, the fact that "no program can be proven to be error free" is used to excuse critical system failures. And as a last resort, one can simply appeal to the complexity of the system. Complex systems are expected to fail. This is like the engineering concept of an "inevitable or normal accident." This concept holds that as the complexity of a system increases so does the likelihood of an accident. The accident should not be attributed to anyone's errors or failures to act. The implication of all of these excuses is that the responsibility for these events is borne by the computer or the complexity of the system rather than by the developer of the computer system. This side-stepping of responsibility by software developers is based on inaccurate computer science. The problem here is more than bad science; these excuses are used to justify the development of systems that are detrimental to society and these excuses inhibit the development of computing as a profession.

The news media like to emphasize catastrophic cases of software development. This emphasis sometimes misleads us into ignoring questions of responsibility in more common cases of software development. Let us look at a common example in computing which can be used to illustrate a fuller, more positive concept of responsibility.

An Inadequate Interface

Fred Consultant, a computer consultant, developed several quality computer systems for the national government of NewLand. He attributed the quality of some of his systems to the good working relationship he had established with potential system users. The government of NewLand has an unnecessarily complex accounting system. The system has so much overhead that administering it wastes significant amounts of taxpayer's money. Jim Midlevel, a local manager of this accounting system, understood where the waste was in the system. Even though he did not understand the day-to-day procedures of the system, he was able to design modifications to the systems which would significantly reduce the overhead costs of running it. Jim convinced his upper-level management to implement his modifications to the system. Because of Fred's previous accomplishments, his company was given the contract to write the first stage of the more efficient accounting system that would be used by the government and would save taxpayers a considerable amount of money. Fred met with Jim to discuss the system and carefully studied the required inputs and outputs of the revised system. Fred asked one of his best software engineers, Joanne Buildscreen, to design the user interface for the system. Joanne studied the required inputs to the system and built an interface for the revised system. The system was developed and shown to Jim Midlevel. Jim was satisfied that the accounting system and the interface contained all of the functionality described in the requirements. The system passed its acceptance test, which proved that all stated requirements had been met. The system was installed, but the user interface was so hard to use that the complaints of Jim's staff were heard by his upper-level management. Because of these complaints, upper-level management decided that it would not invest any more money in the development of the revised accounting system. To reduce staff complaints, they would go back to the original more expensive accounting system.

What is the net result of the development effort described in this case? There is now a general ill will toward Fred's company, and NewLand's officials do not give his company many contracts. The original accounting program is back in place. The continued utilization of this program is a significant burden on the taxpayers. The situation is worse than it had been before this project was undertaken, because now there is little chance of ever modifying the system to make it less expensive.

Side-Steps: Avoiding or Dodging Responsibility

One of the first questions to be asked about this undesirable situation is "Who is responsible?" Generally this question is associated with seeking someone to blame for the problem. One of the reasons why the "blame-game" is so popular is that once it has been decided who is to blame, no one else needs to feel accountable for the problem. Finding a scapegoat to bear the blame for all others who may be involved is just as popular a model in computing as it is in literature.

I believe that there are two primary reasons why CPs side-step the assignment of responsibility, especially after a system failure or a computer disaster. Both of these reasons are errors grounded in misinterpretations of responsibility. These erroneous reasons are the belief that software development is an ethically neutral activity and belief in a malpractice model of responsibility.

Ethical neutrality

The first error is that responsibility is not related to a CP because computing is understood by many CPs to be an ethically neutral practice. There are a number of factors which contribute to this mistake. One reason why CPs expect to look elsewhere for someone to blame is the way they are trained at university. They are trained to solve problems; and the examples used, such as finding the least common multiple (LCM) for a set of numbers, portrays computing as merely a problem-solving exercise. The primary goal of the exercise is to solve the problem exactly as it is presented to the CP. All energy (and responsibility) is focused on finding a solution in an almost myopic fashion. This is analogous to the way people approach crossword puzzles. Solving the puzzle is an interesting exercise, but it generally lacks any significant consequences. There is no responsibility beyond solving the puzzle, other than properly disposing of the paper on which it is written. The same assumptions are made about solving computing problems.

The crossword-puzzle approach to computing problems leads to a failure to realize that computing is a service to the user of the computing artifact. This failure makes it easy to assign blame elsewhere. If there is no responsibility, there is no blame or accountability. The failure to see one's responsibility has other significant consequences. One result of the crossword-puzzle view is seen when we consider the real case of a programmer who was asked to write a program that would raise and lower a large X-ray device above the X-ray table, moving the machine to various fixed positions on a vertical support pole. The programmer wrote and tested his solution to this puzzle. It successfully and accurately moved the device to each of the positions from the top of the support pole to the top of the table. The difficulty with this narrow problem-solving approach was shown when, after installation, an X-ray technician told a patient to get off the table after an X-ray had been taken and then the technician set the height of the device to "table-top-height." The patient had not heard the technician and was later found crushed to death between the machine and the table top. The programmer solved a puzzle but didn't consider any consequences of his solution to the user. If the programmer had considered the broader context, rather than limiting his attention to moving the X-ray machine on the pole, then he might have required an additional confirmation when moving the machine to the table top.

This first misunderstanding of responsibility is dangerous in that it is used to justify a lack of attention to anything beyond the job specification. The absurd degree to which this side-step can be taken is illustrated in the following real case. A defense contractor was asked to develop a portable shoulder-held anti-aircraft system. The specifications required that the shoulder-held system be capable of destroying a particular type of attack helicopter at 1,000 yards with 97 percent efficiency. The system the contractor developed did effectively destroy incoming helicopters. Its kill rate was better than 97 percent. It also had another feature. Because of a software error, the shoulder-held missile launcher occasionally overheated to the extent that it burned off vital portions of the anatomy of the person holding the launcher. The extent of the burns killed the person who launched the missile. The government was, of course, dissatisfied with the product and declined to make the final payment to the contractor. The company took the government to court over the final payment. The company owners declared that they should be paid and that they are not responsible for the deaths because the system they developed "is in full compliance with the specifications given to them by the user." The contractors viewed this problem like a crossword puzzle. They solved a crossword puzzle exactly as it was presented to them, and they denied any further responsibility.

Diffuse responsibility

The second side-step error is based on the belief that responsibility is best understood using a malpractice model which relates responsibility to legal blame and liability. It is important to find the correct parties to blame in order to bring legal action against them. Generally, the concept of blame is tied to a direct action which brought about the undesirable event. A typical approach to determining blame is to isolate the event which immediately preceded and was causally related to the undesirable event, and then blaming the party who brought about the preceding event. In the case of NewLand's inadequate interface, Joanne's design of the interface screens was the direct cause of the user's dissatisfaction with the system. Joanne's screens were the immediate cause of the dissatisfaction, so the tendency is to blame her. If the blame is both severe and public, then others will feel excused from responsibility for the unhappy event.

Joanne will not want to bear the blame and will point to other people's failures as contributing to the problem. This leads to the belief that one can avoid responsibility if the blame can be diffused by being widely distributed. This second side-step is based on the claim that individual software developers are too far from the event which causes the problem. It also distributes the blame so widely that it becomes negligible or cannot be clearly attributed.

This side-step is a paradoxical denial of responsibility since it starts by identifying multiple locations of failure of responsibility, namely the particular irresponsible acts of each member of the development team. This diffusion technique might be used in the Inadequate Interface case. Fred did not behave responsibly because he did not adequately understand the nature of the task. Jim, because of his lack of specific system details, should have coordinated the development activities with the system users. Joanne should have shown preliminary screen designs to the system users. Everyone failed to meet his or her responsibilities. This distribution of failure is then used to deny legal fault or blame. The absurdity is that this identification of multiple individuals failing to meet their system development obligations is also used to deny *each* individual's responsibility. Like the first side-step, this diffusion of responsibility is a very dangerous practice. It follows from the diffusion side-step that whenever there are many people contributing to a project, no individual will be held accountable for contributions to the project. If I am not responsible, then I have no prior commitment to do a competent job or worry about the overall quality of a product.

The diffusion of responsibility has a corollary, which Ladd (1989) has called "task responsibility," which ties responsibility to one narrowly defined task. An example of task responsibility can be generated by giving more details from the Inadequate Interface case. What was the problem that made the interface unusable? The multiple input screens used in the new accounting system did contain fields for all the required data, but the input sequence on the screens was not consistent with the structure of the input forms used by the clerks. To enter the data from a single input form, the clerks had to go back and forth between several screens. Using task responsibility, Joanne would maintain that it is not her job to get copies of the input forms. If "they" wanted the sequence of the data on the screens to match the input forms, then "someone" should have provided her with sample input forms. It is not her job to get the forms.

The association of responsibility with blame leads to a variety of excuses for not being accountable. These excuses include:

1   Absence of a direct and immediate causal link to the unacceptable event (Dunlop and Kling 1991).
2   Denial of responsibility since a responsible act conflicts with one's own self-interest (Harris et al. 1995).
3   Responsibility requires the ability to do otherwise but CPs do most of their work in teams and for large organizations (Johnson 1994).
4   Lack of strength-of-will to do what one thinks is right (Harris et al. 1995).
5   Blaming the computer (Dunlop and Kling 1991).
6   Assuming that science is ethically neutral.
7   Microscopic vision (Davis 1989).

These side-stepping approaches to responsibility are inconsistent with efforts to professionalize computer science and engineering. Any profession should be strongly motivated to pursue the good of society. It should understand its primary function as a service to society. To professionalize computing, therefore, we need to revisit the concept of responsibility, separating it from the legal concept of blame, and separating it from direct and immediate causes of undesirable events. What sense of responsibility would meet these objections and mitigate the urge for side-stepping?

Positive and Negative Responsibility

The philosophical concept of "responsibility" is very rich and is frequently tied to such philosophical conundrums as "free will." Philosophers have long been concerned about the relationship between individual responsibility and free will. This concern derives in part from the implicit connection of the concept of blame with the concept of responsibility. If people have no free will then it is difficult to blame them for their actions. In opposition to this dependency of "responsibility" on the concept of blame and liability, Ladd distinguished the traditional sense of responsibility – which he calls "negative responsibility" from "positive responsibility". Negative responsibility deals with or looks for that which exempts one from blame and liability. An exemption from blame is an exemption from moral responsibility and an exemption from liability is an exemption from legal responsibility. Negative responsibility is distinguished from positive responsibility.

The concept of positive responsibility is consistent with many philosophies. One can extend Ladd's concept of positive responsibility to be justifiable under most philosophical theories. Positive responsibility can be grounded in any of the classical and contemporary theories. Such theories can be organized into a matrix created by the intersection of two of the following dimensions: rules/consequences and collective/individual (see table 1; see also Laudon 1995). The emphasis in positive responsibility is on the virtue of having or being obliged to have regard for the consequences of his or her actions on others. We can place this sense of positive responsibility in each quadrant of the matrix. This sense of responsibility can be founded in: collective rule-based ethics based on the logic of the situation; individual

Table 1

	Rules	Consequences
Collective	Collective rule-based	Collective consequentialist
Individual	Individual rule-based	Individual consequentialist

rule-based ethics based on universal duties applicable to all (Ross 1969); collective consequentialists like J. S. Mill providing the greatest good for the greatest number; or individual consequentialists like Adam Smith, who maintain that the social welfare is advanced by individuals doing good acts which have good consequences for society. No matter which ethical theory is used to justify positive responsibility, the focus of positive responsibility is on what ought to be done rather than on blaming or punishing others for irresponsible behavior.

Positive responsibility is not exclusive. It does not seek a single focus of blame. Negative responsibility, on the other hand, seeks a single focus of blame who, once found, exonerates all others from blame. With positive responsibility, saying that Joanne is responsible and should be held account-able for her failings does not exclude Fred. A virtue of positive responsibility is that several people can be responsible to varying degrees. Not only can we attribute responsibility to Fred, but we can say that he bears more of the responsibility in this case because he knew that Jim was only working with limited knowledge of the system.

This point illustrates a second and more significant virtue of positive responsibility; namely, that it does not require either a proximate or a direct cause. This extension of causal influence beyond the immediate and proxim-ate cause is more consistent with assigning responsibility in the disasters that affect computing. Leveson and Turner (1993), in their article about the technical difficulties of the Therac-25 X-ray machine which led to multiple deaths, conclude that because of the involvement of many hands, respons-ibility for the Therac-25 incidents cannot be assigned. Leveson and Turner use a limited negative concept of responsibility and, after identifying failures of multiple software engineering practices, refer to the deaths that resulted as "accidents." Nissenbaum (1994) correctly criticized such an approach to responsibility when she said, "If we respond to complex cases by not pursuing blame and responsibility, we are effectively accepting agentless mishaps and a general erosion of accountability." The positive sense of responsibility allows the distribution of responsibility to software develop-ment teams, designers, etc. and can apply the concept of responsibility even to large development teams. In the Therac-25 case there may not be a single locus of blame, but under positive responsibility the developers are still responsible.

Any preliminary definition of responsibility starts from the presumption that others are affected by the outcomes of CPs' particular actions or failures to act. This presumption is embodied in many codes of ethics of computing associations. Such codes tend to organize responsibilities by the roles of the people involved. Most codes talk about the CPs' responsibilities to other professionals, to the client or employer, and to society in general. Only a few codes include the obligations of CPs to students. Although such codes try to recognize most of these relationships, most of them make the mistake of not distinguishing employers, clients, and users. In Joanne's case, her employer was Fred, the client was Jim, and the users were the accounting clerks. Because she stood in different relations to each of these parties, she owed them different and perhaps conflicting obligations. Some recent codes, such as the Software Engineering Code of Ethics and Professional Practice, provide the CP with techniques for adjudicating between conflicting obligations.

There are two types of responsibility owed in all of these potential relations. One type of positive responsibility is technically based and the other positive responsibility is based on values. These two types of positive responsibility are both necessary for a concept of professional responsibility.

Positive responsibility points both forward and backward. It points backward when it identifies unmet obligations and what people ought to have done. Fred had an obligation to meet with the clerks to understand the structure of the interface they would need. This sense of responsibility goes beyond the malpractice model. Responsibility is more than just blame, there should also be some lessons learned from failures of responsibility. Thus there should be some lessons learned from the Inadequate Interface case. As a result of this event, Fred is responsible for preventing development failures of similar systems in the future. Knowledge of this kind of failure and its consequences also places responsibility on other computer practitioners and places responsibilities on the profession of computing as a whole. For example, the activity of establishing computing standards of practice is justified by the forward-looking sense of positive responsibility of the CP and the responsibility of the profession.

A Response to Avoidance

The concept of positive responsibility can be used to address several of the responsibility-avoidance techniques referred to earlier. This broader concept of responsibility meets the diffusion side-step and the positive aspect of this concept of responsibility meets the malpractice side-step.

Computing is an emerging profession; indeed, it already bears several of the marks of a profession. In order for computing to be a profession, there must be some agreement among its members of its goals and objectives or ideology. This agreement is of two kinds. One is technological and the other is moral. These match technical positive responsibility and moral positive responsibility. In accordance with the malpractice model, a CP has a responsibility to conform to good standards and operating procedures of the profession. These are generally minimal standards embodied in software development models and model software engineering curricula. This kind of technical knowledge and skill does not distinguish a technician from a professional. To make this distinction one must go beyond mere technical positive responsibility.

A Broader Sense of Responsibility

In a profession, the members pledge to use their skills for the good of society and not merely to act as agents for the client doing whatever a client asks. This commitment is generally embodied in a professional organization's code of ethics. To be a professional, one assumes another layer of responsibility beyond what has been described in positive responsibility. The professional commits to a "higher degree of care" for those affected by the computing product. Most occupations have a principle of "due care" as a standard. For example, a plumber is responsible for ensuring that the results of his work will not injure his customers or users of the plumbing system. But the plumber does not bear the responsibility of advising the customer of potential negative impacts that a new system may have on the customer's business, quality of life, or the environment. The concern to maximize the positive effects for those affected by computing artifacts goes beyond mere "due care," mere avoidance of direct harm. The addition of this layer of responsibility to positive responsibility is what is necessary to change a computing practitioner into a computing professional. The inadequate interface met the contract specifications, but it did not meet the user's needs. Although the system was technically capable of doing all the required functions and met Jim Midlevel's requests, the computing professional had the responsibility of ensuring that the system met the user's needs. The forward-looking sense of positive responsibility also means that the computer professional has the obligation to meet with upper-level management in order to convince them to reinstate the new accounting system. The computing professional has an obligation to the client, the users, and the taxpayers.

This broader sense of responsibility goes beyond the malpractice model. It incorporates moral responsibility and the ethically commendable. This concept of professional responsibility can be used to address the above-mentioned ways used to deny accountability. This sense of responsibility provides a way to address distributed responsibility as well as diffusion of collective responsibility. The ability to deal with collective responsibility is important because it enables meaningful discussion of the "professional responsibility" of organizations which produce software and organizations which represent computing professionals. It is clear that the computing disasters mentioned at the beginning of this chapter would not have occurred if computing practitioners understood and adopted the positive sense of professional responsibility. The recent development by software engineers of a code of ethics and professional practice (Gotterbarn et al. 1999) is an attempt to define for them this sense of professional responsibility.

References

Davis, M. (1989). "Explaining Wrongdoing." *Journal of Social Philosophy* (Spring/Fall): 74–90.

Dunlop, C. and Kling, R. (eds.) (1991). *Computerization and Controversy: Value Conflicts and Social Change*. Academic Press.

Gotterbarn, D., Miller, K., and Rogerson, S. (1999). "Software Engineering Code of Ethics is Approved." *Communications of the ACM*, 42/10: 102–7. (Also in *Computer* (October): 84–9.)

Harris, C. E., Pritchard, M. S., and Rabins, M. J. (eds.) (1995). *Engineering Ethics: Concepts and Cases*. Wadsworth.

Joch, A. (1995). "How Software Doesn't Work." *Byte* (December): 48–60.

Johnson, D. (1994). *Computer Ethics*, 2nd edn. Prentice Hall.

Ladd, J. (1989). "Computers and Moral Responsibility: A Framework for an Ethical Analysis." In C. C. Gould (ed.), *The Information Web: Ethical and Social Implications of Computer Networking*. Westview Press, pp. 207–27.

Laudon, K. (1995). "Ethical Concepts and Information Technology." *Communications of the ACM*, 38/12: 33–40.

Leveson, N. and Turner, C. (1993). "An Investigation of the Therac-25 Accidents." *IEEE Computer Magazine*, 26: 18–41.

Nissenbaum, H. (1994). "Computing and Accountability." *Communications of the ACM*, 37: 73–80.

Ross, W. D. (1969). *Moral Duties*. Macmillan.

Vallee, J. (1982). *The Network Revolution*. And/Or Press.

Basic study questions

1. In the Introduction to this article Gotterbarn describes several cases of computer failures that resulted in serious harm. He says that a "narrow concept of responsibility" contributed to those failures. Explain what he means by this.

2. Gotterbarn describes several "side-stepping" methods that computer practitioners have used in the past to try to avoid being blamed for the harms of computer failure. Briefly describe these side-stepping strategies.

3. Gotterbarn notes that, although the news media tend to report only the catastrophic cases of computer failure, there are less spectacular ones which cause important harm. Describe the example he presents to illustrate this point.

4. According to Gotterbarn, there are two false beliefs about software development that cause computer practitioners to side-step responsibility for the consequences of their work. What are these erroneous beliefs?

5. What is the "crossword-puzzle approach" to computing problems, and why does it lead to a harmful understanding of professional responsibility?

6. To illustrate the damage that the "crossword-puzzle approach" can do, Gotterbarn presents two example cases: the x-ray crusher case and the shoulder-launched missile case. Briefly describe each of these cases.

7. What is the "diffuse responsibility" side-stepping strategy? How is it employed by those who wish to avoid being held responsible? Why does Gotterbarn call it "paradoxical"?

8. According to Gotterbarn, tying the concept of responsibility too closely to that of blame leads to a variety of excuses to avoid blame. What are these excuses?

9. Gotterbarn recommends that computer practitioners adopt a positive sense of responsibility in order to make their activities "more professional." What are the primary features of this positive sense of responsibility, and how do they differ from the relevant features of negative responsibility?

10. Gotterbarn distinguishes two types of positive responsibility. He says that they "are both necessary for a concept of professional responsibility." Briefly describe these two types of positive responsibility.

11. Gotterbarn distinguishes between a "mere technician" and a genuine professional. What is the difference according to Gotterbarn?

Questions for further thought

1. What is a profession, why do professions exist? What is the difference between a profession and professionalism?

2. Are "computer professionals" actually professionals in the same sense as doctors, lawyers and teachers? Are there important differences?

3. What is the proper role of a code of ethics within a profession?

CHAPTER 6

The Ethics of Software Development Project Management

Simon Rogerson

Introduction

It appears universally accepted that the most effective way to develop software is through the use of a project-based organizational structure which encourages individuals to participate in teams with the goal of achieving some common objective. Much has been written about the management of software development projects and no doubt much will be written in the future. The purpose of this chapter is to examine whether typical project management practice effectively deals with the ethical issues surrounding the software development process. For the sake of clarity only one project management approach is discussed, Structured Project Management (SPM). This is used to illustrate the ethical strengths and weaknesses of project management in a technical sphere. The aim is to tease out the fundamental issues and not to dwell on the nuances of one particular approach. In order to do this, a set of ethical principals for the computer professional is derived from the previous work of others. These principles are then mapped onto the methodological framework of SPM, thereby highlighting the areas of ethical concern. Two of the steps within SPM are examined in detail to demonstrate how the application of the relevant ethical principles helps to ensure ethical behavior.

This approach is discussed in more detail in the sections that follow. The next section briefly considers the chosen project management methodology, SPM; the section that follows establishes a set of guiding ethical principles for computer professionals; the fourth section analyzes SPM using these guiding principles; the fifth section considers the critical ethical issues of project management; and, finally, the chapter finishes with some concluding remarks.

Simon Rogerson, "The Ethics of Software Development Project Management." This chapter is a revised version of "Software Project Management Ethics" which was published in C. Myers, T. Hall, and D. Pitt (eds.), *The Responsible Software Engineer* (Springer-Verlag, 1996), ch. 11, pp. 100–6. This version © 2002 by Simon Rogerson.

Table 1   The ten steps of Structured Project Management (SPM)

Step	Description
1	Visualize what the goal is
2	Make a list of the jobs that need to be done
3	Ensure there is one leader
4	Assign people to jobs
5	Manage expectations, allow a margin of error and have a fallback position
6	Use an appropriate leadership style
7	Know what is going on
8	Tell people what is going on
9	Repeat Steps 1 through 8 until Step 10 is achievable
10	Realize the project goal

An Example Approach to Project Management

In his book, *How to Run Successful Projects*, which is part of the British Computer Society Practitioner Series, O'Connell (1994) provides details of the SPM approach. He explains that SPM is a practical methodology which, as De Marco and Lister (1987) state, is a "basic approach one takes to getting a job done." SPM has been chosen for discussion because it is practical rather than conceptual and provides practitioners with realistic guidance in undertaking the vastly complex activity of project management. SPM comprises ten steps (see table 1). The first five steps are concerned with planning and the remaining five deal with implementing the plan and achieving the goal. O'Connell states that most projects succeed or fail because of decisions made during the planning stage, thereby justifying the fact that half of the effort expended in the SPM approach is on preparation.

It is this planning element of project management that lays down the foundations on which the project ethos is built. Here the scope of consideration is established, either implicitly or explicitly, which in turn locates the horizon beyond which issues are deemed not to influence the project or be influenced by the project. How the project is conducted will depend heavily upon the perceived goal.

Visualization of the perceived goal takes place in Step 1, and the first two points in the visualization checklist given by O'Connell are these:

What will the goal of the project mean to all the people involved in the project when the project completes?

What are the things the project will actually produce? Where will these things go? What will happen to them? Who will use them? How will the users be affected by them?

These questions are important because, through answering them, an acceptable project ethos and scope of consideration should be achieved. The problem is that in practice these fundamental questions are often overlooked. It is more likely that a narrower perspective will be adopted, with only the obvious issues in close proximity to the project being considered. The holistic view promoted by the two checklist points requires greater vision, analysis, and reflection; but typically the project manager is under pressure to deliver and so the tendency is to reduce the horizon and establish an artificial boundary around the project.

Steps 2 to 5 are concerned with adding detail and refinements thus arriving at a workable and acceptable plan. Steps 6 to 8 are concerned with implementing the plan, monitoring performance, and keeping those associated with the project informed of progress. Step 9 defines the control feedback loops which ensure that the plan remains focused, current, and realistic. Finally, step 10 is the delivery of the project output to the client and an opportunity to reflect upon what has and has not been achieved.

Principles of Ethics

Relevant ethical principles must now be established in order to identify the ethical issues associated with software development project management in general and SPM in particular.

Ethics comprises both practice and reflection (van Luijk 1994). Practice is the conscious appeal to norms and values to guide one's actions, whilst reflection on practice is the elaboration or defense of norms and values. Norms are collective expectations regarding a certain type of behavior, whilst values are collective ideas about what constitutes a good society. The existence of a plan with a controlling mechanism is the accepted norm in project management, which itself is an accepted value in software development. For the purposes of this chapter, it is sufficient to consider only *ethical practice* (rather than reflection upon ethical ideas), because project management is concerned with action rather than conceptual reflection. Conceptual reflection might manifest itself in, for example, codes of conduct which are concerned with establishing what are the generalized ways of working that are acceptable to a wider community. (See for example the Software Engineering Code of Ethics and Professional Practice which was adopted in 1998 by the IEEE Computer Society and the ACM.) This community would include all potential stakeholders of software development projects. In other words, project management is concerned with how to use and when to apply norms and values, rather than establishing what these norms and values are or should be.

Table 2 Questioning the ethical nature of an action

*	Is it honorable?
~	Is there anyone from whom you would like to hide the action?
*	Is it honest?
~	Does it violate any agreement, actual or implied, or otherwise betray a trust?
*	Does it avoid the possibility of a conflict of interest?
~	Are there other considerations that might bias your judgement?
*	Is it within your area of competence?
~	Is it possible that your best effort will not be adequate?
*	Is it fair?
~	Is it detrimental to the legitimate interests of others?
*	Is it considerate?
~	Will it violate confidentiality or privacy, or otherwise harm anyone or anything?
*	Is it conservative?
~	Does it unnecessarily squander time or other valuable resources?

To be ethical, an action should elicit a positive response to all applicable primary questions (*) and a negative response to each clarification (~).

A useful list of generic questions was devised by John McLeod (in Parker et al. 1990) to help determine the ethical nature of actions within the computing profession. The list is shown in table 2. Within these questions are embedded *norms* which will impact the process of project management.

Software development is about the delivery of a product by a supplier to a client under some agreement. It is irrelevant whether this is an in-house arrangement or whether it is between two independent organizations. According to Velasquez (1992), such an agreement is concerned with product quality and moral product liability. Two parties enter into an agreement to develop a piece of software. Such agreements are often unbalanced, with the client being disadvantaged. Velasquez argues that the principles of due care and social cost must take effect in these situations. There must be due care from the developer over and above what has been accepted in the contract so that adequate steps are taken to prevent any foreseen detrimental effects from occurring through the use of the software. Social cost is measured by the utilitarian idea of minimizing harms and maximizing benefits to society.

By combining the ideas of McLeod and Velasquez, a set of ethical principles can be derived as shown in table 3. The principle of honor is to ensure that actions are beyond reproach. It can be considered as the "umbrella" principle, to which all other principles contribute. Honor demands honesty from the professional. The principle of bias focuses on ensuring decisions and actions are objective rather than subjective. Professional adequacy is

Table 3   Ethical principles for computer professionals

Principle	Related question
Honor	Is the action considered beyond reproach?
Honesty	Will the action violate any explicit or implicit agreement or trust?
Bias	Are there any external considerations that may bias the action to be taken?
Professional adequacy	Is the action within the limits of capability?
Due care	Is the action to be exposed to the best possible quality assurance standards?
Fairness	Are all stakeholders' views considered with regard to the action?
Consideration of social cost	Is the appropriate accountability and responsibility accepted with respect to this action?
Effective and efficient action	Is the action suitable, given the objectives set, and is it to be completed using the least expenditure of resources?

concerned with the ability of individuals to undertake allocated tasks. The principle of due care is linked with the concept of software quality assurance. It is concerned with putting into place the measures by which any undesirable effects can be prevented, which may require additional attention beyond that agreed formally within a contract. Fairness focuses on ensuring that all affected parties are considered in project deliberations. This leads to social cost, which recognizes that it is not possible to abdicate from professional responsibility and accountability. Finally, the principle of effective and efficient action is concerned with completing tasks and realizing goals with the least possible expenditure of resources.

These ethical principles are not mutually exclusive. They were developed to establish a checklist of ethical aspects to be applied whenever an action associated with computer systems takes place. The term action is used to represent any process or task undertaken, which normally includes a human element as the performer of the task or as the beneficiary, or as both performer and beneficiary.

Ethical Project Management

These guiding principles, which are based on ethical concepts, can be easily applied in practical situations. They can be used to analyze, inform, and color practice within the whole of computing and are used here to consider

Table 4 The dominant ethical principles in the steps of SPM

Principle	SPM steps									
	1	2	3	4	5	6	7	8	9	10
1. Honor	X			X		X		X		X
2. Honesty	X			X	X			X		
3. Bias	X	X	X	X				X		X
4. Adequacy			X	X		X				
5. Due care	X		X		X			X	X	
6. Fairness	X				X			X		
7. Social cost	X				X	X				X
8. Action		X	X	X		X	X		X	X
Relationships per step	6	2	4	5	4	4	1	5	2	4

how to undertake ethical project management. The activities within each of the ten steps of SPM have been analyzed in order to identify the dominant ethical issues of each step. The results of the analysis are shown in table 4. It is recognized that most of the eight principles will have some impact on each step, but it is important to identify those that will have a *significant* impact. The mapping in table 4 shows the relationships that are considered significant. Steps 1 and 8 are now considered in further detail to illustrate the implication of the mapping.

Step 1: Visualize what the goal is

As previously mentioned, this step establishes the project ethos, and consequently there are several ethical issues that need to be borne in mind. This is the start of the project, and it is vitally important to be above board at the onset so that a good working relationship is established with the client. The principles of honor and honesty address this point. As can be seen from table 4, bias in decision-making and the undertaking of actions is a major concern throughout the project, including step 1. It is important to take a balanced viewpoint based on economic, technological, and sociological information. The view often portrayed is skewed toward technology and economics, which can have disastrous results leading to major system failure or rejection, as was the case, for example, at the London Ambulance Service (major system failure in 1992; see below, pp. 129–31) and the London Stock Exchange (rejection of new computer system in 1991). This leads to the remaining three dominant principles of due care, fairness, and social cost. Computer systems impact directly and indirectly on many people, and it is important to include all parties in decisions that affect the way in which a project is conducted. Software development projects involve many stakeholders and each is worthy of fair treatment. The principles of due care and social cost will ensure that a longer-term and a broader perspective are adopted.

Step 8: Tell people what is going on

The project is dynamic and exists in a dynamic environment. Step 8 is essential so that everyone is aware of occurring change and so that their assignments can be adjusted accordingly. Being over-optimistic, ultra-pessimistic, or simply untruthful about progress can be damaging not only to the project but also to both the client and supplier organizations. Those involved in this communication would be the project team, the computer department line management, and the client. An honest, objective account of progress, which takes into account the requirements and feelings of all concerned, is the best way to operate. Drawing upon the principles of honor, honesty, bias, due care, and fairness will assist in achieving this.

The ethical verdict

Whilst SPM provides practical guidance on the management of projects, it does not explicitly include an ethical dimension, though it is accepted that there are implicit ethical issues in some parts of the methodology. There is a need for a stronger and more obvious emphasis on ethical issues. The derived mapping provides the framework for this additional ethical perspective within the project management process.

The Ethical Hotspots of Project Management

The mapping of ethical principles onto the steps of the methodology provides overall guidance on how to approach the project management process throughout the life of the project. However, within the project there are numerous activities and decisions to be made and most of these will have an ethical dimension. It is impractical to consider each minute issue in great detail and still hope to achieve the overall project goal. The focus must be on the key issues that are likely to influence the success of the project. These are the ethical hotspots of project management. In (Rogerson and Bynum 1995), ethical hotspots are broadly defined as points where activities and decision-making are likely to include a *relatively* high ethical dimension. More specifically they are those points within any extended human endeavor where there is a relatively high risk of ethical mistakes and where such mistakes have significant consequences for society, its organizations, or its citizens. There are at least two significant ethical hotspots in project management: namely, the defining of the scope of consideration (in step 1 of SPM) and the information dissemination to the client (primarily in step 8 of SPM).

Scope of consideration

It is a common problem with software development projects that decisions concerned with, for example, feasibility, functionality, and implementation, do not take into account the requirements of all those affected by the system once it becomes operational. This is illustrated by the typical cost-benefit analysis activity undertaken at the beginning of most projects, which takes into account only the interests of those involved in the analysis and does not usually consider the rights and interests of *all* parties affected by the proposed system. Such a view is primarily techno-economic rather than techno-*socio*-economic. The potential well-being of many individuals is likely to be at risk, unless an ethically sensitive horizon is established for the scope of consideration. This is more likely to happen if the principles of due care, fairness, and social cost are prevalent during the activity. In this way the project management process will embrace, at the outset, the views and concerns of all parties affected by the project. Concerns over, for example, deskilling of jobs, redundancy, and the break-up of social groupings can be aired at the earliest opportunity and the project goals can be adjusted if necessary.

Information dissemination to the client

The second ethical hotspot is about informing the client. No one likes to get shocking news, and so early warning of a problem and an indication of the scale of the problem are important. Project managers must not see information dissemination to the client as information dissemination to the enemy, which can be the stance in some organizations. The key is to provide factual information in non-emotive words so that the client and project manager can discuss any necessary changes in a calm and professional manner. Confrontational progress meetings achieve nothing. The adoption of the principles of honesty, bias, due care, and fairness would help to ensure a good working relationship with the client.

Conclusions

Without doubt, the project management process for software development is capable of accommodating an ethical perspective. This has been demonstrated by mapping the derived eight ethical principles onto the Structured Project Management methodology. The major criticism of current practice is that any ethical consideration tends to be implicit rather than explicit, which has a tendency to devalue the importance of the ethical dimension. By using ethical principles and the identification of ethical hotspots it is possible to ensure that the key ethical issues are properly addressed.

Quite simply, project management should be guided by a sense of justice, a sense of equal distribution of benefits and burdens and a sense of equal opportunity. In this way software development project management will become ethically aligned. Recent advances by Gotterbarn and Rogerson (see Gotterbarn 2002) have led to the development of the Software Development Impact Statement (SoDIS) process, which is designed to achieve such ethical alignment. The process has been embedded in a project software tool called SoDIS Project Auditor. (See http://www.sdresearch.org)

References

De Marco T. and Lister, T. (1987). *Peopleware*. Dorset House.

Gotterbarn, D. (2002). "Reducing Software Failures: Addressing the Ethical Risks of the Software Development Lifecycle." *Australian Journal of Information Systems*, 9/2: 155–65.

O'Connell, F. (1994). *How to Run Successful Projects*. Prentice Hall.

Parker, D. B., Swope, S., and Baker, B. N. (1990). *Ethical Conflicts in Information and Computer Science, Technology, and Business*. QED Information Sciences.

Rogerson, S. and Bynum, T. W. (1995) "Identifying the Ethical Dimension of Decision Making in the Complex Domain of IS/IT." ETHICOMP95 Conference, De Montfort University, Leicester, UK.

van Luijk, H. (1994). "Business Ethics: The Field and its Importance." In B. Harvey (ed.), *Business Ethics: A European Approach*. Prentice Hall.

Velasquez, M. G. (1992). *Business Ethics: Concepts and Cases*, 3rd edn. Prentice Hall.

Basic study questions

1. What is a software development project, and why did Rogerson choose to focus upon just one approach to such projects?
2. Why, according to Rogerson, is the planning phase of a software development project crucial to the ethical issues that are relevant to the project?
3. What are the ten specific steps in the SPM approach to software development? Which steps constitute the planning phase of the project?
4. Why does Rogerson focus so much attention upon step 1 of SPM?

5. According to Rogerson, what is the difference between norms and values?
6. How does Rogerson derive a set of principles to guide software development projects? What are the eight ethical principles that Rogerson derives?
7. How did Rogerson derive table 4? What is the significance of this table?
8. According to table 4, what six ethical principles are especially relevant to step 1 of SPM?
9. According to table 4, what five ethical principles are especially relevant to step 8 of SPM?
10. What does Rogerson mean by "ethical hotspots"? What are the two main "ethical hotspots" in software development project management?

Questions for further thought

1. What, in your personal view, is the best way to guarantee that appropriate ethical considerations will be applied to software development projects?
2. Why is it important for software engineers to be sensitive to ethical considerations regarding the software that they create?
3. Why are existing risk management and quality assurance procedures used in software development *insufficient* to address effectively the associated ethical issues?

CASE TO ANALYZE: THE LONDON AMBULANCE CASE

A notorious case of poor computer system development involved the London Ambulance Service in London, UK, in 1992. This famous case is described below, and the reader is invited to analyze it using the case-analysis method presented in chapter 3 above.

The London Ambulance Service's Computer-Aided Dispatch Project (LASCAD) used computers in an effort to improve the efficiency and response times of the London Ambulance Service (LAS). LAS is the largest ambulance service in the world, covering 600 square miles. It covers a resident population of some 6.8 million, but its daytime population is larger, especially in central London. In 1992, it handled, on average, about 2,300 medical emergency calls per day (Beynon-Davies 1995).

The primary objective of the LASCAD computer system was to replace the handwritten forms and human dispatchers of the existing ambulance service, because these were thought to be too time-consuming and prone to human error. The proposed LASCAD system was supposed to use faster and more reliable computer technology to receive emergency calls, gather vital information, identify the location of the emergency, identify the nearest appropriate ambulance resources, and dispatch an ambulance to the emergency site.

The specifications for the proposed new computer system were developed with virtually no input from the ambulance drivers and others who would actually be using it. The specifications were very detailed and left little room for new ideas to be incorporated as the project progressed.

The project was put out for public bid, and the lowest bidder was awarded the contract, despite the fact that the company had no prior experience building ambulance dispatch systems. Only the lowest bidder submitted a proposal that fell within the LAS requirements, and the ability of that company to successfully complete the job on time and within budget was never investigated. More experienced bidders said that the desired system could not be built within the cost and timeframe requirements that LAS had set as non-negotiable; and one of the competing companies described the project as "totally and fatally flawed."

On October 26, 1992 LASCAD was put into operation with catastrophic results. A number of things went wrong. Incorrect vehicle information in the system led to incorrect allocation of vehicles. Sometimes multiple vehicles were sent to the same location or the closest vehicles were not dispatched. Calls that did not go through the appropriate protocol were put on a waiting list, which quickly grew extremely large. Important messages scrolled off computer screens. Untrained ambulance crews pressed wrong buttons. Frustrated and frightened patients and their families made many additional calls when ambulances did not appear on the scene quickly. Telephone answering and radio communications slowed down, which generated more frustration and fear among patients, ambulance crews, and LAS staff members. By the next day, the entire system had collapsed; and a number of people may have died because they did not get to hospital on time (Beynon-Davies 1995).

After the LASCAD disaster, there were a number of inquiries into the causes. The general conclusion was that many different failures and mistakes led to the debacle. The findings of the South West Thames Regional Health Authority inquiry, for example, included the following conclusions about the CAD system:

- The CAD system implemented in 1992 was over ambitious and was developed and implemented against an impossible timetable.
- LAS management ignored or chose not to accept advice provided to it from many sources outside of the Service on the tightness of the timetable or the high risk of the comprehensive systems requirement.
- The South West Thames Regional Health Authority procurement rules were followed fully, but these rules emphasized open tendering and the quantitative aspects of procurement (obtaining the best price) rather than the qualitative aspects (doing the job best).
- The project team did not show, or discuss with, the LAS Board independent references on the lead CAD contractor, which raised doubts on their ability to handle such a major project.
- In awarding the contract for CAD to a small software house, with no previous experience of similar systems, LAS management was taking a high risk.
- Project management throughout the development and implementation process was inadequate and at times ambiguous. LAS failed to follow the PRINCE Project Management Method. A major systems integration project such as CAD requires full-time, professional, experienced project management. This was lacking.
- The early decision to achieve full CAD implementation in one phase was misguided. In a project as far reaching as CAD it would have been preferable to implement it in a stepwise approach, proving each phase totally before moving on to the next.
- There was incomplete "ownership" of the system by the majority of its users. The many problems identified with many of the system components over the preceding months had instilled an atmosphere of system distrust in which staff were expecting the system to fail rather than willing it to succeed.

- Satisfactory implementation of the system would require changes to a number of existing working practices. Senior management believed that implementation of the system would, in itself, bring about these changes. In fact, many staff found it to be an operational "strait jacket" within which they still tried to operate local flexibility. This caused further confusion within the system.
- Training provided to Central Ambulance Control staff and to ambulance crews was incomplete and inconsistent.
- The CAD system relied on near perfect information on vehicle location and status being available to it at all times. The project team failed to appreciate fully the impact that a higher level of imperfect information would have on the system.
- The system was not fully tested to a satisfactory level of quality and resilience before full implementation on October 26, 1992.
- The system relied on a technical communications infrastructure that was overloaded and unable to cope easily with the demands that CAD would place upon it, particularly in a difficult communications environment such as London.
- LAS management constantly attributed CAD problems to willful misuse of the system by some ambulance crews. There is no direct evidence of this, but the circumstantial evidence that does exist indicates that it would have been only one of the many contributory factors that led to the CAD failure.
- October 26 and 27, 1992 were not exceptionally busy days in terms of emergency incidents or patients carried. The increase in calls on those days was largely as a result of unidentified duplicate calls and callbacks from the public in response to ambulance delays.
- On October 26 and 27, 1992 the computer system itself did not fail in a technical sense. Response times did on occasions become unacceptable, but overall the system did what it had been designed to do. However, much of the design had fatal flaws that would, and did, cumulatively lead to all of the symptoms of systems failure.

Commenting on the way forward, the Communications Directorate (1993) remarked that, "The lesson to be learnt must be that the particular geographical, social, and political environment in which LAS operates, and the cultural climate within the service itself, require a more measured and participative approach from both management and staff. Management must be willing to have regular and open consultation with staff representatives. By the same token staff and their representatives need to overcome their concerns about previous management approaches, recognize the need for change, and be receptive to discuss new ideas. If ever there was a time and opportunity to cast off the constraints and grievances of the past years and to start a fresh management and staff partnership, that time is now."

ADDITIONAL READINGS AND WEB RESOURCES

Additional readings

Benyon-Davies, P. (1995). "Information Systems 'Failure': the Case of the London Ambulance Service's Computer Aided Dispatch Project." *European Journal of Information Systems*, 4: 171–84.

The Communications Directorate (1993). *Report of the Inquiry Into The London Ambulance Service*. South West Thames Regional Health Authority (February).

Gotterbarn, D. (1996). "Establishing Standards of Professional Practice." In T. Hall, D. Pitt, and C. Meyer (eds.), *The Responsible Software Engineer: Selected Readings in IT Professionalism*. Springer Verlag, ch. 3.

Grodzinsky, F. S. (1999). "The Practitioner from Within: Revisiting the Virtues." *Computers and Society* (March): 9–15.

Johnson, D. G. (2001). *Computer Ethics*, 3rd edn. Prentice-Hall, ch. 3.

Leveson, N. and Turner, C. (1993). "An Investigation of the Therac-25 Accidents." *Computer*, 26/7: 18–41.

Nissenbaum, H. (1994). "Computing and Accountability." *Communications of the ACM*, 37/1: 73–80.

Prior, M., Fairweather, N. B., and Rogerson, S. (2001). *Is IT Ethical? 2000 ETHICOMP Survey of Professional Practice*. UK: Institute for the Management of Information Systems.

Spinello, R. A. (1997). *Case Studies in Information and Computer Ethics*. Prentice Hall.

Web resources

The Association for Computing Machinery, http://www.acm.org

The Australian Computer Society, http://www.acs.org.au/

The British Computer Society, http://www.bcs.org.uk/

Computer Professionals for Social Responsibility, http://www.ccsr.org

Professional Accountability Section of the web site of the Online Ethics Center, http://onlineethics.org/keywords/accountability.html

Professionalism Section of the web site of the Centre for Computing and Social Responsibility, http://www.ccsr.cse.dmu.ac.uk/resources/professionalism/

PART III

Codes of Ethics

We must make the world honest before we can honestly say to our children that honesty is the best policy.

George Bernard Shaw

Editors' Introduction

Functions of Ethics Codes

Codes of ethics for computer professionals can fulfill a variety of functions simultaneously:

1 *Inspiration*   Codes of ethics can serve an inspirational function by identifying values and ideals to which computing practitioners should aspire. In addition, because clients, computer users, and the general public share the same human values and community ideals with computer practitioners, the fact that a professional organization publicly commits itself to such ideals and values helps to inspire public trust and respect for the profession.

2 *Education*   Codes of professional ethics can fulfill several educational functions. For example, they can inform and educate new members of the profession about the values and standards to which the profession is committed. In addition, they can inform public policy-makers, clients, users, and the general public about the profession's ideals, obligations, and responsibilities. Codes of ethics, therefore, can be powerful educational tools.

3 *Guidance*   Ethical principles, values, imperatives, and standards of good practice spelled out in ethics codes can be helpful guides for computer practitioners as they exercise their judgment in making decisions. They also can guide public policy-makers as they perform their public duties regarding information technology.

4 *Accountability*   Codes of ethics reveal to clients and users alike the level of responsibility and care that they should expect – as well as the standards that they should demand – from computing practitioners. In this way, ethics codes can make members of professional organizations accountable to their colleagues and to the public in general.

5 *Enforcement* By providing a basis to identify ethically unacceptable behavior, codes of ethics enable professional organizations to encourage and even to enforce standards of good practice and compliance with responsible norms.

What a Code of Ethics is Not

Even though codes of professional ethics can effectively fulfill all of the above-described functions, there are several roles that they are not intended to fulfill, and that they could not possibly fulfill:

1 *Not laws* Codes of professional ethics are not laws passed by public legislative bodies (although they can provide valuable guidance to such bodies when, for example, creating license-to-practice legislation), and they are not intended to encourage law suits or legal challenges (although they might help to resolve important questions in certain legal disputes).

2 *Not complete ethical frameworks or algorithms* Codes of ethics for computer practitioners are not complete ethical frameworks to cover every possible ethical question that might arise about computing. Indeed, ethics is not a subject that lends itself to such completeness. Even though ethical ideals, values, and principles are very broad, in given situations it is possible for one value or principle to conflict with another. Ethics, therefore, requires deliberation and good judgment that cannot be fully captured in a step-by-step algorithm. The Preamble of the Code of Ethics and Professional Conduct of the Association for Computing Machinery (ACM) explains it this way:

> It is understood that some words and phrases in a code of ethics are subject to varying interpretations, and that any ethical principle may conflict with other ethical principles in specific situations. Questions related to ethical conflicts can best be answered by thoughtful consideration of fundamental principles, rather than reliance on detailed regulations.

3 *Not exhaustive checklists* Since no code of ethics can provide a complete ethical framework, it would be a mistake – indeed a dangerous one – to treat any such code as a "checklist" which one simply runs through to determine if every ethical question has been addressed. (This point is discussed at length below by Fairweather in chapter 7, "No PAPA.") Checklists can, of course, be useful tools in ethical decision-making, because they suggest topics that often need ethical consideration. But, if satisfying a checklist encourages someone to believe that all ethical

matters have been addressed, he or she might overlook some important ethical questions that were not included on the "checklist." As explained in the Preamble of the Code of Ethics of the Institute for the Management of Information Systems (IMIS):

> It is neither desirable nor possible for a Code of Ethics to act as a set of algorithmic rules that, if followed scrupulously, will lead to ethical behavior at all times in all situations. There are likely to be times when different parts of the Code will conflict with each other. . . . At such times, the professional should reflect on the principles and the underlying spirit of the Code and strive to achieve a balance that is most in harmony with the aims of the Code. . . . [I]n cases where it is not possible to reconcile the guidance given by different articles of the Code, the public good shall at all times be held paramount.

A Variety of Formats

In Part II above it is clear that codes of ethics can be useful tools for computer practitioners as they make decisions to fulfill their professional responsibilities. The phrase "codes of ethics" is being used very broadly here to refer to a variety of ideals, rules, imperatives, and guides to behavior. Given this broad meaning, a code of ethics might include, for example, ideals to which a computer practitioner should aspire, such as "respect human dignity," "avoid unethical discrimination," "preserve privacy," and so on. In addition, a more specific code of ethics could be called a "code of conduct" if it lays down rules to govern professional activities – rules such as "maintain professional competence," "honor contracts," "avoid conflicts of interest," and so forth. A code of ethics might even specify accepted standards of good practice, such as "use 'mutation testing' when dealing with life-critical systems" (Gotterbarn et al. 1997). Most codes of ethics adopted by professional organizations of computer practitioners include at least the first two kinds of principle.

Codes of ethics can be organized in a variety of ways. One way is to identify specific ethical principles or ideals associated with the *different roles* that computing professionals fulfill. For example, the Code of Ethics and Professional Conduct of the ACM is organized in this way – the first three sections are devoted to "statements of personal responsibility" associated with a member's role:

- as a human being and member of society (Part 1);
- as a computing practitioner providing services and products (Part 2);
- as a leader in professional organizations (Part 3).

Another way to organize a code of ethics is exemplified by the Code of Ethics of the IMIS, which identifies different groups or individuals to whom a computing professional owes a duty of responsibility:

- to society;
- to organizations;
- to peers;
- to staff;
- to the profession;
- to one's self.

A third way to organize a code of ethics is to identify different types of professional relationships. The Software Engineering Code of Ethics and Professional Practice takes this approach.

Perhaps the most straightforward way to organize a code of ethics is simply to list the major rules and duties that apply to members of the organization. The Code of Ethics of the Institute of Electrical and Electronics Engineers (IEEE) is organized in this way, listing, for example, principles on conflicts of interest, protection of the public, honesty, competence, and fair treatment.

General Ethical Principles

Because an organization and its members are part of society in general, they share the same human values and social ideals as other members of the community. Typically, then, the values and ideals of society are expressed within professional codes. For example, like most other such codes, the Code of Ethics of the Australian Computer Society (ACS) expresses several fundamental values and social ideals:

- be honest, forthright and impartial;
- loyally serve the community;
- advance human welfare;
- consider and respect people's privacy.

Another example is the British Computer Society (BCS) Code of Conduct, where one finds expressions of the following duties:

- have regard for the public health, safety and environment;
- have regard to the legitimate rights of third parties;
- conduct your professional activities without discrimination;
- reject any offer of bribery or inducement.

The broad values and ideals expressed in professional codes of ethics provide an ethical foundation upon which more specific principles and guidelines are developed.

Professional Responsibilities and Duties

Professional codes of ethics normally contain more than just inspirational ideals. They also lay down rules to govern specific professional activities of members. Such rules apply to a wide variety of duties and responsibilities, regarding, for example, professional competence, honest dealings with clients and employers, relevant laws and regulations, assistance to fellow professionals, confidentiality, conflicts of interest, standards of good practice, and so on.

For example, one of the most specific and detailed codes of ethics for computer practitioners is the Software Engineering Code of Ethics and Professional Practice, which includes 80 very specific rules for software engineers. A few examples include:

- Software engineers shall ensure that specifications for software on which they work have been well documented, satisfy the user's requirements, and have the appropriate approvals.
- Software engineers shall use the property of a client or employer only in ways properly authorized, and with the client's or employer's knowledge and consent.
- Software engineers shall take responsibility for detecting, correcting, and reporting errors in software and associated documents on which they work.
- Software engineers shall improve their ability to create safe, reliable, and useful quality software at reasonable cost and within a reasonable time.

Similarly, the IMIS Code of Ethics specifies that members of the IMIS shall, for example,

- endeavor to avoid, identify and resolve conflicts of interest;
- protect the legitimate privacy and property of colleagues and peers;
- actively oppose discrimination at work except on the sole basis of an individual's capacity for the task;
- adhere to relevant and well-founded organizational and professional policies and standards.

Leadership and Management Responsibilities

Computer practitioners regularly serve in leadership and management roles in organizations and businesses. In recognition of this fact, some codes of ethics of professional organizations include principles and imperatives that address responsibilities that come with leadership roles. The ACM Code of Ethics and Professional Conduct, for example, even includes a separate section entitled "Organizational Leadership Imperatives," in which six such imperatives are stated. The following examples are taken from that section of the ACM Code:

- Acknowledge and support proper and authorized uses of an organization's computing and communications resources.
- Create opportunities for members of the organization to learn the principles and limitations of computer systems.

The BCS Code of Conduct also includes some duties specific to leaders and managers. For example:

- You should encourage and support fellow members in their professional development and, where possible, provide opportunities for the professional development of new members, particularly student members. Enlightened mutual assistance between IS professionals furthers the reputation of the profession, and assists individual members.
- You shall accept professional responsibility for your work and for the work of colleagues who are defined in a given context as working under your supervision.

The Software Engineering Code of Ethics and Professional Practice has an entire section devoted to principles for software engineers who also serve as managers. That section states twelve principles, including, for example:

- Assign work only after taking into account appropriate contributions of education and experience tempered with a desire to further that education and experience.
- Provide for due process in hearing charges of violation of an employer's policy or of this Code.

Not every code of professional ethics specifically mentions duties of leaders and managers. Nevertheless, the values and goals of such codes imply that computer practitioners in leadership roles have relevant duties and responsibilities.

Enforcement of Ethical Codes

In the section above entitled "What a Code of Ethics is Not," it was noted that codes of ethics are not laws passed by public legislative bodies. Nevertheless, even if they do not have the force of law, ethical codes can help make members of professional organizations accountable to their colleagues and to the public because they provide a basis to identify ethically unacceptable behavior. This enables an organization to encourage or even to enforce standards of good practice and compliance with responsible norms.

At present, most codes of ethics for computer professionals contain no provisions for enforcement. An exception to this is the ACM Code of Ethics and Professional Conduct, which explicitly states in Part 4 that "if a member does not follow this code by engaging in gross misconduct, membership in ACM may be terminated." The termination process is a complex legal matter involving lawyers on both sides and the Board of Officers of the ACM.

Some critics have noted that even if an irresponsible person loses membership of the ACM, he or she can continue to be a computing practitioner. Such critics have called, instead, for licensing, because the threat of losing a license could be a better tool for enforcing professional codes of ethics. As an illustration of the complexity of this issue, the question of licensing software engineers is discussed at length below by Gotterbarn in chapter 8, "On Licensing Computer Professionals."

Reference

Gotterbarn, D., Miller, K., and Rogerson, S. (1997). "Software Engineering Code of Ethics, version 3." *IEEE Computer.*

CHAPTER 7

No, PAPA: Why Incomplete Codes of Ethics are Worse than None at All

N. Ben Fairweather

Introduction

There has been substantial sustained interest, and there still is current interest, in Richard Mason's 1986 article "Four Ethical Issues of the Information
Age" (for example, Platt and Morrison 1995, pp. 2ff; Barrosso 1996;
Whitman et al. 1998; Timpka 1999). In that article Mason states that "The
ethical issues involved (in the information age) are many and varied," which
is indubitably true, but then he goes on to claim that "it is helpful to focus on
just four. These may be summarized by means of an acronym – PAPA"
(1986, p. 5), standing for privacy, accuracy, property, and accessibility.

Many authors have identified other issues that do not easily fit within
these four categories. For example, three of the "Ten Commandments of
Computer Ethics" (Computer Ethics Institute, undated) do not easily fit
within that framework (despite all the flaws (see Fairweather 2000) of the
"Ten Commandments"). These are the "Commandments" dealing with
"harm to other people," "the social consequences of the program . . . or . . .
system," and "consideration and respect for . . . fellow humans." Other
codes of computer ethics cover a longer list of issues: thus, the Association
for Computing Machinery "Code of Ethics and Professional Conduct"
(Association for Computing Machinery 1992) has 24 imperatives of which
about 11 do not fit within Mason's "four issues;" while the ACM/IEEE-CS
joint "Software Engineering Code of Ethics and Professional Practice"
(Gotterbarn et al. 1998) has 80 imperatives of which perhaps a little over
half do not fit within the "four issues."

N. Ben Fairweather, "No, PAPA: Why Incomplete Codes of Ethics are Worse than None at All." This
chapter was originally presented as a paper at the Conference on Computer Ethics, Linköping
University, Sweden, 1997 and was later published in G. Collste (ed.), *Ethics in the Age of Information
Technology* (Linköping University Press, 2000). © 2000 by N. Ben Fairweather and reprinted by
permission of the author.

The Problem

The problem is that by focusing on the four areas of privacy, accuracy, property, and accessibility, attention may be taken away from other moral issues that could well be realized to be more important on deeper reflection. As I will demonstrate shortly, condemnation of an immoral act may be so highly distorted as to be absurd, or a highly immoral act may not be condemned at all, because the impacts that cause it to be considered immoral do not fit within the PAPA formulation.

Not all important moral issues in information technology can be put under the PAPA headings. I will illustrate this with some examples. It should, however, be clear that these examples are not intended to be a comprehensive list of all the problems with the PAPA formulation.

Weapons

A prime example of the problems with the PAPA formulation is the question of whether technology for use in weapons systems ought to be developed. This is an ethical issue of the information age: information technology comprises the largest part of military spending in the world today. Indeed, the military application of information technology is so substantial that the computing and information industries would be unrecognizable if military spending had not provided an impetus. To give just one example: the Internet itself has developed out of the ARPANET, a military technology (Bissett 1996, p. 87). While the moral issues raised by weapons development may include moral issues of long standing (and thus which may be claimed to be not "of the information age"), the issues of privacy, like those more directly related to weaponry, are of long standing. The information age puts new emphasis on some *parts* of many older moral questions. The moral issues surrounding the development of weaponry are thus a few of the very many possible examples of how an older moral question can take on a new light as technology changes.

Issues of privacy, it may be said, are of relevance to weaponry: after all, being killed violates privacy. However, the violation of privacy is hardly at the heart of what is wrong with being killed. If I were to protest against a war on the grounds that it violated the privacy of its victims, people would think that I had my priorities wrong.

Similarly, accuracy of information systems may be of relevance in weapons systems, because inaccurate data or processing may cause the wrong target to be hit, but the question of whether the system should exist at all is prior to the question about how to get it to do what is intended with a degree of reliability.

The property issues raised by the production, existence, and use of weaponry are important, but they are not the issues of intellectual property and ownership of networks that Mason (1986, pp. 9–10) is interested in. Moreover, again, the property issues raised are not normally considered to be the crucial moral issues to do with weaponry, which are focused around the lives that may be lost in any use of the weaponry, rather than the property destroyed. Of course, it can be argued that the existence of weaponry that is not used can protect property, including intellectual property; however, the possibility that it might be used, destroying life as well as property, *must* be factored into the considerations in a very substantial way.

As with privacy, issues of access to information are of some relevance to consideration of weaponry, but to protest against killing because it will have the consequence of denying the victims access to information is absurdly wrong-headed.

The possibility that weapons may kill is a substantial moral issue that must be considered in any appropriate consideration of weapons technology. All plausibly acceptable moral theories value life (at the very least in its adult human form), even if they can conceive of circumstances in which ending a life might be moral. Thus for all of these moral theories, the possibility that weapons systems might end lives is a morally significant fact, needing morally significant reasons to counter that prima facie objection to weapons.

It may be that, for some people, weapons technology may be justified, if the probability of its use is very low, and/or it will only be used in situations where the war it is used to fight would have been fought anyway using weapons that do even more damage to the things that are valuable in this world, such as life.

But those are very big "ifs," which ought to be considered in depth by anyone considering work on information technology that may have reasonably direct military application, and by those seeking to sell such technology to the military and those allied to the military, both domestically and abroad (and in doing so, they would do well to remember that there may be deception about end use by regimes that may be too willing to put the technology into action in a war).

The possible danger to life of weapons systems, and whether it might be increased or reduced by a new system being developed, is not addressed in any meaningful way by the PAPA issues.

Environmental Impacts

Similarly, there are good reasons for moral concern about the damage that can be done to the environment, and through it to people and animals living in the future (see Attfield 1991, for example), by the materials used in the manufacture of computers, and the consequences of their disposal. Pollution resultant from computer production includes volatile organic compounds, solvents, alkaline cleaning solutions, acids, chromium, oxidizers, carbon slurry, surfactants, phosphorous solutions, glass, alcohol, ammonia, aluminum, particulates, CFCs, nickel, silver, copper, lead, solder, and methyl bromide (classified as a category I acute toxin and another powerful ozone depleter, in addition to the CFCs) (Corporate Watch 1997).

Privacy and accuracy of computer data and information are issues essentially unrelated to the environmental impacts of computing. Property issues in computing will have two tangential relationships to the environment: the cost of software that respects legal intellectual property rights, being a significant portion of the cost of computing, tends to inhibit the increasing use of computers. But the possibility of a return on development costs induces software developers to produce software that requires computers with ever greater computing power, causing users to upgrade hardware far more frequently than wear-and-tear would require. Increasing access to computing would almost certainly need increased production of computers as a prerequisite, and thus increased environmental degradation. Simply considering the PAPA issues gives rise to an apparent call for environmental degradation.

By developing software and facilities that give people a reason to buy computer hardware, the computing and information industries may (often unwittingly) be encouraging others to commit acts that cause pollution (through the production of computers). To cause such pollution is morally reprehensible, in a way that means that moral benefits should come about from the existence of the computers and software, to avoid an overall moral harm. The development of software and facilities itself can have moral benefits greater than the moral harms caused (including through pollution): the development of teleworking technologies that enabled a redistribution of work, and thus wealth, more evenly across the globe would be one possible example.

Teleworking and Telecommuting

The PAPA issues include important ethical issues in teleworking (more frequently called telecommuting in the USA) and questions of privacy and access *are* among the most important moral issues of teleworking. Most of the moral issues related to teleworking are not, however, privacy or access issues. Those issues that are not privacy or access issues are not accuracy issues either, though: the distance between the worker and the conventional workplace does not introduce significant additional accuracy issues.

One of Mason's property issues (1986, p. 10), the issue of bandwidth and ownership of telecommunications networks, is a teleworking issue, as teleworkers rely on sufficient bandwidth to work, whereas on-site workers may be able to do the same job without using bandwidth. However, in the age of graphical interfaces on the Internet, the teleworker can easily be responsible for no more use of bandwidth than on-site workers using the Internet and if (against good employment practice) they have to pay their communications costs, they may well use less bandwidth.

The privacy issue that most clearly accompanies telework is the possible automated collection of data on the employee by the employer. With the unavailability of traditional "over the shoulder" management techniques, there is a temptation for bosses to use technology in an invasive manner to register, for instance, the number of keystrokes per minute which a teleworker makes. The alternative method of management by results is ethically more acceptable (see Fairweather 1999).

Access is an important telework issue because, in the absence of access to the technology, the possible personal advantages that may accrue to a teleworker will be denied. These advantages may include substantial cost and time savings, as commuting is no longer necessary, or the ability to do jobs for employers who would be otherwise be located too far away.

So, PAPA includes some of the important moral issues related to teleworking, but there are others that do not fit within the PAPA framework. Key moral issues of telework include issues of isolation and the moral impact of any changes in the location of work.

The possibility of isolation of employees has for some time been known to be a substantial moral disadvantage to telework. For many people, employment provides a major source of friendship and social contact (Union of Communication Workers 1992, p. 2). Sharing a common workplace also often enables workers to organize unions or employee associations that can negotiate with employers, rather than leave employees completely exposed to whatever bad management is inflicted on them.

Changes in the location of work can have moral consequences because travel to work uses up scarce resources and causes pollution. Telework may possibly lead to office buildings becoming empty, with the resources involved in their building being wasted (British Telecom 1996). If telework enables the worker and employer to be at a great distance, then telework can cause changes in the geographical distribution of wealth, including between continents, and thus could either exacerbate or ameliorate global inequality.

To consider the moral issues of telework without considering those issues that do not fit easily into the PAPA framework is to miss most of the important moral issues.

Protecting the Weak Against the Strong

According to Peter Davis (as quoted in Donaldson 1992, p. 255), one of the key questions to be asked about any moral code is "Does the code support the weak against the strong." All four of the PAPA issues can on occasion be related to protecting the weak against the strong, with access explicitly considering the position of the weak, while protection of property usually protects the *strong* against the weak. To a significant extent this is because having property is itself a type – and probably the most significant type – of strength in western societies and in the global economy. This effect is even stronger when considering computing property, where most of the claims of infringement of property rights are made by massive corporations against smaller businesses. Similarly, claims of a right to privacy (particularly about "commercially sensitive" information) can be used by businesses and "captains of industry" to hinder investigations into corruption and exploitation.

If the fourfold classification gives no indication of priorities, why should access, the aspect that gives greater priority to the position of the weak, take precedence over other issues? The PAPA formulation gives no guidance, and suggests no other considerations that could give guidance about priorities between various issues.

The net result of considering the four key issues for guidance on protecting the strong against the weak is to leave us in a worse position than where we started. As Davis puts it: "Some codes simply do not protect the weak against the strong. They should not be used to legitimate the powerful against the weak" (as quoted in Donaldson 1992, p. 264). PAPA could easily be "used" to legitimate the powerful against the weak, and although it is to some extent equivocal on this, we are left in a worse position than if no advice was given, in part because contradictory advice is very often less helpful than no advice at all.

The Importance of the PAPA Issues

There can be no doubt that there are good reasons for moral consideration of the PAPA issues of privacy, accuracy, property, and accessibility. Immorality in those areas *can* be of such great significance as to destroy some lives, as Mason illustrates:

> Invasions of privacy could enable criminals to build up a profile of where certain people live, and work. Matching data sets in this way could enable the criminals to tell which houses will remain unoccupied during the working day, and thus could be burgled with little chance of detection.

Inaccurate data can lead to denials of credit that prevent participation in mainstream society in the developed world, or worse, to false arrest on very serious charges.

Failure to deal with the property issue of the allocation of bandwidth could prevent safety-critical information such as weather forecasts being received.

Inequalities in access to computing could exacerbate poverty in currently impoverished countries, contributing to an increased number of deaths from starvation. (1986, p. 8)

However, it is implausible that anyone who is seriously worried about the moral consequences of computing would say that the four PAPA issues cover the full range of issues that need consideration: I would not for one moment suggest that is what Mason (1986) was intending to do. To summarize one of my examples in the terminology of computing, weaponry is a safety-critical system, and, as always for safety-critical systems, the safety issue should be given great prominence. I am sure Mason would agree that safety should be given great prominence when considering safety-critical systems, even if PAPA fails to mention it. This chapter is not about criticizing Mason and PAPA *in particular*, but the trap that *many* considerations of a limited range of ethical issues fall into, which Mason's PAPA formulation exemplifies. Other codes of ethics that could give rise to the same fundamental criticism include that of the American Society for Information Systems (1997), or that of the Japan Information Service Industry Association (1993).

Focusing on four areas gives the impression that adherence to the moral requirements in those four areas alone will be enough to ensure moral rectitude. This is far from the case.

The Pressures to Look for Loopholes in Codes

There is a widespread perception that all those involved in businesses pay no heed to morality, and this applies as much to those in the computer and information industries as to those in other industries. Sometimes it is true that people seeking to make a profit, to retain their job, or to keep their business afloat will be guilty of gross immorality.

Often, however, such people in business are very aware of morality and moral obligations. Behavior that seems to critics to be immoral may in fact have a moral motivation: those in business are often aware that they have obligations to shareholders and to others working for the business, and they are also often aware that they have an obligation to members of their family to earn enough income to live on. Such obligations to those immediately around the worker may seem, with a good deal of justification, to be very pressing; it is not surprising if obligations to those less closely connected to the business seem very unimportant by comparison, and get ignored.

The pressures in the commercial world include pressures to meet deadlines – perhaps reinforced by penalty clauses in contracts. This may induce software professionals to claim that a program is ready for the customer by the deadline, when they know that more testing is needed, for instance. The immediate obligations to fellow workers, family, shareholders, etc. may seem much more pressing than the obligation to unknown users of the software – especially when all the tests that have been done seem to give good results. Another common pressure in the commercial world comes from sales targets and pay schemes largely based around commission: in such cases a sales-worker may feel moral obligations to support a family *so keenly* that obligations such as not lying about a system's capabilities seem abstract and unrelated to the real world.

Pressures that work against morally ideal behavior can also be non-financial. One of the greatest pressures on those working as part of a team is the psychological need to fit in; this may lead to participation in the bullying of a member of a minority on the workforce. In other circumstances, deference to superiors can cause problems with moral relevance; where there are clear hierarchies, those in a subordinate role may feel pressure to suppress bad news, or not criticize superiors.[1] These various influences may lead to people committing acts that they personally feel uneasy about.

Equally, it has been known for people to act in ways that others will see as immoral simply out of selfishness, even if the number of such cases is easy to overestimate. Whatever the background, individuals may well be aware that the acts they are about to perform do not meet standards that society will consider to be appropriate for moral behavior. An individual may, nonetheless, feel impelled to act in the way that society will judge immoral by the more immediate pressures. The psychological pressure of this conflict may cause individuals to cast around to find ways to "excuse" their behavior.

In such circumstances, finding what looks like a moral code that *does not condemn* the course of action in question can come as a great relief. Our individual may reason that "the experts who wrote the ethical code know better than the public (or even me) what is right and wrong": or alternatively "the experts understand the pressures on me better than the public." If the "experts" who produced this moral guidance relevant to my field do not condemn what others (and perhaps my own conscience) would condemn, surely I should bow to their expertise.

---

[1]   The most dramatic examples come not from the computing field, but from aviation, where research has linked Australian airlines' good accident record with a greater tendency to insubordination in Australian culture (Independent Radio News 1997).

"What a relief," our individual may think, "I had misgivings, but *look*, it is all right after all!" Meanwhile the "experts" who developed a small piece of moral guidance may be horrified to find that it is being used to excuse behavior that was never meant to be covered by the guidance, simply because it does not mention it at all. I suspect the authors of the IMIS code of conduct would be a little disturbed to find that in a recent survey, 22 percent of the IMIS members who responded agreed that "Employers are entitled to use electronic surveillance to monitor employee's performance without their consent."[2]

Of course, if the pressures to "cut moral corners" are great, then an individual may do so whether or not a code of ethics can be found that fails to condemn her intended acts. The presence or absence of an ethical code *alone* is most unlikely to influence any behavior. Those who write professional codes hope that the code will have an educative function, will tend to push the climate of opinion towards moral behavior and will provide support for those who wish to act in a moral way against those who create a climate of "getting the job done" no matter what immorality that implies. These hopes of those who write professional codes are limited and do not extend as far as stopping the reader from committing an immoral act that they are already committed to.

Similarly, a person finding a "justification" for immorality in an incomplete ethical code may, if denied *that* source of "justification," find "justification" elsewhere: but this is no reason to make the "justification" any more available than it needs to be. Our individual still has ultimate responsibility for her own acts, but authors of ethical codes must also be aware that they may be abused.

Incomplete Moral Codes

Any moral code (whether in computing or elsewhere) can be turned to by someone feeling under pressure to find a relatively easy "way out" of a morally tricky situation. Thus, any moral code could be looked at in the hope that it will provide an excuse for potential immoral acts. Clearly, the more obviously relevant, and the more easily a code comes to hand, the more likely it is that it will be turned to. Further, as we shall see, some ethical codes are more open to such abuse than others are. Nonetheless, moral codes in all fields and sub-fields could be abused in this way if they leave themselves open to it.

It is important for ethical debate to be structured, and in some circumstances such debate will need the enunciation of particular principles or

---

[2] Reanalysis of data collected for Prior et al. 1999. My thanks go to Matt Rowe for the reanalysis.

guidelines for application in particular circumstances. These principles or guidelines may quite clearly not be a complete moral code to those that are taking part in the debate: they may be focused on only one type of issue in very restricted circumstances, for example.

It is quite reasonable to read Mason's PAPA formulation in precisely this way. The problem is that PAPA has been picked up by others in a way that may in turn lead to some people believing consideration of privacy, accuracy, property, and access to be sufficient moral consideration in the field of information technology. Even if Mason's formulation *was*, on the contrary, intended to be a (partial) moral code, there is often the potential for what is intended to be private debate becoming more public and being misinterpreted as an ethical code (albeit a woefully incomplete one).

Similarly, I have to wonder whether the "Ten Commandments of Computer Ethics" were intended as a starting point for thought and a contribution to debate. Whatever the intentions behind them, they are extremely widely quoted (see AltaVista 2000, for example), and often in contexts where they appears to constitute the whole story about computer ethics; yet it is very clear to even undergraduate students with only a little familiarity with computer ethics that these "Ten Commandments" cannot be the whole story.

Another widely quoted "short code" is the list of "fair information principles," dealing with issues of access, collection, use, and storage of personal data (see Kluge 1994, p. 336, for example). Again, while they are generally useful, there are obvious problems with these "principles" in a variety of cases, including, in a medical context, "where the welfare or life of a patient is at stake but no informed patient consent to a breach of confidentiality is possible" (ibid., p. 340).

Whenever consideration of a selection of moral issues is structured around particular suggested principles or guidelines for application in particular circumstances, there is a danger that they may come to be misinterpreted as a moral code. This remains true whatever the intentions of the author.

Equally, it is sensible for moral codes to focus on issues where moral consideration is likely to have the greatest importance. In doing so, moral codes can highlight important issues to great benefit. However, if they allow (however unintentionally) the impression that moral consideration of other issues is not needed, they leave open the possibility of some gross immorality regarding some other issue (or combination of issues) being tacitly accepted by the moral code.

This is particularly likely if, at the time of writing, the focused code assumes that a certain moral or factual basis is prevalent in society. Thus authors of codes of business ethics written at a time of full employment may have considered it to be grossly immoral to make conscientious workers redundant without compensation. But such a possibility would have been considered so implausible that it was not worth including. Now such a possibility *is* plausible, yet not explicitly condemned by codes of business ethics.

Authors of incomplete moral codes risk encouraging others to act in immoral ways with the author's *apparent* sanction.

Complete Moral Codes?

Now comes the question: what constitutes a complete moral code? There must be an obligation on the author of any ethical code, or any other writing that can foreseeably be (mis?)interpreted as an ethical code, to write it so that it covers as many circumstances and issues within its area of competence as possible.

However, an author cannot think through all possible circumstances when writing a code, because the world changes. Moreover, there will inevitably be the boundary questions: what is the edge of the area of competence? – and what should the code say about how to behave beyond that boundary?

Codes should make it clear what their area of competence is (thus a code of computer ethics may make it clear that it will not cover questions of how income generated by using computers should be distributed) but in doing so, it must also make it clear that moral issues outside its area of competence *are* still moral issues, and ones that may be of greater importance than any covered in the code. It is no surprise that Kluge (1994, p. 340) points out that "there is no guarantee that the 'fair information principles' themselves are complete" precisely because of the question of the boundary of their applicability.

Kluge recommends (ibid.) that the best way to develop codes is first "to identify the fundamental ethical principles . . . then identify types of situations that are likely to occur . . . and then derive the rules of behavior . . . by interpreting the principles in the light of the situational requirements." According to Kluge, this method "has the advantage of making it clear from the outset that even though a particular area or type of situation may not currently be covered by a specific rule in an explicit fashion, the general principles themselves still do apply" (ibid.). The logic is impeccable, and the problem of incompleteness is avoided. There is, however, a gaping problem with Kluge's approach.

Attempting to derive a code of ethics, or any similar kind of practical ethical guidance, from fundamental ethical principles is of little practical help, because there is often more dispute about fundamental ethical principles than there is about what the moral thing to do might be in a particular situation. An attempt to derive a code of ethics from a single, coherent basis in fundamental ethical principles will also leave the code open to easy criticism by anyone who has read, or had reported to them the thrust of, one of the huge numbers of texts outlining the difficulties of each particular type of attempt to derive fundamental ethical principles. This sort of criticism mirrors my concerns about how some incomplete codes may fall into disrepute in the face of argument (Fairweather 2000).

To avoid the criticism of incompleteness, it is not necessary for a code to be derived from a consistent set of fundamental ethical principles. Any code that makes absolutely plain that following it is no substitute for careful moral consideration of the individual's actions, and especially in areas or on questions where there is no clear guidance in the code, while not really a complete moral code, avoids the criticism that can be leveled at incomplete codes. Thus the Canadian Information Processing Society's "Code of Ethics and Standards of Conduct" (1996) states that "It should not be construed to deny the existence of other ethical or legal obligations equally imperative, although not specifically mentioned" and the ACM/IEEE-CS joint "Software Engineering Code of Ethics and Professional Practice" (Gotterbarn et al. 1998) says in its preamble that "It is not intended that the individual parts of the Code be used in isolation to justify errors of omission or commission" and that "The list of Principles and Clauses is not exhaustive," before giving some hints for the basis of moral consideration when the code does not provide the answer.

Avoiding Accidental Incomplete "Moral Codes"

Thus we are beginning to come towards an answer to the question that has been implicit in this discussion. "How can discussion of particular issues in the application of morality to the real world be achieved without incomplete moral codes?"

Discussing issues one at a time will tend to guard against the possibility that a consideration of a number together will be mistaken for a moral code, although even in these circumstances it may be a good idea to acknowledge the existence of other, potentially more important, moral issues that are not being discussed. This becomes more important if the circumstances or nature of the moral issues are such that a number *need* to be taken together.

Conclusion

Those who write moral codes (or things that could be mistaken for them) need to be aware of the possibility that they may be abused. Codes that address some issues but not others are very common, and particularly open to such abuse on issues at the edge of their competence. Codes should make it clear what their area of competence is. More importantly, though, authors of codes should always make it clear that their code is no substitute for careful moral consideration, especially in areas or on questions where there is no clear guidance in the code.

References

AltaVista (2000). "Web Results." http://www.altavista.com/cgi-bin/query?sc=on&q=%22commandments+of+computer+ethics%22&kl=XX&pg=q&search.x=35&search.y=7 accessed Jan 6, 2000.

American Society for Information Systems (1997). "Code Of Ethics." http://csep.iit.edu/codes/coe/ASIS_Code.htm accessed Jan 5, 2000.

Association for Computing Machinery (1992). "Code of Ethics and Professional Conduct." In *Communications of the ACM* 35(5), pp. 94–9 The code is at http://www.acm.org/constitution/bylaw17.txt and http://www.ccsr.cse.dmu.ac.uk/resources/professionalism/codes/acm.html both accessed Jan 6, 2000.

Attfield, R. (1991). *The Ethics of Environmental Concern*, 2nd edn. University of Georgia Press.

Barrosso Asenjo, P. (1996). "El PAPA de la Ética de Internet." In P. Barrosso Asenjo et al. (eds.), ETHICOMP96: *Ética y Computadores, III International Conference, Proceedings, Volume 1*. Madrid: Facultad de Ciencas de la Información, Universidad Complutense de Madrid.

Bissett, A. (1996). "Computing Professionals and the 'Peace Dividend', or one Bomb is as Good as Another." In P. Barrosso Asenjo et al. (eds.), ETHICOMP96: *Ética y Computadores, III International Conference, Proceedings, Volume 1*. Madrid: Facultad de Ciencas de la Información, Universidad Complutense de Madrid.

British Telecom (1996). "The Environmental Impact of Teleworking." Research paper at http://www.bt.com/corpinfo/enviro/telework.htm accessed Jan 14, 1997 and Jan 12, 2000.

Canadian Information Processing Society (1996). "Code of Ethics and Standards of Conduct." At http://www.cips.ca/membership/ethics.htm accessed Jan 6, 2000.

Computer Ethics Institute (undated). "Ten Commandments of Computer Ethics." http://www.ccsr.cse.dmu.ac.uk/resources/professionalism/codes/cei_command.html accessed Dec 17, 1999.

Corporate Watch (1997). "The High Cost of High Tech." Online at http://www.corpwatch.org/trac/feature/hitech/computer.html and linked pages accessed May 29, 1997 and Jan 14, 2000.

Donaldson, J. (1992). *Business Ethics: A European Casebook: Principles, Examples, Cases, Codes.* With contributions from Peter Davis, David Huddy, Dirk Lindenbergh, Diana Robertson, and Rob van Es. Academic Press.

Fairweather, N. B. (1999). "Surveillance in Employment: The case of Teleworking." *Journal of Business Ethics*, 22: 39–49; previously presented at ETHICOMP98, Erasmus University Rotterdam, March 25–7, 1998.

Fairweather, N. B. (2000). "Commentary on the 'Ten Commandments for Computer Ethics.'" http://www.ccsr.cse.dmu.ac.uk/resources/professionalism/codes/cei_command_com.html accessed Jan 14, 2000.

Gotterbarn, D. et al. (1998). "Software Engineering Code of Ethics and Professional Practice." http://computer.org/tab/seprof/code.htm accessed Jan 6, 2000.

Independent Radio News (1997). Bulletin broadcast, Jan 13, 1997, by independent local radio stations across the UK.

Japan Information Service Industry Association (1993). "Code of Ethics and Professional Conduct." English Translation http://csep.iit.edu/codes/coe/Japan_Code.htm accessed Jan 5, 2000.

Kluge, E-H. W. (1994). "Health Information, the Fair Information Principles and Ethics." *Methods of Information in Medicine*, 33: 336–45.

Mason, R. O. (1986). "Four Ethical Issues of the Information Age." *MIS Quarterly* 10/1: 5–12.

Platt, R. and Morrison, B. (1995). "Ethical and Social Implications of the Internet." In S. Rogerson and T. W. Bynum (eds.), *ETHICOMP95: An International Conference on the Ethical Issues of Using Information Technology, Proceedings*, 2 vols. De Montfort University, School of Computing Sciences, vol. 1.

Prior, M., Rogerson, S., Fairweather, N. B., Butler, L., and Dixon, S. (1999). *Is IT Ethical? 1998 ETHICOMP Survey of Professional Practice*. Institute for the Management of Information Systems.

Timpka, T. (1999). "Professional Ethics for System Developers in Health Care." *Methods of Information in Medicine*, 38/2: 144–7.

Union of Communication Workers (1992). Pamphlet: *The Teleworking Directory Enquiry Experiment at Inverness*. Union of Communication Workers.

Whitman, M. E., Townsend, A. M., Hendrickson, A. R., and Rensvold, R. B. (1998). "Computer Aversion and Computer-use Ethics in US and Asian Cultures." *Journal of Computer Information Systems*, 38/4: 19–24.

Basic study questions

1. What does the acronym PAPA mean in this article?
2. What, according to Fairweather, is the primary danger or problem with using PAPA to identify ethical issues associated with computing technology?
3. What, according to Fairweather, is the primary moral issue associated with weaponry? Do the ethical questions primarily associated with PAPA directly address this key weaponry issue? Explain.
4. How, according to Fairweather, does focusing primarily upon the PAPA ethical issues actually threaten to do serious environmental harm to the world and thus to the people and animals living in the world?
5. Which important moral issues associated with teleworking and telecommuting are significantly addressed by the PAPA framework? Which important ones are *not* seriously addressed using PAPA?
6. How, according to Fairweather, does focusing upon the PAPA moral issues "leave us in a worse position" with regard to protecting the weak against the strong?

7. Even though the PAPA moral issues are important, there is great danger, according to the author, in focusing primarily upon them when doing computer ethics. Explain what he means.

8. According to Fairweather, various "pressures" in one's everyday life can cause people to behave in ways that seem immoral to others. Describe in detail at least three examples of such "pressures," including financial ones and non-financial ones.

9. According to Fairweather, moral codes can actually be used by people experiencing the "pressures" described in question 8 above to justify *immoral* behavior. Explain how this "abuse" of moral codes can happen. Discuss, in particular, the notion of an "incomplete" moral code.

10. If "incomplete" moral codes can lead to immorality, how can authors of moral codes make certain to create "complete" ones? Explain, in detail, the author's advice regarding this important challenge.

Questions for further thought

1. How are everyday moral ideas, such as helping one's neighbor or doing no harm, related to professional moral codes like those of the British Computer Society (BCS) or the Association for Computing Machinery (ACM)?

2. What is the proper relationship between professional moral codes and the law? For example, should computer professionals adjust their moral codes to take account of government regulations and if so how?

3. How might moral codes be used to reduce the risk of software failure? How are such codes useful retrospectively?

CHAPTER 8

On Licensing Computer Professionals

Donald Gotterbarn

The licensing of computer professionals is a very controversial and political question. Licensing generally means that to claim to practice a certain profession requires a government license, often administered through a professional organization. The general theory is that the licensing process is supposed to help those outside of the licensed profession to judge if someone else is capable of doing certain jobs. Licensing isn't currently required for computer professionals.

The licensing of computing professionals is a complex issue and needs to be clearly discussed. Several reactions to the mention of this topic have only served to confuse the issues. Those opposed to licensing raise issues of freezing technology, limiting research, causing loss of jobs, and unreasonable government interference in the practice of a trade; while those in favor of licensing go to the opposite extreme and talk about licensing as a cure-all for the ills surrounding computing and human interaction with the products of computing. The extremes of both of these positions obfuscate the underlying issues and possibilities of licensing. This chapter develops a broad model of licensing which addresses most of the distracting issues raised by the opponents of licensing, but at the same time it is not founded on the extreme optimism of those who view licensing as a cure-all. Given a level playing field of a viable model of licensing which addresses both the major problems with and the major goals of licensing, a discussion of the real issues should be possible.

Portions of this article were previously published in Joseph M. Kizza (ed.), *The Social and Ethical Effects of the Computer Revolution*. McFarland and Company Inc., 1996. © 2001 by Donald Gotterbarn and reprinted by permission of the author.

Reasons for Current Interest

The current interest in licensing computer professionals comes from a variety of sources. The public has become aware of the impact of computers on their lives and has come to realize that good computing not only impacts on the quality of their lives, it also daily affects their safety. They have been made aware of systems that show the marks of incompetent design, design with malicious intent, and design with fraudulent intent. Licensing is conceived by many as an attempt to control all of these problems. Licensing should not be viewed as an attempt to fully resolve these issues. This overly optimistic view of the effects of licensing has lead to specious arguments against the process of licensing computer professionals. Several of these arguments are considered below.

First, if it is correct to say that licensing is not a cure-all, then why should we be interested in licensing? I argue here that there is a model of licensing which partially addresses these problems and might ameliorate some concerns. Furthermore, establishing a licensing standard will help establish computing as a profession. Those opposed to licensing argue that a movement toward professionalism is a self-serving excuse to justify charging more for providing computer services. This argument ignores some ethically significant aspects of professionalism. Software development already bears important marks of being a profession, viz., computing professionals have a specialized skill which directly impacts the quality and safety of the public.[1] Practice of this profession requires extraordinary trust by the public and justifies a heightened standard of care. The professionalization of computing would make clear the computing professional's responsibility to the public. An example of this is in the Software Engineering Code of Ethics, which gives the following guidance for making an ethical decision:

> These Principles should influence software engineers to consider broadly who is affected by their work; to examine if they and their colleagues are treating other human beings with due respect; to consider how the public, if reasonably well informed, would view their decisions; to analyze how the least empowered will be affected by their decisions; and to consider whether their acts would be judged worthy of the ideal professional working as a software engineer. In all these judgments concern for the health, safety and welfare of the public is primary; that is, the "Public Interest" is central to this Code. (Software Engineering Code of Ethics, Preamble)

---

[1]   In the US, two professional organizations, the Association for Computing Machinery and the IEEE Computer Society, have been working to further the professional standards of software development. They have jointly approved The Software Engineering Code of Ethics and Professional Practice. The IEEE Computer Society has established a standard for certifying software developers which requires 9,000 hours of experience in the field, demonstration of technical knowledge by examination, and adherence to the Software Engineering Code of Ethics.

The discipline of software development has advanced significantly and the public should be assured that the computing professional has knowledge of the best and safest way to develop computing systems. The possession of a computing license is no assurance that a person with this knowledge will not engage in malicious or fraudulent activity, just as being a licensed physician is no guarantee that a physician will avoid malicious or fraudulent activity.

The professionalization of medicine provides at least two forces which discourage such malicious or fraudulent behavior; viz., a code of ethics and professional standards of practice. The physician subscribes to a code of ethics which characterizes the primary obligation of the physician and the purpose of the practice of medicine as the care of the patient. The professionalization of computing would strengthen the concept that computer software has only one function – to perform some service for a client or customer. Recent computing codes of ethics – for example, the ACM/IEEE-CS Software Engineering Code of Ethics and Professional Practice 1999 – have characterized the development of computer software as a service requiring heightened care for the customer. Principle 1.04 of the Software Engineering Code, for example, states: "Disclose to appropriate persons or authorities any actual or potential danger to the user, the public, or the environment, that they reasonably believe to be associated with software or related documents."

Professionalization incorporates both a code of ethics and a set of professional standards. A physician, for example, is encouraged to follow the standards of the medical profession and its code of ethics because failure to do so will lead to revocation of the license to practice. If computer professionals were licensed, they could be encouraged in the same way to follow professional standards. In neither case is it claimed that licensing makes a person competent or ethical. But licensing does make it more likely that a practitioner has knowledge of the discipline's best practices and has some social pressure to "do the right thing."

Without licensing there is no requirement for heightened care and no concept of professional malpractice. In several cases, for example, malpractice suits against software developers have been overturned because they lacked the marks of professionals. In one such case, software development was characterized as "simply a business upon which the public does not particularly entrust its care" (Hospital Computer Systems, Inc. v. Staten Island Hospital, 788 F. Supp. 1351 (D.N.J. 1992)).

Both inside and outside of the profession it is recognized that software development has achieved a certain degree of maturity and that maturity implies both responsibility and accountability. Computing is no longer merely information processing. The software we develop, for example, controls the temperature inside of incubators which directly affects the life or death of infants. A cardiac patient should be able to expect a pacemaker that works. Computing's increased involvement in everyday life requires a heightened sense of both accountability and responsibility.

Negative Reactions

Any discussion of licensing computer professionals generates two types of criticism from software developers: a criticism of the very concept of licensing and a criticism of potential implementations of licensing. Many of these criticisms, however, are misdirected.

Objections to the concept of licensing

Programming is an art and is entitled to the protection of free speech Some have argued that the state has no right to restrict their programming efforts. They believe in "freedom of speech in programming." This view seems to ignore questions of responsibility to users of computing's products. It is true that "freedom of speech," defined as uncontrolled and undisciplined development of software used by the public, would be limited by licensing; but it does not seem to be a bad thing to introduce discipline into the development and testing of software that affects the public. It is not certain whether a program used to control the temperature in an incubator was the product of "free speech or the exercise of an art;" but it is certain that the use of known testing techniques would have discovered the bug in the incubator temperature control software that was responsible for the loss of two children's lives. A similar argument that we should not license a physician because it would prevent "free speech" during a heart transplant seems absurd.

Licensing is just another way to raise taxes Some have argued that "licensing is merely a revenue enhancer or a gimmick by states to make more money." Even if states use licenses or licensing to raise revenues, it does not mean that we ought to eliminate licensing electricians because the state also makes money from it. If the only purpose of licensing were to generate new taxes, then it should be opposed. But there appear to be other good reasons for licensing software professionals.

You can't license a practice that has no standards of practice Two related objections are (1) software development is not yet a fully matured disciple, so there can be no standard of licensing, and (2) licensing will freeze software technology in its immature state.[2] The absence of maturity is a strange standard. Teenage children are not yet fully mature – they don't know all the

---

[2]   Both of these arguments have been offered recently by members of a special committee of the ACM when they recommended that the ACM "withdraw from efforts that promote licensing." http://www.acm.org/serving/se_policy/

right answers – but they are expected to be responsible for those things which they already know. The science of software development is not yet a complete or static body of knowledge. This should not exonerate a software practitioner from following those testing and design principles that are already known. No one would say that because medicine is not a completed science we should not practice the best medicine we can and that we should not hold the medical practitioner responsible for knowing and practicing this "best medicine."

Licensing does not guarantee competence will be applied   Some objections claim that licensing is no guarantee of applied competence. This is correct, but it focuses on the wrong side of the question. The absence of licensing means that we have no way of knowing whether the developer has any knowledge of the current best practices. Licensing will only provide assurances that the developer knows the best practice; and, as stated above, there are other pressures to encourage them to follow these practices.

Pressures of business, such as schedule and budget, override "good practice"   At present, the pressures of budget and schedule are too strong to guarantee that the best practices will be followed. There are no counter-pressures to resist the development of shoddy software justified by budget and schedule pressures. The introduction of licensing, however, would introduce significant counter-pressures. Licensed professionals would put their licenses at risk if they did not follow best practices. Licensing would also introduce the legal pressure of malpractice suits directed at licensees and their employers.

Licensing will establish a software monopoly   This objection would be correct only if a license were universally required to do any software development. Licensing could be required for certain areas of software development, like the avionics systems in airplanes, and optional in other areas. It would limit access to some areas of practice, but that seems better than having life-critical software being developed by practitioners of undetermined skill.

Implementation of licensing

Licensing is sometimes opposed on the quite reasonable grounds that state legislatures do not adequately understand software development. If state legislatures developed licensing standards, then we would all be in difficulty. But most state legislatures would agree with this claim, and that is why standards for licensing are generally established by appropriate professional organizations or by state legislatures working with professional organizations or licensed professionals, as was the case when Texas established licensing for software engineers. The state's responsibility, typically, is merely to administer a test to determine if the professionally established standards have been met and enforce the legal standards associated with licensing. States also charge for this service.

A Model for Licensing Computer Professionals

Many of the objections cited above would be appropriate for some models of licensing, but I believe there is at least one model for licensing software professionals that meets most of the significant objections raised. I propose a model for licensing computer professionals in which there is a national standard supported by computing professionals and implemented by state governments modeled on professional engineer's and paramedic's licensing standards. It would consist of:

1   *A commitment to a body of knowledge – a four-year degree*   This would assure that practitioners would have at least come into contact with current best practices.

2   *A commitment to re-education – a license would expire every five years*   A paramedic's certification expires every two years, and he or she must be re-tested on relevant new medical practices that have been developed. The same principle should apply to computing professionals. Using database design practices of 20 years ago, for example, does not produce the best computing system. This principle contains no specification of how a practitioner must acquire the new knowledge. Before being re-tested, a practitioner would be informed of the new areas to be covered. This emphasis on re-education would completely meet the concern that licensing would freeze technology. Licensing would have the opposite effect: it would require that all licensed practitioners keep up with changing technology.

3   *The skill content would be determined by computer practitioners*   The IEEE and the ACM have done this for undergraduate computer science education by establishing a common curriculum; the IEEE Computer Society has recently published The Software Engineering Body of Knowledge,[3] which specifies ten "knowledge areas" for software developers. In addition, the military and other countries already have skills tests that can be helpful.

---

[3]   *Guide to the Software Engineering Body of Knowledge – SWEBOK*, executive editors: Alain Abran and James W. Moore; editors: Pierre Bourque and Robert Dupuis. Sponsored by the IEEE Computer Society, Computer Society Press, 2001.

4   *Different levels of licensing would be based on skills and areas of competence*
    Paramedics, depending on their competence and training, are certified to
    administer different levels of care to patients. Similarly, computer practi-
    tioners should only undertake tasks that they are competent to complete.
    (This is consistent with the Software Engineering Code – see principle
    2.01: "Provide service in their areas of competence, being honest and
    forthright about any limitations of their experience and education.")

5   *A commitment to the ability to apply theoretical knowledge – three years*
    working with another licensed computer professional   Software develop-
    ment is not a purely theoretical discipline. Competence is gained and
    shown by applying the theories one has learned. This apprenticeship
    requirement is similar to that of CPA's. This standard is less than the
    current 9,000 hours – approximately five years – required by the IEEE
    Computer Society standard. (See the web site http://Computer.ORG/
    Certification.)

6   *A commitment to follow recognized standards – sanctions for violations of the*
    best practices and violations of codes of ethics   This clearly introduces a
    counter pressure for any pressure to develop shoddy products. This pres-
    sure was clearly seen when the Software Engineering Code was used as a
    reference document in a legal case against software developers.

This model of licensing meets the objections cited earlier and provides a basis
for further discussions.

Basic study questions

1. Why, according to Gotterbarn, has the public become interested in the issue of
    licensing computer professionals?
2. According to Gotterbarn, why is it a mistake to view the licensing of computer
    professionals as a cure-all for incompetent, malicious, and fraudulent com-
    puter design?
3. Why, according to Gotterbarn, should computing be viewed as a profession?
4. What is the "free speech" objection to licensing computer professionals, and
    what is Gotterbarn's counter-argument against this objection?
5. What is the "tax-raising" objection to licensing computer professionals, and
    what is Gotterbarn's counter-argument against this objection?
6. What is the "computing is immature" objection to licensing computer profes-
    sionals, and what is Gotterbarn's counter-argument against this objection?
7. What is the "no guarantee of competence" objection to licensing com-
    puter professionals, and what is Gotterbarn's counter-argument against this
    objection?
8. What is the "pressures of budget and schedule" objection to licensing com-
    puter professionals, and what is Gotterbarn's counter-argument against this
    objection?

9.   What is the "monopoly" objection to licensing computer professionals, and what is Gotterbarn's counter-argument against this objection?

10.   What is the "legislators are not competent in computing" objection to licensing computer professionals, and what is Gotterbarn's counter-argument against this objection?

11.   Describe the six major components of Gotterbarn's proposed model for licensing computer professionals. How does this model deal with the objections described in questions 4 to 10 above?

Questions for further thought

1.   Doctors, dentists, lawyers, and public school teachers all need a license or state certification to practice their profession. Are computer practitioners similar enough to these professionals that they should be required to have a license too? Explain you answer in detail.

2.   Does Gotterbarn's model for licensing computer professionals include all of the components that it should have? Would you add anything? – change anything? Explain why.

CASE TO ANALYZE: THE CHEMCO CASE

This is a case about computer professionals' wider obligations to the communities in which they work and live. Codes of ethics can help to understand the nature of these obligations and reduce the risk of disasters occurring, such as the one at Chemco. This thought-provoking case, although it did not actually happen, is similar to real cases that did occur. The reader is invited to analyze it using the case-analysis method presented in chapter 3 above.

Chemco is a major producer of chemical compounds used by most manufacturing industries across the world. It has several plants around the country usually located in sparsely populated regions. The exception to this is the newest plant which is located in a major city in the middle of the country. This was opened 18 months ago and seen as the flagship plant using the latest chemical engineering techniques and heavily dependant on computer systems throughout production management. During the normal consultation process, the local community had expressed concerns about having such a plant within a densely populated region but had been reassured by the planned use of advanced technology to control the plant's operations.

Managers of the new plant were encouraged to seek innovative ways in which to reduce the overhead costs of the plant. The use of latest computer technology and software advances was seen as a key component of this innovative approach. The systems development team would focus on using expert system software based on either neural nets or fuzzy logic to automate the production runs and so increase throughput while reducing existing accepted numbers of production workers. There would be a significant increase in computer-controlled production. It was felt that the front-end input systems for triggering production were tried and tested in existing plants and that all that was needed to realize operational cost savings was to substitute the production control and monitoring subsystems which required significant production worker intervention with the new "intelligent" subsystems.

There would be virtually no operator involvement once the production process was started until the reaction was complete and the chemical compounds were being channeled into the distribution holding tanks. Operators would also have an important role to play in keeping the plant clean, ensuring that residues and waste were correctly disposed of. This cleaning-up process was not automated other than the computer-controlled valves which directed residue and waste away from the open drains. At other plants production workers had suggested that this clean-up phase could be linked automatically to the production phase ensuring a smoother production cycle. Management had rejected this idea on the basis of cost.

The computer specialists and production managers agreed upon a strategy and worked together to develop the new system. The system was tested using new sophisticated simulation software. It passed all tests, which included normal as well as abnormal running situations. The company looked forward to the new plant operating at a new level of efficiency. Following typical minor problems during the commissioning stage, the system had performed well during the first 18 months. Operating costs were well below the average for Chemco and throughput had been increased by 12 percent.

It was the night shift at Chemco's newest plant. As usual, the experienced laboratory worker activated the computer-based batch process input procedure to start the next chemical production. He inadvertently keyed in "tank 593" rather than "tank 693," which introduced the wrong chemical into the production run. The computer system was not designed to capture automatically such errors other than having a data input correction facility if such an error occurred. This was the way the input subsystem worked in other Chemco plants. Experienced laboratory workers were able to double check the data and make adjustments as necessary.

On this occasion, in the new plant, the result was disastrous. The incorrect chemical resulted in a temperature rise in the reactor vat leading to a rupture and subsequent explosion. An administrator observing the error was unable to contact the production operator in time to prevent the accident. The operator did not have the facility to lower the rise in temperature and the new subsystem did not cover this aspect of the production process. The operator summoned the plant's fire brigade. Members of the fire brigade underestimated the danger involved and were not wearing the prescribed safety equipment. They bore the brunt of the explosion. Three people died and nine were seriously injured. There was a wider problem as well. The chemicals spilling from the ruptured vat leaked into the local drainage system before the computer-controlled valves closed. Harmful chemicals contaminated water over a 3-mile radius from the plant.

Chemco's initial reaction to the disaster was to acknowledge the tragic outcome both for the employees and their families, as well as those living in close proximity to the plant. They were keen to stress that the accident had been caused by a series of human errors by Chemco workers on the night shift. The computer specialists, while generally upset about the disaster, felt relieved that the system they had developed and implemented was not seen as a cause of the accident. In the days immediately after the accident there were growing calls for a public inquiry.

ADDITIONAL READINGS AND WEB RESOURCES

Additional readings

Anderson, R. E. (1994). "The ACM Code of Ethics: History, Process, and Implications." In C. Huff and T. Finholt (eds.), *Social Issues in Computing*. McGraw Hill, pp. 48–71.

Gotterbarn, D. (1994). "Software Engineering Ethics." In J. J. Marciniak (ed.), *Encyclopedia of Software Engineering*, vol. 2. John Wiley, pp. 1197–201.

Gotterbarn, D. (1996). "Establishing Standards of Professional Practice." In T. Hall, D. Pitt, and C. Meyer (eds.), *The Responsible Software Engineer: Selected Readings in IT Professionalism*. Springer Verlag, ch. 3.

Gotterbarn, D. (2000). "Computer Professionals and Your Responsibilities: Virtual Information and the Software Engineering Code of Ethics." In D. Langford (ed.), *Internet Ethics*. Macmillan, pp. 200–19.

Rogerson, S., Weckert, J., and Simpson, C. (2000). "An Ethical Review of Information Systems Development: The Australian Computer Society's Code of Ethics and SSADM." *Information Technology and People*, 13/2: 121–36.

Web resources

ACM Position Papers on Software Engineering and Licensing, http://www.acm.org/serving/se_policy/papers.html

Codes of Ethics links on the web site of the Centre for Computing and Social Responsibility, http://www.ccsr.cse.dmu.ac.uk/resources/professionalism/codes/

Commentary on "The Ten Commandments of Computer Ethics," by N. Ben Fairweather, http://www.ccsr.cse.dmu.ac.uk/resources/professionalism/codes/cei_command_com.html

The Software Engineering Ethics Research Institute at East Tennessee State University at Johnson City, TN, USA, http://seeri.etsu.edu/

Appendix:
Example Codes of Ethics

Included here are six example codes of ethics for computer practitioners: the Software Engineering Code of Ethics and Professional Practice, the Association for Computing Machinery's Code of Ethics and Professional Conduct, the Australian Computer Society's Code of Ethics, the British Computer Society's Code of Conduct, the Institute of Electrical and Electronics Engineers Code of Ethics, the Institute for the Management of Information Systems Code of Ethics.

A1 THE SOFTWARE ENGINEERING CODE OF ETHICS AND PROFESSIONAL PRACTICE (VERSION 5.2)

IEEE-CS/ACM Joint Task Force on Software Engineering and Professional Practices*

ABSTRACT   The Software Engineering Code of Ethics and Professional Practice, intended as a standard for teaching and practicing software engineering, documents the ethical and professional obligations of software engineers. The code should instruct practitioners about the standards society expects them to meet, about what their peers strive for, and about what to expect of one another. In addition, the code should also inform the public about the responsibilities that are important to the profession.

Adopted in 1998 by the IEEE Computer Society and the ACM – two leading international computing societies – the code of ethics is intended as a guide for members of the evolving software engineering profession. The code was developed by a multinational task force with additional input from other professionals from industry, government posts, military installations, and educational professions.

Short version: preamble

The short version of the code summarizes aspirations at a high level of abstraction. The clauses that are included in the full version give examples and details of how these aspirations change the way we act as software engineering professionals. Without the aspirations, the details can become legalistic and tedious; without the details, the aspirations can become high-sounding but empty; together, the aspirations and the details form a cohesive code.

*   *About the Joint Task Force*: This Code of Ethics was developed by the IEEE-CS/ACM Joint Task Force on Software Engineering Ethics and Professional Practices. Members are *Executive Committee*: Donald Gotterbarn (Chair), Keith Miller, Simon Rogerson. *Members*: Steve Barber, Peter Barnes, Ilene Burnstein, Michael Davis, Amr El-Kadi, N. Ben Fairweather, Milton Fulghum, N. Jayaram, Tom Jewett, Mark Kanko, Ernie Kallman, Duncan Langford, Joyce Currie Little, Ed Mechler, Manuel J. Norman, Douglas Phillips, Peter Ron Prinzivalli, Patrick Sullivan, John Weckert, Vivian Weil, S. Weisband, Laurie Honour Werth.

Software engineers shall commit themselves to making the analysis, specification, design, development, testing, and maintenance of software a beneficial and respected profession. In accordance with their commitment to the health, safety, and welfare of the public, software engineers shall adhere to the following eight Principles:

1 *Public*   Software engineers shall act consistently with the public interest.
2 *Client and employer*   Software engineers shall act in a manner that is in the best interests of their client and employer, consistent with the public interest.
3 *Product*   Software engineers shall ensure that their products and related modifications meet the highest professional standards possible.
4 *Judgment*   Software engineers shall maintain integrity and independence in their professional judgment.
5 *Management*   Software engineering managers and leaders shall subscribe to and promote an ethical approach to the management of software development and maintenance.
6 *Profession*   Software engineers shall advance the integrity and reputation of the profession consistent with the public interest.
7 *Colleagues*   Software engineers shall be fair to and supportive of their colleagues.
8 *Self*   Software engineers shall participate in lifelong learning regarding the practice of their profession and shall promote an ethical approach to the practice of the profession.

Full version: preamble

Computers have a central and growing role in commerce, industry, government, medicine, education, entertainment, and society at large. Software engineers are those who contribute, by direct participation or by teaching, to the analysis, specification, design, development, certification, maintenance, and testing of software systems. Because of their roles in developing software systems, software engineers have significant opportunities to do good or cause harm, to enable others to do good or cause harm, or to influence others to do good or cause harm. To ensure, as much as possible, that their efforts will be used for good, software engineers must commit themselves to making software engineering a beneficial and respected profession. In accordance with that commitment, software engineers shall adhere to the following Code of Ethics and Professional Practice.

The Code contains eight Principles related to the behavior of and decisions made by professional software engineers, including practitioners, educators, managers, supervisors, and policy-makers, as well as trainees and students of the profession. The Principles identify the ethically responsible relationships in which individuals, groups, and organizations participate and the primary obligations within these relationships. The Clauses of each Principle are illustrations of some of the obligations included in these relationships. These obligations are founded in the software engineer's humanity, in special care owed to people affected by the work of software engineers, and in the unique elements of the practice of software engineering. The Code prescribes these as obligations of anyone claiming to be or aspiring to be a software engineer.

It is not intended that the individual parts of the Code be used in isolation to justify errors of omission or commission. The list of Principles and Clauses is not exhaustive. The Clauses should not be read as separating the acceptable from the unacceptable in professional conduct in all practical situations. The Code is not a simple ethical algorithm that generates ethical decisions. In some situations, standards may be in tension with each other or with standards from other sources. These situations require the software engineer to use ethical judgment to act in a manner that is most consistent with the spirit of the Code of Ethics and Professional Practice, given the circumstances.

Ethical tensions can best be addressed by thoughtful consideration of fundamental principles, rather than blind reliance on detailed regulations. These Principles should influence software engineers to consider broadly who is affected by their work; to examine if they and their colleagues are treating other human beings with due respect; to consider how the public, if reasonably well informed, would view their decisions; to analyze how the least empowered will be affected by their decisions; and to consider whether their acts would be judged worthy of the ideal professional working as a software engineer. In all these judgments concern for the health, safety, and welfare of the public is primary; that is, the "Public Interest" is central to this Code.

The dynamic and demanding context of software engineering requires a code that is adaptable and relevant to new situations as they occur. However, even in this generality, the Code provides support for software engineers and managers of software engineers who need to take positive action in a specific case by documenting the ethical stance of the profession. The Code provides an ethical foundation to which individuals within teams and the team as a whole can appeal. The Code helps to define those actions that are ethically improper to request of a software engineer or teams of software engineers.

The Code is not simply for adjudicating the nature of questionable acts; it also has an important educational function. As this Code expresses the consensus of the profession on ethical issues, it is a means to educate both the public and aspiring professionals about the ethical obligations of all software engineers.

Principles

Principle 1: Public

Software engineers shall act consistently with the public interest. In particular, software engineers shall, as appropriate:

1.01   Accept full responsibility for their own work.

1.02   Moderate the interests of the software engineer, the employer, the client, and the users with the public good.

1.03   Approve software only if they have a well-founded belief that it is safe, meets specifications, passes appropriate tests, and does not diminish quality of life, diminish privacy, or harm the environment. The ultimate effect of the work should be to the public good.

1.04   Disclose to appropriate persons or authorities any actual or potential danger to the user, the public, or the environment, that they reasonably believe to be associated with software or related documents.

1.05   Cooperate in efforts to address matters of grave public concern caused by software, its installation, maintenance, support, or documentation.

1.06   Be fair and avoid deception in all statements, particularly public ones, concerning software or related documents, methods, and tools.

1.07   Consider issues of physical disabilities, allocation of resources, economic disadvantage, and other factors that can diminish access to the benefits of software.

1.08   Be encouraged to volunteer professional skills to good causes and to contribute to public education concerning the discipline.

Principle 2: Client and employer

Software engineers shall act in a manner that is in the best interests of their client and employer, consistent with the public interest. In particular, software engineers shall, as appropriate:

2.01   Provide service in their areas of competence, being honest and forthright about any limitations of their experience and education.

2.02   Not knowingly use software that is obtained or retained either illegally or unethically.

2.03   Use the property of a client or employer only in ways properly authorized, and with the client's or employer's knowledge and consent.

2.04   Ensure that any document upon which they rely has been approved, when required, by someone authorized to approve it.

2.05   Keep private any confidential information gained in their professional work, where such confidentiality is consistent with the public interest and consistent with the law.

2.06   Identify, document, collect evidence, and report to the client or the employer promptly if, in their opinion, a project is likely to fail, to prove too expensive, to violate intellectual property law, or otherwise to be problematic.

2.07   Identify, document, and report significant issues of social concern, of which they are aware, in software or related documents, to the employer or the client.

2.08   Accept no outside work detrimental to the work they perform for their primary employer.

2.09   Promote no interest adverse to their employer or client, unless a higher ethical concern is being compromised; in that case, inform the employer or another appropriate authority of the ethical concern.

Principle 3: Product

Software engineers shall ensure that their products and related modifications meet the highest professional standards possible. In particular, software engineers shall, as appropriate:

3.01   Strive for high quality, acceptable cost, and a reasonable schedule, ensuring significant trade-offs are clear to and accepted by the employer and the client, and are available for consideration by the user and the public.

3.02   Ensure proper and achievable goals and objectives for any project on which they work or propose.

3.03   Identify, define, and address ethical, economic, cultural, legal, and environmental issues related to work projects.

3.04   Ensure that they are qualified for any project on which they work or propose to work, by an appropriate combination of education, training, and experience.

3.05   Ensure that an appropriate method is used for any project on which they work or propose to work.

3.06   Work to follow professional standards, when available, that are most appropriate for the task at hand, departing from these only when ethically or technically justified.

3.07   Strive to fully understand the specifications for software on which they work.

3.08   Ensure that specifications for software on which they work have been well documented, satisfy the user's requirements, and have the appropriate approvals.

3.09   Ensure realistic quantitative estimates of cost, scheduling, personnel, quality, and outcomes on any project on which they work or propose to work and provide an uncertainty assessment of these estimates.

3.10   Ensure adequate testing, debugging, and review of software and related documents on which they work.

3.11   Ensure adequate documentation, including significant problems discovered and solutions adopted, for any project on which they work.

3.12   Work to develop software and related documents that respect the privacy of those who will be affected by that software.

3.13   Be careful to use only accurate data derived by ethical and lawful means, and use it only in ways properly authorized.

3.14   Maintain the integrity of data, being sensitive to outdated or flawed occurrences.

3.15   Treat all forms of software maintenance with the same professionalism as new development.

Principle 4: Judgment

Software engineers shall maintain integrity and independence in their professional judgment. In particular, software engineers shall, as appropriate:

4.01   Temper all technical judgments by the need to support and maintain human values.

4.02   Only endorse documents either prepared under their supervision or within their areas of competence and with which they are in agreement.

4.03   Maintain professional objectivity with respect to any software or related documents they are asked to evaluate.

4.04   Not engage in deceptive financial practices such as bribery, double billing, or other improper financial practices.

4.05   Disclose to all concerned parties those conflicts of interest that cannot reasonably be avoided or escaped.

4.06   Refuse to participate, as members or advisors, in a private, governmental, or professional body concerned with software-related issues in which they, their employers, or their clients have undisclosed potential conflicts of interest.

Principle 5: Management

Software engineering managers and leaders shall subscribe to and promote an ethical approach to the management of software development and maintenance. In particular, those managing or leading software engineers shall, as appropriate:

5.01 Ensure good management for any project on which they work, including effective procedures for promotion of quality and reduction of risk.

5.02 Ensure that software engineers are informed of standards before being held to them.

5.03 Ensure that software engineers know the employer's policies and procedures for protecting passwords, files, and information that is confidential to the employer or confidential to others.

5.04 Assign work only after taking into account appropriate contributions of education and experience tempered with a desire to further that education and experience.

5.05 Ensure realistic quantitative estimates of cost, scheduling, personnel, quality, and outcomes on any project on which they work or propose to work, and provide an uncertainty assessment of these estimates.

5.06 Attract potential software engineers only by full and accurate description of the conditions of employment.

5.07 Offer fair and just remuneration.

5.08 Not unjustly prevent someone from taking a position for which that person is suitably qualified.

5.09 Ensure that there is a fair agreement concerning ownership of any software, processes, research, writing, or other intellectual property to which a software engineer has contributed.

5.10 Provide for due process in hearing charges of violation of an employer's policy or of this Code.

5.11 Not ask a software engineer to do anything inconsistent with this Code.

5.12 Not punish anyone for expressing ethical concerns about a project.

Principle 6: Profession

Software engineers shall advance the integrity and reputation of the profession consistent with the public interest. In particular, software engineers shall, as appropriate:

6.01 Help develop an organizational environment favorable to acting ethically.

6.02 Promote public knowledge of software engineering.

6.03 Extend software engineering knowledge by appropriate participation in professional organizations, meetings, and publications.

6.04 Support, as members of a profession, other software engineers striving to follow this Code.

6.05 Not promote their own interest at the expense of the profession, client, or employer.

6.06 Obey all laws governing their work, unless, in exceptional circumstances, such compliance is inconsistent with the public interest.

6.07 Be accurate in stating the characteristics of software on which they work, avoiding not only false claims but also claims that might reasonably be supposed to be speculative, vacuous, deceptive, misleading, or doubtful.

6.08 Take responsibility for detecting, correcting, and reporting errors in software and associated documents on which they work.

6.09 Ensure that clients, employers, and supervisors know of the software engineer's commitment to this Code of Ethics, and the subsequent ramifications of such commitment.

6.10 Avoid associations with businesses and organizations which are in conflict with this Code.

6.11 Recognize that violations of this Code are inconsistent with being a professional software engineer.

6.12 Express concerns to the people involved when significant violations of this Code are detected unless this is impossible, counterproductive, or dangerous.

6.13 Report significant violations of this Code to appropriate authorities when it is clear that consultation with people involved in these significant violations is impossible, counterproductive, or dangerous.

Principle 7: Colleagues

Software engineers shall be fair to and supportive of their colleagues. In particular, software engineers shall, as appropriate:

7.01 Encourage colleagues to adhere to this Code.

7.02 Assist colleagues in professional development.

7.03 Credit fully the work of others and refrain from taking undue credit.

7.04 Review the work of others in an objective, candid, and properly documented way.

7.05 Give a fair hearing to the opinions, concerns, or complaints of a colleague.

7.06 Assist colleagues in being fully aware of current standard work practices including policies and procedures for protecting passwords, files, and other confidential information, and security measures in general.

7.07 Not unfairly intervene in the career of any colleague; however, concern for the employer, the client, or public interest may compel software engineers, in good faith, to question the competence of a colleague.

7.08 In situations outside of their own areas of competence, call upon the opinions of other professionals who have competence in those areas.

Principle 8: Self

Software engineers shall participate in lifelong learning regarding the practice of their profession and shall promote an ethical approach to the practice of the profession. In particular, software engineers shall continually endeavor to:

8.01   Further their knowledge of developments in the analysis, specification, design, development, maintenance, and testing of software and related documents, together with the management of the development process.

8.02   Improve their ability to create safe, reliable, and useful quality software at reasonable cost and within a reasonable time.

8.03   Improve their ability to produce accurate, informative, and well-written documentation.

8.04   Improve their understanding of the software and related documents on which they work and of the environment in which they will be used.

8.05   Improve their knowledge of relevant standards and the law governing the software and related documents on which they work.

8.06   Improve their knowledge of this Code, its interpretation, and its application to their work.

8.07   Not give unfair treatment to anyone because of any irrelevant prejudices.

8.08   Not influence others to undertake any action that involves a breach of this Code.

8.09   Recognize that personal violations of this Code are inconsistent with being a professional software engineer.

A2 THE ASSOCIATION FOR COMPUTING MACHINERY CODE OF ETHICS AND PROFESSIONAL CONDUCT*
Adopted by ACM Council, October 16, 1992

Preamble

Commitment to ethical professional conduct is expected of every member (voting members, associate members, and student members) of the Association for Computing Machinery (ACM).

This Code, consisting of 24 imperatives formulated as statements of personal responsibility, identifies the elements of such a commitment. It contains many, but not all, issues professionals are likely to face. Section 1 outlines fundamental ethical considerations, while Section 2 addresses additional, more specific considerations of professional conduct. Statements in Section 3 pertain more specifically to individuals who have a leadership role, whether in the workplace or in a volunteer capacity such as with organizations like ACM. Principles involving compliance with this Code are given in Section 4.

The Code shall be supplemented by a set of Guidelines, which provide explanation to assist members in dealing with the various issues contained in the Code. It is expected that the Guidelines will be changed more frequently than the Code.

The Code and its supplemented Guidelines are intended to serve as a basis for ethical decision-making in the conduct of professional work. Secondarily, they may serve as a basis for judging the merit of a formal complaint pertaining to violation of professional ethical standards.

It should be noted that although computing is not mentioned in the imperatives of Section 1, the Code is concerned with how these fundamental imperatives apply to one's conduct as a computing professional. These imperatives are expressed in a general form to emphasize that ethical principles which apply to computer ethics are derived from more general ethical principles.

It is understood that some words and phrases in a code of ethics are subject to varying interpretations, and that any ethical principle may conflict with other ethical principles in specific situations. Questions related to ethical

* This Code and the supplemental Guidelines were developed by the Task Force for the Revision of the ACM Code of Ethics and Professional Conduct: Ronald E. Anderson, Chair, Gerald Engel, Donald Gotterbarn, Grace C. Hertlein, Alex Hoffman, Bruce Jawer, Deborah G. Johnson, Doris K. Lidtke, Joyce Currie Little, Dianne Martin, Donn B. Parker, Judith A. Perrolle, and Richard S. Rosenberg. The Task Force was organized by ACM/SIGCAS and funding was provided by the ACM SIG Discretionary Fund. This Code and the supplemental Guidelines were adopted by the ACM Council on October 16, 1992.
© 1992 by ACM, Inc. Included here by permission.

conflicts can best be answered by thoughtful consideration of fundamental principles, rather than reliance on detailed regulations.

Guidelines

1 General Moral Imperatives

As an ACM member I will . . .

1.1 Contribute to society and human well-being

This principle concerning the quality of life of all people affirms an obligation to protect fundamental human rights and to respect the diversity of all cultures. An essential aim of computing professionals is to minimize negative consequences of computing systems, including threats to health and safety. When designing or implementing systems, computing professionals must attempt to ensure that the products of their efforts will be used in socially responsible ways, will meet social needs, and will avoid harmful effects to health and welfare.

In addition to a safe social environment, human well-being includes a safe natural environment. Therefore, computing professionals who design and develop systems must be alert to, and make others aware of, any potential damage to the local or global environment.

1.2 Avoid harm to others

"Harm" means injury or negative consequences, such as undesirable loss of information, loss of property, property damage, or unwanted environmental impacts. This principle prohibits use of computing technology in ways that result in harm to any of the following: users, the general public, employees, employers. Harmful actions include intentional destruction or modification of files and programs leading to serious loss of resources or unnecessary expenditure of human resources such as the time and effort required to purge systems of "computer viruses."

Well-intended actions, including those that accomplish assigned duties, may lead to harm unexpectedly. In such an event the responsible person or persons are obligated to undo or mitigate the negative consequences as much as possible. One way to avoid unintentional harm is to carefully consider potential impacts on all those affected by decisions made during design and implementation.

To minimize the possibility of indirectly harming others, computing professionals must minimize malfunctions by following generally accepted standards for system design and testing. Furthermore, it is often necessary to assess the social consequences of systems to project the likelihood of any serious harm to others. If system features are misrepresented to users, coworkers, or supervisors, the individual computing professional is responsible for any resulting injury.

In the work environment the computing professional has the additional obligation to report any signs of system dangers that might result in serious personal or social damage. If one's superiors do not act to curtail or mitigate such dangers, it may be necessary to "blow the whistle" to help correct the problem or reduce the risk. However, capricious or misguided reporting of violations can, itself, be harmful. Before reporting violations, all relevant aspects of the incident must be thoroughly assessed. In particular, the assessment of risk and responsibility must be credible. It is suggested that advice be sought from other computing professionals. See principle 2.5 regarding thorough evaluations.

1.3   Be honest and trustworthy

Honesty is an essential component of trust. Without trust an organization cannot function effectively. The honest computing professional will not make deliberately false or deceptive claims about a system or system design, but will instead provide full disclosure of all pertinent system limitations and problems.

A computer professional has a duty to be honest about his or her own qualifications, and about any circumstances that might lead to conflicts of interest.

Membership in volunteer organizations such as ACM may at times place individuals in situations where their statements or actions could be interpreted as carrying the "weight" of a larger group of professionals. An ACM member will exercise care to not misrepresent ACM or positions and policies of ACM or any ACM units.

1.4   Be fair and take action not to discriminate

The values of equality, tolerance, respect for others, and the principles of equal justice govern this imperative. Discrimination on the basis of race, sex, religion, age, disability, national origin, or other such factors is an explicit violation of ACM policy and will not be tolerated.

Inequities between different groups of people may result from the use or misuse of information and technology. In a fair society, all individuals would have equal opportunity to participate in, or benefit from, the use of computer resources regardless of race, sex, religion, age, disability, national origin or other such similar factors. However, these ideals do not justify unauthorized use of computer resources nor do they provide an adequate basis for violation of any other ethical imperatives of this code.

1.5   Honor property rights including copyrights and patents

Violation of copyrights, patents, trade secrets and the terms of license agreements is prohibited by law in most circumstances. Even when software is not so protected, such violations are contrary to professional behavior. Copies of software should be made only with proper authorization. Unauthorized duplication of materials must not be condoned.

1.6   Give proper credit for intellectual property

Computing professionals are obligated to protect the integrity of intellectual property. Specifically, one must not take credit for other's ideas or work, even in cases where the work has not been explicitly protected by copyright, patent, etc.

1.7   Respect the privacy of others

Computing and communication technology enables the collection and exchange of personal information on a scale unprecedented in the history of civilization. Thus there is increased potential for violating the privacy of individuals and groups. It is the responsibility of professionals to maintain the privacy and integrity of data describing individuals. This includes taking precautions to ensure the accuracy of data, as well as protecting it from unauthorized access or accidental disclosure to inappropriate individuals. Furthermore, procedures must be established to allow individuals to review their records and correct inaccuracies.

This imperative implies that only the necessary amount of personal information be collected in a system, that retention and disposal periods for that information be clearly defined and enforced, and that personal information gathered for a specific purpose not be used for other purposes without consent of the individual(s). These principles apply to electronic communications, including electronic mail, and prohibit procedures that capture or monitor electronic user data, including messages, without the permission of users or bona fide authorization related to system operation and maintenance. User data observed during the normal duties of system operation and maintenance must be treated with strictest confidentiality, except in cases where it is evidence for the violation of law, organizational regulations, or this Code. In these cases, the nature or contents of that information must be disclosed only to proper authorities.

1.8 Honor confidentiality

The principle of honesty extends to issues of confidentiality of information whenever one has made an explicit promise to honor confidentiality or, implicitly, when private information not directly related to the performance of one's duties becomes available. The ethical concern is to respect all obligations of confidentiality to employers, clients, and users unless discharged from such obligations by requirements of the law or other principles of this Code.

2 More Specific Professional Responsibilities

As an ACM computing professional I will . . .

2.1 Strive to achieve the highest quality, effectiveness, and dignity in both the process and products of professional work

Excellence is perhaps the most important obligation of a professional. The computing professional must strive to achieve quality and to be cognizant of the serious negative consequences that may result from poor quality in a system.

2.2 Acquire and maintain professional competence

Excellence depends on individuals who take responsibility for acquiring and maintaining professional competence. A professional must participate in setting standards for appropriate levels of competence, and strive to achieve those standards. Upgrading technical knowledge and competence can be achieved in several ways: doing independent study; attending seminars, conferences, or courses; and being involved in professional organizations.

2.3 Know and respect existing laws pertaining to professional work

ACM members must obey existing local, state, province, national, and international laws unless there is a compelling ethical basis not to do so. Policies and procedures of the organizations in which one participates must also be obeyed. But compliance must be balanced with the recognition that sometimes existing laws and rules may be immoral or inappropriate and, therefore, must be challenged. Violation of a law or regulation may be ethical when that law or rule has inadequate moral basis or when it conflicts with another law judged to be more important. If one decides to violate a law or rule because it is viewed as unethical, or for any other reason, one must fully accept responsibility for one's actions and for the consequences.

2.4 Accept and provide appropriate professional review

Quality professional work, especially in the computing profession, depends on professional reviewing and critiquing. Whenever appropriate, individual members should seek and utilize peer review as well as provide critical review of the work of others.

2.5 Give comprehensive and thorough evaluations of computer systems and their impacts, including analysis of possible risks

Computer professionals must strive to be perceptive, thorough, and object-ive when evaluating, recommending, and presenting system descriptions and alternatives. Computer professionals are in a position of special trust, and therefore have a special responsibility to provide objective, credible evaluations to employers, clients, users, and the public. When providing evaluations the professional must also identify any relevant conflicts of interest, as stated in imperative 1.3.

As noted in the discussion of principle 1.2 on avoiding harm, any signs of danger from systems must be reported to those who have opportunity and/or responsibility to resolve them. See the guidelines for imperative 1.2 for more details concerning harm, including the reporting of professional violations.

2.6 Honor contracts, agreements, and assigned responsibilities

Honoring one's commitments is a matter of integrity and honesty. For the computer professional this includes ensuring that system elements perform as intended. Also, when one contracts for work with another party, one has an obligation to keep that party properly informed about progress toward completing that work.

A computing professional has a responsibility to request a change in any assignment that he or she feels cannot be completed as defined. Only after serious consideration and with full disclosure of risks and concerns to the employer or client, should one accept the assignment. The major underlying principle here is the obligation to accept personal accountability for profes-sional work. On some occasions other ethical principles may take greater priority.

A judgment that a specific assignment should not be performed may not be accepted. Having clearly identified one's concerns and reasons for that judgment, but failing to procure a change in that assignment, one may yet be obligated, by contract or by law, to proceed as directed. The computing professional's ethical judgment should be the final guide in deciding whether or not to proceed. Regardless of the decision, one must accept the responsibility for the consequences.

However, performing assignments "against one's own judgment" does not relieve the professional of responsibility for any negative consequences.

2.7   Improve public understanding of computing and its consequences

Computing professionals have a responsibility to share technical knowledge with the public by encouraging understanding of computing, including the impacts of computer systems and their limitations. This imperative implies an obligation to counter any false views related to computing.

2.8   Access computing and communication resources only when authorized to do so

Theft or destruction of tangible and electronic property is prohibited by imperative 1.2 – "Avoid harm to others." Trespassing and unauthorized use of a computer or communication system is addressed by this imperative. Trespassing includes accessing communication networks and computer systems, or accounts and/or files associated with those systems, without explicit authorization to do so. Individuals and organizations have the right to restrict access to their systems so long as they do not violate the discrimination principle (see 1.4). No one should enter or use another's computer system, software, or data files without permission. One must always have appropriate approval before using system resources, including .rm 57 communication ports, file space, other system peripherals, and computer time.

3   Organizational Leadership Imperatives

As an ACM member and an organizational leader, I will . . .

BACKGROUND NOTE   This section draws extensively from the draft IFIP Code of Ethics, especially its sections on organizational ethics and international concerns. The ethical obligations of organizations tend to be neglected in most codes of professional conduct, perhaps because these codes are written from the perspective of the individual member. This dilemma is addressed by stating these imperatives from the perspective of the organizational leader. In this context "leader" is viewed as any organizational member who has leadership or educational responsibilities. These imperatives generally may apply to organizations as well as their leaders. In this context "organizations" are corporations, government agencies, and other "employers," as well as volunteer professional organizations.

3.1 Articulate social responsibilities of members of an organizational unit and encourage full acceptance of those responsibilities

Because organizations of all kinds have impacts on the public, they must accept responsibilities to society. Organizational procedures and attitudes oriented toward quality and the welfare of society will reduce harm to members of the public, thereby serving public interest and fulfilling social responsibility. Therefore, organizational leaders must encourage full participation in meeting social responsibilities as well as quality performance.

3.2 Manage personnel and resources to design and build information systems that enhance the quality of working life

Organizational leaders are responsible for ensuring that computer systems enhance, not degrade, the quality of working life. When implementing a computer system, organizations must consider the personal and professional development, physical safety, and human dignity of all workers. Appropriate human-computer ergonomic standards should be considered in system design and in the workplace.

3.3 Acknowledge and support proper and authorized uses of an organization's computing and communication resources

Because computer systems can become tools to harm as well as to benefit an organization, the leadership has the responsibility to clearly define appropriate and inappropriate uses of organizational computing resources. While the number and scope of such rules should be minimal, they should be fully enforced when established.

3.4 Ensure that users and those who will be affected by a system have their needs clearly articulated during the assessment and design of requirements; later the system must be validated to meet requirements

Current system users, potential users and other persons whose lives may be affected by a system must have their needs assessed and incorporated in the statement of requirements. System validation should ensure compliance with those requirements.

3.5 Articulate and support policies that protect the dignity of users and others affected by a computing system

Designing or implementing systems that deliberately or inadvertently demean individuals or groups is ethically unacceptable. Computer professionals who are in decision making positions should verify that systems are designed and implemented to protect personal privacy and enhance personal dignity.

3.6   Create opportunities for members of the organization to learn the principles and limitations of computer systems

This complements the imperative on public understanding (2.7). Educational opportunities are essential to facilitate optimal participation of all organizational members. Opportunities must be available to all members to help them improve their knowledge and skills in computing, including courses that familiarize them with the consequences and limitations of particular types of systems. In particular, professionals must be made aware of the dangers of building systems around oversimplified models, the improbability of anticipating and designing for every possible operating condition, and other issues related to the complexity of this profession.

4.   Compliance with the Code

As an ACM member I will . . .

4.1   Uphold and promote the principles of this Code

The future of the computing profession depends on both technical and ethical excellence. Not only is it important for ACM computing professionals to adhere to the principles expressed in this Code, each member should encourage and support adherence by other members.

4.2   Treat violations of this code as inconsistent with membership in the ACM

Adherence of professionals to a code of ethics is largely a voluntary matter. However, if a member does not follow this code by engaging in gross misconduct, membership in ACM may be terminated.

A3 THE AUSTRALIAN COMPUTER SOCIETY CODE OF ETHICS*

A Requirement

An essential characteristic of a profession is the need for its members to abide by a Code of Ethics. The Society requires its members to subscribe to a set of values and ideals which uphold and advance the honour, dignity and effectiveness of the profession of information technology.

The code is part of the Society's Regulations and the numbering sequence has been maintained.

4 Code of Ethics

4.1 To uphold and advance the honour, dignity and effectiveness of the profession of information technology and in keeping with high standards of competence and ethical conduct, a member must:

a. be honest, forthright and impartial, and
b. loyally serve the community, and
c. strive to increase the competence and prestige of the profession, and
d. use special knowledge and skill for the advancement of human welfare.

4.2 The personal commitments set out in NR4.3 and NR4.4 bind each member with regard to that member's professional conduct.

4.3 Values and ideals

I must act with professional responsibility and integrity in my dealings with the community and clients, employers, employees and students. I acknowledge:

4.3.1 Priorities: I must place the interests of the community above those of personal or sectional interests.

4.3.2 Competence: I must work competently and diligently for my clients and employers.

4.3.3 Honesty: I must be honest in my representations of skills, knowledge, services and products.

4.3.4 Social Implications: I must strive to enhance the quality of life of those affected by my work.

3.5 Professional Development: I must enhance my own professional development, and that of my colleagues, employees and students.
4.3.6 Information Technology Profession: I must enhance the integrity of the information technology profession and the respect of its members for each other.

4.4 Standards of conduct

The standards of conduct set out in these National Regulations explain how the Code of Ethics applies to a member's professional work. The list of standards is not necessarily exhaustive and should not be read as definitively demarking the acceptable from the unacceptable in professional conduct in all practical situations faced by a member. The intention of the standards of conduct is to illustrate, and to explain in more detail, the meaning of the Code of Ethics in terms of specific behaviour. The fact that a member engages in, or does not engage in, these standards does not of itself guarantee that a member is acting ethically, or unethically, as applicable. A member is expected to take into account the spirit of the Code of Ethics in order to resolve ambiguous or contentious issues concerning ethical conduct.

4.5 Priorities

In accordance with NR4.3.1:

4.5.1 I must endeavour to preserve continuity of information technology services and information flow in my care.
4.5.2 I must endeavour to preserve the integrity and security of the information of others.
4.5.3 I must respect the proprietary nature of the information of others.
4.5.4 I must endeavour to preserve the confidentiality of the information of others.
4.5.5 I must advise my client or employer of any potential conflicts of interest between my assignment and legal or other accepted community requirements.
4.5.6 I must advise my clients and employers as soon as possible of any conflicts of interest or conscientious objections which face me in connection with my work.

4.6 Competence

In accordance with NR4.3.2:

4.6.1 I must endeavour to provide products and services which match the operational and financial needs of my clients and employers.

4.6.2   I must give value for money in the services and products I supply.

4.6.3   I must make myself aware of relevant standards, and act accordingly.

4.6.4   I must respect and protect my clients' and employers' proprietary interests.

4.6.5   I must accept responsibility for my work.

4.6.6   I must advise my clients and employers when I believe a proposed project is not in their best interest.

4.6.7   I must go beyond my brief, if necessary, in order to act professionally.

4.7   *Honesty*

In accordance with NR4.3.3:

4.7.1   I must not knowingly mislead a client or potential client as to the suitability of a product or service.

4.7.2   I must not misrepresent my skills or knowledge.

4.7.3   I must give opinions which are as far as possible unbiased and objective.

4.7.4   I must give realistic estimates for projects under my control.

4.7.5   I must qualify professional opinions which I know are based on limited knowledge or experience.

4.7.6   I must give credit for work done by others where credit is due.

4.8   *Social Implications*

In accordance with NR4.3.4:

4.8.1   I must protect and promote the health and safety of those affected by my work.

4.8.2   I must consider and respect people's privacy which might be affected by my work.

4.8.3   I must respect my employees and refrain from treating them unfairly.

4.8.4   I must endeavour to understand, and give due regard to, the perceptions of those affected by my work.

4.8.5   I must attempt to increase the feelings of personal satisfaction, competence, and control of those affected by my work.

4.8.6   I must not require, or attempt to influence, any person to take any action which would involve a breach of the Code of Ethics.

4.9   *Professional development*

In accordance with NR4.3.5:

4.9.1   I must continue to upgrade my knowledge and skills.

4.9.2   I must increase my awareness of issues affecting the information technology profession and its relationship with the community.

4.9.3   I must encourage my colleagues, employees and students to continue their own professional development.

4.10   *Information technology profession*

In accordance with NR4.3.6:

4.10.1   I must respect, and seek when necessary, the professional opinions of colleagues in their areas of competence.

4.10.2   I must not knowingly engage in, or be associated with, dishonest or fraudulent practices.

4.10.3   I must not attempt to enhance my own reputation at the expense of another's reputation.

4.10.4   I must co-operate in advancing information processing by communication with other professionals, students and the public, and by contributing to the efforts of professional and scientific societies and schools.

4.10.5   I must distance myself professionally from someone whose membership of the Society has been terminated because of unethical behaviour or unsatisfactory conduct.

4.10.6   I must take appropriate action if I discover a member, or a person who could potentially be a member, of the Society engaging in unethical behaviour.

4.10.7   I must seek advice from the Society when faced with an ethical dilemma I am unable to resolve by myself.

4.10.8   I must do what I can to ensure that the corporate actions of the Society are in accordance with this Code of Ethics.

4.10.9   I acknowledge my debt to the computing profession and in return must protect and promote professionalism in information technology.

A4   THE BRITISH COMPUTER SOCIETY CODE OF CONDUCT*
5 September 2001, Version 2.0.

Introduction

This Code sets out the professional standards required by the Society as a condition of membership. It applies to members of all grades, including students, and affiliates, and also non-members who offer their expertise as part of the Society's Professional Advice Register.

Within this document, the term 'relevant authority' is used to identify the person or organisation which has authority over your activity as an individual. If you are a practising professional, this is normally an employer or client. If you are a student, this is normally an academic institution.

The Code governs your personal conduct as an individual member of the BCS and not the nature of business or ethics of the relevant authority. It will, therefore, be a matter of your exercising your personal judgement in meeting the Code's requirements.

Any breach of the Code of Conduct brought to the attention of the Society will be considered under the Society's disciplinary procedures. You should also ensure that you notify the Society of any significant violation of this Code by another BCS member.

The Public Interest

1   You shall carry out work or study with due care and diligence in accordance with the relevant authority's requirements, and the interests of system users. If your professional judgement is overruled, you shall indicate the likely risks and consequences.
    * The crux of the issue here, familiar to all professionals in whatever field, is the potential conflict between full and committed compliance with the relevant authority's wishes, and the independent and considered exercise of your judgement.
    * If your judgement is overruled, you are encouraged to seek advice and guidance from a peer or colleague on how best to respond.
2   In your professional role you shall have regard for the public health, safety and environment.
    * This is a general responsibility, which may be governed by legislation, convention or protocol.

- If in doubt over the appropriate course of action to take in particular circumstances you should seek the counsel of a peer or colleague.

3   You shall have regard to the legitimate rights of third parties.

- The term 'third Party' includes professional colleagues, or possibly competitors, or members of 'the public' who might be affected by an IS project without their being directly aware of its existence.

4   You shall ensure that within your professional field/s you have knowledge and understanding of relevant legislation, regulations and standards, and that you comply with such requirements.

- As examples, relevant legislation could, in the UK, include The UK Public Disclosure Act, Data Protection or Privacy legislation, Computer Misuse law, legislation concerned with the export or import of technology, possibly for national security reasons, or law relating to intellectual property. This list is not exhaustive, and you should ensure that you are aware of any legislation relevant to your professional responsibilities.

- In the international context, you should be aware of, and understand, the requirements of law specific to the jurisdiction within which you are working, and, where relevant, to supranational legislation such as EU law and regulation. You should seek specialist advice when necessary.

5   You shall conduct your professional activities without discrimination against clients or colleagues

- Grounds of discrimination include race, colour, ethnic origin, sexual orientation

- All colleagues have a right to be treated with dignity and respect.

- You should adhere to relevant law within the jurisdiction where you are working and, if appropriate, the European Convention on Human Rights.

- You are encouraged to promote equal access to the benefits of IS by all groups in society, and to avoid and reduce 'social exclusion' from IS wherever opportunities arise.

6   You shall reject any offer of bribery or inducement.

Duty to Relevant Authority

7   You shall avoid any situation that may give rise to a conflict of interest between you and your relevant authority. You shall make full and immediate disclosure to them if any conflict is likely to occur or be seen by a third party as likely to occur.

8   You shall not disclose or authorise to be disclosed, or use for personal gain or to benefit a third party, confidential information except with

the permission of your relevant authority, or at the direction of a court of law.

9   You shall not misrepresent or withhold information on the performance of products, systems or services, or take advantage of the lack of relevant knowledge or inexperience of others.

10   You shall uphold the reputation and good standing of the BCS in particular, and the profession in general, and shall seek to improve professional standards through participation in their development, use and enforcement.

- As a Member of the BCS you also have a wider responsibility to promote public understanding of IS – its benefits and pitfalls – and, whenever practical, to counter misinformation that brings or could bring the profession into disrepute.
- You should encourage and support fellow members in their professional development and, where possible, provide opportunities for the professional development of new members, particularly student members. Enlightened mutual assistance between IS professionals furthers the reputation of the profession, and assists individual members.

11   You shall act with integrity in your relationships with all members of the BCS and with members of other professions with whom you work in a professional capacity.

12   You shall have due regard for the possible consequences of your statements on others. You shall not make any public statement in your professional capacity unless you are properly qualified and, where appropriate, authorised to do so. You shall not purport to represent the BCS unless authorised to do so.

- The offering of an opinion in public, holding oneself out to be an expert in the subject in question, is a major personal responsibility and should not be undertaken lightly.
- To give an opinion that subsequently proves ill founded is a disservice to the profession, and to the BCS.

13   You shall notify the Society if convicted of a criminal offence or upon becoming bankrupt or disqualified as Company Director.

Professional Competence and Integrity

14   You shall seek to upgrade your professional knowledge and skill, and shall maintain awareness of technological developments, procedures and standards which are relevant to your field, and encourage your subordinates to do likewise.

15 You shall not claim any level of competence that you do not possess. You shall only offer to do work or provide a service that is within your professional competence.

  • You can self-assess your professional competence for undertaking a particular job or role by asking, for example,

      i Am I familiar with the technology involved, or have I worked with similar technology before?

      ii Have I successfully completed similar assignments or roles in the past?

      iii Can I demonstrate adequate knowledge of the specific business application and requirements successfully to undertake the work?

16 You shall observe the relevant BCS Codes of Practice and all other standards which, in your judgement, are relevant, and you shall encourage your colleagues to do likewise.

17 You shall accept professional responsibility for your work and for the work of colleagues who are defined in a given context as working under your supervision.

Code of Conduct
5 SEPTEMBER 2001, VERSION 2.03
THE BRITISH COMPUTER SOCIETY, 1 SANFORD STREET,
SWINDON SN1 1HJ
TEL +44 (0)1793 417417
FAX +44 (0)1793 480270
Email: bcshq@hq.bcs.org.uk   web site: www.bcs.org
THE BCS IS A MEMBER OF THE COUNCIL OF EUROPEAN PROFESSIONAL
INFORMATICS SOCIETIES (CEPIS)
THE BCS IS A REGISTERED CHARITY: NUMBER 292786 MTG/CODE/292/
1201

A5   THE INSTITUTE OF ELECTRICAL AND ELECTRONICS ENGINEERS CODE OF ETHICS*

We, the members of the IEEE, in recognition of the importance of our technologies in affecting the quality of life throughout the world, and in accepting a personal obligation to our profession, its members and the communities we serve, do hereby commit ourselves to the highest ethical and professional conduct and agree:

1   to accept responsibility in making engineering decisions consistent with the safety, health, and welfare of the public, and to disclose promptly factors that might endanger the public or the environment;
2   to avoid real or perceived conflicts of interest whenever possible, and to disclose them to affected parties when they do exist;
3   to be honest and realistic in stating claims or estimates based on available data;
4   to reject bribery in all its forms;
5   to improve the understanding of technology, its appropriate application, and potential consequences;
6   to maintain and improve our technical competence and to undertake technological tasks for others only if qualified by training or experience, or after full disclosure of pertinent limitations;
7   to seek, accept, and offer honest criticism of technical work, to acknowledge and correct errors, and to credit properly the contributions of others;
8   to treat fairly all persons regardless of such factors as race, religion, gender, disability, age, or national origin;
9   to avoid injuring others, their property, reputation, or employment by false or malicious action;
10   to assist colleagues and co-workers in their professional development and to support them in following this code of ethics.

Approved by the IEEE Board of Directors
August 1990

A6   THE INSTITUTE FOR THE MANAGEMENT OF INFORMATION SYSTEMS CODE OF ETHICS*

Preamble to Code

The Institute for the Management of Information Systems has a vision to see Information Systems Management regarded as one of the key professions influencing the future of our society. Along with that recognition, however, comes a responsibility for practitioners to adhere to professional level standards of training and codes of conduct.

This Code of Ethics details an ethical basis for the practitioner's professional commitment. It does this by summarising the ethical values that the Institute expects all members to uphold and the ethical standards that a member should strive to achieve. These values and standards should guide the professional conduct of a member at all times.

In common with other Codes of Ethics, the Code is meant to be taken holistically – the conscientious professional should take account of all principles and clauses that have a bearing on a given set of circumstances before reaching a judgement on how to act. Selected parts of the Code should not be used in isolation to justify an action or inaction. Nor should the absence of direct guidance in the Code on a specific issue be seen as excusing a failure to consider the ethical dimensions of an act on or inaction.

It is neither desirable nor possible for a Code of Ethics to act as a set of algorithmic rules that, if followed scrupulously, will lead to ethical behaviour at all times in all situations. There are likely to be times when different parts of the code will conflict with each other. There may also be times when parts of this code will conflict with other ethical codes or generally accepted priorities in the wider world. At such times, the professional should reflect on the principles and the underlying spirit of the Code and strive to achieve a balance that is most in harmony with the aims of the Code. Some indication of relative priority is given within the code where conflict can be anticipated. However, in cases where it is not possible to reconcile the guidance given by different articles of the code, the public good shall at all times be held paramount.

Fundamental Principles

Every Fellow and Member of the Institute (including both Professional and Affiliate Membership grades) shall employ all his or her intelligence, skills, power and position to ensure that the contribution made by the profession to society is both beneficial and respected. In accordance with this commitment, he or she shall at all times uphold the following six fundamental principles:

Principle 1: Society

I will uphold the health, safety and welfare of wider society, future generations and the environment.

Principle 2: Organisations

I will serve my employers and clients honestly, competently and diligently.

Principle 3: Peers

I will respect and support the legitimate needs, interests and aspirations of all my colleagues and peers.

Principle 4: Staff

I will encourage and assist those I supervise both to fulfill their responsibilities and to develop their full potential.

Principle 5: Profession

I will strive to be a fit representative of my profession and to promote the vision of the Institute.

Principle 6: Self

I will be honest in representing myself and will continually strive to enhance both my professional competence and my ethical understanding.

The Code in Detail

1   *Society*: I will uphold the health, safety and welfare of wider society, future generations and the environment.
    1.1   I will strive to ensure that those professional activities for which I have responsibility, or over which I have influence, will not be a cause of avoidable harm to any section of the wider community, present or future, or to the environment.
    1.2   When there is no effective alternative I will bring to the attention of the relevant public authorities any activity by staff I supervise,

colleagues, employers, clients or fellow professionals that is likely to result in harm as described under article 1.1.

1.3 I will contribute to public debate regarding policy formulation in areas where this is in the wider interest, I have technical or professional competence and there is an appropriate opportunity to do so.

1.4 I will use my knowledge, understanding and position to oppose false claims made by others regarding the capabilities, potential or safety of any aspect of Information Systems and Information or Communication Technology.

1.5 I will strive to protect the legitimate privacy and property of individuals and organisations in wider society, where there is a risk that these may be compromised by professional activities for which I am responsible, or over which I have influence.

2 *Organisations*: I will serve my employers and clients honestly, competently and diligently.

2.1 I will endeavour to avoid, identify and resolve conflicts of interest.

2.2 I will accept neither an assignment that I know I will not be able to complete competently, nor an assignment that I suspect I will not be able to complete competently unless the risks are knowingly and freely accepted by all parties concerned.

2.3 I will not knowingly commit a team to a task that cannot be completed within acceptable limits of cost, effort and time, unless the risks are knowingly and freely accepted by all parties concerned.

2.4 I will preserve the legitimate confidentiality of the affairs of my employers and clients.

2.5 I will protect the legitimate property and uphold the legitimate rights of my employers and clients.

2.6 I will adhere to relevant and well founded organisational and professional polices and standards.

2.7 I will ensure, within the extent of my influence, that sufficient and competent staff are deployed on any professional activity.

2.8 I will ensure, within the extent of my influence, compliance with relevant and well-founded technical standards and methods.

2.9 I will ensure that I do not cause my employers or clients to breach applicable legislation or well-founded rules, unless there is a greater ethical priority of sufficient magnitude.

3 *Peers*: I will respect and support the legitimate needs, interests and aspirations of my colleagues and peers.

3.1 I will protect the legitimate privacy and property of my colleagues and peers.

3.2 I will refrain from all conduct that inappropriately undermines my colleagues or peers.

3.3 I will give an honest opinion regarding the competence and potential of my colleagues and peers, when it is appropriate to do so.

3.4 I will act in support of colleagues and peers who uphold what is right above their personal benefit and convenience.

3.5 I will promote teamwork among my colleagues and peers, taking my fair share of the burdens and no more than my fair share of the credit.

4 *Staff*: I will respect and support the legitimate needs, interests and aspirations of those I supervise and I will encourage and assist them both to fulfill their responsibilities and to develop their career potential.

4.1 I will adopt and promote an ethical approach to management.

4.2 I will be fair in my dealings with those I supervise.

4.3 I will be open towards those I supervise, unless constrained by a greater ethical priority.

4.4 I will actively oppose discrimination at work except on the sole basis of an individual's capacity for the task, and will take care that my judgement on this issue is not prejudiced by preconceived notions regarding any group in society.

4.5 I will actively oppose surveillance undertaken without informed consent of the subjects, unless such surveillance is justified by a greater ethical priority.

4.6 I will encourage staff education, training, development and promotion, and will represent the legitimate best interests of those I supervise in developing their careers both within and beyond the organisation.

4.7 I will give an honest opinion regarding the competence and potential of staff I supervise, when it is appropriate to do so.

4.8 I will protect the legitimate privacy and property of those I supervise.

4.9 I will promote adherence to relevant and well-founded specialist codes of conduct.

4.10 I will promote teamwork among those I supervise, taking my fair share of the burdens and no more than my fair share of the credit.

4.11 I will not require those I supervise to breach applicable legislation or well-founded rules.

5 *Profession*: I will strive to be a fit representative of my profession and to promote the vision of the Institute.

5.1 I will act with integrity at all times.

5.2 I will be honest unless constrained by a greater ethical priority.

5.3 I will strive to abide by this Code of Ethics and thereby enhance the public image and standing of the profession.

5.4   I will be willing to perform voluntary work on behalf of the profession, provided that I have the necessary time, resources and capability for the task.

6   *Self*: I will be honest in representing myself and will continually strive to enhance both my professional competence and my ethical understanding.

6.1   I will maintain my personal integrity.

6.2   I will not allow personal interests to influence the advice I give on technical and professional matters.

6.3   I will maintain the continuing development of my technical, professional and ethical understanding and competence.

PART IV

Sample Topics in Computer Ethics

Integrity without knowledge is weak and useless, and knowledge without integrity is dangerous and dreadful.

Samuel Johnson

Computer Security

Editors' Introduction

In this era of "cyber terrorism," computer "viruses," and international spying by distant "hackers,"[1] it is clear that computer security is a topic of concern in the field of computer ethics. The problem is not so much the physical security of hardware (i.e., protecting it from theft, fire, flood, etc.), but rather "logical security," which Spafford, Heaphy, and Ferbrache (Spafford et al. 1989) divide into five aspects:

1 Privacy and confidentiality
2 Integrity – assuring that data and programs are not modified without proper authority
3 Unimpaired service
4 Consistency – ensuring that the data and behavior we see today will be the same tomorrow
5 Controlling access to resources

Malicious software, or "programmed threats," provide a significant challenge to computer security. These include (Spafford et al. 1989):

1 Viruses – which cannot run on their own, but rather are inserted into other computer programs.
2 Worms – which can move from machine to machine across networks, and may have parts of themselves running on different machines.
3 Trojan horses – which give the appearance of being one sort of program, but actually are doing damage behind the scenes.

---

[1] The word "hacker" was originally a positive term for computer specialists who strove to push computer technology to the limits of its capacity. In recent years, however, the word has come more and more to mean a person who breaks into someone else's computer from a distance without permission.

4   Logic bombs – which check for particular conditions and then execute when those conditions arise.
5   "Bacteria" or "rabbits" – which multiply rapidly and fill up the computer's memory.

Computer crimes, such as embezzlement or planting of logic bombs, are normally committed by trusted personnel who have permission to use the computer system. Computer security, therefore, must also be concerned with actions of trusted computer users.

These and many other computer security risks are discussed below by Peter G. Neumann in chapter 9, "Computer Security and Human Values." Neumann points out that computer security can never be perfect; and even in a utopian-like society which is open and completely honest, security measures would be necessary. In addition, computer security is a "double-edged sword" that has not only constructive benefits, but also possible deleterious consequences. Neumann discusses three "gaps" that can lead to undesirable "computer and/or human misbehavior;" and he examines a variety of technological approaches to reduce potential security-related problems.

A significant risk to computer security is the so-called "hacker" who breaks into someone's computer system without permission. Some hackers intentionally steal data or commit vandalism, while others merely "explore" the system to see how it works and what files it contains. These "explorers" often claim to be benevolent defenders of freedom and fighters against rip-offs by major corporations or spying by government agents. These self-appointed vigilantes of cyberspace say they do no harm, and claim to be helpful to society by exposing security risks. However, such hacking is always potentially harmful because it requires a thorough check for inserted malicious code and damaged or lost data. Even if a hacker did indeed make no changes, the system operator must run through a thorough investigation of the compromised system. These and related issues are discussed below by Eugene H. Spafford in chapter 10, "Are Computer Hacker Break-ins Ethical?"

Reference

Spafford, E., Heaphy, K. A., and Ferbrache D. J. (1989). *Computer Viruses: Dealing with Electronic Vandalism and Programmed Threats.* ADAPSO.

CHAPTER 9

Computer Security and Human Values

Peter G. Neumann

Introduction

We focus here on policy issues relating to computer and communication
security, and on the roles that technology can and cannot play in enforcing
the desired policies. In the present context, computer security relates to
measures to provide desired confidentiality, integrity, availability, and, more
generally, prevention against misuse, accidents, and malfunctions, with
respect to both computer systems and the information they contain. We
deliberately take a broad view of what might constitute computer security
as encompassing the prevention of undesirable events, and take a broad
view of undesirable human activities as well. Details are provided in the
following sections.

Security is intrinsically a double-edged sword in computers and communications; it cuts both ways. For example:

- It can be used to protect personal privacy.
- It can be used to undermine freedom of access to false information about
  an individual to which that person should be entitled access; it can also
  be used to undermine other personal rights.

- It can help defend against malicious misuse, such as penetrations, Trojan
  horses, viruses, and other forms of tampering.
- It can significantly hinder urgent repairs and responses to emergencies.

Peter G. Neumann, "Computer Security and Human Values." This article was originally the
"track address" in the Security Track of the National Conference on Computing and Values held
at Southern Connecticut State University, New Haven, CT in August 1991. © by Research Center
on Computing and Society, Southern Connecticut State University and reprinted by permission of
the author.

- It can greatly simplify the concerns of legitimate users.
- It can seriously impair the abilities of legitimate users attempting to protect themselves from calamities, particularly in poorly designed systems with ill conceived human interfaces; it can also hinder routine system use.

- Automated monitoring of computer activities can be used to detect intruders, masqueraders, misuse, and other undesirable events.
- Automated monitoring of computer activities can be used to spy on legitimate users, seriously undermining personal privacy.

Each of these antagonistic pairs illustrates the potential for both constructive and deleterious use – with respect to data confidentiality, integrity, ease of use, and monitoring, respectively.

In the real world, greed, fraud, malice, laziness, curiosity, etc. are facts of life; measures to increase security become a necessity unless it is possible to live in a benign and nonmalevolent environment (e.g., no dial-up lines, no networked access, no easy flow of potentially untrustworthy software, no proprietary rights to protect, ideal hardware reliability, and outstanding administrative procedures – including frequent backups). Even in a perfect world, in which everyone behaves ethically, morally, and wisely, such measures are still needed to protect against accidental misuse, as well as against hardware and environmental problems. On the other hand, attempts to provide greater security invariably cause difficulties that otherwise would not exist. There are numerous potentially detrimental aspects associated with attempts to increase security, varyingly affecting system users and system operations as well as people seemingly not even in the loop (such as innocent bystanders). Effects on users include impediments to the ease of system use, some loss of performance, intensified anxieties, and perhaps increased suspicions or even paranoia resulting from the presence of the security controls and monitoring. Effects relevant to system operations include greater difficulties in maintaining and evolving systems, less facile recovery from failures, and significantly greater effort expended in administering security. There are also second-order effects that are somewhat more subtle, such as the need for emergency overrides to compensate for crashes, deadlocks, lost passwords, etc.; the pervasive use of superuser mechanisms, escapes, and override mechanisms tends to introduce new vulnerabilities that can be intentionally exploited or accidentally triggered.

The attainment of enterprise security is often dependent on adequate system reliability and availability. It also depends on the integrity of underlying subsystems. Thus, we speak of computer-related misbehavior as including user misbehavior that causes a computer system to fail to live up to its desired behavior, and also including system malfunctions due to causes such as hardware problems or software errors (e.g., flaws in design and implementation). Loosely speaking, security involves attempts to prevent such misbehavior.

There has been extensive discussion about whether access requiring no authorization violates the laws that rule against exceeding authority. Irrespective of the laws, Eugene Spafford (1992) concludes that the vast majority of computer break-ins are unethical, along with their would-be justifications. But what good are computer ethics in stopping misuse if computer security techniques and computer fraud laws are deficient? What follows is a relevant quote from Neumann (1990b, p. 535) on that question:

> Some RISKS Forum contributors have suggested that, because attacks on computer systems are immoral, unethical, and (hopefully) even illegal, promulgation of ethics, exertion of peer pressures, and enforcement of the laws should be major deterrents to compromises of security and integrity. But others observe that such efforts will not stop the determined attacker, motivated by espionage, terrorism, sabotage, curiosity, greed, or whatever. . . . It is a widely articulated opinion that sooner or later a serious collapse of our infrastructure – telephone systems, nuclear power, air traffic control, financial, etc. – will be caused intentionally.
>
> Certainly there is a need for better teaching and greater observance of ethics, to discourage computer misuse. However, we must try harder not to configure computer systems in critical applications (whether proprietary or government sensitive but unclassified, life-critical, financially critical, or otherwise depended upon) when those systems have fundamental vulnerabilities. In such cases, we must not assume that everyone involved will be perfectly behaved, wholly without malevolence and errors; ethics and good practices address only a part of the problem – but are nevertheless very important.

There has also been much discussion on whether computer security could become unnecessary in a more open society. Unfortunately, even if all data and programs were freely accessible, there would be a need for computer system and data integrity, to provide defenses against tampering, Trojan horses, faults, and errors.

A natural question is whether computer-related systems raise any value-related issues that are substantively different from those in other kinds of systems. Some partial answers are suggested in Neumann (1991c), and are explored further here:

- People seem naturally predisposed to depersonalize complex systems. Remote and in some cases unattributable computer access intensifies this predisposition. General ambivalence and a resulting sublimation of ethics, values, and personal roles, coupled with a background of increasingly loose corporate manipulations, and anti-ecological abuses seem to encourage in some people a rationalization that unethical behavior is the norm and somehow or other justifiable. Furthermore, encroachments on the rights of other individuals somehow seem less heinous to those who do not realize that they may also be affected.

- Computers permit radically new opportunities, such as remotely perpetrated fraud, distributed attacks, high-speed crosslinking, global searching and matching of enormous databases, internal surveillance of legitimate users that is unknown to those users, external surveillance that is undetectable by systems personnel, detailed tracking of individual activities, etc. These activities were previously impossible, inconceivable, or at least very difficult.

Most professional organizations have ethical codes. Various nations and industries have codes of fair information practice. Teaching and reinforcement of computer-related values are vitally important, alerting system purveyors, users, and would-be misusers to community standards and providing guidelines for handling abusers. But we still need sound computer systems and sound laws. (See, for example, Denning 1990, articles 26–7.)

In the following text, we first identify sources of computer-related misbehavior. We next examine expectations that are placed on computer and communication systems and on people, with respect to security. We also consider various system issues. We then examine different modes of anti-social behavior and their consequences, and consider some specific technological approaches to reducing some of the potential problems. We end with an assessment of future needs, some concluding remarks, and some potential topics for further discussion.

Computer-Related Misbehavior

Approaches to managing the general problem of attaining more meaningful security in a computer-related enterprise have both technological and non-technological components. The former are generally complex, but are becoming better understood and better supported by newer computer systems. The latter are exceedingly broad, including social, economic, political, religious, and other aspects.

By computer-related misbehavior, we mean behavior that is different from what is desired or expected. Such misbehavior may be attributable to a combination of human, computer, and environmental problems. That is, not just system misuse by people, but also people misuse by systems. As noted in Neumann (1988), there are three basic gaps that may permit computer and/or human misbehavior:

1   *Gap 1*: The *technological gap* between what a computer system is actually capable of enforcing and what it is expected to enforce (e.g., its policies for data confidentiality, data integrity, system integrity, availability, reliability, and correctness). This gap includes deficiencies in both hardware and software (for systems and communications) and deficiencies in administration, configuration, and operation. For example, passwords are expected to provide authentication of would-be system users; in practice, passwords are highly compromisible. Instances of this gap may be triggered by people (accidentally or intentionally), or by system malfunction, or by external events (for example).

2   *Gap 2*: The *sociotechnical gap* between the computer-related policies on the one hand and social policies on the other, such as computer-related crime laws, privacy laws, codes of ethics, malpractice codes and standards of good practice, insurance regulations, and other established codifications. For example, the social policy that a system user must not exceed authorization does not translate easily into a system policy that requires no authorization or in which authorization is easily bypassed.

3   *Gap 3*: The *social gap* between social policies (e.g., expected human behavior) and actual human behavior, including cracker activity, misuse by legitimate users, dishonest enforcers, etc. For example, someone accessing a computer system from another country who is bent on misuse of that system may not be very concerned about local expectations of proper human behavior. Similarly, employees who misuse a system because they have been bribed to do so may consider the precedence of a "higher ethic" (money).

The technical gap (Gap 1) can be narrowed by proper development, administration, and use of computer systems and networks that are meaningfully dependable with respect to their given requirements. The sociotechnical gap (Gap 2) can be narrowed by creating well-defined and socially enforceable social policies, although computer-based enforcement depends upon the narrowing of Gap 1. The social gap (Gap 3) can be narrowed to some extent by narrowing Gaps 1 and 2, with some additional help from better education. However, the burden must ultimately rest on better computer systems and computer networks as well as better management and self-imposed discipline on the part of information managers and workers. Detection of misuse then serves to further narrow the gaps – particularly when access controls are inadequately fine-grained so that it is easy for authorized users to misuse their allocated privileges.

A classification of many types of system vulnerabilities and unintentionally introduced flaws that are subject to malicious or accidental exploitation is given in Neumann and Parker (1989). That article provides useful background, although a detailed technical understanding of the different types of attack methods is not essential here.

Given a computer-related misbehavior, there is often a tendency to attempt to place the blame *elsewhere*, i.e., not on the real causes, in order to protect the guilty. For example, it is common to "blame the computer" for mistakes that are ultimately attributable to people. Even disastrous computer-related effects resulting from "acts of God" and hardware mal-functions can in many cases be attributed to a deficiency in the system conception or design. Similarly, it is common to blame computer users for problems that more properly should be attributed to the system designers and, in some cases, to the designers of the human-machine interfaces. In many instances, the blame deserves to be shared widely. A recurring theme in the discussion below involves the relative roles of the three gaps noted above. A suitably holistic view suggests that all three might be involved.

User-View Systems Requirements

There are numerous security-relevant expectations that people may have of a particular computer system, such as the following:

- Preservation of human safety and general personal well-being in the context of computer-related activities. Computer systems in numerous disciplines (transportation, medical, utilities, process control, etc.) are increasingly being called upon to play a key role in life-critical operations.
- Observance of privacy rights, proprietary interests, and other expected attributes. People should be notified when they are being subjected to unusual monitoring activities, and should be given the opportunity to observe and correct erroneous personal data.
- Prevention against undesired human behavior. This includes malicious acts such as sabotage, misuse, fraud, compromise, piracy, and similar antisocial acts. It also includes accidental acts that could have been prevented.
- Prevention against undesired system behavior, such as hardware- or software-induced crashes, wrong results, untolerated fault modes, excess-ive delays, etc.
- Balancing the rights of system users against the rights of system adminis-tration, particularly with respect to resource usage and monitoring.

These requirements are intertwined with value-related issues in a variety of ways, including some related to human foibles in system design, develop-ment, operation, and use, and some related to misplaced trust in systems – e.g., excessive or inadequate.

System Security Requirements

The above human-motivated requirements are typically related to computer system requirements, such as the following: system security requirements, both functional and behavioral. Computer systems should dependably enforce certain agreed-upon system and application security policies such as system integrity, data confidentiality, data integrity, system and application availability, reliability, timeliness, human safety with respect to the system, etc., as needed to enforce or enhance the socially relevant requirements listed in the previous section.

Expectations on Human Behavior

There are also numerous security-relevant expectations that system designers and administrators may wish to make of people involved in particular computer systems and applications. At one extreme are reasonable expectations on supposedly cooperative and benign users, all of whom are trusted within some particular limits; at the other extreme is the general absence of assumptions on human behavior – admitting the possibility of "Byzantine" human behavior such as arbitrarily malicious or deviant behavior by unknown and potentially hostile users. A few of the most important expectations are the following. It is convenient to consider both forms of human behavior within a common set of assumptions, with benign behavior treated as a special case of Byzantine behavior.

- Non-specific expectations relevant across the spectrum of users, e.g., cooperative and uncooperative, remote and local, authorized and un- authorized. Sensible security policies must be established and enforced, with default access attributes that support the user's needs and the administrators' demands for controllable system use.
- User security requirements on generally cooperative users. Even in the presence of friendly users, benignness assumptions are risky, particularly in light of masqueraders and accidents. In relatively constrained or non- hostile environments, it may be reasonable to make some simplifying assumptions, e.g., that there are no external penetrators (as in a classified system that has no external access and only trusted users), and that the likelihood of malicious misuse by authorized users is relatively small, and then to make appropriate checks for deviations.
- User security assumptions on potentially uncooperative users. Designing for Byzantine human behavior is an extremely difficult task, just as it is for Byzantine fault modes. In a totally hostile environment, it may be necessary to assume the worst, including arbitrary malice by individuals

and possible collusion among collaborating hostile authorized users, as well as unreliability of hardware.

Design/Implementation Concerns

Various issues need to be considered relating to system design and implementation:

* Do the system security requirements properly reflect the social requirements? Often there are glaring omissions.
* Are the system security requirements properly enforced by the actual system? There are often flaws in system design and implementation.
* What are the intrinsic limitations as to what can and cannot be guaranteed? Nothing can be absolutely guaranteed. There are always possibilities for undetected exceptions. We can always do better, but cannot be perfect. It is desirable to design systems so that if something undesirable does happen, it may be possible to contain it in some sense relevant to the problem, or to undo it, or to compensate for it.
* Is the system being used in a fundamentally unsound way that clearly violates or permits violations of the desired behavior? In many cases the absence of guarantees combined with the likelihood of serious negative consequences suggests that such use is fundamentally unsound.

Operational Concerns

Even a system that has been ideally designed and implemented can be compromised if it is operationally not soundly administered. Some of the key issues relating to proper administrative management include the following desiderata:

* Ability to recognize and eliminate in a timely fashion various system flaws, configuration vulnerabilities, and procedural weaknesses. Such problems tend to remain of little concern until actually exploited in some dramatic way, at which point a little panic often results in a quick fix that solves only a small part of the problems.
* Ability to react quickly to evident emergencies, e.g., massive penetrations or other computer system attacks. Preparedness is not a natural instinct in the face of unknown or unperceived threats.
* Willingness to communicate the existence of vulnerabilities and ongoing attacks to others who might have similar experiences. In some cases corporate secrecy is important to those who fear negative competitive

impacts from disclosures of losses. In other cases there is a lack of community awareness as to the global nature of the problems. Interchange of information can be an enormous aid to good management.

- Recognizing potential abuses, e.g., insiders privately selling off sensitive information or "fixing" database entries (e.g., removing outstanding warrants from criminal records) and dealing proactively with them.

Antisocial Behaviors

There are various manifestations of antisocial behavior that can be related to computer system design, development, and operation, as well as to specific deviations from ethical, moral, and/or legal behavior.

"Hacking", good and bad

- "Hacker" was originally a benevolent term, not a pejorative term. In light of media responses to recent system misuses, the negative use seems to have prevailed, and has permanently contaminated the term, more or less preempting its use with respect to benevolent hackers. There are many beneficial consequences of an open society in which free exchange of ideas and programmers is encouraged. However, there will always remain serious potentials for misuse.
- Misuse may originate intentionally or accidentally. Both cases represent serious potential problems. (See the next section for a discussion of what to do about these problems.)
- Misuse by authorized users and misuse by unauthorized users are both serious potential problems, although in any particular application either one of these problems may be more important than the other. It depends on the environment.
- What is actually "authorized" in any given application is often unclear, and may be both poorly defined and poorly understood. This is discussed in the next section.

Summary of modes of misuse

- Trap doors and other vulnerabilities represent serious potential sources of security compromise, whether by authorized users or by unauthorized users. Many systems have fundamental security flaws; some flaws can be exploited by people without deep system knowledge, while other flaws cannot.

- Misuse of authority by legitimate users is in some system environments more likely than external intrusions (e.g., where there are much more limited opportunities for intrusions because of the absence of dial-up lines and network connections). Such misuse may be done by partially privileged users as well as by omnipotent users, particularly when vulnerabilities are exploited as well. Note that the distinction between authorized and unauthorized users is a very tricky one, as discussed in System Considerations below.
- There are various modes of abusive system contamination, often lumped together under the rubric of *pest programs*. These include Trojan horses (e.g., time bombs, logic bombs, letter bombs, etc.), human-propagated Trojan horses, self-propagating viruses, malevolent worms, and others. Following the mythology, a Trojan horse is a program (or data or hardware or whatever) that contains something capable of causing an unanticipated and usually undesirable consequence when invoked by an unsuspecting user. The distinctions among the various forms of pest programs tend to cause inordinate philosophical and pseudo-religious arguments among supposedly rational people, but are more or less irrelevant here. So-called personal computer viruses are generally Trojan horse contaminations that are spread inadvertently by human activity. The recent proliferation of old viruses and the continued appearances of new strains of viruses are both phenomena of our times; worse yet, stealth viruses that can hide themselves and in some cases mutate to hinder detection are just beginning to emerge.

Deleterious computer-system-oriented effects

- Losses of confidentiality. Information (e.g., data and programs) may be obtained in a wide variety of ways, including direct acquisition by the obtainer, direct transmittal from a donor, inadvertent access permission from the purveyor or second party, or indirectly. Indirect acquisition includes inferences derived contextually from available information. One form of inference involves the so-called aggregation problem, in which the totality of information is somehow more sensitive than any of the data items taken individually. Another form of indirect acquisition results from the exploitation of a covert channel, which involves a somewhat esoteric signaling through a channel not ordinarily used to convey information, such as the presence or absence of an error message signifying the exhaustion of a shared resource.
- Losses of system integrity, application integrity, and system predictability. There are numerous relevant forms of integrity. System programs, data, and control information may be changed improperly. The same is

true of user programs, data, and control information. Any such changes may prevent the system from dependably producing the desired results. These are basically notions of internal consistency. External consistency is also a serious problem, for example, if the data in a database is not consistent with the real-world data it purports to represent. Erroneous information can have serious consequences in a variety of contexts.

- Denials of service and losses of resource availability. There are deleterious effects that involve neither losses of confidentiality nor losses of integrity. These include serious performance degradations, loss of critical real-time responsiveness, unavailability of data when needed, and other forms of service denial.

- Other misuse. The above list is far from complete, as there are many further types of misuse. For example, misuse may involve undetected thefts of services (e.g., computing time) or questionable applications (e.g., running private businesses from employers' facilities).

Social consequences

- Violation of privacy and related human rights, (e.g., constitutional). Loss of confidentiality can clearly result in serious privacy problems, whether intentionally or unintentionally caused. All of the above modalities of loss of confidentiality can have serious consequences. Furthermore, the effects of erroneous information can be even more serious, in the senses of both internal and external consistency.

- Software piracy. Theft of programs, data, documentation, and other information can result in loss of revenues, loss of recognition, loss of control, loss of responsibility without loss of liability, loss of accountability, and other serious consequences.

- Effects on human safety. Misuse of a life-critical system can result in deaths and injuries, whether it is done accidentally or intentionally.

- Legal issues. The potential legal effects are quite varied. There can be law suits against misusers, innocent users, and system purveyors. Some of those lawsuits would undoubtedly be frivolous or misguided, but nevertheless causing considerable agony to the accused. Computer "crimes" have already been a source of real difficulties for law enforcement communities, as well as for both guilty and innocent defendants.

- Perceptions. Increased interconnectivity, intercommunicability, and use of shared resources are clearly desirable goals. However, fears of Trojan horses, viruses, losses of privacy, theft of services, etc. are likely to create a community that is either paranoid or oblivious to and vulnerable to the social dangers.

System Considerations

There are various techniques, architectures, and methods relating to system development and operation that can help reduce the gap between what is intended and what is actually possible (the technical gap). These include system security measures and administrative procedures. In particular, crucial issues include system accountability, with user identification, authentication, and authorization, and (sub)system identification, authentication, and authorization as well; better system designs, implementing finer-grain security policies with fewer security vulnerabilities; and judicious monitoring of system usage. These problems are particularly relevant in highly distributed systems (e.g., Neumann 1990a).

Some authors have attempted to make distinctions between intentional and accidental misuse. Even a cursory examination shows that it is essential in many systems and applications to anticipate both types of misuse, including system misbehavior (e.g., hardware faults) as well as human misbehavior. There are examples of one type that can cause (or have caused) serious disasters that could not be detected as instances of the other type. (See Neumann 1991b.)

Identification, authentication, and authorization

One of the most difficult problems related to security is in determining what "authorized usage" means. Computer fraud and abuse laws generally imply that unauthorized use is illegal. But in many computer systems there is no explicit authorization required for malicious or other harmful use. A simple illustrative example is provided by the Internet Worm (e.g., Denning 1990, articles 10–15), in which four mechanisms were exploited: the *sendmail debug* option, the *finger* program, the *.rhosts* tables for accessing remote systems, and the encrypted password file. Surprising to some, perhaps, none of these required any explicit authorization for their misuse. If enabled by the system configuration, the *sendmail debug* option can be used by anyone. The *finger* program bug (relying on a flawed program *gets*) permitted anyone to exploit a widely available program designed to give out information about another user. The *.rhosts* tables permit remote access to anyone logged in with no further authorization. Finally, encrypted password files are typically readable, and subject to off-line or on-line dictionary attacks if any of the passwords are indeed dictionary words. The exploitation of each of these four mechanisms is clearly not what was intended as proper use, but authorization is not what distinguishes "good" (or proper) usage from "bad" (or improper). Perhaps the problem lies in system administrators and users unwisely trusting untrustworthy mechanisms, and with vendors promoting systems that are fundamentally limited.

Without the knowledge of who is doing what to whom (in terms of computer processes, programs, data, etc.), authorization is of very limited value. Thus, some reasonably non-spoofable form of authentication is often essential to provide some assurance that the presumed identity is indeed correct.

In the absence of meaningful authorization, the laws tend to be muddled. For example, the current (i.e. 1991) computer abuse laws in California can actually be construed as making certain perfectly legitimate computer uses illegal. Prosecutors have been quoted as saying that this presents no problems, because no such cases would be prosecuted. But clearly there are problems because it becomes impossible to close the sociotechnical gap.

Access controls

The existence of the technical gap noted above is fairly pervasive in most computer and communication systems. Ideally, the system access controls should permit only those accesses that are actually desirable. In practice, many forms of undesirable user behavior are actually permitted. Thus, the system controls should as closely as possible permit authorized access only when that access actually corresponds to desired behavior.

Uses of encryption technologies

Encryption has traditionally been an approach for achieving communication secrecy. It is now emerging as a partial solution for many other security-related functions, such as providing encrypted and non-forgeable authenticators, transmitting encrypting and decrypting keys in an encrypted form, identification and authentication, digital signatures, tickets for trusted transactions such as registry and notarization functions, non-forgeable integrity seals, non-tamperable date and time stamps, and messages that once sent legitimately cannot easily be non-repudiated as forgeries. Thus, there is a burgeoning assortment of interesting new applications.

Unfortunately, government restrictions on research, use, and export of encryption techniques makes some of these applications difficult.

Accountability and monitoring

User identification and authentication are both essential for adequate accountability. In the absence of adequate user identification, accountability is of limited value.

Anonymous use presents some potential problems. Typical restrictions permit reading only for information that is freely available, while forbidding external modification; unless the system is to be a sandbox or public blackboard, appending of new material should also be restricted, to prevent directory saturation denials of service.

Monitoring is itself a critical security issue. It must be generally non-subvertible (non-bypassable, non-alterable, and otherwise non-compromisable), and must respect privacy requirements.

Monitoring can serve many different purposes, including seeking to detect anomalies relating to confidentiality, integrity, availability, reliability, human safety, etc. With respect to security monitoring, there are two fundamentally different, but interrelated, types – monitoring of use to detect intruders (which may be a benefit to legitimate users) and monitoring to detect misuse by (supposedly) legitimate users. Management has a responsibility to inform legitimate users as to what type of monitoring is in place, although unfortunately it may be desirable to hide the detailed algorithms, because they may imply the existence of particular vulnerabilities. This is a difficult issue. (See, for example, Denning et al. 1987.)

Security remains an especially serious problem in highly distributed systems, in which accountability and monitoring take on an even greater role. Examples of systems for real-time audit-trail analysis are given by Lunt (1988), while a particular instance of a system that has been carefully designed and implemented to provide extensive restrictions on what can be audited and how the audit data can be controlled is given by Lunt and Jagannathan (1988).

Future Needs

The pervasive existence of the three gaps noted above suggests that efforts are needed to narrow each of the gaps. Some needs for the future include the following.

- Better systems, providing more comprehensive security with greater assurance – systems that are easier to use and to administer, easier to understand with respect to what is actually happening, more representative of the security policy that is really desired, etc. (Gap 1)
- Professional standards. Existing professional associations have established ethical codes. But are they adequate? – or adequately invoked? (Gap 2)
- Better education relating to ethics and values, in the context of the technology, particularly in relation to computer and communication systems, and also relating to the risks of computerization (cf. Neumann 1991a). (Gap 2)

- Better understanding of the responsibilities and rights of system administrators, users, misusers, and penetrators. (Gaps 2 and 3)
- A population that is more intelligent and more responsible, including designers, programmers, operations personnel, users, and lay people who are in many ways forced to be dependent on computerization, whether they like it or not. Holistically, we need a kinder and gentler society, but realistically that is too utopian. (Gap 3)
- In the absence of a utopian world, it seems necessary that we must strive to improve our computer systems and communications, our standards, our expectations of education, and our world as a whole, all at the same time, although the needs of our society will tend to dictate certain priorities among those contributing directions. Unfortunately, commercial expedience often dictates that emphasis be placed on seemingly easy and palliative solutions that in the long run are inadequate. (Gaps 1, 2, 3, addressed together from an overall perspective)

Conclusions

In this chapter, we have considered security somewhat broadly, encompassing not only protection against penetrations and internal misuse, but also protection against other types of undesirable system and user behavior. This perspective is important, because attempts to address a narrower set of problems are generally shortsighted.

Overall, awareness of computer system vulnerabilities and security countermeasures is greater than it was a few years ago. In retrospect, computer security has been getting steadily better, but so have the crackers and stealthy misusers of authority. Further, the potential opportunities and gains from insider misuse seem to be increasing. However, our society does not seem to be getting significantly more moral on the whole, despite some determined efforts on the part of a few individuals and groups. Gap 1 has actually been closing a little; Gap 2 needs still more work; Gap 3 remains a potentially serious problem.

At a conference in 1969, I heard "2001" author Arthur Clarke talk about how it was getting harder and harder to write good science fiction; he lamented: "The future isn't what it used to be." Yogi Berra might have remarked that Clarke's observation was "déjà vu all over again." By transitive closure, I think it is appropriate to combine those two aphorisms. Déjà vu isn't what it used to be all over again – it seems to be getting worse. And there seem to be enough people around who subscribe to Tom Lehrer's title for a song he never wrote (because it would have been an anticlimax): "If I had it to do all over again, I'd do it all over you." In the absence of better computer and communication systems, better system operations, better laws, better educational programs, better ethical practices, and better people, we are all likely to have it done to us, over and over again.

Some Topics for Discussion

One of the purposes of this chapter is to stimulate further discussion of the vital issues relating to values in the use of computers. What follows are a few topics of potential interest. They are stated here because of the pervasive nature of the problems, and the dangers of attempting to compartmentalize the relations between causes and effects.

1   Can the three gaps discussed above (technical, sociotechnical, and social, respectively) ever be closed in any realistic sense, in the face of the antisocial behaviors discussed above? Are we converging or diverging, or both? Remember, there is *no* perfect security.

2   Are the existing laws an adequate representation of the need to close Gaps 2 and 3? What are the appropriate roles of "intent," "exceeding authority," and "misusing authority," particularly in situations in which no authorization is required, and what are the implications on attempts to close Gap 1?

3   What are the intrinsic limitations of technological security measures by themselves, administrative and operational security measures by themselves, and all of these together? See design and implementation concerns discussed above.

4   What are the essential limitations of trying to maintain privacy, particularly in light of the demands for compromising it? The implications of emergency overrides and other exceptional mechanisms provide conflicting needs.

5   How can we best balance personal rights with needs for monitoring? For example, consider the FBI monitoring on-line newsgroups, and corporations monitoring inbound and outbound email and general system usage. (See accountability and monitoring discussed above.)

6   Consider the Free Software Foundation (FSF) philosophy of open access and free distribution, and its implications. Note that security has many more purposes than just providing confidentiality. For example, preventing Trojan horses and other types of sabotage is clearly an important goal. (Added note: Ironically, just before I completed this article, abuse of the FSF computers became rampant, including using the open accounts to trash the FSF software and to gain free access to other Internet systems. Richard Stallman of the FSF reluctantly admitted that they had had to institute passwords. See the *Boston Globe*, August 6, 1991, front-page article.)

7 Can we realistically "place the blame" for undesired system and human behavior, with respect to crackers, malfeasors, designers, programmers, system administrators, marketers, corporate interests, US and other governments, etc., across the broad spectrum of security-related problems? Attempts to place blame are often misguided, and tend to lose sight of the underlying problems. Furthermore, blame can usually be widely distributed. There is also the danger of shooting the messenger. (Contrast this distributed notion of blame with the *I Ching* concept of "no blame"!) (See also Denning 1991.)

8 How can the needs of encryption for privacy, integrity, and other purposes noted above be balanced with needs for "national security" and other governmental constraints? Consider the social implications of private-key versus public-key encryption, export controls, corporate and national interests, international cooperation, etc.

9 How does security aid or interfere with other social issues? Might it seriously impede access by handicapped and disadvantaged people? Or if it does not, would it present intrinsic vulnerabilities that could be exploited by others? There are challenges both ways. For example, physically disabled or otherwise handicapped individuals might be able to vote from their homes, via telephone or computer hook-up. Such systems might also encourage fraudulent voting. If serious security measures were invoked, the benefits might be lost.

10 Are we creating a bipolar society of computer-literate insiders and everyone else? Or a multipolar society of various distinct categories? Are we disenfranchising any sectors of society, such as ordinary mortals and people who do not have computer resources?

11 What are the implications of computer security on scholarly research? Unnecessary secrecy is clearly one concern. So is inadequate privacy. Loss of integrity is another concern, with the possibility of having experimental data and research results altered or forged. Authenticity (the ability to provide assurance that something is genuine) and subsequent non-repudiatability (the ability to provide some assurance that something attributed to an individual really was correctly attributed) are illustrative technical issues that relate to this question.

12 Do existing transnational data exchange regulations present serious obstacles to international cooperation, including dissemination of knowledge, programs and other on-line information? If those regulations were relaxed, would there be serious consequences, e.g., with respect to social, economic, political issues, and national integrity? Could computer security help to provide controls that would permit national boundaries to be safely transcended? Or must it be an impediment? Or are both of these alternatives actually true at the same time?

The above itemization is by no means complete. It merely suggests a few of the thornier topics that might be of interest for further discussion.

Further Background

Further background on computer security is found in Clark et al. (1990), while various examples of system misuse are analyzed in Denning (1990) and Hoffman (1990). Examples of accidental and intentional events that have resulted in serious computer-related problems are summarized in Neumann (1991a). (For the latest version of Neumann's *Risks Digest*, see the following URL: http://catless.ncl.ac.uk/Risks.)

References

Clark, David D. et al. (1990). *Computers at Risk: Safe Computing in the Information Age.* National Research Council, National Academy Press, 2101 Constitution Ave., Washington, DC 20418, December 5. Final report of the System Security Study Committee, ISBN 0-309-04388-3. (A full list of committee members is given in the report accessed at http//www7.nationalacademies.org/cstb/pub_computersatrisk.htm)

Denning, Dorothy E. (1991). "Responsibility and Blame in Computer Security." In Terrell Ward Bynum, Walter Maner, and John L. Fodor (eds.), *Computing Security.* Research Center on Computing and Society, 1992.

Denning, Dorothy E., Neumann Peter G., and Parker Donn B. (1987). "Social Aspects of Computer Security." *Proceedings of the 10th National Computer Security Conference.* Baltimore MD, September.

Denning, Peter J. (ed.) (1990). *Computers Under Attack: Intruders, Worms, and Viruses,* ACM Press, 1990. See particularly chapters on The Internet Worm (articles 10–15), social, legal, and ethical implications (articles 26–37), ACM order number 706900.

Hoffman, L. J. (ed.) (1990). *Rogue Programs: Viruses, Worms, and Trojan Horses.* Van Nostrand Reinhold.

Lunt, Teresa F. (1988). "Automated Audit Trail Analysis and Intrusion Detection: A Survey." *11th National Computer Security Conference,* Baltimore MD, October.

Lunt, Teresa F., and Jagannathan, R. (1988). "A Prototype Real-Time Intrusion-Detection Expert System." *Proceedings of the 1988 Symposium on Security and Privacy,* IEEE Computer Society, Oakland CA, April, pp. 59–66.

Neumann, Peter G. and Parker, Donn (1989) "A Summary of Computer Misuse Techniques." *Proceedings of the 12th National Computer Security Conference,* Baltimore MD, October 10–13, pp. 396–407.

Neumann, P. G. (1988). "The Computer-Related Risk of the Year: Computer Abuse." *Proceedings of COMPASS (Computer Assurance),* June, pp. 8–12. IEEE 88CH2628–6.

Neumann, P. G. (1990a). "The Computer-Related Risk of the Year: Distributed Control." *Proceedings of COMPASS (Computer Assurance),* June, pp. 173–7. IEEE 90CH2830.

Neumann, P. G. (1990b). "A Perspective from the RISKS Forum." Article 39 in Peter J. Denning (ed.), *Computers Under Attack*. ACM Press, pp. 535–43.

Neumann, P. G. (1991a). "Illustrative Risks to the Public in the Use of Computer Systems and Related Technology." *SEN*, 16/1 (January): 2–9. (Index to the published RISKS archives.)

Neumann, P. G. (1991b). "The Roles of Structure in Safety and Security." Position paper for an IFIP Workshop on Reliability, Safety, and Security of Computer Systems: Accidental vs Intentional Faults, Grand Canyon, February 22–4.

Neumann, P. G. (1991c). "Computers, Ethics, and Values, Inside Risks." *Communications of the ACM*, July, inside back cover.

Spafford, Eugene (1992). "Are Computer Hacker Break-Ins Ethical?" *Journal of Systems and Software*, January. [Chapter 10 below, p. 227.]

Basic study questions

1. Describe how the application of computer security can function as "a double-edged sword." Include some of Neumann's examples.
2. Name and describe some of the potentially negative effects that can occur with the increase of computer security.
3. Discuss the need for instruction on ethical issues that are computer-related.
4. Name and describe the three fundamental gaps that can allow for computer-related misbehavior.
5. Why would computer security be necessary even if there were no intentional misuse?
6. Describe the range of expectations of computer security that users tend to have.
7. What are some security considerations that need to be taken into account when designing and implementing computer systems?
8. What kinds of operational concerns does Neumann identify and describe with regard to computer systems administrators?
9. Describe some of the various social consequences that Neumann identifies with regard to antisocial behaviors involving computer systems.
10. How does authorization affect identification and accountability for computer misbehavior?

Questions for further thought

1. Given that computer security can *never* be perfect, can the three "gaps" discussed by Neumann ever be closed to some reasonable extent?
2. What is the relationship between privacy and computer security? How can privacy be both an aid and a hindrance to computer security?
3. Is computer security good or bad for scholarly research? – good or bad for business? – good or bad for national defense? Why?

CHAPTER 10

Are Computer Hacker Break-ins Ethical?

Eugene H. Spafford

Introduction

Recent incidents [i.e., in the late 1980s and early 1990s] of unauthorized computer intrusion have brought about discussion of the ethics of breaking into computers. Some individuals have argued that as long as no significant damage results, break-ins may serve a useful purpose. Others counter with the expression that the break-ins are almost always harmful and wrong.

This article lists and refutes many of the reasons given to justify computer intrusions. It is the author's contention that break-ins are ethical only in extreme situations, such as a life-critical emergency. The article also discusses why no break-in is "harmless."

On November 2, 1988, a program was run on the Internet that replicated itself on thousands of machines, often loading them to the point where they were unable to process normal requests (Seeley 1989, Spafford 1989a and b). This Internet Worm program [see box 1] was stopped in a matter of hours, but the controversy engendered by its release raged for years. Other recent incidents, such as the "wily hackers"[1] tracked by Cliff Stoll (1989), the "Legion of Doom" members who are alleged to have stolen telephone company 911 software (Schwartz 1990), and the growth of the computer virus problem (Spafford et al. 1989; Hoffman 1990; Stang 1990; Denning 1991) have added to the discussion. What constitutes improper access to computers? Are some break-ins ethical? Is there such a thing as a "moral hacker" (Baird et al. 1987)?

---

[1] I realize that many law-abiding individuals consider themselves *hackers* – a term formerly used as a compliment. The press and general public have co-opted the term, however, and it is now commonly viewed as a pejorative. Here, I will use the word as the general public now uses it.

Eugene H. Spafford, "Are Computer Hacker Break-Ins Ethical?" This chapter was first published in the *Journal of Systems and Software*, 1992. An earlier version appeared in *Information Technology Quarterly*, IX (1990). © 1991, 1997 by Eugene H. Spafford, all rights reserved. Reprinted by permission of the author.

Box 1   The Internet Worm

On the evening of November 2, 1988, a self-replicating program was released upon the Internet. This program (a worm) invaded VAX and Sun-3 computers running versions of Berkeley UNIX, and used their resources to attack still more computers. Within the space of hours this program had spread across the US, infecting hundreds or thousands of computers and making many of them unusable due to the burden of its activity. The Internet had never been attacked in this way before, although there had been plenty of speculation that an attack was in store. Most system administrators were unfamiliar with the concept of worms, and it took some time before they were able to establish what was going on and how to deal with it (Seeley 1989).

This whole episode should cause us to think about the ethics and laws concerning access to computers. The technology we use has developed so quickly that it is not always simple to determine where the proper boundaries of moral action may be. Many senior computer professionals started their careers years ago by breaking into computer systems at their colleges and places of employment to demonstrate their expertise. However, times have changed and mastery of computer science and computer engineering now involves a great deal more than can be shown by using intimate knowledge of the flaws in a particular operating system. Entire businesses are now dependent, wisely or not, on computer systems. People's money, careers, and possibly even their lives may be dependent on the undisturbed functioning of computers. As a society, we cannot afford the consequences of condoning or encouraging behavior that threatens or damages computer systems. As professionals, computer scientists and computer engineers cannot afford to tolerate the romanticization of computer vandals and computer criminals (Spafford 1989c).

It is important that we discuss these issues. The continuing evolution of our technological base and our increasing reliance on computers for critical tasks suggests that future incidents may well have more serious consequences than those we have seen to date. With human nature as varied and extreme as it is, and with the technology as available as it is, we must expect to experience more of these incidents.

In this article, I will introduce a few of the major issues that these incidents have raised, and present some arguments related to them. For clarification, I have separated a few issues that have often been combined when debated; it is possible that most people are in agreement on some of these points once they are viewed as individual issues.

What is Ethical?

Webster's Collegiate Dictionary defines ethics as: "The discipline dealing with what is good and bad and with moral duty and obligation." More simply, it is the study of what is *right* to do in a given situation – what we *ought* to do. Alternatively, it is sometimes described as the study of what is *good* and how to achieve that good. To suggest whether an act is right or wrong, we need to agree on an ethical system that is easy to understand and apply as we consider the ethics of computer break-ins.

Philosophers have been trying for thousands of years to define right and wrong, and I will not make yet another attempt at such a definition. Instead, I will suggest that we make the simplifying assumption that we can judge the ethical nature of an act by applying a deontological assessment: regardless of the effect, is the act itself ethical? Would we view that act as sensible and proper if everyone were to engage in it? Although this may be too simplistic a model (and it can certainly be argued that other ethical philosophies may also be applied), it is a good first approximation for purposes of discussion. If you are unfamiliar with any other formal ethical evaluation method, try applying this assessment to the points I raise later in this paper. If the results are obviously unpleasant or dangerous in the large, then they should be considered unethical as individual acts.

Note that this philosophy assumes that *right* is determined by actions and not by results. Some ethical philosophies assume that the ends justify the means; our current society does not operate by such a philosophy, although many individuals do. As a society, we profess to believe that "it isn't whether you win or lose, it's how you play the game." This is why we are concerned with issues of due process and civil rights, even for those espousing repugnant views and committing heinous acts. The process is important no matter the outcome, although the outcome may help to resolve a choice between two almost equal courses of action.

Philosophies that consider the results of an act as the ultimate measure of good are often impossible to apply because of the difficulty in understanding exactly what results from any arbitrary activity. Consider an extreme example: the government orders 100 cigarette smokers, chosen at random, to be beheaded on live nationwide television. The result might well be that many hundreds of thousands of other smokers would quit "cold turkey," thus prolonging their lives. It might also prevent hundreds of thousands of people from ever starting to smoke, thus improving the health and longevity of the general populace. The health of millions of other people would improve as they would no longer be subjected to secondary smoke, and the overall impact on the environment would be very favorable as tons of air and ground pollutants would no longer be released by smokers or tobacco companies.

Yet, despite the great good this might hold for society, everyone, except for a few extremists, would condemn such an *act* as immoral. We would likely object even if only one person was executed. It would not matter what the law might be on such a matter; we would not feel that the act was morally correct, nor would we view the ends as justifying the means.

Note that we would be unable to judge the morality of such an action by evaluating the results, because we would not know the full scope of those results. Such an act might have effects favorable or otherwise, on issues of law, public health, tobacco use, and daytime TV shows for decades or centuries to follow. A system of ethics that considered primarily only the results of our actions would not allow us to evaluate our current activities at the time when we would need such guidance; if we are unable to discern the appropriate course of action prior to its commission, then our system of ethics is of little or no value to us. To obtain ethical guidance, we must base our actions primarily on evaluations of the actions and not on the possible results.

More to the point of this paper, if we attempt to judge the morality of a computer break-in based on the sum total of all future effects, we would be unable to make such a judgment, either for a specific incident or for the general class of acts. In part, this is because it is so difficult to determine the long-term effects of various actions, and to discern their causes. We cannot know, for instance, if increased security awareness and restrictions are better for society in the long term, or whether these additional restrictions will result in greater costs and annoyance when using computer systems. We also do not know how many of these changes are directly traceable to incidents of computer break-ins.

One other point should be made here: it is undoubtedly possible to imagine scenarios where a computer break-in would be considered to be the preferable course of action. For instance, if vital medical data were on a computer and necessary to save someone's life in an emergency, but the authorized users of the system cannot be located, breaking into the system might well be considered the right thing to do. However, that action does not make the break-in ethical. Rather, such situations occur when a greater wrong would undoubtedly occur if the unethical act were not committed.

Similar reasoning applies to situations such as killing in self-defense. In the following discussion, I will assume that such conflicts are not the root cause of the break-ins; such situations should very rarely present themselves.

Motivations

Individuals who break into computer systems or who write *vandalware* usually use one of a few rationalizations for their actions. (See, for example, Landreth 1984 and the discussion in Adelaide et al. 1990.) Most of these individuals would never think to walk down a street, trying every door to find one unlocked, then search through the drawers of the furniture inside. Yet, these same people seem to give no second thought to making repeated attempts at guessing passwords to accounts they do not own, and once on to a system, browsing through the files on disk.

These computer burglars often present the same reasons for their actions in an attempt to rationalize their activities as morally justified. I present and refute some of the most commonly used ones in what follows; motives involving theft and revenge are not uncommon, and their moral nature is simple to discern, so I shall not include them here.

The hacker ethic

Many hackers argue that they follow an ethic that both guides their behavior and justifies their break-ins. This hacker ethic states, in part, that all information should be free (see Baird et al. 1987). This view holds that information belongs to everyone, and there should be no boundaries or restraints to prevent anyone from examining information. Richard Stallman (1986) states much the same thing in his GNU Manifesto. He and others have further stated in various forums that if information is free, it logically follows that there should be no such thing as intellectual property, and no need for security.

What are the implications and consequences of such a philosophy? First and foremost, it raises some disturbing questions of privacy. If all information is (or should be) free, then privacy is no longer a possibility. For information to be free to everyone, and for individuals to no longer be able to claim it as property, means that anyone may access the information if they please. Furthermore, as it is no longer property of any individual, that means that anyone can alter the information. Items such as bank balances, medical records, credit histories, employment records, and defense information all cease to be controlled. If someone controls information and controls who may access it, the information is obviously not free. But without that control, we would no longer be able to trust the accuracy of the information.

In a perfect world, this lack of privacy and control might not be a cause for concern. However, if all information were to be freely available and modifiable, imagine how much damage and chaos would be caused in our real world by such a philosophy! Our whole society is based on information whose accuracy must be assured. This includes information held by banks and other financial institutions, credit bureaus, medical agencies and professionals, government agencies such as the IRS, law enforcement agencies, and educational institutions. Clearly, treating all their information as "free" would be unethical in any world where there might be careless and unethical individuals.

Economic arguments can be made against this philosophy, too, in addition to the overwhelming need for privacy and control of information accuracy.

Information is not universally free. It is held as property because of privacy concerns, and because it is often collected and developed at great expense. Development of a new algorithm or program, or collection of a specialized database, may involve the expenditure of vast sums of time and effort. To claim that it is free or should be free is to express a naive and unrealistic view of the world. To use this as a justification for computer break-ins is clearly unethical. Although not all information currently treated as private or controlled as proprietary needs such protection, that does not justify unauthorized access to it or to any other data.

The security arguments

These arguments are the most common ones within the computer community. A common argument was the same one used most often by people attempting to defend the author of the Internet Worm program in 1988: break-ins illustrate security problems to a community that will otherwise not note the problems.

In the Worm case, one of the first issues to be discussed widely in Internet mailing lists dealt with the intent of the perpetrator – exactly why the worm program had been written and released. Explanations put forth by members of the community ranged from simple accident to the actions of a sociopath. A common explanation was that the Worm was designed to illustrate security defects to a community that would not otherwise pay attention. This was not supported by the testimony during the author's trial, nor is it supported by past experience of system administrators.

The Worm author, Robert T. Morris, appears to have been well known at some universities and major companies, and his talents were generally respected. Had he merely explained the problems or offered a demonstration to these people, he would have been listened to with considerable attention. The month before he released the Worm program on the Internet, he discovered and disclosed a bug in the file transfer program ftp; news of the flaw spread rapidly, and an official fix was announced and available within a matter of weeks. The argument that no one would listen to his report of security weaknesses is clearly fallacious.

In the more general case, this security argument is also without merit. Although some system administrators might have been complacent about the security of their systems before the Worm incident, most computer vendors, managers of government computer installations, and system administrators at major colleges and universities have been attentive to reports of security problems. People wishing to report a problem with the security of a system need not exploit it to report it. By way of analogy, one does not set fire to the neighborhood shopping center to bring attention to a fire hazard in one of the stores, and then try to justify the act by claiming that firemen would otherwise never listen to reports of hazards.

The most general argument that some people make is that the individuals who break into systems are performing a service by exposing security flaws, and thus should be encouraged or even rewarded. This argument is severely flawed in several ways. First, it assumes that there is some compelling need to force users to install security fixes on their systems, and thus computer *burglars* are justified in "breaking and entering" activities. Taken to extremes, it suggests that it would be perfectly acceptable to engage in such activities on a continuing basis, so long as they might expose security flaws. This completely loses sight of the purpose of the computers in the first place – to serve as tools and resources, not as exercises in security. The same reasoning would imply that vigilantes have the right to attempt to break into the homes in my neighborhood on a continuing basis to demonstrate that they are susceptible to burglars.

Another flaw with this argument is that it completely ignores the technical and economic factors that prevent many sites from upgrading or correcting their software. Not every site has the resources to install new system software or to correct existing software. At many sites, the systems are run as turnkey systems – employed as tools and maintained by the vendor. The owners and users of these machines simply do not have the ability to correct or maintain their systems independently, and they are unable to afford custom software support from their vendors. To break into such systems, with or without damage, is effectively to trespass into places of business; to do so in a vigilante effort to force the owners to upgrade their security structure is presumptuous and reprehensible. A burglary is not justified, morally or legally, by an argument that the victim has poor locks and was therefore "asking for it."

A related argument has been made that vendors are responsible for the maintenance of their software, and that such security breaches should immediately require vendors to issue corrections to their customers, past and present. The claim is made that without highly visible break-ins, vendors will not produce or distribute necessary fixes to software. This attitude is naive, and is neither economically feasible nor technically workable. Certainly, vendors should bear some responsibility for the adequacy of their software (McIlroy 1990), but they should not be responsible for fixing every possible flaw in every possible configuration.

Many sites customize their software or otherwise run systems incompatible with the latest vendor releases. For a vendor to be able to provide quick response to security problems, it would be necessary for each customer to run completely standardized software and hardware mixes to ensure the correctness of vendor-supplied updates. Not only would this be considerably less attractive for many customers and contrary to their usual practice, but the increased cost of such "instant" fix distribution would add to the price of such a system – greatly increasing the cost borne by the customer. It is unreasonable to expect the user community to sacrifice flexibility and pay a much higher cost per unit simply for faster corrections to the occasional security breach. That assumes it was even possible for the manufacturer to find those customers and supply them with fixes in a timely manner, something unlikely in a market where machines and software are often repackaged, traded, and resold.

The case of the Internet Worm is a good example of the security argument and its flaws. It further stands as a good example of the conflict between ends and means valuation of ethics. Various people have argued that the Worm's author did us a favor by exposing security flaws. At Mr Morris's trial on Federal charges stemming from the incident, the defense attorneys also argued that their client should not be punished because of the good the Worm did in exposing those flaws. Others, including the prosecuting attorneys for the government, argued that the act itself was wrong no matter what the outcome. Their contention has been that the result does not justify the act itself, nor does the defense's argument encompass all the consequences of the incident.

This is certainly true; the complete results of the incident are still not known. There have been many other break-ins and network worms since November 1988, perhaps inspired by the media coverage of that incident. More attempts will possibly be made, in part inspired by Mr Morris's act. Some sites on the Internet have restricted access to their machines, and others were removed from the network; I have heard of sites where a decision has been made not to pursue a connection, even though this will hinder research and operations. Combined with the many decades of person-hours devoted to cleaning up afterwards, this seems to be a high price to pay for a claimed "favor."

The legal consequences of this act are also not yet known. For instance, many bills were introduced into Congress and state legislatures in subsequent years as a (partial) result of these incidents. One piece of legislation introduced into the House of Representatives, HR-5061, entitled "The Computer Virus Eradication Act of 1988," was the first in a series of legislative actions that had the potential to affect significantly the computer profession. In particular, HR-5061 was notable because its wording would have prevented it from being applied to true computer viruses.[2] The passage of similar well-intentioned but poorly defined legislation could have a major negative effect on the computing profession as a whole.

---

[2]   It provided penalties only in cases where programs were introduced into computer systems; a computer virus is a segment of code attached to an existing program that modifies other programs to include a copy of itself (Spafford et al. 1989).

The idle system argument

Another argument put forth by system hackers is that they are simply making use of idle machines. They argue that because some systems are not used at any level near their capacity, the hacker is somehow entitled to use them.

This argument is also flawed. First of all, these systems are usually not in service to provide a general-purpose user environment. Instead, they are in use in commerce, medicine, public safety, research, and government functions. Unused capacity is present for future needs and sudden surges of activity, not for the support of outside individuals. Imagine if large numbers of people without a computer were to take advantage of a system with idle processor capacity: the system would quickly be overloaded and severely degraded or unavailable for the rightful owners. Once on the system, it would be difficult (or impossible) to oust these individuals if sudden extra capacity was needed by the rightful owners. Even the largest machines available today would not provide sufficient capacity to accommodate such activity on any large scale.

I am unable to think of any other item that someone may buy and maintain, only to have others claim a right to use it when it is idle. For instance, the thought of someone walking up to my expensive car and driving off in it simply because it is not currently being used is ludicrous. Likewise, because I am away at work, it is not proper to hold a party at my house because it is otherwise not being used. The related positions that unused computing capacity is a shared resource, and that my privately developed software belongs to everyone, are equally silly (and unethical) positions.

The student hacker argument

Some trespassers claim that they are doing no harm and changing nothing – they are simply learning about how computer systems operate. They argue that computers are expensive, and that they are merely furthering their education in a cost-effective manner. Some authors of computer viruses claim that their creations are intended to be harmless, and that they are simply learning how to write complex programs.

There are many problems with these arguments. First, as an educator, I claim that writing vandalware or breaking into a computer and looking at the files has almost nothing to do with computer education. Proper education in computer science and engineering involves intensive exposure to fundamental aspects of theory, abstraction, and design techniques. Browsing through a system does not expose someone to the broad scope of theory and practice in computing, nor does it provide the critical feedback so important to a good education (cf. Denning et al. 1989; Tucker et al. 1991). Neither does writing a virus or worm program and releasing it into an unsupervised environment provide any proper educational experience. By analogy, stealing cars and joyriding does not provide one with an education in mechanical engineering, nor does pouring sugar in the gas tank.

Furthermore, individuals "learning" about a system cannot know how everything operates and what results from their activities. Many systems have been damaged accidentally by ignorant (or careless) intruders; most of the damage from computer viruses (and the Internet Worm) appear to be caused by unexpected interactions and program faults. Damage to medical systems, factory control, financial information, and other computer systems could have drastic and far-ranging effects that have nothing to do with education, and could certainly not be considered harmless.

A related refutation of the claim has to do with knowledge of the extent of the intrusion. If I am the person responsible for the security of a critical computer system, I cannot assume that any intrusion is motivated solely by curiosity and that nothing has been harmed. If I know that the system has been compromised, I must fear the worst and perform a complete system check for damages and changes. I cannot take the word of the intruder, for any intruder who actually caused damage would seek to hide it by claiming that he or she was "just looking." In order to regain confidence in the correct behavior of my system, I must expend considerable energy to examine and verify every aspect of it.

Apply our universal approach to this situation and imagine if this "educational" behavior was widespread and commonplace. The result would be that we would spend all our time verifying our systems and never be able to trust the results fully. Clearly, this is not good, and thus we must conclude that these "educational" motivations are also unethical.

The social protector argument

One last argument, more often heard in Europe than the US, is that hackers break into systems to watch for instances of data abuse and to help keep "Big Brother" at bay. In this sense, the hackers are protectors rather than criminals. Again, this assumes that the ends justify the means. It also assumes that the hackers are actually able to achieve some good end.

Undeniably, there is some misuse of personal data by corporations and by the government. The increasing use of computer-based record systems and networks may lead to further abuses. However, it is not clear that breaking into these systems will aid in righting the wrongs. If anything, it will cause those agencies to become even more secretive and use the break-ins as an excuse for more restricted access. Break-ins and vandalism have not resulted in new open-records laws, but they have resulted in the introduction and passage of new criminal statutes. Not only has such activity failed to deter "Big Brother," but it has also resulted in significant segments of the public urging more laws and more aggressive law enforcement – the direct opposite of the supposed goal.

It is also not clear that these are the individuals we want "protecting" us. We need to have the designers and users of the systems – trained computer professionals – concerned about our rights and aware of the dangers involved with the inappropriate use of computer monitoring and record-keeping. The threat is a relatively new one, as computers and networks have become widely used only in the last few decades. It will take some time for awareness of the dangers to spread throughout the profession. Clandestine efforts to breach the security of computer systems do nothing to raise the consciousness of the appropriate individuals. Worse, they associate that commendable goal (heightened concern) with criminal activity (computer break-ins), discouraging proactive behavior by the individuals in the best positions to act in our favor. Perhaps it is in this sense that computer break-ins and vandalism are most unethical and damaging.

Concluding Remarks

I have argued here that computer break-ins, even when no obvious damage results, are unethical. This must be the considered conclusion even if the result is an improvement in security, because the activity itself is disruptive and immoral. The results of the act should be considered separately from the act itself, especially when we consider how difficult it is to understand all the effects resulting from such an act.

Of course, I have not discussed every possible reason for a break-in. There might well be an instance where a break-in might be necessary to save a life or to preserve national security. In such cases, to perform one wrong act to prevent a greater wrong may be the right thing to do. It is beyond the scope or intent of this paper to discuss such cases, especially as no known hacker break-ins have been motivated by such instances.

Historically, computer professionals as a group have not been overly concerned with questions of ethics and propriety as they relate to computers. Individuals and some organizations have tried to address these issues, but the whole computing community needs to be involved to address the problems in any comprehensive manner. Too often, we view computers simply as machines and algorithms, and we do not perceive the serious ethical questions inherent in their use.

When we consider, however, that these machines influence the quality of life of millions of individuals, both directly and indirectly, we understand that there are broader issues. Computers are used to design, analyze, support, and control applications that protect and guide the lives and finances of people. Our use (and misuse) of computing systems may have effects beyond our wildest imagining. Thus, we must reconsider our attitudes about acts demonstrating a lack of respect for the rights and privacy of other people's computers and data.

We must also consider what our attitudes will be towards future security problems. In particular, we should consider the effect of widely publishing the source code for worms, viruses, and other threats to security. Although we need a process for rapidly disseminating corrections and security information as they become known, we should realize that widespread publication of details will imperil sites where users are unwilling or unable to install updates and fixes.[3] Publication should serve a useful purpose; endangering the security of other people's machines or attempting to force them into making changes they are unable to make or afford is not ethical.

Finally, we must decide these issues of ethics as a community of professionals and then present them to society as a whole. No matter what laws are passed, and no matter how good security measures might become, they will not be enough for us to have completely secure systems. We also need to develop and act according to some shared ethical values. The members of society need to be educated so that they understand the importance of respecting the privacy and ownership of data. If locks and laws were all that kept people from robbing houses, there would be many more burglars than there are now; the shared mores about the sanctity of personal property are an important influence in the prevention of burglary. It is our duty as informed professionals to help extend those mores into the realm of computing.

References

Adelaide, J. P. B., Bluefire, R. J., Brand, R., Stoll, C., Hughes, D., Drake, F., Homeboy, E. J., Goldstein, E., Roberts, H., Gasperini, J., JIMG, Carroll, J. R., Felsenstein, L., Mandel, T., Horvitz, R., Stallman, R., Tenney, G., Acid Phreak, and Phiber Optik. (1990). "Is Computer Hacking a Crime?" *Harper's Magazine*, 280/1678: 45–57.

Baird, B. J., Baird Jr., L. L., and Ranauro, R. P. (1987). "The Moral Cracker?" *Computers and Security*, 6/6 (December): 471–8.

Denning, P. J. (ed.) (1991). *Computers Under Attack: Intruders, Worms, and Viruses.* ACM Books/Addison-Wesley.

Denning, P. J., Comer, D. E., Gries, D., Mulder, M. C., Tucker, A., Turner, A. J., and Young, P. R. (1989). "Computing as a Discipline". *Communications of the ACM*, 32/1 (January): 9–23.

---

[3]   To anticipate the oft-used comment that the "bad guys" already have such information: not every computer burglar knows or will know every system weakness – unless we provide them with detailed analyses.

Hoffman, L. (ed.) (1990). *Rogue Programs: Viruses, Worms, and Trojan Horses.* Van Nostrand Reinhold.

Landreth, B. (1984). *Out of the Inner Circle: A Hacker's Guide to Computer Security.* Microsoft Press.

McIlroy, M. D. (1990). "Unsafe at Any Price." *Information Technology Quarterly,* IX/2: 21–3.

Schwartz, J. (1990). "The Hacker Dragnet," *Newsweek,* 65/18 (April).

Seeley, D. (1989). "A Tour of the Worm." *In Proceedings of the Winter 1989 Usenix Conference* (January). Usenix Association.

Spafford, E. H. (1989a). "The Internet Worm: Crisis and Aftermath." *Communications of the ACM,* 32/6 (June): 678–98.

Spafford, E. H. (1989b). "An Analysis of the Internet Worm." In C. Ghezzi and J. A. McDermid (eds.), *Proceedings of the 2nd European Software Engineering Conference.* Springer-Verlag, pp. 446–68.

Spafford, E. H. (1989c). "The Internet Worm Program: An Analysis." *ACM Computer Communication Review,* 19/1: 17–57.

Spafford, E. H., Heaphy, K. A., and Ferbrache, D. J. (1989). *Computer Viruses: Dealing with Electronic Vandalism and Programmed Threats.* ADAPSO.

Stallman, R. (1986). *GNU EMacs Manual,* "The GNU Manifesto." Free Software Foundation, pp. 239–48.

Stang, D. J. (1990). *Computer Viruses,* 2nd edn. National Computer Security Association.

Stoll, C. (1989). *Cuckoo's Egg.* Doubleday.

Tucker, A. B., Barnes, B. H., Aiken, R. M., Barker, K., Bruce, K. B., Cain, J. T., Conry, S. E., Engel, G. L., Epstein, R. G., Lidtke, D. K., Mulder, M. C., Rogers, J. B., Spafford, E. H., and Turner, A. J. (1991). *Computing Curricula 1991.* IEEE Society Press.

Basic study questions

1. According to Spafford, what two ethical models can be used to determine the morality of an act? Which approach does Spafford prefer and why?

2. Does Spafford recognize any circumstances in which it might be ethical to break into someone else's computer without permission? If yes, explain what such circumstances would be like.

3. What, according to Spafford, is wrong with the view that all information should be free?

4. Discuss the so-called "improved security" argument to justify hacker break-ins. In particular, explain why the argument fails to be convincing.

5. What is the "idle system" argument, and how is it flawed?

6. What is the "student hacker" argument and how is it flawed?

7. What is the "social protector" argument and how is it flawed?

8. According to Spafford, *all* unauthorized hacker break-ins are harmful, even those in which the hacker allegedly "did no harm." Explain Spafford's point.

Questions for further thought

1. Is hacking into someone's computer without permission the same, ethically, as the crime of "breaking and entering" into someone's house or office? Why or why not?

2. What is the difference, if any, between citizen vigilantes who take it upon themselves to enforce the law without actually being police officers and "hackers" who take it upon themselves to "protect society" from alleged "criminals" in corporations or government agencies? Would you want to live in a society where anyone who suspects others of committing crimes decides to become a vigilante and enforce the law himself?

CASE TO ANALYZE: A FLIGHT OF FANCY AT AEROWRIGHT

Although the case presented below did not actually happen, it is similar to a number of cases that did occur. It illustrates the tensions and risks that can arise when the need for security is confronted by a desire for convenience and ease of access. The reader is invited to analyze this case using the methods described in chapter 3 above.

In the highly competitive worldwide aerospace industry, communication of key information is vital for those involved in negotiating complex design contracts. This can make the difference between winning or losing a huge contract to design and manufacture components of the next generation of aircraft. AeroWright is a major player in this industry. Although relatively small compared with its competitors, AeroWright has flourished by having technically able and gifted negotiators backed by a globally accessible information network known as AirNET. AeroWright is constantly upgrading AirNET to take advantage of the latest technological advances.

A recent decline in demand for new aircraft by airline operators worldwide led AeroWright to review once more the appropriateness of the current version of AirNET. It had become clear that information now needed to be available on demand during actual negotiations. Previously, negotiators had accessed AirNET prior to meetings. This was done from the international offices of AeroWright or its agents. Arthur Daly, the commercial director who was responsible for contract negotiation, undertook the review. It was done from a business perspective.

Daly believed that the current configuration of AirNET was still appropriate in that it provided unlimited access to all information held on the company databases. The problem lay in negotiators not being able to link to AirNET virtually anywhere at any time. The solution, as Daly saw it, was to provide a way in which the negotiators could use their laptops or hand-held computers to connect to AirNET while they were in meetings. He recalled having attended a seminar recently on wireless local area networks (WLAN), where he had been impressed by the concluding remarks about WLAN providing the infrastructure that warrants a broad-based move to wireless for employees needing anyplace, up-to-the-minute access to information. This seemed to be exactly what was required.

Daly contacted a WLAN supplier to find out more. He was told that wireless technology offered many benefits, including convenience, ease of connection, and less structural upheaval. The cost of upgrading existing computers was minimal and overall set-up and running costs were low. In fact it appeared that savings could be made through reducing network facilities at the international offices that would offset virtually all the new expenditure. What was particularly attractive was the very short lead-time in deploying WLAN. Each computer needed to be upgraded to enable a wireless connection to AirNET. Negotiators would be using the same application systems to give them unlimited access to the AeroWright databases. Existing security procedures would still be operative. Such upgrades seemed to be within the remit of Daly's department rather than having to involve directly the IT department.

The decision was made to provide wireless access to AirNET using the upgraded laptops and hand-held computers of the negotiators. A brief conversation with the system security engineer took place before the final order was placed. He warned of network security issues associated with such unprecedented openness to AeroWright's internal systems. Using AirNET with WLAN could be multifaceted and complex. Daly felt that this was an automatic response by security personnel who are always ultra cautious. What was proposed was not a major change, and AirNET had never suffered from any form of security breach.

The work went ahead to install WLAN. It took just two weeks before all negotiators had the improved access capability to AirNET. It was an immediate success. The convenience and speed of information access made negotiators more responsive in meetings. Negotiators started to use AirNET even more and started to access new types of information. Six months after WLAN was installed, Daly felt satisfied that the right action had been taken. Market demand, however, was still declining. AeroWright was winning orders, but the orders were small and margins were minimal. AeroWright was struggling to survive, as were many of its competitors. The success of each subsequent contract negotiation seemed to become more critical.

Last week AirNET suffered a security breach. This was carried out using a dictionary-building attack that, after analysis of approximately one day's traffic, allowed real-time automated decryption of traffic on AirNET. Key company confidential information was accessed and then posted on all the bulletin boards used by the aerospace industry. It resulted in AeroWright losing a major contract it desperately needed to win and suffering a very serious loss of credibility in the marketplace. Yesterday AirNET was infiltrated again. All the design documents for the wing of a new wide-body jet were destroyed. Daly resigned. The system security engineer resigned on a matter of principle. Tomorrow, it is feared, AeroWright will be out of business.

ADDITIONAL READINGS AND WEB RESOURCES

Additional readings

Denning, P. J. (ed.) (1991). *Computers Under Attack: Intruders, Worms, and Viruses.* ACM Books/Addison-Wesley.

Manion, M. and Goodrum, A. (2000). "Terrorism or Civil Disobedience: Toward a Hacktivist Ethic." *Computers and Society*, 30/2 (June): 14–19.

Neumann, P. G. (1995). *Computer Related Risks.* ACM Press/Addison-Wesley.

Spafford, E., Heaphy, K. A., and Ferbrache, D. J. (1989). *Computer Viruses: Dealing with Electronic Vandalism and Programmed Threats.* ADAPSO.

Tavani, H. T. (2000). "Defining the Boundaries of Computer Crime: Piracy, Break-Ins, and Sabotage in Cyberspace." *Computers and Society*, 30/3 (September): 3–9.

Web resources

Center for Education and Research in Information Assurance and Security (CERIAS) at Purdue University, Eugene H. Spafford, Director. http://www.cerias.purdue.edu/

Computer Security Group, Cambridge University, UK.
http://www.cl.cam.ac.uk/Research/Security/

Computer Security Institute. http://www.gocsi.com/

Computer Security Research Center, London School of Economics.
http://csrc.lse.ac.uk/

The Risks Digest: Forum On Risks To The Public In Computers And Related Systems, ACM Committee on Computers and Public Policy, Peter G. Neumann, Moderator.
http://catless.ncl.ac.uk/Risks

Privacy and Computing

Editors' Introduction

In the late nineteenth century, the term "privacy" referred primarily to *non-intrusion* into someone's home, onto someone's property, or into someone's "personal space" such as a hotel room or a cabin on a ship. By the middle of the twentieth century, the meaning of "privacy" had broadened to include *non-interference* into personal or family decisions that affect one's health, love life, or family planning. And by the end of the twentieth century, especially in industrialized nations, the term "privacy" had become "informationally enriched" by computer technology (see James H. Moor in chapter 1 above). The meaning of "privacy" expanded to include – even to emphasize – one's ability to control or restrict access to personal information about oneself.

Why did information and communication technology (ICT) have such an impact on the concept of privacy? And why did ICT dramatically increase concern that personal privacy is eroding and slipping away? The answers to these important questions lie in the nature of ICT and in its rapid development in the late twentieth century.

Digitization   In the 1930s and 1940s, with the invention of electronic computers, it became possible to digitize information and then process it at very high speeds. Initially, the information and processing were mathematical in nature; but it soon became clear that all kinds of information could be encoded digitally and processing could include logical manipulation.

Massive databases and high-speed retrieval   At first, digitized information was physically stored in objects such as punch cards and paper tape; however, electronic storage on magnetic tapes, discs, and drums soon followed. Huge quantities of information could then be electronically stored and quickly retrieved. By the early 1960s, massive databases containing information about individual persons became commonplace, especially in government agencies like tax departments, census bureaux, criminal justice departments, military agencies, and departments of public health. In industrialized countries, people began to worry about "Big Brother government" prying into their personal lives, and so, in the early 1970s, governments in America and Europe began to establish privacy laws to protect citizens from inappropriate access to their personal data.

Computer networks   In the 1970s, government, educational, and business computer networks became common; and many large corporations developed massive databases of personal information about clients and customers. By the 1980s the Internet had been created and had grown to global proportions – connecting together not only government, educational, and business computers, but even "personal computers" that individuals had in their homes.

The World Wide Web   In the 1990s the World Wide Web emerged and expanded rapidly. The so-called "global information infrastructure" or "information super highway" electronically connected more than 200 countries of the world.

Data-gathering, data-matching, and data-mining   In the late twentieth century, a wide variety of methods were developed to extract, collect, store, categorize, and interpret massive amounts of information about individual persons. Such information was gathered from government and business databases, credit cards, debit cards, smart cards, supermarket "scan cards," Internet "surfing" records, web site cookies, and many other sources. Data-matching, data-mining, pattern recognition, and a variety of other techniques were employed to enrich already existing records. Data-matching and data-profiling became a way of combating various kinds of fraud. In the United States, buying and selling "personal profiles" of information about individuals became a multibillion dollar industry.

Organizations are increasingly computerizing the processing of personal information. This may be without the consent or knowledge of the individuals concerned. The advances in computer technology have led to the growth of databases holding personal and other sensitive information in multiple formats, including text, pictures, and sound. The scale of data collected, its type, and the scale and speed of data exchange have all changed with the advent of computers. The potential to breach the privacy of people at less cost and to greater advantage continues to increase. Responsible organizations will ensure that the privacy of the individual is protected while they pursue their business activities.

Protecting the Right to Privacy

All of these developments have concerned many governments and people who worry that individual citizens may be harmed if their personal information is inappropriately accessed – information about their health, lifestyle, economic situation, buying habits, political preferences, religious preferences, gender, genetic make-up, ethnic heritage, and many other personal matters.

According to James H. Moor, in chapter 11, entitled "Towards a Theory of Privacy in the Information Age," once personal information is digitized and entered into a computer on a network, the information becomes "greased data" that can easily slip across networks and into many different computers. As a result, personal information may no longer be controlled and people may access it who have no right to do so. Moor presents a theory of privacy to analyze this thorny problem and develop ways to preserve our right to privacy in the information age.

In the United States, privacy laws were passed in the 1970s primarily to protect citizens from government interference in their private lives. Possible invasions of privacy by businesses, on the other hand, have for the most part remained unregulated by government in the USA. Instead, the American business community has essentially been allowed to regulate itself with regard to privacy.

In Europe, however, governments have taken a much more active role, passing "data protection" laws intended to defend the right to privacy by regulating the collection and processing of personal data. A good example of the European approach is the United Kingdom's "Data Protection Acts," which are described in chapter 12, "Data Protection in a Changing World," by Elizabeth France, who is the Information Commissioner of the UK.

CHAPTER 11

Towards a Theory of Privacy in the Information Age

James H. Moor

Greased Data

When we think of ethical problems involving computing, probably none is more paradigmatic than the issue of privacy. Given the ability of computers to manipulate information – to store endlessly, to sort efficiently, and to locate effortlessly – we are justifiably concerned that in a computerized society our privacy may be invaded and that information harmful to us will be revealed. Of course, we are reluctant to give up the advantages of speedy and convenient computerized information. We appreciate the easy access to computerized data when making reservations, using automatic teller machines, buying new products on the web, or investigating topics in computer databases. Our challenge is to take advantage of computing without allowing computing to take advantage of us. When information is computerized, it is *greased* to slide easily and quickly to many ports of call. This makes information retrieval quick and convenient. But legitimate concerns about privacy arise when this speed and convenience lead to the improper exposure of information. Greased information is information that moves like lightning and is hard to hold onto.

Consider, for example, listed telephone numbers which have been routinely available through a telephone operator and a telephone book but which are now available, along with address information, in giant electronic phone books on the Internet. The Hanover, New Hampshire telephone book (the telephone book for where I live) is rather hard to locate in most places in the world, but now anyone anywhere with access to the Internet can easily find out my phone number, who my wife is, and where I live. It is even possible to retrieve a map of my residential area. I don't consider this to be a

James H. Moor, "Towards a Theory of Privacy in the Information Age." This chapter was first published in *Computers and Society*, 27 (September 1997), pp. 27–32. © 1997 by James H. Moor. Reprinted by permission of the author.

breach of privacy, but I use it to point out how the same information, which has technically been public for a long time, can dramatically change levels of accessibility practically speaking when put into electronic form on computer networks. It is ironic that my name may be hard to find in the Internet phone book because it is listed there anachronistically in an abbreviated form. "James" is abbreviated as "Jas.," an abbreviation I never use and have seen only in old print phone books, presumably introduced to save print space but needlessly copied when put on the Internet. Don't tell anyone!

The greasing of information makes information so easy to access that it can be used again and again. Computers have elephant memories – big, accurate, and long term. The ability of computers to remember so well for so long undercuts a human frailty that assists privacy. We, humans, forget most things. Most short-term memories don't even make it to long-term memory. Every time I go to a busy supermarket I am a new customer. Who can remember what I bought the last time I was there? Actually, a computer does. Most of the time I shop at a cooperative food store that gives a rebate at the end of the year. When I buy food, I give the checkout person my account number (I can remember at least that most days). The checkout person scans my purchases, which appear on a screen by the name of the item and its price. This information is definitely greased. It appears as quickly as the checker can move the items across the bar-code reader. Then my total is displayed and the information is added to my grand total of purchases on which I get a certain percentage back each year. Notice that in addition to the total of my purchases, the market also has information about what I have purchased. It helps the market keep track of its inventory. But, it also means that the store has a profile on my buying habits. They know how much wine I purchase, my fondness for Raisin Bran cereal, and the kind of vegetables I prefer. In principle, such evidence could be subpoenaed if my eating habits were relevant to a court case. Does this accumulation of information violate my privacy? I suppose not, but it is greased so that it moves easily and is more accessible over a longer period of time than ever before. Practically speaking, the information is never forgotten. A documented history of purchases generates the possibility for an invasion of privacy that does not exist without it.

In the case of my food shopping the collection of information is obvious to me. I can see my eating habits and my limited will power flash on the display screen as the calories tumble by on the conveyor. But information about us can be collected subtlety when we don't realize it. The greasing of information allows other computers to capture and manipulate information in ways we do not expect. Consider a final personal example to illustrate this. Not long ago I lived for a few months in Edinburgh. On days I didn't feel like cooking, I would sometimes order a pizza. The pizza was delivered to my apartment and hence was a convenient way to get a quick meal. However,

I was somewhat taken aback the second time I phoned the pizza establishment. Before I had placed my order, the pizza-makers already seemed to know my address and my favorite pizza. Did I want to have another medium pepperoni and mushroom delivered? I hadn't been in Edinburgh very long. How could they possibly know my taste (or lack of taste) so quickly? The answer, of course, was their use of caller ID. No mystery here. I had called before and given information about my pizza preference and my delivery address, and they had linked it with my phone number. When I called the second time, my phone number was captured electronically by the pizza parlor and used to select the other information from my first call. Had my privacy been invaded? Probably not, but I confess that I initially felt some mild indignation that my pizza profile had been stored away without my knowing it. If I were a frequent customer in a fine restaurant and the waiter had memorized my tastes, I would feel complimented that he remembered me. But, as efficient as the caller ID/computer system was, I found no gain in self-worth by having a pizza parlor computer recall my intake of pepperoni and mushroom pizza.

I mention these three examples – the Internet phone book, the supermarket refund policy based on bar-code data, and the pizza parlor caller ID – not because they represent some deep treachery, but because they are perfectly ordinary activities and illustrate how effortlessly information is collected and transmitted without any of us giving it a second thought. Once information is captured electronically for whatever purpose, it is greased and ready to go for any purpose. In a computerized world we leave electronic footprints everywhere and data collected for one purpose can be resurrected and used elsewhere. The problem of computer privacy is to keep proper vigilance on where such information can and should go.

For the most part, the need for privacy is like good art: you know it when you see it. But sometimes our intuitions can be misleading and it is important to become as clear as possible what privacy is, how it is justified, and how it is applied in ethical situations. In this chapter I will assemble pieces of an overall theory of privacy and try to defend it. In the computer age, during a period when information technology is growing rapidly and its consequences are difficult to predict more than a few days in advance, if at all, it is more important than ever to determine how privacy should be understood and guarded.

Grounding Privacy

From the point of view of ethical theory privacy is a curious value. On the one hand, it seems to be something of very great importance and something vital to defend, and, on the other hand, privacy seems to be a matter of individual preference, culturally relative, and difficult to justify in general. Is privacy a primary value? How can we justify or ground the importance of privacy?

I will discuss two standard ways of justifying privacy, both of which I have used before, and describe the limitations of these two approaches. Then I will present a third way to justify the importance of privacy which I now find more defensible. Philosophers frequently distinguish between instrumental values and intrinsic values. Instrumental values are those values that are good because they lead to something else which is good. Intrinsic values are values that are good in themselves. Instrumental values are good as means: intrinsic values are good as ends. My computer is good as a means to help me write papers, send email and calculate my taxes. My computer has instrumental value. However, the joy I gain from using my computer is good in itself. Joy doesn't have to lead to anything to have value. Joy has intrinsic value. And, as philosophers since Aristotle have pointed out, some things, such as health, have both instrumental and intrinsic value. This familiar philosophical distinction between instrumental and intrinsic values suggests two common ways to attempt to justify privacy.

Almost everyone would agree that privacy has instrumental value. This is its most common justification. Privacy offers us protection against harm. For example, in some cases, if a person's medical condition were publicly known, then that person would risk discrimination. If the person tests HIV+, an employer might be reluctant to hire him and an insurance company might he reluctant to insure him. Examples of this nature are well known and we need not amass examples further to make a convincing case that privacy has instrumental value. But, so do toothpicks. To justify the high instrumental value of privacy we need to show that not only does privacy have instrumental value, but that it leads to something very, very important. One of the best known attempts to do this has been given by James Rachaels. Rachaels suggests that privacy is valuable because it enables us to form varied relationships with other people (1975, p. 323). Privacy does enable us to form intimate bonds with other people that might he difficult to form and maintain in public. But the need to relate to others differently may not ground privacy securely because not everyone may want to form varied relationships, and those who do may not need privacy to do it. Some people simply do not care how they are perceived by others.

The justification of privacy would be more secure if we could show that it has intrinsic value. Deborah Johnson has suggested a clever way of doing this. Johnson proposes that we regard "privacy as an essential aspect of autonomy" (1994, p. 89). So, assuming that autonomy is intrinsically valuable and privacy is a necessary condition for autonomy, we have the strong and attractive claim that privacy is a necessary condition for an intrinsic good. If privacy is not an intrinsic good itself, it is the next best thing. But, is it true that "autonomy is inconceivable without privacy" (ibid.)?

I have proposed a thought experiment about Tom, an electronic eaves-dropper, which, I believe, shows Johnson's claim to he incorrect (Moor 1989, pp. 61–2). In this thought experiment Tom is very good with computers and electronics and has a real fondness for knowing about you – all about you. Tom uses computers secretly to search your financial records, your medical records, and your criminal records. He knows about your late mortgage payments, your persistent hemorrhoids, and that driving-while-intoxicated charge that you thought was long forgotten. Tom is so fascinated with your life that he has clandestine cameras installed which record your every movement. You know nothing about any of this, but Tom really enjoys watching you, especially those instant replays. "For Tom, watching your life is like following a soap opera – The Days of Your Life" (ibid., p. 62). I think most of us will agree that there is something repugnant about Tom's peeping. But what is it? It is not that he is directly harming you. He doesn't use any of this information to hurt you. He doesn't share the information with anyone else or take advantage of you in any way whatsoever. More-over, you have complete autonomy, just no privacy. Thus, it follows that privacy is not an essential condition for autonomy. It is conceivable to have autonomy without privacy. Nevertheless, I would agree that some people, including myself, regard privacy as intrinsically valuable, not merely instru-mentally valuable.

Now let me consider a third approach to justifying the importance of privacy. I wish to maintain that there is a set of values, which I call the "core values," which are shared and fundamental to human evaluation. The test for a core value is that it is a value found in all human cultures. Here is a list of some of the values that I believe are at the core: *life, happiness, freedom, knowledge, ability, resources,* and *security.* My claim is an empirical one. I am claiming that all sustainable human cultures will exhibit these values. I am not suggesting for a moment that all cultures are moral or that these goods are fairly distributed in every culture. Regrettably, they almost never are. An ethical theory requires an account of fairness as well as an account of the core values. What I am claiming is that every viable culture will exhibit a preference for these values. Consider the most primitive, immoral culture you can imagine. As barbaric and repulsive as it is, its members must find nourishment and raise their young if the culture is to survive. These activit-ies require at least implicit acknowledgment of the core values. To abandon the core values completely is to abandon existence.

Is privacy a core value? I wish it were. It would make the justification of privacy so much easier. But, upon reflection, it is clear that it is not in the core. One can easily imagine sustainable and flourishing human cultures that place no value on privacy. Consider a man and a woman who live together but give each other no privacy and who couldn't care less about priv-acy. Presumably, many couples live this way and have no trouble existing.

Now imagine a family or small tribe with equal disinterest in privacy. Everybody in the group can know as much as they want about everybody else. They might believe that their society functions better without secrets. An anti-Rachaelsean in the society might maintain that they have better and more varied human relationships just because they can know everything about everybody! The concept of privacy has a distinctly cultural aspect which goes beyond the core values. Some cultures may value privacy and some may not.

How then should we justify privacy? How is it grounded? Let me propose a justification of privacy by using the core values. The core values are the values that all normal humans and cultures need for survival. Knowledge, for example, is crucial for the ongoing survival of individuals and cultures. The transmission of culture from one generation to the next by definition involves the transmission of knowledge. I emphasize the core values because they provide a common value framework, a set of standards, by which we can assess the activities of different people and different cultures (Moor 1998). The core values allow us to make transcultural judgments. The core values are the values we have in common as human beings. To focus on the core is to focus on similarities. But, now let us focus on the differences. Individuals and cultures articulate the core values differently depending on environment and circumstances. The transmission of knowledge is essential for the survival of every culture, but it is not the same knowledge that must he transmitted. Resources such as food are essential for everyone, but not everyone must prefer the same kind of food. So, though there is a common framework of values, there is also room for much individual and cultural variation within the framework. Let's call the articulation of a core value for an individual or a culture the "expression of a core value".

Although privacy is not a core value per se, it is the expression of a core value, viz., the value of security. Without protection, species and cultures don't survive and flourish. All cultures need security of some kind, but not all need privacy. As societies become larger, highly interactive, but less intimate, privacy becomes a natural expression of the need for security. We seek protection from strangers who may have goals antithetical to our own. In particular, in a large, highly computerized culture in which lots of personal information is greased, it is almost inevitable that privacy will emerge as an expression of the core value, security.

Consider once again the dichotomy between instrumental and intrinsic values. Because privacy is instrumental in support of all the core values, it is instrumental for important matters; and because privacy is a necessary means of support in a highly computerized culture, privacy is instrumentally well grounded for our society. Moreover, because privacy is an expression of the core value of security, it is a plausible candidate for an intrinsic good in the context of a highly populated, computerized society. Tom, the electronic eavesdropper, who doesn't harm his subject when he spies, nevertheless seems to be doing something wrong intrinsically. The subject's security is being violated by Tom, even if no other harm befalls the person. People have a basic right to be protected, which, from the point of view of our computerized culture, includes privacy protection.

I have argued that in using the core value framework, privacy can be grounded both instrumentally and intrinsically – instrumentally, as a support of all the core values, and intrinsically, as an expression of security. I am, however, concerned that the traditional instrumental/intrinsic understanding may be misleading. Traditionally, instrumental/intrinsic analyses push us in the direction of a search for a *summum bonum*, a greatest good. We try to find the one thing to which all other things lead. In the core value approach that I am advocating some values may be more important than others, but there is not a *summum bonum*. Rather, the model is one of an intersupporting framework. The core values, like the beams of a truss, are in support of each other. Asking whether a core value or the expression of a core value is instrumental or intrinsic is like asking whether a beam of a truss is supporting or supported. It is essentially both. The core values for all of us are mutually supporting. Some people will emphasize some values more than others. An athlete will emphasize ability, a businessperson will emphasize resources, a soldier will emphasize security, a scholar will emphasize knowledge, and so forth. However, everyone and every culture needs all of the core values to exist and flourish. Privacy, as an expression of security, is a critical, interlocking member in our systems of values in our increasingly computerized culture.

The Nature of Privacy

Understanding privacy as the expression of the core value of security has the advantage of explaining the changing conception of privacy over time. Privacy is not mentioned explicitly either in the United States Declaration of Independence or in its Constitution (Moor 1990). It is strange that a value that seems so important to us now was not even mentioned by the revolutionary leaders and statesmen who were so impressed with the ideals of individual freedoms. The concept of privacy has been evolving in the US from a concept of non-intrusion (e.g., the Fourth Amendment to the US Constitution offering protection against unreasonable governmental searches and seizures), to a concept of non-interference (e.g., the Roe v. Wade decision giving a woman the right to choose to have an abortion), to limited information access (e.g., the Privacy Act of 1974 restricting the collection, use, and distribution of information by Federal agencies). Privacy is a concept that has been dramatically stretched over time as it developed.

In our computer age the notion of privacy has become stretched even further. Now the concept of privacy has become so informationally enriched (Moor 1998; see also chapter 1 above) that "privacy" in contemporary use typically refers to informational privacy, though, of course, other aspects of the concept remain important.

Consider a useful distinction that helps to avoid some misunderstandings about the nature of privacy. The term "privacy" is sometimes used to designate a situation in which people are protected from intrusion or observation by natural or physical circumstances. Someone spelunking by herself would be in a naturally private (and probably dangerous) situation. Nobody can see her in the cave she is exploring. In addition to natural privacy there is normative privacy. A normatively private situation is a situation protected by ethical, legal, or conventional norms. Consultations with a lawyer or doctor would be normatively private situations. Obviously, many normatively private situations are naturally private as well. We send mail in sealed envelopes. When an unauthorized entry is made into a normatively private situation, privacy has not only been lost, it has been breached or invaded.

Now if we put the evolving conceptions of privacy together with the distinction between normative and natural privacy we get a useful account of the nature of privacy:

> An individual or group has normative privacy in a situation with regard to others if and only if in that situation the individual or group is normatively protected from intrusion, interference, and information access by others. (Culver et al. 1994, p. 6)

I use the general term "situation" deliberately because it is broad enough to cover many kinds of privacy: private *locations* such as one's diary in a computer file, private *relationships* such as email to one's pharmacy, and private *activities* such as the utilization of computerized credit histories.

The situations which are normatively private can vary significantly from culture to culture, place to place, and time to time. This doesn't show that the privacy standards are arbitrary or unjustified; they are just different. For example, at a private college faculty salaries are kept confidential, but at some state colleges faculty salaries, at least salaries above a certain level, are published. Presumably, the private colleges believe that protecting salary information will reduce squabbling and embarrassment; whereas state colleges (or the state legislatures) believe that the taxpayers who support the institution have the right to know how much faculty members are being paid. These are different but defensible policies for protecting and releasing information.

Clearly some personal information is very sensitive and should be protected. We need to create zones of privacy, a variety of private situations, so that people can ensure that information about themselves which might be damaging if generally released will be protected. With different zones of privacy, one can decide how much personal information to keep private and how much to make public. Notice that on my account the notion of privacy really attaches to a situation or zone and not to the information itself. For instance, if an Internal Revenue Service employee uses a computer to call up and process a movie star's income tax return, then the employee is not invading the star's privacy. He is allowed in this situation to investigate the star's tax return. However, if that same employee were to call up that same star's tax return on his computer after hours just to browse around, then the employee would be violating the star's privacy although the employee may gain no new information. The employee has legitimate access in the first situation but not the second.

The theory I am proposing is a version of the restricted access view of privacy (Moor 1990, pp. 76–80). The major opposing view is the control theory of privacy. One proponent of this view, Charles Fried, writes: "Privacy is not simply an absence of information about us in the minds of others, rather it is the *control* we have over information about ourselves" (Fried 1984, p. 209). I agree that it is highly desirable that we control information about ourselves. However, in a highly computerized culture this is simply impossible. We don't control vast amounts of information about ourselves. Personal information about us is well greased and slides rapidly through computer systems around the world, around the clock. Therefore, to protect ourselves we need to make sure the right people, and only the right people, have *access* to relevant information at the right time. Hence, the restricted access view puts the focus on what we should be considering when developing policies for protecting privacy. However, the restricted access account, at least in the form I am proposing it, has all the advantages of the control theory for one of the goals in setting policies to give individuals as much control (informed consent) over personal data as realistically possible. For this reason I will label my account as a "control/restricted access" theory of privacy.

The control/restricted access conception of privacy has the advantage that polices for privacy can be fine-tuned. Different people may be given different levels of access for different kinds of information at different times. A good example occurs in a modern, computerized hospital. Physicians are allowed access to on-line medical information which secretaries are not given. However, physicians are generally not allowed to see all the information about a patient that a hospital possesses. For example, they don't have access to most billing records. In some hospitals some medical information such as psychiatric interviews may be accessible to some physicians and not others. Rather than regarding privacy as an all or nothing proposition – either only I know or everybody knows – it is better to regard it as a complex of situations in which information is authorized to flow to some people some of the time. Ideally, those who need to know do, those who don't don't.

The control/restricted access conception also explains some anomalies about private situations. Usually, when we consider privacy, we are thinking about situations in which individuals possess possibly damaging personal information they want to keep others from knowing. But situations can be private in other circumstances. Imagine a situation in a restaurant with scores of people dining. A couple begin to argue loudly and eventually each shouts to the other about a marital problem they are having. They go into excruciating detail about various kinds of sexual dysfunction and bodily needs. Everyone can hear them and many patrons of the restaurant feel uncomfortable as they proceed with their meal. Finally, the waiter, who thinks he can help, cannot stand it any longer. He walks over to the couple and asks whether they would like his advice. The couple in unison tell him, "No. it's a private matter."

As ironic as their comment may be, it does make sense on several levels. In private situations the access to information can be blocked in both directions. This couple did not want to allow information from the waiter although they themselves had been indiscreet in revealing details to the entire population of the restaurant. Moreover, in our culture some activities are required to be done in private. Discussions of one's intimate marital problems may be one of them. Privacy is a form of protection and it can protect the general population as well as individuals.

Setting and Adjusting Policies for Private Situations

So far I have commented on the greasing effect computerization has on information and the potential problems for privacy computerization poses. I have proposed a justification for privacy as an expression of one of the core values and as an essential member of the central framework of values for a computerized society. I have characterized the nature of privacy as an evolving concept which has become informationally enriched with the development of computing. And I have argued that privacy is best understood in terms of a control/restricted access account. Now it is time to focus on practical policies for the protection of privacy. As an example I will use information gathered from genetic testing. This is an interesting case because, practically speaking, genetic testing would not be possible without information technology and with information technology genetic testing is one of the greatest potential threats to our individual privacy. Improper disclosure of our genetic information may be the ultimate violation of our privacy.

Suppose a patient decides to have herself tested for a breast cancer gene. She does not have breast cancer, but breast cancer runs in her family and she wants to know whether she is genetically disposed to have breast cancer. She goes to the hospital for tests for the gene and the results are positive. The results are put in her medical record so that the information is available to physicians to encourage aggressive testing for the disease in the future. The information will be computerized, which means that many health care providers throughout the state may have access to the information. The patient's health insurance company will also have access to it. Information of this kind could be detrimental to the patient when obtaining life insurance or future health insurance, and eventually, if the information slides through enough computer networks, it could be detrimental to the patient's children when obtaining insurance and applying for employment, though they have shown no signs of the disease and have never been tested.

In formulating policies we should try to minimize excess harm and risk. In cases like this, it may be hard to do. Clearly, the medical records should be treated confidentially, but that may not be enough to protect the patient. Because the records are computerized, and hence well greased, information will be sent rapidly along networks and gathered by third parties who may find their own self-interested uses for it. New legal policies might he helpful here, including the passage of statutes protecting patients from discrimination on the basis of genetic testing. Also, the hospital might consider setting up a zone of privacy for patients who want only predictive testing done. There is a difference between predictive genetic testing in which the patient is tested for genetic information that may be indicative of future disease and diagnostic testing in which the patient is tested for genetic information that may confirm a diagnosis of an existing disease. The hospital could establish a private situation for predictive testing so that the patient's records were not incorporated into the regular medical file. These records would be computerized but not accessible to all of those who have access to the general medical record. This is a way of adjusting the access conditions to increase the level of privacy for the patient. Of course, the patient should he told what will happen to the test information. The patient might prefer to have the information included in her medical record.

One of the principles that should guide the establishment of policies for privacy is the Publicity Principle:

> *The Publicity Principle*   Rules and conditions governing private situations should be clear and known to the persons affected by them.

In effect, we can plan to protect our privacy better if we know where the zones of privacy are and under what conditions and to whom information will be given. If an employer can read one's email, then applying for a new job is done more discreetly by not using email. The publicity principle encourages informed consent and rational decision-making.

Once policies are established and known, circumstances sometimes arise which invite us to breach the policy. Obviously, policy breaches should be avoided as much as possible as they undermine confidence in the policy. However, sometimes truly exceptional circumstances occur. Suppose that after some predictive genetic tests are run, new information about the consequences of the test results are uncovered. New scientific evidence in combination with the test results show that the patient surely must have transmitted a devastating disease to her offspring but that the disease can be treated effectively if caught in time. In such circumstances it would seem that the hospital should notify not only the patient but also her adult offspring, even though that was not part of the original agreement. The harm caused by the disclosure will be so much less than the harm prevented that the breach is justified.

> *The Justification of Exceptions Principle*   A breach of a private situation is justified if and only if there is a great likelihood that the harm caused by the disclosure will be so much less than the harm prevented that an impartial person would permit a breach in this and in morally similar situations.

These exceptional circumstances should not be kept secret from future users of the policy. Hence, we need a principle for disclosure and adjustment in the policy statement itself:

> *The Adjustment Principle*   If special circumstances justify a change in the parameters of a private situation, then the alteration should become an explicit and public part of the rules and conditions governing the private situation.

In this example those who continued to have predictive genetic testing would know what information would be released in the stated exceptional circumstances. They would know the possible consequences of their decision to have predictive genetic testing and could plan accordingly. The control/restricted access theory can give individuals as much personal choice as possible while still being concerned about information flow beyond individual control.

Conclusion

In a computerized society information is greased. It moves like lightning and will have applications and re-applications that are impossible to imagine when initially entered into a computer. In a computerized society the concern for privacy is legitimate and well grounded. Privacy is one of our expressions of the core value of security. Individuals and societies that are not secure do not flourish and do not exist for long. It is, therefore, imperative that we create zones of privacy that allow citizens to rationally plan their lives without fear. The zones of privacy will be contained private situations with different kinds and levels of access for different individuals. It is important to think of privacy in terms of a control/restricted access account, because this conception encourages informed consent as much as possible and fosters the development of practical, fine-grained and sensitive policies for protecting privacy when it is not.

References

Culver, C., Moor, J., Duerfeldt, W., Knapp, M., and Sullivan, M. (1994). "Privacy." *Professional Ethics*, 3/3, 4: 3–25.

Fried, C. (1984). "Privacy," In F. D. Schoeman (ed.), *Philosophical Dimensions of Privacy*. Cambridge University Press, pp. 203–22.

Johnson, D. G. (1994). *Computer Ethics*, 2nd edn. Prentice-Hall.

Moor, J. (1985). "What is Computer Ethics?" *Metaphilosophy*, 16/4: 266–75.

Moor, J. (1989). "How to Invade and Protect Privacy with Computers." In Carol C. Gould (ed.), *The Information Web*. Westview Press, pp. 57–70.

Moor, J. (1990). "Ethics of Privacy Protection." *Library Trends*, 39/1, 2: 69–82.

Moor, J. (1998). "Reason, Relativity, and Responsibility in Computer Ethics." *Computers and Society*, 28/1: 14–21. [Chapter 1 above, p. 21]

Rachels, J. (1975). "Why is Privacy Important?" *Philosophy and Public Affairs*, 4 (Summer): 323–33.

Basic study questions

1. What does Moor mean by "greased data" and why does he call it greased?
2. Moor gives three examples of how information about us is easily collected when we are going about our daily lives. Describe these three examples briefly and clearly.
3. Explain the difference between "instrumental" and "intrinsic" values.
4. Explain how privacy can be viewed as an instrumental value.
5. Deborah Johnson has argued that privacy has intrinsic value because it is necessary for autonomy. What is autonomy?
6. Describe the case of "Peeping Tom." How does Moor use this case to argue against Johnson's view that privacy has intrinsic value?
7. What does Moor mean by the term "core values"? Give five examples of core values that Moor identifies in his article.
8. Why, according to Moor, is privacy *not* a core value? Even though, according to Moor, privacy is not a core value, he says that it is "an expression of a core value". Explain clearly and carefully what he means.
9. Explain clearly and carefully what "natural privacy" is and also what "normative privacy" is.

10. Explain clearly and fully what Moor means by "zones of privacy."
11. Explain in detail Moor's "control/restricted access" account of privacy.
12. Explain Moor's three principles for formulating new privacy policies.

Questions for further thought

1. Discuss the advantages and disadvantages of greased data in people's daily lives. Are there more harms or benefits? Are there ways to maximize the benefits and minimize the harms?
2. What can computer users do to help themselves keep personal information private?
3. Is there a way for a company to keep track of a person's habits (shopping, web surfing, etc.) without invading his/her privacy? Explain.

CHAPTER 12

Data Protection in a Changing World

Elizabeth France

Some Historical Highlights

Data Protection Law has been found on the statute books in an increasing number of countries since Sweden set the pace in the 1970s; and since October 2001 there has been substantive implementation of a European Union (EU) Directive[1] which seeks to harmonize data protection law across Europe. That Directive began life in draft in 1990. The first general EU Directive of this kind, it builds on two previous international instruments, both of which appeared a decade earlier. In 1980 the OECD (Organization for Economic Cooperation and Development) guidelines on privacy and transborder flows of personal data were established and the following year the Council of Europe Convention, Treaty 108, was open for ratification.[2]

The Council of Europe Convention led directly to the development of the first United Kingdom Data Protection Act. A series of UK reports published during the 1970s – Crowther in 1971; Younger in 1972; and Lindop in 1978 – had made reference to the need for protection of individual privacy, but their articulation of the risks had not been sufficient to lead the government to take action. There was a shortage of information about just how data processing would impact on most members of the public. Indeed, Younger, in the chapter of his report[3] which dealt with computing, admitted that the situation was currently one of "apprehension and fears and not so far one of facts and figures." By 1978 Lindop was persuaded of the need for legislation

---

[1]   Directive 95/46/EC on the protection of individuals with regard to the processing of personal data and on the free movement of such data, adopted by the Council on July 24, 1995.
[2]   Council of Europe Convention of the protection of individuals with regard to automatic processing of personal data. European Treaty Series No. 108, Strasbourg 1981.
[3]   The Younger Report (1972) Cmnd 5012.

and an independent data protection authority;[4] but it was the need to ratify Council of Europe Treaty 108 for the purposes of trade, rather than a real recognition by the government of the risk to privacy, which led to the passage of the 1984 Data Protection Act.

A Fundamental Right and Eight Principles of Fair Information Handling

The Data Protection Act 1984 came fully into force in 1987. The nature of the drafting of that Act gives little hint of the fundamental rights background evident in the international instruments on which it is based. Indeed, the mood of the time would not have justified it. Nevertheless, early annual reports of the first Data Protection Registrar, Eric Howe, show a clear understanding of the underlying philosophy, an understanding that data protection law provides a statutory framework which protects the right to respect for private life in relation to the processing of personal data. In his first annual report in June 1985, the Registrar said: "A primary further objective must be to establish a significant measure of public awareness of the rights of the individual under the Act and an understanding of the way in which those rights may be exercised. At the same time it is important that data users are aware of their responsibilities."[5]

The eight enforceable principles of fair information handling practice set out in a Schedule to the 1984 Act were at the heart of the law. It was those principles that reflected both the OECD principles and the Council of Europe Treaty provisions. It is those principles that can be found in varied form in any data protection law anywhere in the world, and which provide the link between the 1984 Act and the UK's current law. Indeed, in summary there is little variation between them (see table 1). The structure of the 1984 Act, however, gave an emphasis to the bureaucratic process of "registration," which dominated the perception of many as to the primary purpose of the Act. There was a danger that it was seen to be no more than an exercise in form-filling designed to obstruct the exploitation by business of new technology. That was never its role, but the view was perhaps reinforced by the relatively low level of concern about their privacy rights expressed by individuals ("data subjects" as the law describes them). In the days of main-frame computing people were less readily aware that processing of their personal data was going on, and the knowledge of potential risks was held by relatively fewer people than today.

---

[4]   The Lindop Report (1978) Cmnd 7341.
[5]   First Report of the Data Protection Registrar, June 1985, HMSO, ISBN 0-10-247085-J.

Table 1   UK Data Protection Acts, 1984 and 1998

Data Protection Act 1984 The Principles[a]	Data Protection Act 1998 The Principles[b]
A data user must:	Data must be:
1. obtain and process personal data fairly and lawfully;	1. fairly and lawfully processed;
2. hold the data only for the purposes specified in your Register entry;	2. processed for limited purposes; 3. adequate, relevant and not excessive;
3. use the data only for the purposes, and disclose only to the people, listed in your Register entry;	4. accurate;
4. only hold data which are adequate, relevant and not excessive in relation to the purpose for which the data are held;	5. not kept for longer than is necessary; 6. processed in line with data subjects' rights;
5. ensure personal data are accurate and where necessary, kept up-to-date;	7. secure;
6. hold the data for no longer than is necessary;	8. not transferred to countries outside the European Economic Area unless there are adequate safeguards.
7. allow individuals access to information held about them and, where appropriate, correct it or erase it;	
8. take security measures to prevent unauthorized or accidental access to, alteration, disclosure, or loss and destruction of information.	

[a] For full text see Schedule 1 of the Data Protection Act 1984
[b] For full text see Schedule 1 of the Data Protection Act 1998

A Broader Scope

The 1984 Act survived as a valuable tool into the age of the networked PC and the smart card because the enforceable principles were written in a way that was not technology specific. It was also possible, in anticipation of the changes in the law which the EU Directive brought, to begin to move the focus away from registration and more clearly onto individual rights. It was 1995 by the time the EU Directive reached its final form. That Directive was brought into domestic law in the United Kingdom by the Data Protection Act 1998, which was given Royal Assent in July of that year. An extensive transitional period, taking until October 24, 2001, was allowed for those who process personal information (referred to in the Act as 'data controllers') to apply the changes in the law to any processing which was already under way. For the United Kingdom the new law was not in any way a change of direction. It built upon the old. Those who processed personal data in a way that was fully in line with the requirements of the old law should not have found it difficult to comply with the new. However, there are some key differences, largely in the *scope* of the legislation.

Without exhaustively detailing the scope of the first Data Protection Act it may be helpful to set out three of the key definitions to be found in the new law:

What is a data controller?   A data controller is a person who, (either alone or jointly or in common with other persons), determines the purposes for which and the manner in which any personal data are, or are to be processed.

What is personal data?   Personal data means data which relate to a living individual who can be identified (a) from those data, or (b) from those data and other information which is in the possession of or likely to come into the possession of the data controller.

What is processing?   "Processing" means obtaining, recording, or holding the data or carrying out any operation or set of operations on the data including:
1   organization, adaptation or alteration of the data;
2   retrieval, consultation or use of the data;
3   disclosure of the data by transmission, dissemination or otherwise making available; or
4   alignment, blocking, erasure or destruction of the data.

These three definitions taken together give a feel for the breadth of the 1998 Act. Other key definitions are those for data, which shows the extension of the law to cover some manual files, and for "sensitive" data included separately and with more safeguards required, for the first time. Put at its simplest, in an age where information is all around us and so much of it relates to individuals, it is likely that doing anything with that information, indeed even simply holding such information, will bring the data controller within the scope of the legislation. Although there are many who would like to suggest that such a broad scope inhibits processing, that is to misunderstand the law. The role of the legislation is, in fact, designed to ensure the free flow of information to meet business needs. To ensure that there can be such a free flow it sets out a framework of obligations which, if adhered to, will ensure respect for the private lives of individuals. It applies to all sectors, and must be interpreted in context.

A Model Code of Practice: Closed Circuit Television

An early example of how the new law could be applied to a specific area of technology without the primary legislation itself having made any such references lies in the way that we developed a code of practice for the use of closed circuit television (CCTV) in public places. As the foreword which I produced to that code of practice says, CCTV surveillance is an increasing feature of daily lives in the United Kingdom. There is an ongoing debate over how effective CCTV is in reducing and preventing crime, but one thing is certain: its deployment is commonplace in a variety of areas to which members of the public have free access. We might be caught on camera while walking down the street, visiting a shop or bank, or traveling through a railway station or airport. The House of Lords Select Committee on Science and Technology expressed its view that if public confidence in CCTV systems was to be maintained there needed to be some tighter control over their deployment and use (5th Report – Digital Images as Evidence).

There was no statutory basis for systematic legal control of CCTV surveillance over public areas until the Data Protection Act 1998 came into force. Because, as has been explained, definitions in this new Act are broader than those of the Data Protection Act 1984, they more readily cover the processing of images of individuals caught by CCTV cameras than did the previous data protection legislation. The same legally enforceable information handling standards as have previously applied to those processing personal data on computer can now be seen to cover CCTV.

One important new feature of the 1998 Act is a power to issue a Commissioner's code of practice (section 51(3)(b), Data Protection Act 1998) setting out guidance for the following of good practice. In my 14th Annual Report to Parliament, I signaled my intention to use this power to provide guidance on the operation of CCTV as soon as those new powers became available to me. Work is also going on to produce a code of practice for employers on their use of personal data, but the code of practice on the use of CCTV in public places was the first Commissioner's code to be issued under the Data Protection Act 1998.

The code deals with surveillance in areas to which the public have largely free and unrestricted access because, as the House of Lords Committee highlighted, there is particular concern about a lack of regulation and central guidance in this area. Although the Data Protection Act 1998 covers other uses of CCTV, the code of practice addresses the area of widest concern. Many of its provisions will be relevant to other uses of CCTV and will be referred to as appropriate when we develop other guidance. There are some existing standards that have been developed by representatives of CCTV system operators and, more particularly, the British Standards Institute. While such standards are helpful, they are not legally enforceable. The changes in data protection legislation mean that for the first time legally enforceable standards will apply to the collection and processing of images relating to individuals.

The code of practice on the use of CCTV in public places has the dual purpose of assisting operators of CCTV systems to understand their legal obligations while also reassuring the public about the safeguards that should be in place. It sets out the measures which must be adopted to comply with the Data Protection Act 1998, and it goes on to set out guidance for the following of good data protection practice. The code makes clear what the standards are which must be followed to ensure compliance with the Data Protection Act 1998, and then it indicates those standards which are not strict legal requirements but do represent the following of good practice.

The pattern developed in producing this code of practice has set a model for us. It allows flesh to be put on the bones of the law so that high-level statements can be explained in context. Codes of practice within a statutory framework allow flexibility, for they can more readily be amended than the law itself, while giving assistance to those trying to comply with the law by indicating how the enforcement body will interpret it in particular circumstances.

Electronic Government

The nature of the law also allows comment on emerging government policy. It has been pleasing to see the way in which those responsible for policy development at the national and local levels increasingly recognize the importance of their obligations in relation to the processing of personal information and seek advice before finalizing policy. The recognition, particularly in the context of e-government, of the importance of ensuring that the citizen is confident about what is being done with personal data is apparent.

Sometimes called "joined-up government," sometimes "information age government," sometimes "electronic government," the government's vision has several strands. There is a target of delivering 100 percent of government services electronically by 2005 through mechanisms such as the government portal, call centers, and one-stop shops. In general terms, the challenge is simple: to ensure that the system works in the way in which it is supposed to. If it doesn't, citizens will lose confidence and interest. Setting and meeting data protection standards is a key component. It is always important for a regulator to work with those it regulates, and in this context we will continue to work with relevant parts of government (currently the Office of the e-Envoy and the Cabinet Office) to develop these standards. In the area of on-line authentication and identification, in particular, there is still much work to be done.

In promoting e-government, stress is often laid upon the use of technology to deliver the same services in a smarter way. For instance, a "joined-up" change-of-address service has recently been piloted. In other scenarios the whole point of the deployment of new technology is that it allows different objectives to be achieved through the use of data-mining and profiling. Whereas, previously, benefit claims or tax returns might be sampled for accuracy, today it is possible to check, say, all applications for taxi licenses against all applications for benefit, to identify all possible cases of error and to automatically rank cases in order of the likelihood of fraud. Not only does this raise questions as to whether the "quality" of the data is sufficient to support the conclusions that are drawn, it also raises questions about transparency. Is information about how data are to be used and the purposes for which they are disclosed made sufficiently clear to data subjects? Without transparency, the necessary public debate about the extent to which it is right that individual conduct should be routinely monitored can never take place.

Another strand of the modernizing agenda of e-government is the use of information technology to reconfigure service delivery. For example joint initiatives between Social Services Departments and National Health Service Trusts depend upon the sharing of information about clients between partners who do not necessarily have the same attitudes towards issues such as confidentiality. One of the ways in which data protection and privacy concerns have been addressed within multi-agency environments has been through the development of local information-sharing protocols. In some cases national model protocols have been successfully developed, allowing local agreements to be put in place relatively easily; but this has not always been the case, and too often local bodies are struggling to agree upon standards.

In July 2001, I also set out in my annual report[6] the importance of improving data quality. Data quality is a critical issue in looking at large databases in the public and the private sectors and one which the Data Protection Act requires to be addressed, particularly to ensure that the quality of the data is fit for the purpose that the data are intended to fulfill.

Complaints and Requests for Assessment

What of individuals' perspectives in this changing world? The fact that today most people in the UK are aware that their personal information is being processed, and that many people will be processing information about others in their workplace, has made them far more appreciative of the risks to respect for private life which processing of personal data can bring. The number of

---

[6]   Information Commissioner annual report and accounts for the year ending March 31, 2001, HMSO, June 2001, ISBN 0-10-291017-0.

individuals who come to us alleging that there has been a breach of their rights is at an all-time height.

Section 42 of the Data Protection Act 1998 provides that persons who believe that they are directly affected by any processing of personal data may request the Commissioner to make an assessment whether the processing is likely or unlikely to have been carried out in compliance with the Act. In practice, most requests for assessment are complaints from individuals who believe that their personal data have not been processed in compliance with the Act. In a considerable number of cases, even though it is clear that the person making the request has concerns regarding the processing in question, we are not provided with sufficient information to enable us to make an assessment, but we are able to provide authoritative advice. Such cases, where we provide written advice, are counted as inquiries. These are to be distinguished from requests from data controllers for advice regarding their own compliance. Alleged breaches of the Telecommunications Regulations are not technically requests for assessment but are included in our caseload figures.

The total of requests for assessment, and those "complaints" where an assessment is not made but which are recorded as enquiries, may be broadly compared with the annual totals of complaints received under the Data Protection Act 1984. The 2000/01 annual total of some 8,875 requests for assessment and enquiries the office had dealt with by March 31, 2001 (including 1,721 complaints of breaches of the Telecommunications Regulations), therefore, indicate a very significant increase in casework for compliance staff. Especially as this is in addition to work undertaken in closing 1,121 complaints received under the Data Protection Act 1984 (see figure 1). Requests were received about:

Consumer Credit	24.5%
Telecommunications	16.6%
Direct Marketing	4.0%
Other	47.9%

What happens if it appears that there has been a breach of the law? An independent supervisory authority must be able to apply sanctions. Where there has been a breach of principle, enforcement action is possible, designed to remedy the breach. The approach of the Office over the years has been to seek to achieve compliance with the law without the need to resort to formal action. Indeed, the number of formal actions taken is small, but there are many occasions on which the knowledge that the failure to move to compliant processing would lead to such action has assisted the change.

For some individuals, remedying a breach may provide no relief. If, for example, inaccurate information is corrected, or a name on a mailing list is successfully suppressed, or a breach in security is remedied, or information

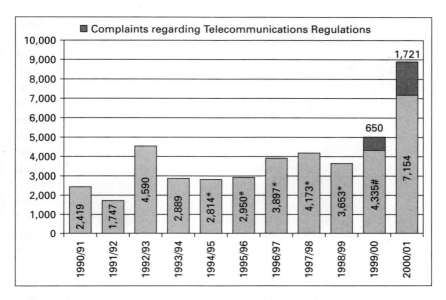

* Figures since 1994/95 refer to the financial year commencing April 1 and ending March 31 rather than using the previous reporting period for the Data Protection Registrar's Annual Report, which ran from June 1 to May 31.

This figure for the financial year 1999/2000 is based on the number of complaints recived for the eleven months to February 29, 2000, adjusted to provide a 12-month estimate.

Figure 1   Complaints/requests for assessment received 1990 to 2001

required in response to a subject access request is belatedly provided, the individual may still have been damaged and distressed by the original failure of compliance. In those circumstances individuals can seek compensation in the court.

There are also some criminal offences which I can, as Information Commissioner, prosecute. These relate to the requirement of notifying and to the unsavory practice of those people and organizations who seek to obtain other people's personal details by deception and then pass them on at a price.

European and Global Considerations

While the European Union Directive is intended to harmonize data protection across Europe, the detail of the law and the nature of enforcement powers will vary, reflecting culture and legal systems. [For an example of a data-protection issue between the EU and another region of the world, see box 2.] The Directive itself recognized the need to be proactive about

Box 2   The Safe Harbor Agreement

The EU passed its data protection directive in 1998. It states that data must be: fairly and lawfully processed for limited purposes, adequate, relevant and not excessive, accurate, not kept longer than necessary, processed in accordance with the data subject's rights, secure and not transferred to countries without adequate protection.

This last point prompted a dispute with the US where people do not have the same level of protection as in the EU. The US has a "safe harbor" arrangement under which American companies agree to give a certain level of protection and this is self-regulated. The EU has now accepted the "safe harbor" principle but the agreement is controversial as many people find the US system as inadequate. The US Federal Trade Commission published a report to the US Congress in May 2000 which found that only 20 percent of companies were complying with the US fair information practice principles (EUBusiness (2001). "EU data protection overview". *EUBusiness*. Item 1923. http://www.eubusiness.com/item/19123).

working to achieve the greatest possible harmonization. To that end, meetings of Commissioners are held regularly to advise government representatives. These are, however, global issues. Beyond Europe, informal networks and working groups of various kinds meet to address common problems.

Starting points for consideration of data protection issues vary: language used and legal contexts vary; our own law might benefit from change. A review of the Directive will give the UK government an opportunity to comment.[7] However, the concept and approach provided in UK law has shown itself to be of value in a fast changing world. While technological development moves ever faster, the fundamental rights to be protected are unchanging.

Basic study questions

1. How long have data protection laws existed in at least some European countries, and when was the first European-Union-wide data protection directive fully implemented?
2. State the "fundamental right" that data protection laws are intended to protect.
3. The UK Data Protection Act 1984 and the UK Data Protection Act 1998 share eight "principles of fair information handling." What are these principles?
4. Three important ideas included in the Data Protection Act 1998 are "data controller," "personal data," and "data processing." Define these important terms.
5. What is the overall goal of the Data Protection Act 1998?

---

[7]   Data Protection Act 1998: Post-Implementation Appraisal. Summary of responses to September 2000 consultation. Lord Chancellor's Department. CP(R)99/01, December 2001.

6.   What is a "code of practice" and how does it differ from a law like the Data Protection Act 1998? (Use, as an example to illustrate your answer, the UK code of practice for the use of CCTV in public places.)

7.   What are the benefits of adopting codes of practice to supplement laws like the Data Protection Act 1998?

8.   What is e-government? Why are data protection laws needed to make e-government possible?

9.   Why is "data quality" an important consideration for data protection?

10.   What explains the dramatic increase in "complaints" and "requests for assessment" from individual citizens during recent years?

11.   What happens when the Office of the Information Commissioner determines that the Data Protection Act 1998 has been violated by a person or an organization?

Questions for further thought

1.   Even though different countries have different cultures and different legal systems, there are many on-going efforts around the world to harmonize data protection laws and practices from country to country. Why is this happening, and how likely is it that these efforts will eventually succeed?

2.   Explain how the "codes of practice" described above by Elizabeth France are related to James Moor's notion of "zones of privacy."

3.   Data subjects under European legislation are living people. Consider the privacy ramifications of this restriction with the advent of, for example, genetic data.

4.   CCTV raises many privacy issues. With the advent of computer face recognition Smart CCTV is now being used in public spaces. What additional issues does this raise and how might they be addressed?

CASE TO ANALYZE: A SMALL MATTER OF PRIVACY

The imagined case presented below illustrates the risks to privacy that can occur when information management technology is deployed to help solve pressing human and social problems. In this case, the areas of medical research and medical information management are involved; but similar risks are present in many other human endeavors. The reader is invited to analyze this case using the case-analysis method described in chapter 3 above.

Jimmy Small, aged 39, lives in a small rural community where his family has lived for generations. His extended family is one of the largest families in the area. Local people often comment on how Small women live a lot longer than Small men. Indeed it is small wonder that Jimmy is teased about how his sisters will be around long after Jimmy. The Smalls are generally of good health but nevertheless are all, including Jimmy, registered with one of the doctors at the Micham Medical Center (MMC), which is one of three medical centers in the area. Tradition is prevalent with the Smalls, and they have used MMC since it was formed over 70 years ago.

MMC has steadily grown from its meager beginnings and now provides a full range of medical care. Clinicians comprise six doctors, five nurses, two midwives, one counselor and one physiotherapist. These are supported by the medical practice manager and six administrators. MMC prides itself on being at the forefront of medical practice and administration. Since 1990 MMC has used computer systems to support both medical practice and administration. Currently there is a network of 25 computers used by clinicians and administrators. Clinicians directly enter information onto electronic patient records (EPR). Administrators transpose clinical information from other sources onto EPRs. Pathology results and X-ray reports are received electronically and added to the EPRs by administrators.

As part of the regional medical network (RMN) MMC links into Medlink, which enables EPRs to be transferred between hospitals, medical practices, medical research centers, and a group of authorized organizations, including pharmacists, social care organizations, and medical appliance services. MedLink has been fully operational for nine months. A recent report has been issued by the RMN which suggests that EPR transfer is helping to provide a more effective and efficient service to individuals and with an additional benefit of providing new evidence for medical researchers in the area of public health and healthcare.

One month ago Jimmy Small had to visit his doctor, Dr Measures at MMC, as he was complaining of unusual tiredness. It is standard practice at MMC for doctor and patient to share and contribute to the EPR as part of the consultation. Dr Measures asked Jimmy some searching questions about his condition and entered the details onto Jimmy's EPR. The two of them discussed the information on Jimmy's EPR. He had had few medical ailments throughout his life. Dr Measures suggested that a set of routine tests should be undertaken, the results of which would be back in 10 days. Jimmy made an appointment to discuss the results.

By the time he returned to see Dr Measures, the results of the test had been added to the EPR. But Dr Measures had some additional information for Jimmy that was to radically change his life. One of the medical research centers in the RMN had for sometime been investigating life expectancy and natural causes of death in the region's population. This research used empirical data as well as genetic data. Use had been made of the region's EPRs that were now available on Medlink. It had enabled families to be studied in detail. This had led to a predictive life expectancy and cause of death model being developed which was to be used in the long-term planning of medical resources in the region covered by RMN.

It turned out that the Small family was a unique case. Genetic data from Jimmy's predecessors had revealed a rare medical condition that meant Small males were likely to die prematurely due to a medical disorder. This made them susceptible to a range of illnesses and diseases. The last ten Small males had each died of a different cause, but it had been triggered by this hereditary disorder. Once triggered, there was little chance of recovery. When Jimmy's test results had arrived at MMC, the Medical Research Center had also received them and sent a communication to MMC about their findings. Dr Measures explained to Jimmy that the trigger had been set and that his condition would deteriorate gradually over 5 years. After that, life expectancy was unpredictable.

Devastated, Jimmy left MMC in a daze. Since then, he seemed to have been living in a dream world. Today, Jimmy was in the local shop when Sharon Webb, who worked as an administrator at MMC, walked in. She was a friend of Jimmy and had been one of those who had teased him about the Small women. Today was different; she smiled and apologized for the teasing she had done in the past. Jimmy was shocked that Sharon seemed to know about his condition. He went home where he found the mail had arrived. There was a renewal notice for his medical insurance. He discovered that his premiums had been tripled due to a profiling exercise that the company had just completed. "Is there anyone who does not know about my condition?" thought Jimmy.

ADDITIONAL READINGS AND WEB RESOURCES

Additional readings

Elgesem, D. (1999). "The Structure of Rights in Directive 95/46/EC on the Protection of Individuals with regard to the Processing of Personal Data and the Free Movement of Such Data." *Ethics and Information Technology*, 1: 283–93.

Introna, L. I. (1997). "Privacy and the Computer: Why We Need Privacy in the Information Society." *Metaphilosophy*, 28/3: 259–75.

Nissenbaum, H. (1997). "Toward an Approach to Privacy in Public: Challenges of Information Technology." *Ethics and Behavior*, 7/3: 207–19.

Tavani, H. T. (1999). "Informational Privacy, Data Mining and the Internet." *Ethics and Information Technology*, 1: 137–45.

Tavani, H. T., and Moor, J. H. (2001). "Privacy Protection, Control of Information, and Privacy-Enhancing Technologies." In R. A. Spinello and H. T. Tavani (eds.), *Readings in CyberEthics*. Jones and Bartlett, pp. 378–91.

van den Hoven, J. (1997). "Privacy and the Varieties of Informational Wrong-doing." *Computers and Society*, 27: 33–7.

Web resources

The Electronic Privacy Information Center at http://www.epic.org

The Information Commissioner of the United Kingdom at
http://www.dataprotection.gov.uk

The Office of the Federal Privacy Commissioner, Australia at
http://www.privacy.gov.au

Privacy International at http://www.privacy.org/pi/

Privacy.net at http://www.privacy.net

Privacy.org at http://www.privacy.org

Computing and
Intellectual Property

Editors' Introduction

"Greased" Property

With recent advances in computer technology, most forms of intellectual property can now be digitized – for example, novels, stories, essays, poems, diaries, journals, magazines, newspapers, charts, diagrams, maps, drawings, photos, databases, musical recordings, movies, television programs, university courses, and on and on. But digitizing intellectual property has led to a nest of thorny ethical problems that could take decades to resolve. How did information technology bring about such a crisis for intellectual property? The answer lies in the fact that ownership essentially involves the right to *control* what one owns, and digitizing one's property can cause one to lose control of it.

Copies of digital entities are essentially identical to their originals. And, as Moor has pointed out (see chapter 11 above), once an item has been digitized and entered into a networked computer system, it becomes "greased data" that can easily slip from computer to computer across the network. Owners can thereby lose control of their property. Perhaps the most important loss for most owners is the ability to sell, lease, or rent the property and thereby make a profit. The ease and trivial costs of digital copying have thereby "greased" the world's intellectual properties, making them vulnerable to worldwide dissemination free of charge. Famous examples of this phenomenon include Napster-disseminated music files [see box 3] and Morpheus-enabled swapping of movies and television programs. New possibilities like these have led to major "policy vacuums" requiring significant revision of ownership laws, treaties, and acceptable business practices. Society might even be forced to rethink the fundamental concept of "ownership" itself.

Box 3   Napster

The most well publicized IPR [intellectual property rights] issue on the Internet involves the digital exchange of music. The very existence of Napster (and related software such as Gnutella) raises pressing ethical questions. The Napster software program was originally created to allow Internet users to quickly and easily exchange files for free over the Internet. However, Napster is primarily used for the exchange of copyrighted songs. A product whose only use is for illegal activities is clearly unethical, but a product which has both legal and illegal uses is more problematic. If a product is created for legal purposes but is then used almost exclusively for illegal acts, is the creator responsible?

Napster has been involved in an ongoing legal battle with major music companies who are trying to prevent their songs from being downloaded with the software. This issue is such a complex one that it has even caused rifts within the community of musicians.

Music companies claim that they are losing tremendous amounts of profits because potential customers are stealing music online instead of purchasing it directly from the companies. The companies are supported in their claims by several top musicians, notably the hard rock band Metallica who brought on the original lawsuit.

On the other side of the argument are unknown musicians who see Napster as an opportunity to spread their music. The purpose of IPR laws is to expand knowledge and intellectual property. Unknown musicians say that this can happen just as well through Napster. Many musicians also see Napster as a way to free themselves from the high fees of music companies, allowing them to directly reach their fans.

Source: From Gros, M. and Meir, A. (2001). *Values for Management*. 6 (April). http://www.besr.org/journal/besr_newsletter_6.html

What is Ownership and How Can It Be Justified?

What does it mean to say that someone "owns" a house, a car, a musical composition, or a computer program? Ownership is typically explained as having *a set of rights to control one's property, including the right to use it as well as the right to say whether and how others may use it*. If you own a house, for example, you have the right to live in it, to raise your family in it, to entertain friends in it, and so on. You also have the right to determine who else may use your house and for what purposes. This includes the right to sell it or lease it to others, or give it away as a gift, or leave it to someone in your will.

The right to control one's property, however, is not absolute. For example, a person may not burn down his house if doing so will endanger a neighbor's house. If someone owns a knife, she has the right to use it for a variety of purposes, but she does not have the right to plunge it into someone else's chest or to give another person permission to do so. A person may drive his car down the street, but only at an appropriate speed and only on the proper side of the road. Ownership, then, is typically defined as a limited set of rights to control what one owns. But how does one acquire these rights? Philosophers have offered a number of theories to ethically justify ownership.

The labor theory of ownership   Perhaps the most famous theory of ownership is that of the English philosopher John Locke. He argued that a person who mixes his labor with resources that are not owned by others, and thereby creates a product, has gained the right to own the resulting product. Because the laborer has invested a part of his life to create the item, and no one else did the same, the laborer has a right to control what he has created. Locke added an important proviso that the laborer must leave "as much and as good" of the original resources for the next person, so that anyone else could also mix her labor with those resources to create a product for herself. Although Locke applied his theory of ownership to physical objects created from natural resources (e.g., log cabins in the wilderness), his theory can easily be extended to cover intangible entities – intellectual property – like poems created from the words of a language, or musical compositions created from the notes of a music scale, or a computer program created from the resources of a computer language. Creating items from these resources leaves as much and as good for everyone else to make their own intellectual properties.

The personality theory of ownership   Another justification of ownership, used by the German philosopher Hegel, is the "personality theory." This theory is similar in many ways to Locke's, and it applies most easily to intellectual property. A poem, a musical composition, a painting, or some other product of human creativity is considered to be an expression or extension of the creator's personality. The creator, therefore, has the right to control it – that is, to use it and to say whether and under what circumstances others may use it.

The utilitarian theory of ownership   According to this view, property rights should be recognized, promoted, and protected in order to maximize happiness and well-being within the community and minimize pain and sorrow. Humanity benefits when people invent new products and processes that are useful, informative, or entertaining. Property rights provide incentives for creative people to generate a continuous flow of new creations, which in turn will contribute to the greatest happiness for the greatest number of people.

The social contract theory of ownership   This account of ownership explains and justifies property by making it part of a complex social agreement. The community agrees to pass laws and create conditions that are conducive to property ownership. The owners, in return, agree to use their property in ways that society considers appropriate. Owners and society must keep their promises to each other by fulfilling their contracts. If the overall goal within a given community is to maximize happiness and minimize harm, then the social contract theory becomes a version of the utilitarian theory. But a community might aim, instead, at *different* ends like obeying the commands of a god, or establishing a meritocracy, or some other non-utilitarian goal; so the social contract theory is *not* just the utilitarian theory under a different name.

Today, many countries of the world use primarily utilitarian grounds for establishing and defending intellectual property rights. In the United States, for example, the Constitution (Article I, Section 8) grants to Congress the power to "Promote the Progress of Science and useful Arts, by securing for limited Times to Authors and Inventors the exclusive Right to their respective Writings and Discoveries." The rights of ownership, therefore, are used as incentives for the creation or discovery of useful new products and processes that will likely benefit society as a whole.

Current Varieties of Ownership of Intellectual Property

The three most common forms of ownership for intellectual property are (a) copyrights, (b) patents, and (c) trade secrets.

Copyrights

When an author writes a literary work, or a composer makes a musical composition, or an artist creates a painting, he or she can acquire a copyright for that work in any country that has signed the Berne Convention for the Protection of Literary and Artistic Works (149 countries by early 2002). The Berne Convention protects nearly all text-based items, as well as musical creations, works of art, films, videos, photographs, etc. In 1996 the World Intellectual Property Organization (WIPO) Treaty explicitly added computer programs to the list of copyright-protected works (see Article 4 of that treaty).

By 1996, when the WIPO Treaty was adopted, most industrialized nations had already granted copyright protection to software (e.g., the United States did so in 1980). Nevertheless, even today, after decades of scholarly debate and court cases, there are issues of software ownership that have not been fully settled. Copyright law is complex and constantly evolving, and additional decades will likely be needed to resolve the important issues. In spite of this, American courts have already identified several aspects of computer programs that can be copyright protected, including (a) the original source code, (b) any translation of the source code (including machine translations), (c) the "look and feel" of some computer programs, and (d) the "structure, sequence and organization" of the elements of some programs.

Copyright is a long-lasting form of ownership which extends 70 years beyond the death of the creator. It prevents others from directly copying, distributing, or publicly performing a work without permission from the copyright holder. On the other hand, copyright is a rather *weak* form of ownership because it does not provide monopoly control to the owner. Thus, if someone independently creates a work that is very similar to or even identical to an already copyrighted work, the original copyright holder cannot prevent the new creator from using and disseminating the work. In addition, the burden of proof is on the copyright owner if he or she believes that others have copied the original.

For owners of computer programs, an important shortcoming of copyright protection is the fact that copyrights do not protect the *algorithm* – the underlying sequence of computer commands embedded within the program. For most owners of a computer program, the algorithm is exactly the part that most needs protection, since it is the "functional" part that gives software the power to control a computer. In addition, creating the algorithm normally requires the most time, resources and creativity.

Patents

A stronger kind of ownership is the *patent*, which provides *monopoly control* of one's intellectual property for 17 years (often renewable for 5 more years). For example, if someone has a patent on a piece of software, he or she can stop anyone else – for 17–22 years – from using, copying, distributing, or marketing that software without permission. Even if the other person did not copy the original program, but instead created it independently, the patent holder can nevertheless prevent the new creator from using his own independent creation.

Because patents give monopoly control to owners, it is understandable that software writers would want patents to protect their programs. Until the early 1980s, however, courts in the United States were reluctant to grant patents for software. Even though most computer programs did fulfill the usual requirements of being "useful, novel and non-obvious," they were not considered able to meet the test of being "a process, machine, manufacture or composition of matter." Also, a computer program was viewed as a sequence of ideas or mathematical formulas, and these are not supposed to be patented because they are "the building blocks of science and technology." Patenting them would remove them from the public domain and thereby impede progress in science and technology. This would defeat the primary goal of patents, which is to encourage new scientific and technological discoveries and inventions.

In 1981 the watershed case of Diamond v. Diehr led American courts to view many computer programs as similar to step-by-step manufacturing processes. As a result, after 1981 the sequences of commands (algorithms) embedded in many software programs were allowed to be patented. This new development opened the floodgates, and tens of thousands of computer programs were patented after 1981. Many people today are alarmed by this new situation because they worry that significant aspects of science and mathematics are being removed from the public domain. In addition, it has now become very expensive to conduct a patent search in order to make sure that one's new software does not infringe on thousands of already patented programs. Only very wealthy corporations can afford to conduct such searches, and this puts small software companies and individual programmers at a huge disadvantage. Instead of encouraging new developments in science and technology, which patents are supposed to do, software patents may actually be hindering such progress. It should be noted that, currently, in many other countries software patents are unlikely to be granted.

Trade secrets

A third form of ownership for intellectual property is trade secrecy. This type of ownership allows a company to create something in-house and then use it within the company to carry on the business. A trade secret might be, for example, a manufacturing process, a food recipe, a chemical formula, or a software program used within the company. To qualify as a trade secret the protected entity must be novel, the company has to make a significant investment of effort and resources to create it, and the company must also make a significant effort to keep it a secret from potential competitors. License agreements, employee contracts, encryption efforts, and other devices are typically used to preserve secrecy.

Trade secrecy can be used to protect the same kinds of intellectual property as copyrights and patents combined. Nevertheless, trade secrecy has some significant shortcomings as a form of ownership. For example, if a competitor happens to create or discover the same thing independently, the competitor may be allowed to use it without permission of the original owner. In some cases, the competitor might even file for a patent or copyright and force the original company to pay royalties. In addition, if the secret somehow leaks out, the property may no longer be protected by law.

Trade secrecy is an especially troublesome form of ownership for software, because most software is created for distribution to large numbers of licensees. In spite of licensing agreements that are intended to preserve secrecy, once thousands of copies of the software have been distributed relevant secrets may be revealed and ownership by trade secrecy may be lost.

Do Current Forms of Ownership Ethically Protect Software?

In chapter 13, entitled "Proprietary Rights in Computer Software," Deborah G. Johnson raises a key question about the current forms of software ownership: *Do copyrights, patents, and trade secrets adequately and justly protect the property rights of software owners?* To answer this question, she adopts the utilitarian theory of ownership because that is the theory employed in the US Constitution. She concludes that the relevant laws are "not bad laws," because they are "right on target in seeking to create an environment in which invention can flourish." However, given the kind of problems and shortcomings described above, Johnson suggests that current laws may have to be modified, perhaps even abandoned, for computer-related inventions. She concludes:

> Whatever changes one supports, it seems clear that we must keep in mind that our ends should be the same as those of the patent and copyright systems, to create an environment in which creativity and invention are encouraged and facilitated.

Unlike Johnson, Richard Stallman argues, in chapter 14, "Why Software Should Be Free," that current forms of ownership for computer programs are unjust and immoral, and therefore should be eliminated. Software ownership, he says, inflicts many kinds of harm upon society. He also uses the utilitarian theory of ownership; but, unlike Johnson, he concludes that current laws restrict and discourage creativity and invention and therefore should be abandoned in favor of free software.[1]

---

[1]   Stallman's call for "free software" eventually led to the so-called "open source movement." This, in turn, led to free software like the LINUX operating system and the email software SENDMAIL that is used globally on the Internet. See the article "The Cathedral and the Bazaar," by Eric Raymond, listed in the Bibliography.

CHAPTER 13

Proprietary Rights in Computer Software: Individual and Policy Issues

Deborah G. Johnson

Introduction

In this paper I want to focus on two central moral issues surrounding the ownership of computer software. These are the individual moral question and the policy issue. The individual moral issue is simply this: Is it morally wrong for an individual (or company) to make an illegal copy of a piece of proprietary software? Here the question is one of what is right or wrong for an individual to do, given the law, and not a question of what the law should be. The policy issue centers on what the law should be and includes the following questions: Should computer software be private property? Does the extant system of copyright, patent, and trade secrecy protection adequately protect computer software? Does the system produce good consequences? I want to sketch positions on both of these issues, taking the copying issue first, but recognizing that the two are somewhat interdependent.

Is it Wrong to Copy Proprietary Software?

The issue here must be clarified in at least two ways. First, making a backup copy of a piece of software (which you have purchased) for your own protection may not be illegal. Second, while I have used the label "individual" moral issue, it is not just an issue for individuals but applies as well to collective units such as companies, agencies, and institutions. The typical cases that I have in mind are cases in which either you make a copy of a piece of

Deborah G. Johnson, "Proprietary Rights in Computer Software: Individual and Policy Issues." This chapter was originally presented as a paper at the National Conference on Computing and Values held at Southern Connecticut State University, New Haven, CT in August 1991. © by Research Center on Computing and Society, Southern Connecticut State University and reprinted by permission of the author.

proprietary software to give to a friend, or you borrow a piece of software from someone who has purchased it and you make a copy for your own use. These cases do not seem to differ significantly from the case in which a company buys a single copy of a piece of software and makes multiple copies for use within the company in order to avoid purchasing more.

The intuition that copying a piece of software is not wrong is understandable. Making a copy of a piece of proprietary software is easy, seems harmless, and the laws aimed at preventing it seem ill-suited for doing the job. Nevertheless, when I examine the arguments that are made (or might be made) to support the conclusion, I find that I can not "buy in." I am compelled to conclude that it is morally wrong to make an illegal copy of a piece of software, because it is illegal. The key issue here has little to do with software per se, and everything to do with the relationship between law and morality.

Perhaps the best way to begin is by laying out what I take to be the strongest arguments for the moral permissibility of individual copying. The strongest arguments claim (1) that the laws protecting computer software are bad, and, then, either: (2a) making a copy of a piece of software is not intrinsically wrong, or (2b) making a copy of a piece of software does no harm, or (2c) not making a copy of a piece of software may do some harm.

I will address premise (1) in the next section of this paper when I examine complaints about the law. For now, however, it is important to get clear on what might be claimed in premise (1). Here are some of the possibilities: (1a) all property law in America is unjust and the software laws are part of this; (1b) all intellectual property laws are unjust and software laws are part of this; (1c) most property law in America is just, but the laws surrounding computer software are not; (1d) while the laws surrounding the ownership of software are not unjust, they could be a lot better. The list could go on and just which position one holds makes much of the difference in the copying argument.

I do not want to take the time to run through these arguments so I am going to short-cut my argument here by just proclaiming that my position (to be elaborated in the next section) is that the system of intellectual property rights in America (in particular the patent and copyright systems) may not be the best of all possible systems in every detail, but both copyright and patent law have good ends and aim at the right balance between what can and what cannot be owned. In other words, while I recognize that the extant system of copyright and patent protection for software could be improved, I do not believe that these systems of law are blatantly unjust or wholly inappropriate for computer software.

The next step in my argument is to claim that an individual has a prima facie obligation to obey the laws of a roughly just system of law. "Prima facie" means "all things being equal" or "unless there are overriding reasons."

The prima facie obligation to obey the law could be overridden by higher order obligations or by special circumstances which justify disobedience. Higher order obligations will override when, for example, obeying the law will lead to greater harm than disobeying. Higher order obligations may even require civil disobedience. That is, if the law is immoral, then disobedience is morally obligatory. Special circumstances could justify disobedience to an otherwise good law when harm would come from obeying the law this one time. For example, the law prohibiting one to drive on the left side of the road is a good law, but one would be justified in breaking it in order to avoid hitting someone.

So I am not claiming that one always has an obligation to obey the law. I argue only that the burden of proof is on those who would disobey roughly good laws.

Given that extant laws regarding computer software are roughly good – which I am simply proclaiming for the moment – and given that one has a prima facie obligation to obey roughly good laws, the second premise carries the weight of any argument for the moral permissibility of copying. Hence premises (2a) to (2c) have to be examined carefully.

I agree with premise (2a) that there is nothing intrinsically wrong with making a copy of a piece of software. If there were no laws against it, such acts would not be wrong. Indeed, I have argued elsewhere that property rights are not natural or moral in themselves (Johnson 1993). They acquire moral significance only when they are created by law and only in relatively just systems of law. However, premise (2a) does not support the argument for copying because copying has been made illegal and as such it is prima facie wrong.

According to premise (2b), making a copy of a piece of software for personal use harms no one. If we think of copying taking place, as in (2a), in a state of nature, this premise appears to be true, i.e., no one is harmed. However, once we are in a society of laws, the laws create legal rights, and it seems that one harms others by depriving them of their legal rights. When one makes a copy of a piece of software, one deprives the owner of the legal right to control the use of that software and to require payment in exchange for the use of the software, and this is a harm. Those who think this is not a harm should talk to small software companies or individual entrepreneurs who have gone into the business of developing software, invested time and money, only to be squeezed out of business by customers who buy one copy and make others instead of buying more. So, premise (2b) is false in that making a copy of a piece of software does harm someone.

Premise (2c) has the most promise, for if it were true that one would actually be doing harm by obeying the law, then one might have a moral reason for overriding the law, even if it were relatively good. Richard Stallman (1990) and Helen Nissenbaum (1991) have both made arguments of this kind. Both argue that there are circumstances in which not making a copy or not making a copy and providing it to a friend does some harm. However, in their arguments, the harm referred to does not seem of the kind to counterbalance the effects of a relatively just system of property rights. Both give examples of how an individual might be able to help a friend out by providing an illegal copy of a piece of proprietary software. Both argue that this discourages altruism. But this argument ignores the harm to the copyright holder or patent holder.

Even if I were to grant that not providing a copy to a friend is doing harm, we have to compare the harms and choose the lesser one. Given what I said above about the prima facie obligation to obey the law, it follows that there may be some situations in which copying will be justified, namely when some fairly serious harm can only be prevented by making an illegal copy of a piece of proprietary software and using it. In most cases, however, the claims of the software owner to her legal rights would seem to be much stronger than the claims of someone who needs a copy to make her life easier.

If the position I have just sketched seems odd, consider an analogy with a different sort of property. Suppose I own a private swimming pool and I make a living by renting the use of it to others. I do not rent the pool everyday and you figure out how to break in undetected and use the pool when it is not opened and I am not around. The act of swimming is not intrinsically wrong, and swimming in the pool does no obvious harm to me (the owner) or anyone else. Nevertheless, you are using my property without my permission. It would hardly seem a justification for ignoring my property rights if you claimed that you were hot and the swim in my pool made your life easier. Similarly, if you argued that you had a friend who was very uncomfortable in the heat and you, having the knowledge of how to break into the pool, thought it would be selfish not to use that knowledge to help your friend break into the pool.

Of course, there are circumstances under which your illegal entry into my pool might be justified. For example, if someone else had broken in, was swimming, and began to drown. You were innocently walking by, saw the person drowning, and broke in, in order to save the other person. Here the circumstances justify overriding my legal rights.

There seems to be no moral difference between the two cases. Breaking into the pool and making a copy of a proprietary piece of software are both acts which violate the legal rights of the owner. And they are legal rights created by reasonably good laws. I will grant that these laws do prevent others from acting altruistically, but this, I believe, is inherent to private property. Private property is individualistic, exclusionary, and, perhaps, selfish. So, if Stallman and Nissenbaum want to launch an attack on all private property laws, I am in sympathy with their claims. However, I would press them to explain why they had picked out computer software law when private ownership of other things, such as natural resources or corporate conglomerates, seems much more menacing.

I conclude that it is prima facie wrong to make illegal copies of proprietary software because to do so is to deprive the owners of their legal rights, and this is to harm them. I admit that this has been a sketchy discussion of a topic that needs much more attention, but it is a topic that needs to be put on the table here.

Is Our System of Copyright and Patent Protection for Computer Software Good?

To put the policy issue in a moral or value framework, let me begin by saying that while in earlier work (Johnson 1985), I toyed with moral arguments supporting the ownership of software, namely a Lockean labor-theory argument, I now believe that property rights do not have a moral basis in the sense that they would exist prior to a society of laws. That is, I believe that property rights are social or conventional or artificial. This is entirely consistent with copyright and patent law in America, for both these systems of law are utilitarian in character. Both systems aim to produce good consequences for society in the long run. Debate and discussion about what the law should be with regard to computer software should, then, be framed in utilitarian theory.

In the late 1970s and early 1980s, a good deal of concern was being expressed that neither copyright nor patent law would adequately protect computer software. A sizeable literature described the extent and impact of software piracy and illegal copying, and expressed fear that software development would be significantly impeded because software companies would not be able to recover the costs of development, let alone profit from their creations. The incentive to create would be significantly dampened.

In the late 1980s and early 1990s, more and more concern is being expressed that there is too much protection for computer software; that is, that too much has become proprietary. The concern now is that copyright and patent protection are being extended too far. They now get in the way of software development (Kahin 1990).

This shift of concern goes to the heart of the aims of our intellectual property laws, for both copyright and patent law aim to create an environment in which invention is encouraged. This is done, on the one hand, by granting ownership in things such that the owner can put the new invention into the marketplace and profit when the invention is useful. On the other hand, invention is facilitated by insuring that the "building blocks" of the technological arts and sciences are not owned. Ownership of the building blocks would interfere with invention insofar as new inventors would have to seek permission to use these building blocks from private owners – owners who could refuse to grant permission (to avoid competition, out of personal whim, or for any reason whatsoever), or drive the price of invention prohibitively high.

When it comes to copyright, you can own the expression of an idea, but not the idea itself; when it comes to patents, you can receive a monopoly on the use of your invention as long as your invention is not, or does not, pre-empt use of a law of nature, abstract idea, mathematical formula, etc. The rationale for these restrictions is the same in both cases. To grant ownership of ideas, laws of nature, mathematical formulas, etc. would interfere with progress in the technological arts and sciences because others could not freely use these building blocks.

So, both patent and copyright law aim at facilitating invention; that is, both aim at producing good consequences in the technological arts and sciences. In order to do this, both systems of law must draw a very careful line between what can and cannot be owned. However, the line is particularly difficult to draw in the case of computer software because the distinctions traditionally used to draw the line, such as that between idea and expression, or that between mathematical formula and application, get very blurry for software and other computer technology.

Patents

The shift in concern about patent protection on software from the early 1980s to the early 1990s can be traced to a shift in the policies and practices of the Patent Office and the Court of Customs and Patent Appeals (CCPA) after the Diamond v. Diehr case (Samuelson 1990). Up until Diamond v. Diehr the Patent Office had been extremely reluctant to grant patents on computer related claims, though its reluctance had been challenged by the CCPA. After Diamond v. Diehr the Patent Office began granting patents and the CCPA found new reasons to grant more. While only a handful of software related patents had been granted before Diamond v. Diehr, thousands have been granted since then (Kahin 1990).

The new concerns about patent protection on software go to the heart of the patent system's aim, for they suggest that because so much is owned, invention is now being inhibited. The subject-matter limitation on what can be patented aims to insure that the building blocks of science and technology should not be owned so that continued development will flourish, yet complaints suggest that the building blocks may now be owned. The situation is described roughly as follows: Because so many patents have been granted, before putting new software on the market, one must do an extensive and expensive patent search. If overlapping patents are found, licenses must be bought. Even if no overlapping patents are found, there is always the risk of late-issuing patents. Patent searches are not guaranteed to identify all potential infringements because the Patent Office has a poor classification system for software. Hence, there is always the risk of a lawsuit due to patent infringement. One may invest a great deal in developing a product, invest even more in a patent search, and then find at the last minute that the new product infringes on something already claimed. These factors make software development a risky business and constitute barriers to development of new software. In particular, the costs and risks are barriers to small entrepreneurs.

I have argued elsewhere that computer algorithms should not be patentable and these criticisms lend support to that position. Depending on how the term "algorithm" is defined, these criticisms suggest that an even broader subject-matter limitation for program-related patent claims should be implemented. Stallman (1990) proposes that we pass a law that excludes software from the domain of patents. Samuelson (1990) argues that the Patent Office and the CCPA have over-extended the meaning of the Supreme Court's decision in the Diamond v. Diehr case.

Copyright

The situation with regard to copyright is less clear and I am not going to spend as much time on it. Copyright protection has the legal advantage that the Copyright Act was amended in 1980 to explicitly specify that it applies to computer software. On the other hand, the meaning of copyright protection is unclear in the sense that it is not clear what aspect of a piece of software you own.

Copyright protection is easier to acquire in the sense that if you develop a new program on your own, even though the new software may duplicate something already copyrighted, you do not infringe as long as you were unfamiliar with the copyrighted program while you were developing your own. This is an advantage from the point of view of acquiring protection, but a disadvantage in that the protection you acquire is weak.

It is becoming increasingly apparent that the idea/expression distinction, which is the conceptual heart of copyright law, may not be adequate to handle computer software. The uncertainty of the application of copyright law is itself enough to get in the way of development in the field.

Not Bad Laws

Note that these criticisms of patent and copyright protection are not directed at the fundamental character of the laws. The aims and strategies of copyright and patent law seem right on target in seeking to create an environment in which invention can flourish. In this respect they are not bad laws. But while their aims are right, they seem to lack the conceptual tools to handle the issues posed by computer technology. It appears that copyright law and patent law will have to be modified or abandoned for computer-related invention. Whatever changes one supports, it seems clear that we must keep in mind that our ends should be the same as those of the patent and copyright systems, to create an environment in which creativity and invention are encouraged and facilitated.

References

Johnson, D. G. (1993). "A Reply to 'Should Computer Programs Be Ownable?' " *Metaphilosophy*, 24: 85–90.

Johnson, D. G. (1985). *Computer Ethics*. Prentice-Hall.

Kahin, B. (1990). "The Software Patent Crisis." *Technology Review*, 93/1 (April): 543–58.

Nissenbaum, H. (1991). "A Plea for Casual Copying." In T. W. Bynum, W. Maner, and J. L. Fodor (eds.), *Software Ownership and Intellectual Property Rights*. Research Centre on Computing and Science. Available at www.southernct.edu/organizations/rccs/resources/research/intellectual_property/intel_prop_contents.html (accessed December 7, 2002).

Samuelson, P. (1990). "Benson Revisted: The Case Against Patent Protection for Algorithms and Other Computer Program-Related Inventions." *Emory Law Journal*, 39/4 (Fall): 1025–154.

Stallman, R. (1990). Conference paper, American Philosophical Association Meetings, December.

Basic study questions

1. Describe the two "central moral issues" that Johnson identifies regarding the ownership of software.
2. Why does Johnson conclude that it is morally wrong to make an illegal copy of a piece of software?
3. What, according to Johnson, are the two strongest arguments for the moral permissibility of individual copying of owned software? Why does she consider these arguments to be unacceptable?
4. According to Johnson, when – if ever – is one morally justified in breaking a law?
5. Does Johnson consider copying a piece of software intrinsically wrong? What is the reasoning behind her position?
6. Does Johnson agree that making a copy of a piece of software harms no one? Why, or why not?
7. Are patents and copyrights the same thing? If not, explain the differences between them with respect to the ownership of software.

8. Given her criticism of copyright and patent laws, why does Johnson believe that one still has a moral obligation to obey them? Explain in detail.
9. What, according to Johnson, should be the major goal of any modifications to traditional copyright and patent laws?

Questions for further thought

1. What is the "classical" theory of ownership developed by English philosopher John Locke? This theory seems to fit well with ownership of physical objects like log cabins in the forest, but how well does it fit with "non-physical" intellectual property like computer software? Explain in detail.
2. What is the difference between law and ethics? Can some actions be ethical but illegal? Can some actions be legal but unethical? Explain your answers with examples (not necessarily involving software or computing).
3. Do you agree with Johnson's view that "property rights are not natural or moral in themselves" – that if there were no laws and no societies, no one would have the right to own anything? Explain in detail why you think so.

CHAPTER 14

Why Software Should Be Free

Richard Stallman

Introduction

The existence of software inevitably raises the question of how decisions about its use should be made. For example, suppose one individual who has a copy of a program meets another who would like a copy. It is possible for them to copy the program? Who should decide whether this is done? The individuals involved? Or another party, called the "owner"?

Software developers typically consider these questions on the assumption that the criterion for the answer is to maximize developers' profits. The political power of business has led to the government adoption of both this criterion and the answer proposed by the developers: that the program has an owner, typically a corporation associated with its development.

I would like to consider the same question using a different criterion: the prosperity and freedom of the public in general.

This answer cannot be decided by current law – the law should conform to ethics, not the other way around. Nor does current practice decide this question, although it may suggest possible answers. The only way to judge is to see who is helped and who is hurt by recognizing owners of software, why, and how much. In other words, we should perform a cost-benefit analysis on behalf of society as a whole, taking account of individual freedom as well as production of material goods.

In this essay, I will describe the effects of having owners, and show that the results are detrimental. My conclusion is that programmers have the duty to encourage others to share, redistribute, study, and improve the software we write: in other words, to write free software, the word "free" in "free software" refers to freedom, not to price; the price paid for a copy of a free program may be zero, or small, or (rarely) quite large.

How Owners Justify Their Power

Those who benefit from the current system where programs are property offer two arguments in support of their claims to own programs: the emotional argument and the economic argument.

The emotional argument goes like this: "I put my sweat, my heart, my soul into this program. It comes from me, it's *mine!*" This argument does not require serious refutation. The feeling of attachment is one that programmers can cultivate when it suits them; it is not inevitable. Consider, for example, how willingly the same programmers usually sign over all rights to a large corporation for a salary; the emotional attachment mysteriously vanishes. By contrast, consider the great artists and artisans of medieval times, who didn't even sign their names to their work. To them, the name of the artist was not important. What mattered was that the work was done – and the purpose it would serve. This view prevailed for hundreds of years.

The economic argument goes like this: "I want to get rich (usually described inaccurately as 'making a living'), and if you don't allow me to get rich by programming, then I won't program. Everyone else is like me, so nobody will ever program. And then you'll be stuck with no programs at all!" This threat is usually veiled as friendly advice from the wise. I'll explain later why this threat is a bluff. First, I want to address an implicit assumption that is more visible in another formulation of the argument.

This formulation starts by comparing the social utility of a proprietary program with that of no program, and then concludes that proprietary software development is, on the whole, beneficial, and should be encouraged. The fallacy here is in comparing only two outcomes – proprietary software versus no software – and assuming there are no other possibilities.

Given a system of intellectual property, software development is usually linked with the existence of an owner who controls the software's use. As long as this linkage exists, we are often faced with the choice of proprietary software or none. However, this linkage is not inherent or inevitable; it is a consequence of the specific social/legal policy decision that we are questioning: the decision to have owners. To formulate the choice as between proprietary software versus no software is begging the question.

The Argument Against Having Owners

The question at hand is: "Should development of software be linked with having owners to restrict the use of it?"

In order to decide this, we have to judge the effect on society of each of those two activities independently: the effect of developing the software (regardless of its terms of distribution), and the effect of restricting its use (assuming the software has been developed). If one of these activities is helpful and the other is harmful, we would be better off dropping the linkage and doing only the helpful one. To put it another way, if restricting the distribution of a program already developed is harmful to society overall, then an ethical software developer will reject the option of doing so.

To determine the effect of restricting sharing, we need to compare the value to society of a restricted (i.e., proprietary) program with that of the same program, available to everyone. This means comparing two possible worlds. This analysis also addresses the simple counter-argument sometimes made that "the benefit to the neighbor of giving him or her a copy of a program is cancelled by the harm done to the owner." This counter-argument assumes that the harm and the benefit are equal in magnitude. The analysis involves comparing these magnitudes, and shows that the harm is much greater. To elucidate this argument, let us apply it in another area – road construction.

It would be possible to fund the construction of all roads with tolls. This would entail having toll booths at all street corners. Such a system would provide a great incentive to improve roads. It would also have the virtue of causing the users of any given road to pay for that road. However, a toll booth is an artificial obstruction to smooth driving – artificial, because it is not a consequence of how roads or cars work. Comparing free roads and toll roads by their usefulness, we find that (all else being equal) roads without toll booths are cheaper to construct, cheaper to run, safer, and more efficient to use. In a poor country, tolls may make the roads unavailable to many citizens. The roads without toll booths thus offer more benefit to society at less cost; they are preferable for society. Therefore, society should choose to fund roads in another way, not by means of toll booths. Use of roads, once built, should be free.

When the advocates of toll booths propose them as merely a way of raising funds, they distort the choice that is available. Toll booths do raise funds, but they do something else as well: in effect, they degrade the road. The toll road is not as good as the free road; giving us more or technically superior roads may not be an improvement if this means substituting toll roads for free roads. Of course, the construction of a free road does cost money, which the public must somehow pay. However, this does not imply the inevitability of toll booths. We who must in either case pay will get more value for our money by buying a free road.

I am not saying that a toll road is worse than no road at all. That would be true if the toll were so great that hardly anyone used the road – but this is an unlikely policy for a toll collector. However, as long as the toll booths cause significant waste and inconvenience, it is better to raise the funds in a less obstructive fashion.[1]

To apply the same argument to software development, I will now show that having "toll booths" for useful software programs costs society dearly: it makes the programs more expensive to construct, more expensive to distribute, and less satisfying and efficient to use. It will follow that program construction should be encouraged in some other way. Then I will go on to explain other methods of encouraging and (to the extent actually necessary) funding software development.

The Harm Done by Obstructing Software

Consider for a moment that a program has been developed, and any necessary payments for its development have been made; now society must choose either to make it proprietary or allow free sharing and use. Assume that the existence of the program and its availability is a desirable thing. One might regard a particular computer program as a harmful thing that should not be available at all, like the Lotus Marketplace database of personal information, which was withdrawn from sale due to public disapproval. Most of what I say does not apply to this case, but it makes little sense to argue for having an owner because the owner will make the program less available. The owner will not make it completely unavailable, as one would wish in connection with a program whose use is harmful. Restrictions on the distribution and modification of the program cannot facilitate its use. They can only interfere. So the effect can only be negative. But how much? And what kind?

Three different levels of material harm come from such obstruction:

- fewer people use the program;
- none of the users can adapt or fix the program;
- other developers cannot learn from the program, or base new work on it.

Each level of material harm has a concomitant form of psychosocial harm. This refers to the effect that people's decisions have on their subsequent feelings, attitudes, and predispositions. These changes in people's ways of

---

[1]   The issues of pollution and traffic congestion do not alter this conclusion. If we wish to make driving more expensive to discourage driving in general, it is disadvantageous to do this using toll booths, which contribute to both pollution and congestion. A tax on gasoline is much better. Likewise, a desire to enhance safety by limiting maximum speed is not relevant; a free access road enhances the average speed by avoiding stops and delays, for any given speed limit.

thinking will then have a further effect on their relationships with their fellow citizens, and can have material consequences.

The three levels of material harm waste part of the value that the program could contribute, but they cannot reduce it to zero. If they waste nearly all the value of the program, then writing the program harms society by at most the effort that went into writing the program. Arguably, a program that is profitable to sell must provide some net direct material benefit.

However, taking account of the concomitant psychosocial harm, there is no limit to the harm that proprietary software development can do.

Obstructing Use of Programs

The first level of harm impedes the simple use of a program. A copy of a program has nearly zero marginal cost (and you can pay this cost by doing the work yourself), so in a free market, it would have nearly zero price. A license fee is a significant disincentive to use the program. If a widely useful program is proprietary, far fewer people will use it.

It is easy to show that the total contribution of a program to society is reduced by assigning an owner to it. Each potential user of the program, faced with the need to pay to use it, may choose to pay, or may forego use of the program. When a user chooses to pay, this is a zero-sum transfer of wealth between two parties. But each time someone chooses to forego use of the program, this harms that person without benefiting anyone. The sum of negative numbers and zeros must be negative.

But this does not reduce the amount of work it takes to develop the program. As a result, the efficiency of the whole process, in delivered user satisfaction per hour of work, is reduced. This reflects a crucial difference between copies of programs and cars, chairs, or sandwiches. There is no copying machine for material objects outside of science fiction. But programs are easy to copy; anyone can produce as many copies as are wanted, with very little effort. This isn't true for material objects because matter is conserved: each new copy has to be built from raw materials in the same way that the first copy was built.

With material objects, a disincentive to use them makes sense, because fewer objects bought means less raw materials and work needed to make them. It's true that there is usually also a start-up cost, a development cost, which is spread over the production run. But as long as the marginal cost of production is significant, adding a share of the development cost does not make a qualitative difference. And it does not require restrictions on the freedom of ordinary users. However, imposing a price on something that would otherwise be free is a qualitative change. A centrally imposed fee for software distribution becomes a powerful disincentive.

What is more, central production as now practiced is inefficient even as a means of delivering copies of software. This system involves enclosing physical disks or tapes in superfluous packaging, shipping large numbers of them around the world, and storing them for sale. This cost is presented as an expense of doing business; in truth, it is part of the waste caused by having owners.

Damaging Social Cohesion

Suppose that both you and your neighbor would find it useful to run a certain program. In ethical concern for your neighbor, you should feel that proper handling of the situation will enable both of you to use it. A proposal to permit only one of you to use the program, while restraining the other, is divisive; neither you nor your neighbor should find it acceptable.

Signing a typical software license agreement means betraying your neighbor: "I promise to deprive my neighbor of this program so that I can have a copy for myself." People who make such choices feel internal psychological pressure to justify them, by downgrading the importance of helping one's neighbors – thus public spirit suffers. This is psychosocial harm associated with the material harm of discouraging use of the program.

Many users unconsciously recognize the wrong of refusing to share, so they decide to ignore the licenses and laws, and share programs anyway. But they often feel guilty about doing so. They know that they must break the law in order to be a good neighbor, but they still consider the laws authoritative, and they conclude that being a good neighbor (which they are) is naughty or shameful. That is also a kind of psychosocial harm, but one can escape it by deciding that these licenses and laws have no moral force.

Programmers also suffer psychosocial harm knowing that many users will not be allowed to use their work. This leads to an attitude of cynicism or denial. A programmer may describe enthusiastically the work that he finds technically exciting; then, when asked, "Will I be permitted to use it?," his face falls, and he admits the answer is no. To avoid feeling discouraged, he either ignores this fact most of the time or adopts a cynical stance designed to minimize the importance of it.

Since the age of Reagan, the greatest scarcity in the United States has not been technical innovation, but rather the willingness to work together for the public good. It makes no sense to encourage the former at the expense of the latter.

Obstructing Custom Adaptation of Programs

The second level of material harm is the inability to adapt programs. The ease of modification of software is one of its great advantages over older technology. But most commercially available software isn't available for modification, even after you buy it. It's available for you to take it or leave it, as a black box – that is all.

A program that you can run consists of a series of numbers whose meaning is obscure. No one, not even a good programmer, can easily change the numbers to make the program do something different.

Programmers normally work with the "source code" for a program, which is written in a programming language such as Fortran or C. It uses names to designate the data being used and the parts of the program, and it represents operations with symbols such as + for addition and – for subtraction. It is designed to help programmers read and change programs. Here is an example; a program to calculate the distance between two points in a plane:

```
double distance (p0, p1) struct point p0, p1;
double xdist = p1.x – p0.x;
double ydist = p1.y – p0.y;
return sqrt (xdist * xdist + ydist * ydist);
```

Here is the same program in executable form, on the computer I normally use:

1314258944	–232267772	–231844864	1634862
1411907592	–231844736	2159150	1420296208
–234880989	–234879837	–234879966	–232295424
1644167167	–3214848	1090581031	1962942495
572518958	–803143692	1314803317	.

Source code is useful (at least potentially) to every user of a program. But most users are not allowed to have copies of the source code. Usually, the source code for a proprietary program is kept secret by the owner lest anybody else learn something from it. Users receive only the files of incomprehensible numbers that the computer will execute. This means that only the program's owner can change the program.

A friend once told me of working as a programmer in a bank for about six months, writing a program similar to something that was commercially available. She believed that if she could have gotten source code for that commercially available program, it could easily have been adapted to their needs. The bank was willing to pay for this, but was not permitted to – the source code was a secret. So she had to do six months of make-work, work that counts in the GNP but was actually waste.

The MIT Artificial Intelligence (AI) lab received a graphics printer as a gift from Xerox around 1977. It was run by free software to which we added many convenient features. For example, the software would notify a user immediately on completion of a print job. Whenever the printer had trouble, such as a paper jam or running out of paper, the software would immediately notify all users who had print jobs queued. These features facilitated smooth operation.

Later, Xerox gave the AI lab a newer, faster printer, one of the first laser printers. It was driven by proprietary software that ran in a separate dedicated computer, so we couldn't add any of our favorite features. We could arrange to send a notification when a print job was sent to the dedicated computer, but not when the job was actually printed (and the delay was usually considerable). There was no way to find out when the job was actually printed; you could only guess. And no one was informed when there was a paper jam, so the printer often went for an hour without being fixed.

The system programmers at the AI lab were capable of fixing such problems, probably as capable as the original authors of the program. Xerox was uninterested in fixing them, and chose to prevent us, so we were forced to accept the problems. They were never fixed.

Most good programmers have experienced this frustration. The bank could afford to solve the problem by writing a new program from scratch, but a typical user, no matter how skilled, can only give up.

Giving up causes psychosocial harm – to the spirit of self-reliance. It is demoralizing to live in a house that you cannot rearrange to suit your needs. It leads to resignation and discouragement, which can spread to affect other aspects of one's life. People who feel this way are unhappy and do not do good work.

Imagine what it would be like if recipes were hoarded in the same fashion as software. You might say, "How do I change this recipe to take out the salt?," and the great chef would respond, "How dare you insult my recipe, the child of my brain and my palate, by trying to tamper with it? You don't have the judgment to change my recipe and make it work right!"

"But my doctor says I'm not supposed to eat salt! What can I do? Will you take out the salt for me?"

"I would be glad to do that; my fee is only $50,000." Since the owner has a monopoly on changes, the fee tends to be large. "However, right now I don't have time. I am busy with a commission to design a new recipe for ship's biscuit for the Navy Department. I might get around to you in about two years."

Obstructing Software Development

The third level of material harm affects software development. Software development used to be an evolutionary process, where a person would take an existing program and rewrite parts of it for one new feature, and then another person would rewrite parts to add another feature; in some cases, this continued over a period of 20 years. Meanwhile, parts of the program would be "cannibalized" to form the beginnings of other programs.

The existence of owners prevents this kind of evolution, making it necessary to start from scratch when developing a program. It also prevents new practitioners from studying existing programs to learn useful techniques or even how large programs can be structured.

Owners also obstruct education. I have met bright students in computer science who have never seen the source code of a large program. They may be good at writing small programs, but they can't begin to learn the different skills of writing large ones if they can't see how others have done it.

In any intellectual field, one can reach greater heights by standing on the shoulders of others. But that is no longer generally allowed in the software field – you can only stand on the shoulders of the other people in *your own company*.

The associated psychosocial harm affects the spirit of scientific cooperation, which used to be so strong that scientists would cooperate even when their countries were at war. In this spirit, Japanese oceanographers abandoning their lab on an island in the Pacific carefully preserved their work for the invading US Marines, and left a note asking them to take good care of it.

Conflict for profit has destroyed what international conflict spared. Nowadays scientists in many fields don't publish enough in their papers to enable others to replicate the experiment. They publish only enough to let readers marvel at how much they were able to do. This is certainly true in computer science, where the source code for the programs reported on is usually secret.

It Does Not Matter How Sharing Is Restricted

I have been discussing the effects of preventing people from copying, changing, and building on a program. I have not specified how this obstruction is carried out, because that doesn't affect the conclusion. Whether it is done by copy protection, or copyright, or licenses, or encryption, or ROM cards, or hardware serial numbers, if it *succeeds* in preventing use, it does harm.

Users do consider some of these methods more obnoxious than others. I suggest that the methods most hated are those that accomplish their objective.

Software Should be Free

I have shown how ownership of a program – the power to restrict changing or copying it – is obstructive. Its negative effects are widespread and important. It follows that society shouldn't have owners for programs.

Another way to understand this is that what society needs is free software, and proprietary software is a poor substitute. Encouraging the substitute is not a rational way to get what we need.

Vaclav Havel has advised us to "Work for something because it is good, not just because it stands a chance to succeed." A business making proprietary software stands a chance of success in its own narrow terms, but it is not what is good for society.

Why People Will Develop Software

If we eliminate intellectual property as a means of encouraging people to develop software, at first less software will be developed, but that software will be more useful. It is not clear whether the overall delivered user satisfaction will be less; but if it is, or if we wish to increase it anyway, there are other ways to encourage development, just as there are ways besides toll booths to raise money for streets. Before I talk about how that can be done, I want to question how much artificial encouragement is truly necessary.

Programming is Fun

There are some lines of work that no one will embark on except for money – road construction, for example. There are other fields of study and art in which there is little chance to become rich, which people enter for their fascination or their perceived value to society. Examples include mathematical logic, classical music, and archaeology; and political organizing among working people. People compete, more sadly than bitterly, for the few funded positions available, none of which is funded very well. They may even pay for the chance to work in the field, if they can afford to.

Such a field can transform itself overnight if it begins to offer the possibility of getting rich. When one worker gets rich, others demand the same opportunity. Soon all may demand large sums of money for doing what they used to do for pleasure. When another couple of years go by, everyone connected with the field will deride the idea that work would be done in the field without large financial returns. They will advise social planners to ensure that these returns are possible, prescribing special privileges, powers, and monopolies as necessary to do so.

This change happened in the field of computer programming in the past decade. Fifteen years ago, there were articles on "computer addiction": users were "onlining" and had $100-a-week habits. It was generally understood that people frequently loved programming enough to break up their marriages. Today, it is generally understood that no one would program except for a high rate of pay. People have forgotten what they knew 15 years ago.

When it is true at a given time that most people will work in a certain field only for high pay, it need not remain true. The dynamic of change can run in reverse, if society provides an impetus. If we take away the possibility of great wealth, then after a while, when the people have readjusted their attitudes, they will once again be eager to work in the field for the joy of accomplishment.

The question, "How can we pay programmers?" becomes an easier question when we realize that it's not a matter of paying them a fortune. A mere living is easier to raise.

Funding Free Software

Institutions that pay programmers do not have to be software houses. Many other institutions already exist which can do this.

Hardware manufacturers find it essential to support software development even if they cannot control the use of the software. In 1970, much of their software was free because they did not consider restricting it. Today, their increasing willingness to join consortiums shows their realization that owning the software is not what is really important for them.

Universities conduct many programming projects. Today, they often sell the results, but in the 1970s, they did not. Is there any doubt that universities would develop free software if they were not allowed to sell software? These projects could be supported by the same government contracts and grants which now support proprietary software development.

It is common today for university researchers to get grants to develop a system, develop it nearly to the point of completion and call that "finished", and then start companies where they really finish the project and make it usable. Sometimes they declare the unfinished version "free;" if they are thoroughly corrupt, they instead get an exclusive license from the university. This is not a secret; it is openly admitted by everyone concerned. Yet if the researchers were not exposed to the temptation to do these things, they would still do their research.

Programmers writing free software can make their living by selling services related to the software. I have been hired to port the GNU C compiler to new hardware, and to make user-interface extensions to GNU Emacs. (I offer these improvements to the public once they are done.) I also teach classes for which I am paid.

I am not alone in working this way; there is now a successful, growing corporation which does no other kind of work. Several other companies also provide commercial support for the free software of the GNU system. This is the beginning of the independent software support industry – an industry that could become quite large if free software becomes prevalent. It provides users with an option generally unavailable for proprietary software, except to the very wealthy.

New institutions such as the Free Software Foundation can also fund programmers. Most of the Foundation's funds come from users buying tapes through the mail. The software on the tapes is free, which means that every user has the freedom to copy it and change it, but many nonetheless pay to get copies. (Recall that "free software" refers to freedom, not to price.) Some users who already have a copy order tapes as a way of making a contribution they feel the programmers deserve. The Foundation also receives sizable donations from computer manufacturers.

The Free Software Foundation is a charity, and its income is spent on hiring as many programmers as possible. If it had been set up as a business, distributing the same free software to the public for the same fee, it would now provide a very good living for its founder.

Because the Foundation is a charity, programmers often work for the Foundation for half of what they could make elsewhere. They do this because the Foundation free of bureaucracy, and because they feel satisfaction in knowing that their work will not be obstructed from use. Most of all, they do it because programming is fun. In addition, volunteers have written many useful programs for the Foundation (recently, even technical writers have begun to volunteer).

This confirms that programming is among the most fascinating of all fields, along with music and art. We don't have to fear that no one will want to program.

What Do Users Owe to Developers?

There is a good reason for users of software to feel a moral obligation to contribute to its support. Developers of free software are contributing to the users' activities, and it is both fair and in the long-term interest of the users to give them funds to continue. However, this does not apply to proprietary software developers, since obstructionism deserves a punishment rather than a reward.

We thus have a paradox: the developer of useful software is entitled to the support of the users, but any attempt to turn this moral obligation into a requirement destroys the basis for the obligation. A developer can either deserve a reward or demand it, but not both.

I believe that an ethical developer faced with this paradox must act so as to deserve the reward, but should also entreat the users for voluntary donations. Eventually the users will learn to support developers without coercion, just as they have learned to support public radio and television stations.

What Is Software Productivity?

If software were free, there would still be programmers, but perhaps fewer of them. Would this be bad for society?

Not necessarily. Today the advanced nations have fewer farmers than in 1900, but we do not think this is bad for society, because the few deliver more food to the consumers than the many used to do. We call this improved productivity. Free software would require far fewer programmers to satisfy the demand, because of increased software productivity at all levels:

- wider use of each program that is developed;
- the ability to adapt existing programs for customization instead of starting from scratch;
- better education of programmers;
- the elimination of duplicate development effort.

Those who object to cooperation because it would result in the employment of fewer programmers, are actually objecting to increased productivity. Yet these people usually accept the widely held belief that the software industry needs increased productivity. How is this?

"Software productivity" can mean two different things: the overall productivity of all software development, or the productivity of individual projects. Overall productivity is what society would like to improve, and the most straightforward way to do this is to eliminate the artificial obstacles to cooperation which reduce it. But researchers who study the field of "software productivity" focus only on the second, limited, sense of the term, where improvement requires difficult technological advances.

Is Competition Inevitable?

Is it inevitable that people will try to compete, to surpass their rivals in society? Perhaps it is. But competition itself is not harmful; the harmful thing is combat.

There are many ways to compete. Competition can consist of trying to achieve ever more, to outdo what others have done. For example, in the old days, there was competition among programming wizards – competition for who could make the computer do the most amazing thing, or for who could make the shortest or fastest program for a given task. This kind of competition can benefit everyone, as long as the spirit of good sportsmanship is maintained.

Constructive competition is enough competition to motivate people to great efforts. A number of people are competing to be the first to have visited all the countries on Earth; some even spend fortunes trying to do this. But they do not bribe ship captains to strand their rivals on desert islands. They are content to let the best person win.

Competition becomes combat when the competitors begin trying to impede each other instead of advancing themselves – when "Let the best person win" gives way to "Let me win, best or not." Proprietary software is harmful, not because it is a form of competition, but because it is a form of combat among the citizens of our society.

Competition in business is not necessarily combat. For example, when two grocery stores compete, their entire effort is aimed at improving their own operations, not at sabotaging the rival. But this does not demonstrate a special commitment to business ethics; rather, there is little scope for combat in this line of business short of physical violence. Not all areas of business share this characteristic. Withholding information that could help everyone advance is a form of combat.

Business ideology does not prepare people to resist the temptation to combat the competition. Some forms of combat have been banned with anti-trust laws, truth in advertising laws, and so on, but rather than generalizing this to a principled rejection of combat in general, executives invent other forms of combat which are not specifically prohibited. Society's resources are squandered on the economic equivalent of factional civil war.

"Why Don't You Move to Russia?"

In the United States, any advocate of other than the most extreme form of laissez-faire selfishness has often heard this accusation. For example, it is leveled against the supporters of a national health care system, such as is found in all the other industrialized nations of the free world. It is leveled against the advocates of public support for the arts, also universal in advanced nations. The idea that citizens have any obligation to the public good is identified in America with Communism. But how similar are these ideas?

Communism as it was practiced in the Soviet Union was a system of central control where all activity was regimented, supposedly for the common good, but actually for the sake of the members of the Communist party, and where copying equipment was closely guarded to prevent illegal copying. The American system of intellectual property exercises central control over distribution of a program, and guards copying equipment with automatic copying protection schemes to prevent illegal copying.

By contrast, consider a system where people are free to decide their own actions; in particular, free to help their neighbors, and free to alter and improve the tools which they use in their daily lives. A system based on voluntary cooperation, and decentralization.

Clearly it is the software owners, if anyone, who ought to move to Russia.

The Question of Premises

I make the assumption in this paper that a user of software is no less important than an author, or even an author's employer. In other words, their interests and needs have equal weight, when we decide which course of action is best.

This premise is not universally accepted. Many maintain that an author's employer is fundamentally more important than anyone else. They say, for example, that the purpose of having owners of software is to give the author's employer the advantage he deserves – regardless of how this may affect the public.

It is no use trying to prove or disprove these premises. Proof requires shared premises. So most of what I have to say is addressed only to those who share the premises I use, or at least are interested in what their consequences are. For those who believe that the owners are more important than everyone else, this paper is simply irrelevant.

But why would a large number of Americans accept a premise which elevates certain people in importance above everyone else? Partly because of the belief that this premise is part of the legal traditions of American society. Some people feel that doubting the premise means challenging the basis of society.

It is important for these people to know that this premise is not part of our legal tradition. It never has been. Thus, the Constitution says that the purpose of copyright is to "promote the progress of science and the useful arts." The Supreme Court has elaborated on this, stating in Fox Film v. Doyal that "The sole interest of the United States and the primary object in conferring the (copyright) monopoly lie in the general benefits derived by the public from the labors of authors."

We are not required to agree with the Constitution or the Supreme Court. (At one time, they both condoned slavery.) So their positions do not disprove the owner supremacy premise. But I hope that the awareness that this is a radical right-wing assumption rather than a traditionally recognized one will weaken its appeal.

Conclusion

We like to think that our society encourages helping your neighbor; but each time we reward someone for obstructionism, or admire them for the wealth they have gained in this way, we are sending the opposite message.

Software hoarding is one form of our general willingness to disregard the welfare of society for personal gain. We can trace this disregard from

Ronald Reagan to Jim Baker, from Ivan Boesky to Exxon, from failing banks to failing schools. We can measure it with the size of the homeless population and the prison population. The antisocial spirit feeds on itself, because the more we see that other people will not help us, the more it seems futile to help them. Thus society decays into a jungle.

If we don't want to live in a jungle, we must change our attitudes. We must start sending the message that a good citizen is one who cooperates when appropriate, not one who is successful at taking from others. I hope that the free software movement will contribute to this: at least in one area, we will replace the jungle with a more efficient system which encourages and runs on voluntary cooperation.

Basic study questions

1. What does Stallman mean by "free" when he says that software should be "free"?
2. According to Stallman, in trying to answer the question "Should software be owned?," we cannot decide by looking at what the current law says. Why not? How does Stallman propose to answer this question?
3. Stallman rejects the so-called "emotional argument" in favor of ownership of software. State the emotional argument and then explain why Stallman rejects it.
4. Stallman rejects the so-called "economic argument" in favor of ownership of software. State the economic argument and then explain why Stallman rejects it.
5. In defense of his view that software should not be owned, Stallman makes an analogy with toll roads. Present this analogy and explain how Stallman applies it to the question of the ownership of software.
6. According to Stallman, allowing the ownership of software inflicts a variety of harms upon society. Explain the harm he mentions regarding the number of people who can use a piece of software.
7. Explain the harm that Stallman mentions with regard to adapting and fixing software.
8. Explain the harm that Stallman mentions with regard to learning from software.
9. Explain the harm that Stallman mentions with regard to building upon already existing software.
10. Explain the harm that Stallman mentions with regard to human relationships and social cohesion.
11. According to Stallman, if the law did not permit people to own software, many people would nevertheless continue to create it. Why does he think so? State his three reasons.
12. According to Stallman, permitting the ownership of software leads to destructive "combat" rather than constructive competition. Explain his arguments on this topic.

Questions for further thought

1. Critics of Stallman claim that his "emotional argument" is a flawed distortion of the classical defense of ownership by British philosopher John Locke. What is Locke's theory of ownership? Is Stallman's "emotional argument" really a distortion of Locke's classical theory?
2. Do you agree with Stallman that "the law should conform to ethics"? If so, how can we tell whether current software ownership laws are ethical laws?
3. Using Internet-based resources, such as Eric Raymond's web site "The Cathedral and the Bazaar," explain the basic ideas of the so-called "open source movement" using the LINUX operating system as an example to illustrate the key points: http://www.tuxedo.org/~esr/writings/cathedral-bazaar/
4. What policies need to be in place to realize a free software industry?

CASE TO ANALYZE: FREE-RANGE PROPERTY

Although this imagined case did not actually happen, it is very similar to cases that have occurred in the past. It illustrates the kinds of challenge to intellectual property ownership that information technology has frequently generated. The reader is invited to analyze this case using the case-analysis method presented in chapter 3 above.

George Freestuff, aged 15, is in love with computers. He owns five of them and keeps them in his room at home. At the age of 13, he built one of his computers himself with various parts that he bought on the Internet. Two additional computers are gifts that he received when he was 14, one from his real mother and one from his new step-mother. Last summer, George earned extra money beyond his generous allowance by installing digital TV and music systems for his father's wealthy neighbors. He also got a newspaper delivery job to earn even more money so that he could purchase a "really cool" high-speed computer that "does everything." That new computer is now his favorite one, although he is also delighted with the "amazing" new laptop that his father just gave him for his excellent achievements at school.

George spends all his spare time with the computers in his room. Instead of playing physical games outside or at the gym, George plays computer games of all kinds. He loves to surf the Web, playing "neat" games, participating in "dungeons" and chat rooms, and exchanging "tons of email" with his on-line friends. He gets lots of physical exercise, however, by running or walking on a "really outrageous" treadmill in his room while wearing virtual-reality equipment. This "utterly cool" equipment makes it seem as if George is running through underground caves, or climbing a steep hill while surrounded by dangerous animals, or chasing beautiful girls across a meadow.

A few months ago, George made several on-line friends who are "really into open source stuff." He agreed with his new friends that "information wants to be free," and that large software companies are "ripping people off by charging a fortune for their software and constantly making upgrades that you have to buy." He also agreed that music distributors and film companies are "charging much too much for CDs and DVDs." He was very excited to find "such cool friends" on-line.

George Freestuff and his friends have been working for more than two months creating a new software program which they call "Free-Range Property" (or "FRP," for short). They named it after "free-range" farm animals that are permitted to roam across the farm, instead of being confined to barns and cages. George and his friends are designing FRP to send digitized files – *any* digitized files – across the Internet free of charge. This "awesome" program will use "open source" code that anyone in the world can get free on the Internet. FRP has two important parts: namely, "The Capsule" and "The Share List":

The Capsule This "utterly cool" electronic "envelope" is like an electronic safe into which you can place any digitized file – music, video programs, films, texts, software, graphics, games, – "*any* digitized stuff whatsoever!". The file is hidden inside of the encrypted "walls" of the capsule. As the capsule travels across the Internet, anyone who intercepts it will be unable to tell what's inside, except for the person who is supposed to receive it. (That person has been emailed the decryption password.) In this way, electronic "water marks" and other ways of identifying or tracking particular digital items can be defeated, and people can share computer files without fear of being hassled by "their so-called owners".

The Share List Also hidden inside the capsule is a list of electronic addresses where this same digital file, as well as many other similar files, can be acquired free of charge. The "neat" thing about the share list is that it is constantly being updated and expanded by people who received the same file in the past. Each person who receives an FRP capsule is supposed to add to the list any similar files he is willing to share and also new electronic addresses where similar files can be acquired. In this way, the share list keeps expanding and changing to take account of new developments. When the list gets bigger than a certain size, it is automatically cut in half, with the latest entries preserved and the earliest ones deleted.

George and his on-line friends are really excited about FRP because it has so many "really awesome" features. The share list feature, for example, makes it possible for people to share files with each other over the Internet – and find new files to acquire and share – without the need for a specific server or web site to function as a source or coordinator. In this way, there is no server or web site that anyone could shut down to prevent sharing on the Internet. All digitized intellectual properties, therefore, will be able to "range freely over the net with no fences or cages to confine them!"

George is very proud, because he believes that he is helping to overcome "horrible injustices" in the world. "Poor people and poor countries of the world will be able to get all sorts of benefits free – benefits that they have been denied in the past," he said. "The world's music and films will be available to everyone! Libraries, works of art, games and newspapers will be free! Huge corporations will no longer be able to rip off the little people! Struggling artists and musicians will be able to share their works with the world and become famous! This is going to be really awesome!"

When George told all this to his school friend Lizzy, she was not impressed. Indeed, she began to lecture George about companies that will go out of business, and artists who won't be able to earn a living from selling their works. "Movie studios will stop making movies, because there won't be any income!" she said.

George just laughed and said, "Oh, Lizzy, businesses will just have to find new ways to make money. Information wants to be free! And tomorrow me and my friends will set it free on the Internet with FRP. Set it free with FRP! Set it free with FRP!"

ADDITIONAL READINGS AND WEB RESOURCES

Additional readings

Barlow, J. P. (1994). "The Economy of Ideas: A Framework for Rethinking Patents and Copyrights in the Digital Age (Everything You Know About Intellectual Property is Wrong)." *Wired* (March): 85–129.

Johnson, D. G. (2001). "Property Rights in Computer Software." *Computer Ethics*, 3rd edn. Prentice Hall, pp. 137–67.

McFarland, M. C. (1999). "Intellectual Property, Information and the Common Good." In R. A. Spinello, and H. T. Tavani (eds.), *Readings in CyberEthics*. Jones and Bartlett, pp. 252–62.

Samuelson, P. (1997). "The US Digital Agenda at WIPO." *Virginia Journal of International Law Association*, 37: 369–439.

Web resources

Electronic Frontier Foundation, "Intellectual Property Online: Patent, Trademark, Copyright." Archive http://www.eff.org/pub/Intellectual_property

Raymond, E. "The Cathedral and the Bazaar." A web site on the open source movement. http://www.firstmonday.dk/issues/issue3_3/raymond/

Software Ownership and Intellectual Property Rights: A Monograph (see especially the article "A Plea for Casual Copying," by Helen Nissenbaum). http://www.southernct.edu/organizations/rccs/resources/research/intellectual_property/ownership_mono/ownership_contents.html

Volkman, R., "Softward Ownership and Natural Rights." http://www.southernct.edu/organizations/rccs/resources/research/intellectual_property/volkman_nat-rights.html

World Intellectual Property Organization. http://www.wipo.org

Global Information Ethics

Editors' Introduction

According to James H. Moor's influential definition of the field of computer ethics (see chapter 1), information technology is so powerful and so flexible that it enables people and organizations to do things that they never could do before. Because such things were never done before, there may be no laws or standards of good practice or shared expectations to regulate them or to guide one's judgments about how to proceed. In Moor's view, it is the role of computer ethics to identify and analyze such "policy vacuums" and to recommend new policies to fill those vacuums.

In chapter 15, Krystyna Gorniak-Kocikowska points out that the Internet makes possible – for the first time in history – a genuinely global discussion about ethics and human values. This is a worldwide discussion that was not possible before the invention of information and communication technology, and it has implications for social policy that we can only begin to imagine. Traditional borders and barriers between countries have now become less meaningful because people and organizations in most countries are interconnected by the Internet. For this reason, individuals, companies, and organizations in every culture can engage in global business transactions, distance education, cyber-employment, discussions of social and political issues, sharing and debating of values and perspectives. Will this global "conversation" bring about better understanding between peoples and cultures? – new shared values and goals? – new national and international laws and policies? Or will individual cultures become "diluted," homogenized, and blurred? These are just a few of the many social and ethical issues emerging from the "globalization" brought about by information and communication technology.

The worldwide nature of the Internet has already led to many policy vacuums to clarify and resolve. For example, if sexually explicit materials are provided on a web site in a culture in which they are permitted, and then they are accessed by someone in a different culture where such materials are outlawed as "obscene," whose laws and values should apply? Should the "offending" person in the first culture be extradited to the second culture and prosecuted there as a purveyor of pornography? Should the values of the first culture be permitted to undermine those of the second culture via the Internet? How can such cultural clashes be reasonably resolved?

One suggestion that is sometimes offered to help avoid or resolve cultural clashes on the Internet is to avoid doing anything that might offend someone – to be sensitive to the values and beliefs of cultures other than one's own. But how does one know what could be offensive to others? Almost anything could offend somebody somewhere; so does this mean that we should simply stop using the Internet? These and related questions are examined by John Weckert in chapter 16, "Giving Offense on the Internet."

Another set of "policy vacuums" generated by the Internet concerns business transactions in cyberspace: Whose laws apply to business on the Internet? When people in one country purchase goods and services from merchants in another country, who should regulate or tax the transactions? And how will "cyberbusiness" in a global market affect local business? – local tax collections? – local unemployment? What new laws, regulations, rules, and practices should be adopted, and who should create or enforce them? What policies would be fair to all concerned?

How will global cyberbusiness affect the gap between rich and poor nations? Will that gap get even wider? Will the Internet lead to a "new colonialism" in which the information rich lord it over the information poor? Will economic and political rivalries emerge to threaten peace and security? What kinds of conflict and misunderstanding might arise, and how should they be handled? – and by whom?

Or consider cyber medicine: Medical advice and psychological counseling on the Internet, "keyhole" surgery conducted at a distance, medical tests and examinations over the net, "cyber prescriptions" for medicine written by doctors in one part of the world for patients in other parts of the world – these are just a few of the medical services and activities that already exist in cyberspace. How safe is cyber medicine? Who will have access to sensitive information held in electronic patient records? Who should regulate, license, and control cyber medicine?

Or consider education in cyberspace: Hundreds of universities and colleges worldwide now offer educational credit for courses and modules. But when students earn university credits from all around the globe, who should set the standards? Who should award degrees and certify "graduates"? Will there be a "Cyber University of the World"? Will thousands of "ordinary" teachers be replaced by a handful of "Internet-superstar teachers"? – or perhaps by teams of multimedia experts? – or even by educational software? Would such developments be wonderful new learning opportunities, or instead be educational disasters? What policies, rules, and practices should be adopted and who should develop them?

At the social and political level of education, what will be the impact upon previously uneducated peoples of the world when they suddenly gain access to libraries, museums, newspapers, and other sources of knowledge? How will access to the world's great newspapers affect "closed" societies with no free press? Are democracy and human rights necessary consequences of an educated population with access to a free press? Will the Internet foster global democracy? – or will it become a tool for control and manipulation of the masses by a handful of powerful governments? – or powerful corporations?

It is clear from the above discussion that "global information ethics" is a vast and growing area of computer ethics with a wide diversity of newly emerging policy vacuums to be analyzed and resolved. Individuals, organizations, communities, whole societies, and humankind in general will be coping with such challenges for decades to come. The articles and other resources presented in this part of the present book are mere examples of the wide diversity of issues in this important field of research and human endeavor.

CHAPTER 15

The Computer Revolution
and Global Ethics

Krystyna Gorniak-Kocikowska

Introduction

This paper is based upon my view of the nature of the Computer Revolution that is currently transforming the world. That view can be summarized by the following five points:

1 The Computer Revolution causes profound changes in peoples' lives worldwide. In cyberspace, there are no borders in the traditional sense. The borders, as well as the links between individuals worldwide, will be increasingly defined in terms of the degree of an individual's ability to penetrate cyberspace.

2 Because of the global character of cyberspace, problems connected with or caused by computer technology actually or potentially have a global character. This includes ethical problems. Hence, computer ethics has to be regarded as global ethics.

3 Up to the present stage of evolution of humankind there has not been a successful attempt to create a universal ethic of a global character. The traditional ethical systems based on religious beliefs were always no more powerful than the power of the religion they were associated with. And no religion dominated the globe, no matter how widespread its influence was. The ethical systems that were not supported by religion had an even more restricted influence.

4 The very nature of the Computer Revolution indicates that the ethic of the future will have a global character. It will be global in a spatial sense,

Krystyna Gorniak-Kocikowska, "The Computer Revolution and Global Ethics." This is a shortened version of "The Computer Revolution and the Problem of Global Ethics", presented at ETHICOMP95 and published in the conference proceedings, ed. Simon Rogerson and Terrell Ward Bynum. Reprinted in *Science and Engineering Ethics*, 2:2 (special issue, 1996), pp. 177–190. © 1995 by Krystyna Gorniak-Kocikowska and reprinted by permission of the author.

since it will encompass the entire globe. It will also be global in the sense that it will address the totality of human actions and relations.

5   The future global ethic will be a computer ethic because it will be caused by the Computer Revolution and it will serve the humanity of a Computer Era. Therefore, the definition of computer ethics ought to be wider than that proposed, for example, by James Moor in his classic paper, "What Is Computer Ethics?" (1985). If this is the case, computer ethics should be regarded as one of the most important fields of philosophical investigation.

The Computer Revolution

In his presentation of the anatomy of the Computer Revolution, Moor (1985) uses an analogy with the Industrial Revolution in England. He notes that the first stage of the Industrial Revolution took place during the second half of the eighteenth century, and the second stage during the nineteenth century. This is a span of about 150 years. Let me compare this with what happened after the printing press was invented in Europe. (Of course, books were printed in China already around the year 600 CE.[1])

Johann Gutenberg printed the "Constance Mass Book" in 1450, and in 1474 William Caxton printed the first book in the English language. Already in 1492 "the profession of book publishers emerges, consisting of the three pursuits of type founder, printer and bookseller" (Grun 1982). This was, roughly speaking, 40 years after the invention of the printing press, the same amount of time Moor says the Computer Revolution needed for its introduction stage. In 1563, the first printing presses were used in Russia. (This was the same year in which the term "Puritan" was first used in England, one year before the horse-drawn coach was introduced in England from Holland, and two years before pencils started to be manufactured in England.) And in 1639, the same year in which the English settled at Madras, two years after English traders were established in Canton and the Dutch expelled the Portuguese from the Gold Coast, the first printing press was installed in North America, at Cambridge, Massachusetts. This is about 140 years from the first publication of Gutenberg's printed text – almost the same amount of time Moor considers for both stages of the Industrial Revolution.[2]

---

[1]   The fact that print did not revolutionize life in China the way it did in Europe is itself an interesting subject for analysis.

[2]   Timetables for the Industrial Revolution vary greatly depending upon sources and criteria. The timetable chosen by Moor is very popular, but the view that the Industrial Revolution began with the invention of the printing press is very popular as well.

Another point made by Moor in "What is Computer Ethics?" is just *how* revolutionary the computer is. He argues that *logical malleability* makes the computer a truly revolutionary machine – computers can be used to do almost any task that can be broken down into simple steps. Moor challenges the "popular conception of computers in which computers are understood as number crunchers, i.e., essentially as numerical devices" (1985, p. 269). He further writes:

> The arithmetic interpretation is certainly a correct one, but it is only one among many interpretations. Logical malleability has both a syntactic and a semantic dimension. . . . Computers manipulate symbols but they don't care what the symbols represent. Thus, there is no ontological basis for giving preference to numerical applications over non-numerical applications. (Ibid., p. 270)

Here, too, the similarity between a computer and a printing press seems to be evident. Like the printing press, computers serve to transmit thoughts. The appearance of the printing press meant both a technological revolution, as well as a revolution in the transport of ideas – communication between human minds. The same can be said about a computer.

On the other hand, the function of the most important machines invented at the end of the eighteenth century – the steam engine and the spinning machine – was replacement of manual labor. But the primary function of the printing press, and the computer as well, lies in the fact that both increase so incredibly the efficiency of the labor of human minds – and not only the individual mind. Computers, like the printing press, allow human minds to work faster and more efficiently, because of their ground-breaking impact on the communication and exchange of ideas. Like the printing press, they are creating a new type of network between human individuals, a community existing despite the spatial separation of its members.

I have written elsewhere about the impact of the printing press on the Western hemisphere. (Gorniak-Kocikowska 1986) Here, I would like to mention only two of the many changes caused by the invention of movable typeface. Mass-production of texts, and hence their growing accessibility, made reading and writing skills *useful* and caused a profound change in the very idea of education. Gradually, the ability to read and write became an indispensable condition of a human being's effectiveness in functioning in the world.

Printed texts also made it possible to acquire knowledge *individually* (i.e., not through oral public presentation) and *freely* (i.e., without control of either the individual tutor or the owner of the collection of manuscripts). One of the results of this situation was the loss of belief that knowledge means possession of a mystery, a *secret* wisdom, inaccessible to outsiders. Knowledge became an instrument which everyone could and should use. Faith in the power and universal character of the individual human mind was born – and with it a new concept of the human being. The masses of believers who used to obey the possessors of knowledge discovered that they were rational individuals capable of making their own judgments and decisions. This paved the way for the two new ethical theories that were ultimately created by Immanuel Kant and Jeremy Bentham.

The Printing Press and Ethics

Since many authors who write on the subject of computer ethics, including such prominent scholars as James Moor, Terrell Bynum and, above all, the author of the first major textbook in the field, Deborah Johnson, use the ethics of Bentham and Kant as the point of reference for their investigations, it is important to make clear that both these ethical systems arrived *at the end* of a certain phase of profound and diverse changes initiated by the invention of movable printing type.[3] The question is: were these ethical systems merely solving the problems of the past or were they vehicles driving humankind into the future?

The ethical systems of Kant and Bentham were created during the time of the Industrial Revolution, but they were not a reaction to, nor a result of, the Industrial Revolution of the eighteenth and nineteenth centuries. There was no *immediate* reaction in the form of a new ethical theory to the invention of the printing press. Rather, problems resulting from the economic, social, and political changes that were caused by the circulation of printed texts were at first approached with the ethical apparatus elaborated during the high Middle Ages and at the time of the Reformation. Then, there was a period of growing awareness that a new set of ethical rules was necessary. The entire concept of human nature and society had to be revised. Hobbes, Locke, Rousseau, and others did that work. Finally, new ethical systems like those of Kant and Bentham were established. These ethics were based on the concept of a human being as an independent individual, capable of making rational judgments and decisions, freely entering "the social contract." Such a concept of the human being was able to emerge in great part because of the wide accessibility of the printed text.

The ethics of Bentham and Kant, then, were both manifestations of and summaries of the European Enlightenment. They were created at a time when Europeans were experimenting with the idea of society's being a result of an agreement (a "social contract") between free and rational human individuals, rather than submission to divine power or to the power of

---

[3] Of course, the printing press was not the *only* cause of such profound changes, but neither was the steam engine or the spinning machine. I do recognize the tremendous complexity of the processes we are talking about.

Nature. Moreover, such a new, contractual society could have been created in *separation* from traditional social groups. The conquest of the world by Europeans – called by them geographic "discoveries" and colonization of "new" territories – made it possible. Locke's definition of property as appropriation of nature by one's own labor, plus lack of a concept of private property in most of the invaded societies, helped that task.

Thus, despite their claims to universalism, Kant's as well as Bentham's concept of human being refers to European man as defined by the Enlightenment – free and educated enough to make rational decisions. "Rational" means here the type of rationality that grew out of Aristotelian and scholastic logic and those mathematical theories of the time of the printing press revolution. This tradition was strengthened by ideas from Pascal, Leibniz, and others; and it permitted one to dismiss from the ranks of *partners in discourse* all individuals who did not follow the iron rules of that kind of rationality. The term "mankind" did not really apply to such individuals. Finally, this tradition turned into Bentham's computational ethics and Kant's imperialism of duty as seen by calculating reason.

The nature of both these ethical systems must be very attractive and tempting for computer wizards, especially for those who grew up within the influence of the "Western" set of values. It is quite easy to imagine that there could be a "yes" answer to a question asked by James Moor – "Is Ethics Computable?" (1996) – if one has Bentham's or even Kant's ethical systems in mind.

It now seems to me very likely that a similar process of ethical theory development will occur, although probably less time will be needed for all phases to be completed. The Computer Revolution *is* revolutionary; already computers have changed the world in profound ways. At present, though, we are able to see only the tip of the iceberg. Computer technology generates many new situations and many new problems, and some of these are ethical in nature. There are attempts to solve these problems by applying existing ethical rules and solutions. This procedure is not always successful, and my claim is that the number and difficulty of the problems will grow. Already, there is a high tide of discussions about an ethical crisis in the United States. It is starting to be noticeable that traditional solutions do not work anymore. The first reaction is, as is usual in such situations, "let's go back to the old, good values." However, the more computers change the world as we know it, the more irrelevant the existing ethical rules will be and the more evident will be the need for a new ethic. This new ethic will be the computer ethic.

The Global Character of Ethics in the Computer Era

Revolution, more than any other kind of change, means that two processes take place simultaneously: the process of creation and the process of destruction. The problem is that in a human society this usually causes conflict, because both creation and destruction can be regarded as a positive (good) or negative (bad/evil) process. The assessment depends on the values accepted by the people (individuals or groups) who are exposed to the revolutionary changes.

Moor writes: "On my view, computer ethics is a dynamic and complex field of study which considers the relationships among facts, conceptualizations, policies and values with regard to constantly changing computer technology" (1985, p. 267). This is a broad enough definition to be accepted by almost everybody; but a problem arises when we realize how many people may be affected by and interested in those "facts, conceptualizations, policies and values" – how diverse this group is. In my opinion, we are talking about the whole population of the globe! Computers do not know borders. Computer networks, unlike other mass media, have a truly global character. Hence, when we are talking about computer ethics, we are talking about an emerging global ethic – and we are talking about all areas of human life, since computers affect them all. What does this mean for the understanding of what computer ethics is?

For one thing, computer ethics cannot be just another professional ethics. Writers like Deborah Johnson (1994) and Donald Gotterbarn (1992) sometimes appear to assert that computer ethics is simply a kind of professional ethics. I support wholeheartedly the idea of a code of ethics for computer professionals. However, at least two problems arise if we take computer ethics to be just a type of professional ethics:

1   Unlike, say, physicians or lawyers, computer professionals cannot prevent or regulate activities that are similar to their own but performed by non-professionals. Therefore, although many of the rules of conduct for physicians or lawyers do not apply to those outside of the profession, the rules of computer ethics, no matter how well thought through, will be ineffective unless respected by the vast majority of – maybe even all – computer users. This means that, in the future, the rules of computer ethics should be respected by the majority (or all) of the human inhabitants of the Earth. In other words, computer ethics should become universal, it should be a global ethic.

2   Let us assume that computer ethics applies only to computer professionals. Such professionals are not totally isolated from the society in which they function. The role of their profession is significantly determined by the general structure of the society in which they are included. At present, there exist various societies and cultures on earth. Many of them function within different ethical systems than those predominantly accepted in the United States or even in the "western world". Hence, professional ethics, including ethical codes for computer professionals,

may differ among cultures to the point of conflict. And even if they do not differ, conflict may still be unavoidable. Example: Computer professionals in two countries who happen to be at war may obey the *same* rule that computers should be used to strengthen national security. In such a situation, computers may become a weapon more deadly than the atomic bomb. Discussions such as those about scientists responsible for the use of nuclear energy may now apply to computer professionals. And given the power of computer technology, the potential for destruction may be even greater than the case of the atomic bomb.

Or consider another example: It is well known that the United States' CIA monitors the Internet for security reasons. However, the question arises whether this means that certain ethical rules, such as respecting privacy, do not apply to certain people? If the CIA does not need to respect an ethical code, who else is entitled to break the rules and on what grounds? If one country can do it, what *moral* imperatives should stop other countries from doing the same? Let us assume that such moral rules could be found. If they are better, why shouldn't they be applied on a global scale?

Problems like those described above will become more obvious and more serious in the future when the global character of cyberspace makes it possible to affect the lives of people in places very distant from the acting subject's location. This happens already today, but in the future it will have a much more profound character. Actions in cyberspace will not be local. Therefore, the ethical rules for such actions cannot be rooted in a particular local culture, unless the creators of computer ethics accept the view that the function of computers is to serve as a tool in gaining and maintaining dominion over the world by one particular group of humans. I would like very much to believe that this is not the case. I would like to believe Smarr's optimistic comment (quoted in Broad 1993, p. C10):

> It's the one unifying technology that can help us rise above the epidemic of tribal animosities we're seeing worldwide. One wants a unifying fabric for the human race. The Internet is pointing in that direction. It promotes a very egalitarian culture at a time when the world is fragmenting at a dizzying pace.

This may be yet another example of wishful thinking, though. And I worry that scholars in computer ethics may contribute to the problem if they do not fully realize the importance of their undertaking. It seems to me that, unfortunately, the scholars who have chosen to explore the field of computer ethics have been too modest in defining the area of investigation, as well as the importance of the subject.

References

Broad, W. J. (1993). "Doing Science on the Network: A Long Way from Gutenberg." *The New York Times*, Tuesday, May 18.

Gorniak-Kocikowska, K. (1986). "Dialogue – A New Utopia?" In *Conceptus. Zeitschrift für Philosophie*, XX/51: 99–110 (in German). English translations published in *Occasional Papers on Religion in Eastern Europe*, Princeton, VI/5 (October): 13–29, and in *Dialectics And Humanism*, Warsaw, XVI/3–4: 133–47.

Gotterbarn, D. (1992). "The Use and Abuse of Computer Ethics." In T. W. Bynum, W. Maner, and J. L. Fodor (eds.), *Teaching Computer Ethics*. Research Center on Computing and Society, pp. 73–83.

Grun, B. (1982). *The Timetables of History: A Horizontal Linkage of People and Events*, new, updated edn. Based on Werner Stein's *Kulturfahrplan*, Simon and Schuster, Touchstone Edition.

Johnson, D. G. (1994). *Computer Ethics*, 2nd edn. Prentice Hall.

Moor, J. H. (1985). "What is Computer Ethics?" *Metaphilosophy*, 16: 226–75.

Moor, J. H. (1996). "Is Ethics Computable?" *Metaphilosophy*, 27: 1–21.

Basic study questions

1. Briefly describe two important social changes brought about by the invention of movable printing type.
2. According to Gorniak, the philosophers Kant and Bentham both presuppose the same conception of human nature. What is it?
3. What are some of the similarities between the printing press revolution and the Computer Revolution?
4. Why, according to Gorniak, must computer ethics be considered a global ethics?
5. What two reasons does Gorniak offer to believe that computer ethics is much more than a kind of professional ethics?
6. What important concern about computer ethics does Gorniak express at the end of her article?

Questions for further thought

1. Discuss the idea that the Computer Revolution is bringing about an alternative reality to Nature – a "second world" for humans to inhabit.
2. According to Gorniak, a genuine social revolution involves two processes that inevitably lead to conflict. Describe the two processes and how they relate to the Computer Revolution.

CHAPTER 16

Giving Offense on the Internet

John Weckert

Introduction

A concept, central to Internet ethics but rarely examined in that context, is offense. This concept underlies much of the discussion of freedom of speech and censorship, especially where the discussion has a global setting as it does on the Internet, a setting where various religions, customs, and moralities come into contact. In this paper we examine the notion of offense, and argue that its importance arises because of its close links with respect for others and with self-respect. This then gives a basis for attempting to discover what, if anything, is wrong with giving offense. We then propose and defend criteria for the acceptable and unacceptable giving of offense. Clearly not all offense giving can be outlawed. One would be condemned to silence. These criteria are discussed particularly in relation to pornography, cultural, racial, and religious vilification on the Internet. Our argument is that an examination of offense can help to give guidelines for conduct on the Internet.

If one believes the popular press and politicians, there seems to be a plethora of offensive material on the Internet which some people want banned, some want restricted and some want protected. The US Communications Decency Act talks of material which is "patently offensive" (Communications Decency Act 1996), the new Internet content legislation in Australia talks of offensive material and of "offensive fetishes" (Broadcasting Services Amendment (Online Services) Bill 1999), a recently published paper is entitled "Illegal and Offensive Content on The Information Highway" (Sansom 1995), and in "Content on the Internet: Free or Unfettered", Burton (1996) repeatedly speaks of offensive material.

John Weckert, "Giving Offense on the Internet." This chapter was originally presented as a paper at The Computer Ethics Conference, Linköping University, Sweden. It was first published in G. Collste (ed.), *Ethics and Information Technology* (New Academic Publishers, 1998), pp. 104–18. © 1997 by John Weckert. Reprinted by permission of the author.

A number of important issues underlie discussions of *offensive material*. One of these issues is that we know what offensive material is, and another is that offense can be used as a criterion for drawing a line between what is acceptable material or communication on the Internet and what is not. These questions will be considered in turn.

What Is Offense?

We get an idea of what is thought offensive by looking at some of the discussions mentioned above. The Communications Decency Act (1996) has a quite clear account where it talks of:

> any comment, request, suggestion, proposal, image, or other communication that, in context, depicts or describes, in terms patently offensive as measured by contemporary community standards, sexual or excretory activities or organs. (Section 223 (2) (d) (1) (B))

From this it appears that offensive material is sexual in content. The one virtue of this is that it seems to give a fairly simple way of establishing whether or not some material is offensive: just see if it is sexual.

While sexual material, or certain types, can be offensive to some, perhaps even to most, equating 'offensive' with 'sexual' is very odd when we consider what typically offends us and what typically offends others. All sorts of things offend, and different people are offended by different things. Burton raises two pertinent points with respect to this:

> [W]hat offends me may not offend you: have I the right to say you should not view it or read it? Attitudes to material which could be deemed offensive are so often part of a nation's culture, and so will differ widely: consider the example of the Netherlands [attitude to soft drugs] quoted earlier, or the difference between Scandinavian and Middle Eastern attitudes to nudity. Jack Schofield has recently raised similar questions: could fundamentalists ban discussion on theories of evolution, or could the Vatican seek to ban sites on birth control? (1996, p. 5)

Religious (or anti-religious) statements can offend, as can those on politics, gender, and race, to mention just a few of the more important. What is obvious from this is that if offensiveness is to be used as a criterion for censorship, it will need to be spelt out much more carefully. This is what will be attempted now.

Strictly speaking, we are not offended by things, but by people. I might not be offended by a rock formation which looks much like part of a human's anatomy, but very offended by a photograph of that same part, or even, in the right context, by a photograph of the rock formation. The difference is *intention*. This need not necessarily be the intention to offend, but the utterance, picture, or whatever must have been the intended result of some human action. It is not easy to spell out clearly just what it is to have intentions, but here it is sufficient to say that if a person P performs action A intentionally, then P performs A in order to achieve some goal G. P believes that performing A will achieve G. The goal G might be to offend, but it might be something completely harmless or even beneficial. If someone is offended by A, it will typically be because it is thought that the goal G is an inappropriate goal. The reason that this is worth saying is that talk of *offensive material* gives the impression that things offend, whereas the discussion should focus on people offending other people.

At what is offense taken? I might be offended by a chance remark about my new shirt, by not being invited to a party, or by jokes mocking stereotypical Australian traits. An Australian newspaper has recently carried items about teachers and parents who find an increase in education bureaucrat's salary offensive, about the offensiveness of the policies of a new political party, and about how the homosexual community is offended by a statement of a government minister. The same newspaper also published a large, digitally altered, version of Leonardo da Vinci's *The Last Supper* with a well-known local food critic seated at one end of the table, in earnest discussion with several of the disciples. The picture accompanied an article on that critic. This alteration would undoubtedly be considered offensive to many Christians, and perhaps also by some art lovers. Many other examples are supplied by Feinberg, ranging from public nudity and copulating to racist and religious actions. The least offensive he calls "offensive nuisances," while the more serious are termed "profound offenses" (Feinberg 1985).

First, what is offense and what is involved in giving offense? Offense, typically, is a sort of unease, unhappiness, mental distress, or mental suffering of some variety. An offended person has his or her feelings hurt in some way. A central point is that something will only offend someone if that person *takes* offense. We cannot offend in quite the same way that we can punch. Offense is closely related to beliefs, attitudes, feelings, and so on. I cannot offend meat-eaters by eating meat in front of them, but a vegetarian might find such behavior offensive. Giving offense, then, is not quite the same as causing physical harm, even though in some sense it might harm. I can only harm a person by offending that person if he or she has *particular* beliefs, attitudes, or feelings. It might be that people only take offense if they are overly sensitive or if they cherish certain beliefs too much. In a sense, therefore, if they are hurt by something said or shown, they have only themselves to blame. But this is too swift. In fact, while it is good not to take offense too easily, there can be something a little sad, perhaps even pathetic, about people who never take offense, even though they may be objects of ridicule or discrimination, but for some reason do not realize it, or have such low self-esteem that they see it as just. We might even question whether we respect people who are never offended by things which degrade them.

Offense and Respect

In an effort to learn more about what offense really is, we will ask two questions: (1) What, if anything, is wrong with giving offense, and (2) why do people take offense? In answer to (1), one may be inclined to say that there is nothing really wrong with giving offense. After all, if people are so silly or sensitive that they become offended at something heard or seen, so much the worse for them. We cannot spend all of our lives worrying about who might not like what we say or do. While this contains an element of truth, it is a bit hard, as we saw a moment ago. It is probably true that any offense taken at the mocking of a football team might not matter much, but the mocking of a physical disability or a tragedy, for example, might not only be in bad taste, but also extremely hurtful even for those not overly sensitive. Even if no offense is taken in the sense of feelings or pride being hurt, it might be that painful memories are awakened. However, not all offense is like this. People are offended by blasphemy, language to do with sexual activity, ridicule of race, class, occupation, political belief, and a host of other things. Some of these seem not too worrying; however, others are troublesome.

We will attempt to answer (2), why people take offense, before looking for a solution to (1). Obviously, offense is taken for different reasons by different people and over a wide range of areas. We will look at three areas, the first of which concerns things which are not necessarily directed at any person or group, such as sexually explicit language and nudity (but excluding pornography, which raises other issues). Some people are offended by certain language and pictures. Part of the explanation for the offense taken clearly has to do with upbringing and socialization. This, however, is not a complete explanation. Why offense rather than anger? There might be anger where something is not liked because it is thought that it will have harmful consequences, for example that it will contribute to the corruption of youth, or the general lowering of standards in the community. Offense seems to involve something more than this. If I find something offensive, I take it personally in some way. I am *hurt*, not just angered. A reasonable explanation of why I am hurt is that I identify closely with beliefs that this sort of behavior is wrong, and in a way I feel violated. If you expose me to these things that you know I do not like, then you are not showing me the respect that I deserve as a person. Even if it was not directed at me in particular, I may feel that people like me are not respected enough. In both cases, that is, where it is directed at us in particular and where it is not, we may feel devalued as persons.

The second area is the ridiculing or even just criticizing of beliefs and commitments, particularly perhaps religious and political. A reason that offense is taken here is that we tend to identify with a set of beliefs or with a group in a way that makes those beliefs or that group part of our self-image. So when ridicule is directed at those beliefs or that group, we feel that we are being ridiculed, and again can feel that we are not being respected as persons.

The third and final area is the offense taken at language or conduct which is racist or sexist or which "makes fun of" or otherwise denigrates those with mental or physical disabilities or the victims of accidents or crimes. What these all share is that there is no choice involved in being a member of any of these groups. There is a real sense here in which our identity and self-image is inextricably linked with the group of this type of which we find ourselves members. Offense will almost always be bound up with self-respect.

These three examples all show that there is a close connection between the taking of offense and respect, both respect for others and self-respect or esteem. When someone makes a remark or exhibits conduct that we find offensive, we may feel that we are not being respected as persons in the way that we ought to be. Our self-respect may be lessened to some extent. Too much of this conduct can cause us to see ourselves as people of little worth. If something which is an integral part of me is mocked – say, my height, race, gender, or intelligence – this is evidence that others do not value me as a person. They are not showing me the respect that I deserve as a person. If I identify very closely with a football team or with a religion and if that team or religion is ridiculed, I may feel the same (although it will be argued later that there are relevant differences in these cases). So perhaps we can say that what is wrong with giving offense in general is that it is showing a lack of respect for others and that it may cause them to lose some of their self-respect.

The argument is not that all lack of respect causes loss of self-respect, nor does it imply that all that is wrong with showing a lack of respect is this link with self-respect. However, it is claimed that there is an important link. The respect under consideration is respect for *persons*, as distinct from respect for a *role* occupied by a person. I might show little respect for someone *as a professor*, for example, but still respect him or her as a person. This is not a sharp distinction, particularly in societies where people are to a large extent identified with their occupations, but it is still a viable one. If someone shows me lack of respect as a person, and if I recognize this, it is difficult for my self-respect not to be dented. However, if I am not respected as a professor by someone who believes that universities ought to be places for the totally free exchange of ideas, with no academic hierarchy, there is nothing to take as a personal slight, except perhaps in the sense that I am willingly participating in a corrupt system.

There are two respects in which this account fits in with commonly held beliefs. First, it explains why offense connected with race, gender, and physical disability, for example, seems to be much more serious than offense related to football or political allegiances or non-pornographic pictures of naked humans. If we choose to make a commitment to something, or admit that we do not like something, we should be prepared, to some extent anyway, to accept the consequences of making that commitment or admission. At any rate, there is an important difference between areas in which we have some choice, like football team allegiance, and those in which we do not – for example, race.

There are, of course, some cases which are anything but clear-cut. Religious belief is one example. That there is some choice possible in religious commitment is obvious. People do choose to join or leave particular religious groups. But religious beliefs are also closely connected with culture, and we do not have much choice regarding the culture in which we are raised. This perhaps partly explains why offense at criticisms or ridicule of religious beliefs is often so deep. Our culture helps make us what we are, and so do our religious beliefs. Mature, thinking adults, however, cannot plausibly maintain that they have no choice in their religious beliefs. They may have had no choice in the faith in which they grew up, but once mature and aware of other faiths, the choice is there to abandon their original beliefs, and this regularly happens. So criticism of the religious beliefs of a university-educated person is not showing any lack of respect, or not necessarily, while doing the same to an uneducated peasant who has had no real opportunity to choose may be. In the former case it may even be showing respect, in that we consider the person to be mature and intelligent enough to be able to cope with criticism.

The second way that this account of offense fits in with common feelings is that it also helps to explain why it seems more objectionable to mock or ridicule the disadvantaged than the advantaged. If someone takes offense at some mockery of an advantaged group, that person must first identify him or herself with that group, that is, they must see themselves as privileged in some way. If they can only take offense to the extent that they identify with some favored section of society, they are unlikely to have their self-respect dented.

Offense and Harm

Is an action harmful because it is offensive, or offensive because it is harmful (or both)? If an action is offensive because it is harmful, the notion of offense is unimportant as a criterion for restricting freedoms. If X is harmful, there is a ground for restricting it regardless of whether or not it is offensive as well. It is of little concern that inflicting physical bodily harm can be offensive. That it harms is enough for there to be laws against it.

Is something harmful because it is offensive? In one sense, yes. If offense is a kind of unhappiness or mental distress, even if mild, then it is a kind of harm. This is even more so if, as was argued, offense is closely related to self-respect. In this sense something is harmful by virtue of being offensive. My not being invited to the party is harmful to me simply because it offended me. In another sense, however, we distinguish between offense and harm. A common debate regarding pornography is whether or not it is harmful, or merely offensive. Arguments for its restriction or banning often concern its supposed harmful effects, rather than its undoubted offensiveness to many. Racial vilification might be condemned on similar grounds. It certainly is offensive, but it can also harm its target groups by inciting racial hatred and perhaps even violence.

The relationship, then, between offense and harm is not straightforward. In one sense offense is harm, and in another it is not. It is tempting to argue that in the sense in which it is harm, it is of a pretty mild variety, and so need not be taken into consideration when examining reasons for restricting freedom of speech and expression. While it probably is mild harm in most cases, it is not necessarily so in all. The ridiculing of dearly held beliefs, particularly religious ones, can cause deep distress, even if there is no other harm involved.

This leads to another distinction, one raised by Feinberg, that is the distinction between something considered wrong because it is offensive and something being offensive because it is believed wrong (Feinberg 1985). One difference that Feinberg claims is important between offensive nuisances and profound offenses is that the former are considered wrong because they are offensive, while the latter offensive because they are wrong. While this distinction is certainly not sharp, it does have some plausibility. Perhaps the wrongness of publishing pictures of naked human bodies on the Internet attaches purely to its offensiveness. In other contexts, in medical texts for example, such pictures might not be offensive, and so not wrong. On the other hand, an anti-abortionist is unlikely to claim that abortion is wrong because it is offensive. For him or her it is offensive because it is wrong. Similarly, the manipulated copy of Leonardo's *The Last Supper* mentioned earlier, might not be thought wrong because it is offensive to many Christians, but offensive because it is wrong to make light of one of Christianity's most significant events.

The relationship between offense and harm on the one hand and offense and wrongness on the other is important. The argument that offense is a kind of harm is more plausible in the case where offense is taken because something is thought wrong, than when something is thought wrong just because it is offensive.

Offense on the Internet

Discussions of offense on the Internet seem to arise most often when there is talk of regulating its content. And, as we saw earlier, offensive material is frequently identified with the sexual. While discussions of sex do seem to fascinate, there are also concerns about material which is offensive because of its racial, religious, or cultural nature, and which arise in contexts other than that of regulation. One of these areas is web page design. Designing one's own web pages is a feature of the Internet that is new. It shares features with paintings, drawings, and other art work, as well as the designing of book covers, posters, television images, and so on, but it allows people to be on the world stage, as it were, much more easily. Few people get to design book covers, posters, and so on, which will go on display to the world, but many design and create web pages accessible worldwide. There are various reasons why someone might consider a web page offensive; for example, language, images, layout, or colors. Mullet and Sano give a few examples of icons which might offend (1995, p. 198). These include images depicting death or violence (guns, skull and crossbones, hatchets, tombstones), the thumbs up or down signs, which have different meanings in different cultures, and others. There are pragmatic as well as moral reasons why this should be taken into account by web page designers, whether individuals or corporations. The moral argument simply is that in general we should not offend intentionally if it can be avoided, given what was said earlier concerning the relationship between respect and offense. Pragmatically, giving offense to potential customers is not a wise thing if one is trying to sell goods or services. If web pages are part of an electronic commerce effort, it would be good business as well as morally admirable to be sensitive to what might be offensive to those likely to view the page.

While this issue of offensiveness in web page design is one which deserves more attention, as was said previously it is in the area of Internet content regulation that giving offense raises its head most frequently, and to this we now turn.

Offense as a Criterion for Internet Censorship

It has been argued that giving offense is sometimes serious. It therefore should be taken into consideration in discussions of freedom of speech and expression, and censorship. Clearly, however, there cannot be a law against giving offense in general. Almost anything might offend some sensitive soul, so we would be reduced to virtual silence. On the other hand, some offense seems serious enough to warrant restriction. Feinberg suggests two conditions which must be satisfied before coercion is justified with respect to offense. One is *universality* and the other *reasonable avoidability*. Of the former he says:

> For offensiveness . . . to be sufficient to warrant coercion, it should be the reaction that could be expected from almost any person chosen at random from the nation as a whole, regardless of sect, faction, race, age or sex. (1973, p. 44)

Of reasonable avoidability he writes:

> No one has a right to protection from the state against offensive experiences if he can effectively avoid those experiences with no unreasonable effort or inconvenience. (Ibid.)

We will consider these in turn.

The obvious problem with universality in the context of the Internet is that it is too weak to be useful. Given the global nature of the Internet, probably very little will be offensive to all. Ridiculing Christianity would not be universally offensive, as it might be in a Christian country. Mocking a national group will not offend too widely, apart from the members of that nationality. A supporter of this universality principle could, of course, happily go along with all of this, and claim that all it shows is that nothing on the Internet should be restricted just on the grounds of offensiveness. (It could be argued though that this is a reasonable criterion when considering restrictions in any one country.)

The main problem, however, with universality, is not its *weakness* when applied to the Internet context, but rather its *implausibility* when considered in the light of the previous discussion of the nature of offense. Let us see why. Things that are most offensive are commonly not those which are universally offensive, but rather those that single out individuals or groups. To begin with a trivial example, I feel more offended if I alone amongst my group of friends do not get invited to the party than I do if most of us do not. The reason is obvious. If I alone am singled out, I feel slighted, and unjustly treated. I feel that I have not been treated with the respect that I deserve. A similar point can be seen in jokes against a particular group. I may be offended at jokes against Australians if told by non-Australians, but I am not offended by such jokes when told by Australians. Again, the reason is simple. In the second case I am not being 'put down' or slighted by someone who is portraying him or herself as being superior to me, as the joke-teller would be in the former case.

While the party and joke examples might not be too important in themselves, they do show what is wrong with the universality principle. Offense which singles out individuals and groups is more serious than that which is offensive to all (or most). It is more serious simply because it treats that individual or group as being of less consequence, or less worthy of respect, than other individuals or groups, or less worthy than me, or my group. Our own self-respect and self-esteem are not totally determined by our perceived status relative to others, but that relativity is certainly important. Conduct or material which is offensive to just certain types of individuals and groups imply that they are in some way inferior.

Feinberg's second principle is reasonable avoidability, and this does have some plausibility. If I am offended by certain World Wide Web sites, I can easily avoid them, and consequently there seems to be no good reason why they should be banned on the ground of giving offense. This situation is very different from one where I am confronted by offensive material each time I log on to the Internet, say by a particular welcoming message or the wording of a prompt or image of an icon. If I am offended by the sight of nude humans on the Internet, I seem to have little cause for complaint if I can only access such images via tortuous paths punctuated by warnings.

The problem with this is that it is really only plausible in the case of milder offenses – actions which are only thought wrong because they offend, and not those which offend because they are thought wrong. If something is found offensive because it is believed wrong, those offended will not be placated by just keeping it away from their eyes and ears, any more than most of us are willing to condone murder which occurs away from us. That it is happening at all is offensive. Wolgast is right in her criticism of Feinberg's argument about pornography, which he puts thus:

> When printed words hide decorously behind covers of books sitting passively on bookstore shelves, their offensiveness is easily avoided. . . . [T]here is nothing like the evil smell of rancid garbage oozing right out through the covers of a book. When an "obscene" book sits on the shelf, who is there to be offended? Those who want to read it for the sake of erotic stimulation presumably will not be offended (or else they wouldn't read it), and those who choose not to read it will have no experience by which to be offended. (Feinberg 1973, p. 45)

Wolgast's response is:

> The felt insult and indignity that women protest is not like a noise or bad odor, for these are group-neutral and may offend anyone, while pornography is felt to single women out as objects of insulting attention. . . . [W]ith pornography there is a felt hostile discrimination. (1987, p. 112)

If offense is related to respect for others and to self-respect, as was argued earlier, the issue of reasonable avoidability does not arise. If women or some race or any particular group is singled out for treatment which shows lack of respect and which is of the type to lower self-respect, it is not an issue whether or not someone can easily avoid some instance of that treatment.

One woman might avoid seeing pornography on one occasion, and one member of the racial group might avoid hearing some racially offensive language, but these individuals are still being shown less respect than they deserve, simply because they are members of these targeted groups.

Even if reasonable avoidability were a useful criterion in some contexts, it is not so clear that it is on the Internet. Looking for material on the Internet is not much like performing that task in a library or in a bookshop, where to a large extent we do "judge a book by its cover." We see a title or author and explore further. On the Internet we seek out material on the basis of words, phrases, or names using search engines, and have little control over what is discovered. Innocuous search terms can find sites containing almost any sort of material, so reasonable avoidability does not have much force here.

It has been argued in this paper that offense does need to be taken seriously, not in the sense that there should be legislation against giving offense in general – that would be just silly; but in the sense that there needs to be careful examination of offensive behavior to see which, if any, should be subject to regulation. It has also been argued that the universality and reasonable avoidability criteria proposed by Feinberg do not help much. Offense is of particular importance on the Internet, because it is offense which causes much of the distress and other kinds of worry. It is also important because of the previously mentioned global nature of the Internet. Material which may offend no one within a particular country may be offensive to many on the Internet, where it is available to people of other beliefs, customs, and race.

Where does this discussion leave us with respect to the vexed question of curtailing freedom of speech and expression on the Internet? A useful distinction is that between activities, words, pictures, and so on, which offend because of characteristics over which people have no control – for example, race, gender, and physical appearance – and those which offend because of characteristics over which there is some control – for instance, political beliefs, football team allegiance, and dress. It is fairly obviously worse to ridicule a person because of the color of his or her skin than because of the color of his or her shirt. While both may offend, the former is showing much less respect, and is much more detrimental to self-respect. I can always change my shirt to end the ridicule if I cannot cope with it. Cases can, of course, arise where a shirt cannot easily be changed, say because of poverty. But this does not weaken the usefulness of the distinction; rather it indicates why ridiculing someone living in poverty is worse than ridiculing the more affluent.

J. S. Mill argued that one of the strengths of freedom of speech is that it forces people to continually re-examine their beliefs, and that, as a result, those beliefs, or the ones that survive, would be stronger and more lively.

Beliefs unexamined wither and die (Mill 1859). On these grounds, freedom of speech and expression can override worries about giving offense in the case of ridiculing or criticizing beliefs and commitments. The same argument can apply to the case in which certain language or pictures are taken as offensive in themselves. To the extent that such language or pictures might be seen as offensive just because of beliefs, these beliefs should be open to challenge. To the extent that the offense is not based on beliefs but purely on something like taste, it seems not too important. This might seem to suggest that offense is no ground for censoring pornography. However, pornography singles out a certain group, women, and can be seen as degrading to them, regardless of the beliefs of individual women.

The argument Mill offers does not apply where the offense concerns race, gender, appearance, or other factors over which we have no control. No amount of freedom of speech is going to change my race, gender, or appearance, even if I want it to. A plausible argument can be made that freedom of speech and expression ought to be restricted where its offensiveness harms, or is likely to harm, someone's self-respect, by showing a lack of respect for a person or group, where that person or group is identified by traits which they cannot change. Racial vilification language would be a case in point, and, as we have argued, pornography could also be.

Offense, in summary, is a relevant consideration in censorship, but only in those areas where self-respect is at stake, and primarily where individuals or groups are singled out by characteristics which they have no power to change. On these grounds there is reason to restrict conduct on the Internet which offends, for example, racial groups and women, but not, in general, religious or political groups or any groupings defined by their beliefs.

Finally, there is another issue of relevance in censorship of the Internet. The effective censoring activity on the Internet will not be easy, given current technology, without limiting its usefulness. While it may not be good that certain sorts of things are communicated, things which may harm or offend some people, it may well be worse overall in some cases if this form of communication is restricted in ways which would limit the Internet's effectiveness. Offense must be taken into account, but only serious cases should be restricted. Not too many babies should be thrown out with the bath water. An attempt has been made in this paper to show which cases are the serious ones.

References

Broadcasting Services Amendment (Online Services) Bill (1999). Accessed July 6, 1999, at http://www.aph.gov.au/parlinfo/billsnet/bills.htm.
Burton, P. F. (1996). "Content on the Internet: Free or Unfettered." Revised version of a paper presented at the 10th Annual Computers in Libraries International

Conference, London, February 20, 1996, accessed July 6, 1999, at http://www.dis.strath.ac.uk/people/paul/CIL96.html.

Communications Decency Act (1996). Enacted by the US Congress on February 1, 1996. Text provided by the Electronic Privacy Information Center, accessed July 6, 1999, at http://www.fcc.gov/Reports/tcom1996.txt.

Feinberg, J. (1973). *Social Philosophy*. Prentice-Hall.

Feinberg, J. (1985). *The Moral Limits of the Criminal Law*. Vol. 2: *Offense to Others*. Oxford University Press.

Mill, J. S. (1859). *On Liberty*.

Mullet, K. and Sano, D. (1995). *Designing Visual Interfaces*. Prentice-Hall.

Sansom, G. (1995). *Illegal and Offensive Content on the Information Highway: A Background Paper*. Long Range Planning and Analysis (DPP), Spectrum, Information Technologies and Telecommunications Sector (SITT), Canada, June 19. Available at http://insight.mcmaster.ca/org/efc/pages/doc/offensive.html.

Wolgast, E. H. (1987). *The Grammar of Justice*. Cornell University Press.

Basic study questions

1. What are the two key issues regarding offense that Weckert identifies in the introduction of this article?
2. Name five types of materials on the Internet which, according to Weckert, are often considered offensive.
3. According to Weckert, "we are not offended by things, but by people." Explain what he means.
4. According to Weckert, "something will only offend someone if that person *takes* offense." Does this mean that a person should never take offense at anything? Explain your answer.
5. According to Weckert, being offended involves more than mere anger. What else is involved and why?
6. What is the close relationship that Weckert identifies between offense and respect?
7. Why, according to Weckert, is offense connected with race, gender or physical disability more serious than offense connected with one's favorite football team? (Hint: What is the role of choice?)
8. According to Weckert, "there cannot be a law against giving offense in general." Why?
9. State Feinberg's two conditions that must be satisfied before censorship would be justified.
10. Why, according to Weckert, is Feinberg's "universality principle" unacceptable?
11. Why, according to Weckert, does Feinberg's "reasonable avoidability principle" *not* apply to the Internet?
12. Why does Weckert say that only "serious cases" of offense should be censored on the Internet? What, according to Weckert, makes an offense serious?

Questions for further thought

1. What is Weckert's view of someone who never takes offense at anything? Do you agree with his view? Why or why not?
2. How are offense and harm related to each other? Is every case of offense harmful? Is every case of harm offensive? Why do you think so? Give examples.
3. While designing web pages, should a person be concerned about the possibility of offending people who view those pages? Why?

CASE TO ANALYZE: A CLEVER IDEA

The overall case described below did not really happen, but something very much like it could easily occur in the future, and some of the events described here did occur. This case illustrates some of the challenges that the world faces because of the global reach of the Internet and the many policy vacuums that have resulted. The reader is invited to analyze this case using the method described in chapter 3 above.

Joe Clever is very excited about his future. He has just earned a degree in international law, and he has hit upon an idea for a new kind of law firm. "This is going to make me a multimillionaire!" he thought to himself. Joe's plan is to create a law firm that specializes in lawsuits based upon "value clashes" on the Internet.

While he was a law student, Joe learned about a number of "messy legal cases" that resulted from the global reach of the Internet and the fact that different societies and communities have different values. In one of those cases, a powerful judge in France objected to "hate web sites" based in America and protected by the "free speech" amendment of the US Constitution. The judge decided to ban those web sites in France and prosecute companies and individuals from America who make "hate sites" accessible to French citizens over the Internet. The judge was spurred into action by many angry French citizens who were outraged that Nazi hate messages and Nazi memorabilia were available to French citizens over the Internet, even though they were outlawed in France.

Many American citizens, even though they abhor Nazism and wish that it did not exist, were nevertheless angered by the French judge's actions. They saw him as trying to impose French law upon Americans in their own country and trying to undermine the First Amendment "freedom of speech" protection of the US Constitution. "The French have no right to meddle with American democracy and freedom!" said Americans who were angry with the French judge. "If they don't like American web sites, they don't have to sign onto them!"

Another case that Joe studied in law school involved a legal tangle between two states *within* the United States. A man in Tennessee, which has strict anti-pornography laws, objected to a pornographic Internet bulletin board based in a region of California where pornography is legal. For a fee, the man, who lied as part of a police "sting" operation, had downloaded sexually explicit pictures into his home computer in Tennessee. He was angry because children in his community managed to access that same bulletin board, even though it was supposed to be for adults only. The angry man went to the police to have the bulletin board owners in California extradited and tried for selling pornography in Tennessee. The extradition took place and the California bulletin board owners were tried and convicted in Tennessee. The bulletin board owners' lawyer argued in court that they had not sold pornography in Tennessee, because the server that has the bulletin board is in California and the business transaction took place on that server. The Tennessee lawyers, however, argued that the Californians had indeed sold pornography in Tennessee, since the pornographic materials were received on a computer in Tennessee and the purchaser never left the state when he bought the pornographic materials.

Internet companies and web site publishers in many countries are very worried about the implications of such cases. If people are subject to arrest and prosecution in other states, or even other countries, for actions which were perfectly legal in their own home towns, how can people do anything at all on the Internet? Just about anything they do might offend someone, somewhere! Doesn't this undermine the usefulness of the Internet?

Joe Clever thought all this was wonderful. "This is going to generate an endless supply of very profitable, very messy legal cases for us," Joe enthusiastically told his future law partners. "This is terrific! Imagine all the legal cases of people gambling on the Internet in countries where gambling is illegal! Or creating controversial political, sexual, racial, and ethnic web sites that will offend people all around the globe!"

As soon as his new law firm opened for business, Joe Clever hired an "Internet business stimulator" to generate business for the firm. The "business stimulator's" job was to get onto the Internet, using chat rooms, bulletin boards, and email to stir up conflicts among people in different states and different countries with different laws and values. "The more heated conflicts we stir up," said Joe, "the more highly profitable lawsuits we will get for our law business! We are all going to be millionaires!"

ADDITIONAL READINGS AND WEB RESOURCES

Additional readings

Barlow, J. P. (1991). "Coming Into The Country", *Communications of the ACM*, 34/3 (March): 19–21.

Ess, C. (2002). "Cultures in Collision: Philosophical Lessons from Computer-Mediated Communication." In J. H. Moor, and T. W. Bynum (eds.), *Cyber Philosophy: The Intersection of Philosophy and Computers*. Blackwell, pp. 219–42.

Johnson, D. G. (1997). "Is the Global Information Infrastructure a Democratic Technology?" *Computers and Society* 20–6.

Lessig, L. (2001). "The Laws of Cyberspace." In R. A. Spinello, and H. T. Tavani (eds.), *Readings in CyberEthics*. Jones and Bartlett, pp. 124–34.

Web resources

The Cyber Rights Working Group, Computer Professionals for Social Responsibility, http://www.cpsr.org/cpsr/nii/cyber-rights/

"The Global Culture of Digital Technology and Its Ethics", abstract of a paper by Krystyna Gorniak-Kocikowska, http://www.ccsr.cse.dmu.ac.uk/conferences/ccsrconf/ethicomp2001/abstracts/gorniak.html

The Internet Society – an international organization for global cooperation, http://www.isoc.org/isoc/

UNESCO's Info-Ethics Program, The United Nations, http://www.unesco.org/webworld/infoethics/infoethics.htm

A Final Case to Analyze

Given all that you have learned from this textbook about various computer ethics issues and methods, you are now in a position to apply the case-analysis method presented in chapter 3 to the following imagined, but realistic, case. There are several computer ethics issues lurking here – some of which have already been dealt with in the chapters above, and some new ones. Your newly acquired knowledge in computer ethics, when combined with your freshly honed case-analysis skills, should enable you to unpack and clarify the major issues successfully.

Corner-Shop Goes Virtual

Corner-Shop retail chain outlets sell a wide range of groceries, newspapers and magazines, and some home maintenance products. Services such as cleaning, photographic processing, and floral deliveries are provided. With the advent of shopping at the hypermarket and out-of-town superstore, Corner-Shop has found it increasingly difficult to compete. The formula of slightly increased prices in return for local, customized service no longer seems to be attractive to the consumer. Two years ago Corner-Shop was close to collapsing. Enter the new chief executive Jean Webb, whose job it was to reinvent Corner-Shop and return the chain to profitability.

Given the advances in Internet technologies and a growing expansion of electronic commerce, Webb believed that the company's future was in providing a range of services and products via the Internet. She hired a consulting firm to investigate the commercial potential of electronic commerce for Corner-Shop. The resulting report confirmed Webb's belief. It reported that there were many benefits to be gained, including: the creation of a larger global market place, improved competitiveness, the ability to customize services and products for all its customers, shortened or eradicated supply chains, and substantial cost savings. consequently, the board backed her proposal to reorganize the business, transforming it into an electronic retailer within two years. The decision was also taken to phase out over a two-year period the existing Corner-Shop outlets, which would result in a large reduction in shop assistants and shop managers.

The chain is now back in profit. It now runs E.Shop as an electronic shopping service available on the World Wide Web via a personal computer or digital television. Customers can buy goods that can be found in a traditional supermarket and have them delivered to their homes or collect them from a local distribution point. This distribution network is slowly expanding. All major cities in the country are now covered and pilot projects are nearing completion in six other countries.

The pricing policy has used the reduction in overheads to set prices lower than the supermarkets and set the same prices when goods are delivered to the customer. The range of goods has been expanded to cover large household items such as furniture and domestic appliances. Other services are now offered including full electronic banking facilities. Gradually, customers are being encouraged, via incentives, to use this facility to pay for their shopping. Webb's intention is to make customers dependant upon the chain for all their daily household needs and transactions and so enable the chain to exploit fully the trader–customer relationship.

A potential customer has to complete an on-line registration form to become a shopper at E.Shop. Credit-worthiness is checked and, if satisfactory, the person is accepted and a customer profile is set up which, over time, contains a complete history of customer purchases and visits to E.Shop. Jean Webb explains that this history of customer activity enables goods and services to be tailored to individual customers, and customers can also be targeted with new promotions that they would find interesting based on their past activity. Analysis of financial activity is dealt with separately so that valued customers are automatically given credit limit increases as they near their existing limits. Much of this profile-driven marketing and customer servicing is done in a way that keeps it unnoticed by customers, because, as Webb explains, "customers simply want to gain quick access to our virtual shop, quickly buy the goods that they need, and leave. They are not interested in the question of how we are able to direct them to the goods they are most likely to want. That suits both them and us."

The profile of customers has changed since Corner-Shop became E.Shop. Generally, the new customers are financially better off and have easy access to at least one Internet facility. Webb welcomes this shift, for she sees a greater potential for increasing sales to these customers than to those who shopped at Corner-Shop outlets. Those customers tended to buy small amounts several times a week and spend quite a lot of time in conversation with staff, which was inefficient and costly. There have been a number of complaints from community groups about the loss of small local shops and the impact upon local customers. But how those customers are now serviced is of no concern to Webb or her board, because they see their future as E.Shop.

Webb believes that the success of E.Shop is based a lot upon image. They have worked hard to get customers to trust them. This has been achieved by using the leading Trust Mark agency to verify their authenticity as an electronic trader and so enable them to display the Trust Mark on their site. The site is backed by the leading electronic commerce software vendor, and their mark is also displayed on the site, which further instills customer confidence. The whole image presented is one of a large organization, backed by leading computer technology suppliers, and in close contact with its customers. In reality, E.Shop is operated with a very small number of staff. The provision, storage, and delivery of goods are all done by local subcontractors who automatically receive orders and customer details as the customers shop electronically. E.Shop maintains a secure link with its subcontractors as well as having reasonably secure Internet access. It is the responsibility of subcontractors to insure that information passed to them by E.Shop is held in a secure environment. E.Shop drew up a contract with subcontractors that makes subcontractors liable for information once received from E.Shop. E.Shop assume that subcontractors will have adequate security in place given this contractual clause and therefore do not monitor security arrangements. Overall uniform branding promotes this image of a large organization rather than a group of much smaller organizations tied together by legal contracts.

Jean Webb is proud of the progress the chain has made under her leadership. When she took it over, it was a floundering retail chain dealing directly with customers with small buying potential in little shops in the outskirts of many towns. Today it is seen as a model electronic retailer providing all the goods and services that busy people require in the modern world. Its virtual doors are open 24 hours a day, and it delivers to its customers when and where they require. Over the next 12 months, the pilots in the six other countries will be transformed into fully operational services. Webb sees this as the inevitable move to a global operation of shared services, shared cost, and shared information. It is founded on a technological infrastructure that is capable of exploiting economies of scale and global market potential.

Bibliography

ACM and IEEE-CS (1991). *Computing Curricula 1991*. Available at http://www. computer.org/education/cc1991/

Anderson, R. E. (1994). "The ACM Code of Ethics: History, Process, and Implications." In C. Huff and T. Finholt (eds.), *Social Issues in Computing*. McGraw Hill, pp. 48–71.

Anderson, R., Johnson D. G., Gotterbarn D., and Perrolle, J. (1993). "Using the New ACM Code of Ethics in Decision Making." *Communications of the ACM*, 36 (February): 98–107.

Baase, S. (2002). *A Gift of Fire: Social, Legal, and Ethical Issues in Computing*, 2nd edn. Prentice-Hall.

Baird, R. M., Rosenbaum, S. E., and Ramsower, R. M. (eds.) (2000). *Cyberethics: Social and Moral Issues in the Computer Age*. Prometheus Books.

Barlow, J. P. (1991). "Coming into The Country." *Communications of the ACM*, 34/3 (March): 19–21.

Barlow, J. P. (1994). "The Economy of Ideas: A Framework for Rethinking Patents and Copyrights in the Digital Age (Everything You Know About Intellectual Property is Wrong)." *Wired*: 85–129.

Bayles, M. (1981). *Professional Ethics*. Wadsworth.

Benyon-Davies, P. (1995). "Information Systems 'Failure': the Case of the London Ambulance Service's Computer Aided Dispatch Project." *European Journal of Information Systems*, 4: 171–84.

Bowyer, K. W. (ed.) (2000). *Ethics and Computing: Living Responsibly in a Computerized World*, 2nd edn. Wiley-IEEE Press.

Brey, P. (2000). "Disclosive Computer Ethics." *Computers and Society*, 30/4 (December): 10–16.

Bynum, T. W. (1993). "Computer Ethics in the Computer Science Curriculum." In T. W. Bynum, W. Maner, and J. L. Fodor (eds.) (1993). *Teaching Computer Ethics*. Research Center on Computing and Society (also available at http://www. computerethics.org).

Bynum, T. W. (1999). "The Foundation of Computer Ethics." A keynote address at the AICEC99 Conference, Melbourne, Australia, July 1999. (Published in *Computers and Society*, June 2000: 6–13.)

Bynum, T. W. (2001). "Computer Ethics: Basic Concepts and Historical Overview." In E. Zalta (ed.), *Stanford Encyclopedia of Philosophy*, on-line at http://plato.stanford.edu/entries/ethics-computer

Bynum, T. W. and Rogerson, S. (1996). *Global Information Ethics*. Published as *Science and Engineering Ethics*, 2/2.

Bynum, T. W. and Schubert, P. (1997). "How to Do Computer Ethics: A Case Study – The Electronic Mall Bodensee." In M. J. van den Hoven (ed.), *Computer Ethics: Philosophical Enquiry – Proceedings of CEPE'97*, Erasmus University Press, pp. 85–95 (also available at http://www.computerethics.org).

Chadwick, R. (ed.) (2001). *The Concise Encyclopedia of Ethics of New Technologies*. Academic Press.

Collins, W. R., Miller, K. W., Spielman B. J., and Wherry, P. (1994). "How Good is Good Enough?" *Communications of the ACM*, 37 (January): 81–91.

Conry, S. (1992). "Interview on Computer Science Accreditation." In T. W. Bynum, and J. L. Fodor, (creators) *Computer Ethics in the Computer Science Curriculum* (video program). Educational Media Resources.

Denning, P. J. (ed.) (1991). *Computers Under Attack: Intruders, Worms, and Viruses*. ACM Books and Addison-Wesley.

Dhillon, G. (2002). *Social Responsibility in the Information Age: Issues and Controversies*. Idea Group Publishing.

Edgar, S. L. (2002). *Morality and Machines: Perspectives on Computer Ethics*, 2nd edn. Jones and Bartlett.

Eichmann, D. (1994). "Ethical Web Agents." Proceedings of the Second International World Wide Web Conference: Mosaic and the Web, Chicago, IL, October 18–20, pp. 3–13 (see also: http://archive.ncsa.uiuc.edu/SDG/IT94/Proceedings/Agents/eichmann.ethical/eichmann.html).

Elgesem, D. (1996). "Privacy, Respect for Persons, and Risk." In C. Ess (ed.), *Philosophical Perspectives on Computer-Mediated Communication*. State University of New York Press.

Elgesem, D. (1999). "The Structure of Rights in Directive 95/46/EC on the Protection of Individuals with Regard to the Processing of Personal Data and the Free Movement of Such Data." *Ethics and Information Technology*, 1: 283–93.

Epstein, R. G. (1996). *The Case of the Killer Robot*. John Wiley and Sons.

Ermann, M. D., Williams, M. B., and Shauf, M. S. (1997). *Computers, Ethics and Society*. Oxford University Press.

Ess, C. (2002). "Cultures in Collision: Philosophical Lessons from Computer-Mediated Communication." In J. H. Moor, and T. W. Bynum (eds.), *Cyberphilosophy: The Intersection of Philosophy and Computers*. Blackwell (also in *Metaphilosophy*, January 2002).

Fairweather, N. B. and Rogerson, S. (2001). "A Moral Approach to Electronic Patient Records." *Medical Informatics and the Internet in Medicine*, 26/3: 219–34.

Fodor, J. L. and Bynum, T. W. (creators) (1992). *What Is Computer Ethics?* (video program). Educational Media Resources.

Ford, P. J. (2000). *Computers and Ethics in the Cyberage*. Prentice-Hall.

Forester, T. and Morrison, P. (1994). *Computer Ethics: Cautionary Tales and Ethical Dilemmas in Computing*, 2nd edn. MIT Press.

Fried, C. (1984). "Privacy." In F. D. Schoeman (ed.), *Philosophical Dimensions of Privacy*. Cambridge University Press.

Gleason, D. H. (1999). "Subsumption Ethics." *Computers and Society*, 29: 29–36.

Goodman, K. W. (ed.) (1997). *Ethics, Computing and Medicine: Informatics and the Transformation of Health Care*. Cambridge University Press.

Gorniak-Kocikowska, K. (1996). "The Computer Revolution and the Problem of Global Ethics." *Science and Engineering Ethics*, 2 (April): 177–90.

Gotterbarn, D. (1991). "Computer Ethics: Responsibility Regained." *National Forum: The Phi Beta Kappa Journal*, 71: 26–31.

Gotterbarn, D. (1992). "You Don't Have the Right to Do It Wrong." Available at www-cs.etsu-tnedu/gotterbarn/Artpp4.htm (accessed December 7, 2002).

Gotterbarn, D. (1994). "Software Engineering Ethics." In J. J. Marciniak (ed.), *Encyclopedia of Software Engineering*, vol. 2. John Wiley and Sons, pp. 1197–201.

Gotterbarn, D. (1996). "Establishing Standards of Professional Practice." In T. Hall, D. Pitt, and C. Meyer (eds.), *The Responsible Software Engineer: Selected Readings in IT Professionalism*. Springer Verlag, ch. 3.

Gotterbarn, D. (2000). "Computer Professionals and Your Responsibilities: Virtual Information and the Software Engineering Code of Ethics." In D. Langford (ed.), *Internet Ethics*. Macmillan, pp. 200–19.

Gotterbarn, D., Miller, K., and Rogerson, S. (1997). "Software Engineering Code of Ethics." *Communications of the ACM*, 40/11: 110–18.

Goujon, P. and Dubreuil, B. H. (eds.) (2001). *Technology and Ethics: A European Quest for Responsible Engineering*. Peeters.

Grodzinsky, F. S. (1999). "The Practitioner from Within: Revisiting the Virtues." *Computers and Society* (March): 9–15.

Halbert, T. and Ingulli, E. (2001). *Cyberthethics*. South-Western College Publishing.

Hamelink, C. J. (2000). *The Ethics of Cyberspace*. Sage.

Hester, M. and Ford, P. J. (eds.) (2001). *Computers and Ethics in the Cyberage*. Prentice Hall.

Himanen, P. (2001). *The Hacker Ethic and the Spirit of the Information Age*. Random House.

Huff, C. and Finholt, T. (eds.) (1994). *Social Issues in Computing: Putting Computing in its Place*. McGraw-Hill, Inc.

IEEE-CS and ACM (2001). *Computing Curricula 2001*. Available at: http://www.acm.org/sigcse/cc2001/

Introna, L. I. (1997). "Privacy and the Computer: Why We Need Privacy in the Information Society." *Metaphilosophy*, 28/3: 259–75.

Jefferies, P. and Rogerson, S. (2003). "Using Asynchronous Computer Conferencing to Support the Teaching of Computing and Ethics: A Case Study." *Annals of Cases on Information Technology*, V.

Johnson, D. G. (1985). *Computer Ethics*. Prentice-Hall (2nd edn 1994; 3rd edn 2001).

Johnson, D. G. (1997) "Ethics On-Line." *Communications of the ACM*, 40/1 (January): 60–9.

Johnson, D. G. (1997). "Is the Global Information Infrastructure a Democratic Technology?" *Computers and Society* (September): pp. 20–6.

Johnson, D. G. (1999). "Computer Ethics in the 21st Century." A keynote address at the ETHICOMP99 Conference, Rome, Italy, October.

Johnson, D. G. and Nissenbaum, H. F. (eds.) (1995). *Computers, Ethics and Social Values*. Prentice-Hall.

Kesar, S. and Rogerson, S. (1998). "Managing Computer Misuse". *Social Science Computer Review*, 16/3 (Fall): 240–51.

Kizza, M. J. (2001). *Computer Network Security and Cyber Ethics*. McFarland.

Ladd, J. (1989). "Computers and Moral Responsibility: A Framework for an Ethical Analysis." In C. C. Gould (ed.), *The Information Web: Ethical and Social Implications of Computer Networking*. Westview Press, pp. 207–27.

Langford, D. (1999). *Business Computer Ethics*. Addison Wesley.

Langford, D. (ed.) (2000). *Internet Ethics*. St Martin's Press.

Lessig, L. (2001). "The Laws of Cyberspace." In R. A. Spinello, and H. T. Tavani (eds.) (2001). *Readings in CyberEthics*. Jones and Bartlett, pp. 124–34.

Leveson, N. and Turner, C. (1993). "An Investigation of the Therac-25 Accidents." *Computer*, 26/7: 18–41.

Maner, W. (1980). *Starter Kit in Computer Ethics*. Helvetia Press (published in co-operation with the National Information and Resource Center for the Teaching of Philosophy). (Originally self-published by Maner in 1978.)

Maner, W. (1996). "Unique Ethical Problems in Information Technology." *Science and Engineering Ethics*, 2/2: 137–54.

Maner, W. (2002). "Heuristic Methods for Computer Ethics." In J. H. Moor, and T. W. Bynum (eds.), *Cyberphilosophy: The Intersection of Philosophy and Computing*, Blackwell (see also: http://csweb.cs.bgsu.edu/maner/heuristics).

Manion, M. and Goodrum, A. (2000). "Terrorism or Civil Disobedience: Toward a Hacktivist Ethic." *Computers and Society*, 30/2 (June): 14–19.

Marx, G. T. (1996). "Privacy and Technology." *Telektronikk*, 1: 40–8.

Mason, R. O. (1986). "Four Ethical Issues of the Information Age." *MIS Quarterly*, 10/1: 5–12.

Mason, R. O., Mason, F. M., and Culnan, M. J. (1995). *Ethics of Information Management*. Sage.

McFarland, M. C. (1999). "Intellectual Property, Information and the Common Good." In R. A. Spinello, and H. T. Tavani (eds.) (2001), *Readings in CyberEthics*. Jones and Bartlett, pp. 252–62.

Miller, A. R. (1971). *The Assault on Privacy: Computers, Data Banks, and Dossiers*. University of Michigan Press.

Moor, J. H. (1979). "Are There Decisions Computers Should Never Make?" *Nature and System*, 1: 217–29.

Moor, J. H. (1985). "What Is Computer Ethics?" In T. W. Bynum (ed.), *Computers and Ethics*. Blackwell, pp. 266–75. (Published as the October 1985 issue of *Metaphilosophy*.) (Also available at: http://www.computerethics.org)

Moor, J. H. (1996) "Is Ethics Computable?" *Metaphilosophy*, 27: 1–21.

Moor, J. H. (1999). "Just Consequentialism and Computing." *Ethics and Information Technology*, 1: 65–9.

Moor, J. H. (2001). "The Future of Computer Ethics: You Ain't Seen Nothin' Yet." *Ethics and Information Technology*, 3/2.

Neumann, P. G. (1995). *Computer Related Risks*. ACM Press and Addison-Wesley.

Nissenbaum, H. (1994). "Computing and Accountability." *Communications of the ACM,* 37/1: 73–80.

Nissenbaum, H. (1997). "Toward an Approach to Privacy in Public: Challenges of Information Technology." *Ethics and Behavior,* 7/3: 207–19.

Nissenbaum, H. (1998). "Protecting Privacy in an Information Age: The Problem of Privacy in Public." *Law and Philosophy,* 17: 559–96.

Nissenbaum, H. (1999). "The Meaning of Anonymity in an Information Age." *The Information Society,* 15: 141–4.

Parker, D. (1968). "Rules of Ethics in Information Processing." *Communications of the ACM,* 11: 198–201.

Parker, D. (1978). *Ethical Conflicts in Computer Science and Technology.* AFIPS Press.

Parker, D., Swope, S., and Baker, B. N. (1990). *Ethical Conflicts in Information and Computer Science, Technology, and Business.* QED Information Sciences.

Perrolle, J. A. (1987). *Computers and Social Change: Information, Property, and Power.* Wadsworth.

Pratchett, L., Birch, S., Candy, S., Fairweather, N. B., Rogerson, S., Stone, V., Watt, R., and Wingfield, M. (2002). *The Implementation of Electronic Voting in the UK.* LGA Publications.

Prior, M., Fairweather, N. B., and Rogerson, S. (2001). *Is IT Ethical? 2000 ETHICOMP Survey of Professional Practice.* UK: Institute for the Management of Information Systems.

Prior, M., Rogerson, S., and Fairweather, N. B. (2002). "The Ethical Attitudes of Information Systems Professionals: Outcomes of an Initial Survey." *Telematics and Informatics,* 19/1: 21–36.

Rahanu, R., Davies, J., and Rogerson, S. (1999). "Ethical Analysis of Software Failure Cases." *Failure and Lessons Learned in Information Technology Management,* 3: 1–22.

Raymond, E. (2000). *The Cathedral and the Bazaar* (a book and a web site at http://www.tuxedo.org/~esr/writings/cathedral-bazaar/cathedral-bazaar).

Rogerson, S. (1996). "The Ethics of Computing: The First and Second Generations." *The UK Business Ethics Network News* (Spring): 1–4.

Rogerson, S. (1998). *Ethical Aspects of Information Technology: Issues for Senior Executives.* Institute of Business Ethics.

Rogerson, S. and Bynum, T. W. (1995). "Cyberspace: The Ethical Frontier." *Times Higher Education Supplement, The Times,* June 9.

Rogerson, S., Weckert, J., and Simpson, C. (2000). "An Ethical Review of Information Systems Development: the Australian Computer Society's Code of Ethics and SSADM." *Information Technology and People,* 13/2: 121–36.

Salehnia, A. (ed.) (2002) *Ethical Issues of Information Systems.* Idea Group Publishing.

Samuelson, P. (1997). "The US Digital Agenda at WIPO." *Virginia Journal of International Law Association,* 37: 369–439.

Spafford, E. (1992). "Are Computer Hacker Break-Ins Ethical?" *Journal of Systems and Software,* 17 (January): 41–7.

Spafford, E., Heaphy, K. A., and Ferbrache D. J. (1989). *Computer Viruses: Dealing with Electronic Vandalism and Programmed Threats.* ADAPSO.

Spier, R. E. (ed.) (2002). *Science and Technology Ethics.* Routledge.

Spinello, R. A. (1997). *Case Studies in Information and Computer Ethics.* Prentice-Hall.

Spinello, R. A. (2000). *Cyberethics: Morality and Law in Cyberspace*. Jones and Bartlett.

Spinello, R. and Tavani, H. (eds.) (2001). *Readings in CyberEthics*. Jones and Bartlett.

Stallman, R. (1992). "Why Software Should Be Free." In T. W. Bynum, W. Maner, and J. L. Fodor (eds.) (1992). *Software Ownership and Intellectual Property Rights*. Research Center on Computing and Society, pp. 35–52 (also available at: http://www.computerethics.org).

Stoll, C. (1989). *The Cuckoo's Egg: Tracking a Spy Through the Maze of Computer Espionage*. Doubleday.

Tavani, H. T. (1999). "Informational Privacy, Data Mining and the Internet." *Ethics and Information Technology*, 1: 137–45.

Tavani H. T. (2000). "Defining the Boundaries of Computer Crime: Piracy, Break-Ins, and Sabotage in Cyberspace." *Computers and Society*, 30/3 (September): 3–9.

Tavani, H. T. and Moor, J. H. (2001). "Privacy Protection, Control of Information, and Privacy-Enhancing Technologies." In R. A. Spinello and H. T. Tavani (eds.), *Readings in CyberEthics*. Jones and Bartlett, pp. 378–91.

The League for Programming Freedom (1992). "Against Software Patents." In T. W. Bynum, W. Maner, and J. L. Fodor (eds.) (1992). *Software Ownership and Intellectual Property Rights*. Research Center on Computing and Society (also available at http://www.computerethics.org).

Turkle, S. (1984). *The Second Self: Computers and the Human Spirit*. Simon and Schuster.

Turner, A. J. (1991). "Summary of the ACM/IEEE-CS Joint Curriculum Task force Report: Computing Curricula, 1991." *Communications of the ACM*, 34/6 (June): 69–84.

van den Hoven, J. (1997). "Privacy and the Varieties of Informational Wrongdoing." *Computers and Society*, 27: 33–7.

van Speybroeck, J. (1994). "Review of *Starter Kit on Teaching Computer Ethics*" (by T. W. Bynum, W. Maner, amd J. L. Fodor (eds.)), *Computing Reviews* (July): 357–8.

Weckert, J. (2002), "Lilliputian Computer Ethics." In J. H. Moor, and T. W. Bynum (eds.), *Cyberphilosophy: The Intersection of Philosophy and Computing*. Blackwell.

Weckert, J. and Adeney, D. (1997). *Computer and Information Ethics*. Greenwood Publishing Group.

Weizenbaum, J. (1976). *Computer Power and Human Reason: From Judgment to Calculation*. Freeman.

Westin, A. R. (1967). *Privacy and Freedom*. Atheneum.

Wiener, N. (1948). *Cybernetics: or Control and Communication in the Animal and the Machine*. Technology Press.

Wiener, N. (1950). *The Human Use of Human Beings: Cybernetics and Society*. Houghton Mifflin. (2nd rev. edn, Doubleday Anchor, 1954).

Wood-Harper, A. T., Corder, S., Wood, J. R. G., and Watson, H. (1996). "How We Profess: The Ethical Systems Analyst." *Communications of the ACM*, 39/3 (March): 69–77.

Index